NETWORK CONTROL AND ENGINEERING FOR QoS, SECURITY AND MOBILITY IV

T0205684

IFIP – The International Federation for Information Processing

IFIP was founded in 1960 under the auspices of UNESCO, following the First World Computer Congress held in Paris the previous year. An umbrella organization for societies working in information processing, IFIP's aim is two-fold: to support information processing within its member countries and to encourage technology transfer to developing nations. As its mission statement clearly states,

> *IFIP's mission is to be the leading, truly international, apolitical organization which encourages and assists in the development, exploitation and application of information technology for the benefit of all people.*

IFIP is a non-profitmaking organization, run almost solely by 2500 volunteers. It operates through a number of technical committees, which organize events and publications. IFIP's events range from an international congress to local seminars, but the most important are:

• The IFIP World Computer Congress, held every second year;
• Open conferences;
• Working conferences.

The flagship event is the IFIP World Computer Congress, at which both invited and contributed papers are presented. Contributed papers are rigorously refereed and the rejection rate is high.

As with the Congress, participation in the open conferences is open to all and papers may be invited or submitted. Again, submitted papers are stringently refereed.

The working conferences are structured differently. They are usually run by a working group and attendance is small and by invitation only. Their purpose is to create an atmosphere conducive to innovation and development. Refereeing is less rigorous and papers are subjected to extensive group discussion.

Publications arising from IFIP events vary. The papers presented at the IFIP World Computer Congress and at open conferences are published as conference proceedings, while the results of the working conferences are often published as collections of selected and edited papers.

Any national society whose primary activity is in information may apply to become a full member of IFIP, although full membership is restricted to one society per country. Full members are entitled to vote at the annual General Assembly. National societies preferring a less committed involvement may apply for associate or corresponding membership. Associate members enjoy the same benefits as full members, but without voting rights. Corresponding members are not represented in IFIP bodies. Affiliated membership is open to non-national societies, and individual and honorary membership schemes are also offered.

NETWORK CONTROL AND ENGINEERING FOR QoS, SECURITY AND MOBILITY, IV

Fourth IFIP International Conference on Network Control and Engineering for QoS, Security and Mobility, Lannion, France, November 14-18, 2005

Edited by

Dominique Gaïti
Université de Technologie de Troyes, France

 Springer

Network Control and Engineering for QoS, Security and Mobility IV

Edited by D. Gaïti

p. cm. (IFIP International Federation for Information Processing, a Springer Series in Computer Science)

ISSN: 1571-5736 / 1861-2288 (Internet)

Printed on acid-free paper

ISBN 978-1-4419-4320-0   eISBN: 13: 978-0-387-49690-0

9 8 7 6 5 4 3 2 1
springer.com

NETCON'05

Unreduced Dynamic Complexity: Towards the Unified Science of Intelligent Communication Networks and Software

Andrei P. Kirilyuk

Solid State Theory Department, Institute of Metal Physics
36 Vernadsky Avenue, 03142 Kiev-142, Ukraine
kiril@metfiz.freenet.kiev.ua

Operation of autonomic communication network with complicated user-oriented functions should be described as unreduced many-body interaction process. The latter gives rise to complex-dynamic behaviour including fractally structured hierarchy of chaotically changing realisations. We recall the main results of the universal science of complexity based on the unreduced interaction problem solution and its application to various real systems, from nanobiosystems and quantum devices to intelligent networks and emerging consciousness. We concentrate then on applications to autonomic communication leading to fundamentally substantiated, exact science of intelligent communication and software. It aims at unification of the whole diversity of complex information system behaviour, similar to the conventional, "Newtonian" science order for sequential, regular models of system dynamics. Basic principles and first applications of the unified science of complex-dynamic communication networks and software are outlined to demonstrate its advantages and emerging practical perspectives.

1 Introduction

Although any information processing can be described as interaction between participating components, communication and software tools used today tend to limit this interaction to *unchanged*, preprogrammed system configuration, which reduces underlying interaction processes to a very special and rather trivial type of a sequential and regular "Turing machine". It does not involve any genuine novelty emergence (with the exception of thoroughly avoided failures), so that the occurring "normal" events do not change anything in system configuration and are supposed to produce only *expected* modification in particular register content, etc. In terms of fundamental science, one deals here with a rare limiting case of exactly solvable, *integrable* and certainly *computable* interaction problem and dynamics. The latter property, associated with total *regularity, predictability*, and *decidability*, forms even a major *purpose* and invariable operation principle of all traditional information processing and communication systems (it can be generalised to all man-made tools and engineering approaches). One can say also that usual ICT systems do not possess any genuine *freedom*, or unre-

Please use the following format when citing this chapter:

Kirilyuk, A. P., 2007, in IFIP International Federation for Information Processing, Volume 229, Network Control and Engineering for QoS, Security, and Mobility, IV, ed. Gaïti, D., (Boston: Springer), pp. 1–20.

duced, *decision-taking* autonomy, which is totally displaced towards the human user side. One should not confuse that truly autonomic, *independent* kind of action with a high degree of man-made *automatisation* that can only (usefully) *imitate* a decision making process, while preserving the basic predictability and computability of such "intelligent" machine behaviour.

In the meanwhile, unreduced interaction processes involving essential and *noncomputable* system configuration change conquer practically important spaces at a catastrophically growing rate. On one hand, this rapid advance of unreduced interaction complexity occurs inevitably in communication networks and related software themselves as a result of strong increase of user numbers, interests, and functional demands (i.e. desired "quality of service"). On the other hand, it is due to simultaneous, and related, growth of popularity of *complex-dynamical applications* of ICT tools, which can be truly efficient only if those tools possess corresponding levels of *unreduced, interaction-driven complexity* and autonomy. It can appear either as unacceptably growing frequency of complicated system *failures*, or else as the transition to a fundamentally different operation mode that uses inevitable uncertainties of complex interaction dynamics to strongly *increase system performance quality*.

The second aspect has its deep, objective origin in today's specific moment of development, where one can *empirically* modify, *for the first time* in history, the *whole* scale of natural system complexity at *all* its levels, from ultimately small, quantum systems (high-energy physics) to the most complicated, biological, ecological, and conscious systems (genetics, industrial transformation, social and psychological changes). However, the genuine *understanding* of complex dynamics we *strongly modify* is persistently *missing* from modern science, which gives rise to multiple and real *dangers* (c.f. [1]) and determines the *urgency* of *complexity transition* in major ICT *instruments of progress*. In fact, any progress becomes blocked when zero-complexity, regular computing instruments encounter the unreduced, *noncomputable* complexity of real systems.

Those reasons determine increased attention to autonomic, complex, "bio-inspired" operation of communication networks and software tools that appears within various overlapping research initiatives, such as "pervasive computing", "ambient intelligence", "autonomic communication networks", "knowledge-based networks", "context awareness", "semantic grid/web", "complex software", etc. (see e.g. [2–8] for overview and further references). In fact, such kind of development has become a major, rapidly growing direction of ICT research. However, as big volumes of "promising" results and "futuristic" expectations accumulate, the need for a *unified* and *rigorous* framework, similar to exact science for non-complex, regular models, becomes evident.

Although creation of "intelligent" ICT structures has *started* from applied, *engineering* studies (*contrary* to traditional science applications), the emerging *qualitative* novelties call for a *new kind* of *fundamental knowledge* as a basis for those practically oriented efforts, without which there is a *serious risk* to "miss the point" in unlimited diversity of unreliable guesses. The created *proto-science* state of autonomic communication and complex software should now be extended to the *genuine scientific knowledge* of a new kind. This *exact science* should provide *rigorously specified and unified* description of *real*, not "model", complex systems with *unreduced* interaction of "independent" components, leading to *explicitly emerging*, "unexpected" structures and properties.

One can call such unreduced interaction process *generalised autonomic network*, even though it is realised eventually in *any* kind of unreduced interaction process, including *complex software* systems. We deal here with an important quality of new knowledge, absent in the model-based and intrinsically split usual science: once the *truly consistent understanding* of real complex interaction is established, it should *automatically* be applicable to any other, maybe externally quite different case of equally complex many-body interaction.[1] Thus, truly autonomic communication networks may show basically the same patterns of behaviour and evolution as full-scale nanobiosystems, biological networks in living organisms and ecosystems, or intelligent neural networks. It is a fortunate and non-occasional circumstance, since those complex-dynamic ICT tools will be properly suited to their material basis and application objects, complex systems from the "real world", so that finally there is *no separation and basic difference* between complex behaviour of "natural", real-world and "artificial", ICT systems: *everything* tends to be irreducibly complex, interconnected, *and* man-made, whereupon the necessity of a unified and realistic understanding of emerging new, *explicitly complex* world becomes yet more evident.

Note again the essential difference with the prevailing usual science approach, where the unreduced complexity of real structures is *artificially* reduced, i.e. *completely destroyed*, so that "computer simulation" of such basic structures as elementary particles or biomolecules takes the highest existing "supercomputer" (or grid) powers and still cannot provide a really useful, unambiguous result. In view of such situation one can have justified doubts in the ability of usual, scholar science to describe truly complex systems without losing the underlying rigour (objectivity) of the scientific method itself (see e.g. [1,9–12]).

In this report we describe a theory of arbitrary many-body interaction leading to a universally applicable concept of dynamic complexity [13–26] (Sect. 2). The resulting *universal science of complexity* provides a working prototype of the new kind of science claimed by modern development of information and communication systems [21]. We then specify its application to emerging complex software and autonomic communication systems (Sect. 3). We finally summarise the key features of the "new mathematics of complexity" as a fundamental and rigorous basis for the new science of intelligent information systems (Sect. 4) and draw major development perspectives (Sect. 5).

---

[1] This difference from the usual, "Newtonian" science (including its versions of "new physics" and "science of complexity") stems from the fact that it does *not* propose any *solution* to the *unreduced*, realistic interaction problem and does not really aim at obtaining the related *complete explanation* of the analysed phenomena, replacing it with a mathematically "exact" (analytically "closed"), but extremely simplified, unrealistic, and often guessed "models" and "postulates", which are then mechanically adjusted to separate, subjectively chosen observation results.

2 Complex Dynamics of Unreduced Interaction Process

2.1 Multivalued Dynamics and Unified Complexity Concept

We begin with a general equation for arbitrary system dynamics (or many-body problem), called here *existence equation* and simply fixing the fact of interaction between the system components (it generalises various model equations):

$$\left\{\sum_{k=0}^{N}\left[h_k\left(q_k\right)+\sum_{l>k}^{N}V_{kl}\left(q_k,q_l\right)\right]\right\}\Psi\left(Q\right)=E\Psi\left(Q\right),\qquad(1)$$

where $h_k\left(q_k\right)$ is the "generalised Hamiltonian" of the k-th system component, q_k is the degree(s) of freedom of the k-th component, $V_{kl}\left(q_k,q_l\right)$ is the (arbitrary) interaction potential between the k-th and l-th components, $\Psi\left(Q\right)$ is the system state-function, $Q\equiv\{q_0,q_1,...,q_N\}$, E is the generalised Hamiltonian eigenvalue, and summations are performed over all (N) system components. The generalised Hamiltonian, eigenvalues, and interaction potential represent a suitable measure of dynamic complexity defined below and encompassing practically all "observable" quantities (action, energy/mass, momentum, information, entropy, etc.). Therefore (1) can express unreduced interaction configuration of arbitrary communication/software system. If interaction potential (system configuration) depends explicitly on time, one should use a time-dependent form of (1), where eigenvalue E is replaced with the partial time derivative operator.

It is convenient to separate one of the degrees of freedom, e.g. $q_0\equiv\xi$, representing a naturally selected, usually "system-wide" entity, such as component coordinates or "connecting agent" (here now $Q\equiv\{q_1,...,q_N\}$ and $k,l\geq1$):

$$\left\{h_0(\xi)+\sum_{k=1}^{N}\left[h_k(q_k)+V_{0k}(\xi,q_k)+\sum_{l>k}^{N}V_{kl}(q_k,q_l)\right]\right\}\Psi(\xi,Q)=E\Psi(\xi,Q),$$

$$(2)$$

We express the problem in terms of known free-component solutions for the "functional", internal degrees of freedom of system elements ($k\geq1$):

$$h_k\left(q_k\right)\varphi_{kn_k}\left(q_k\right)=\varepsilon_{n_k}\varphi_{kn_k}\left(q_k\right),\qquad(3)$$

$$\Psi\left(\xi,Q\right)=\sum_{n}\psi_n\left(\xi\right)\varphi_{1n_1}\left(q_1\right)\varphi_{2n_2}\left(q_2\right)...\varphi_{Nn_N}\left(q_N\right)\equiv\sum_{n}\psi_n\left(\xi\right)\Phi_n\left(Q\right),\quad(4)$$

where $\{\varepsilon_{n_k}\}$ are the eigenvalues and $\{\varphi_{kn_k}\left(q_k\right)\}$ eigenfunctions of the k-th component Hamiltonian $h_k\left(q_k\right)$, forming the complete set of orthonormal functions, $n\equiv\{n_1,...,n_N\}$ runs through all possible eigenstate combinations, and $\Phi_n\left(Q\right)\equiv\varphi_{1n_1}\left(q_1\right)\varphi_{2n_2}\left(q_2\right)...\varphi_{Nn_N}\left(q_N\right)$ by definition. The system of equations for $\{\psi_n\left(\xi\right)\}$ is obtained then in a standard way, using the eigen-solution orthonormality (e.g. by multiplication by $\Phi_n^*\left(Q\right)$ and integration over Q):

$$[h_0(\xi)+V_{00}(\xi)]\psi_0(\xi)+\sum_{n}V_{0n}(\xi)\psi_n(\xi)=\eta\psi_0(\xi)$$

$$[h_0(\xi)+V_{nn}(\xi)]\psi_n(\xi)+\sum_{n'\neq n}V_{nn'}(\xi)\psi_{n'}(\xi)=\eta_n\psi_n(\xi)-V_{n0}(\xi)\psi_0(\xi),\qquad(5)$$

where $n, n' \neq 0$ (also below), $\eta \equiv \eta_0 = E - \varepsilon_0$, $\eta_n = E - \varepsilon_n$, $\varepsilon_n = \sum_k \varepsilon_{n_k}$,

$$V_{nn'}(\xi) = \sum_k \left[V_{k0}^{nn'}(\xi) + \sum_{l>k} V_{kl}^{nn'} \right] , \tag{6}$$

$$V_{k0}^{nn'}(\xi) = \int_{\Omega_Q} dQ \Phi_n^*(Q) V_{k0}(q_k, \xi) \Phi_{n'}(Q) , \tag{7}$$

$$V_{kl}^{nn'}(\xi) = \int_{\Omega_Q} dQ \Phi_n^*(Q) V_{kl}(q_k, q_l) \Phi_{n'}(Q) , \tag{8}$$

and we have separated the equation for $\psi_0(\xi)$ describing the generalised "ground state" of system elements, i. e. the state with minimum complexity. The obtained system of equations expresses the same problem as the starting equation (2) but now in terms of "natural" variables, and therefore it results from various starting models, including time-dependent and formally "nonlinear" ones.

We can try to solve the "nonintegrable" system of equations (5) with the help of generalised effective, or optical, potential method [27], where one expresses $\psi_n(\xi)$ through $\psi_0(\xi)$ from equations for $\psi_n(\xi)$ using the standard Green function technique and then inserts the result into the equation for $\psi_0(\xi)$, obtaining thus the *effective existence equation* that contains *explicitly* only "integrable" degrees of freedom (ξ) [13–17, 25, 26]:

$$h_0(\xi) \psi_0(\xi) + V_{\text{eff}}(\xi; \eta) \psi_0(\xi) = \eta \psi_0(\xi) , \tag{9}$$

where the operator of *effective potential (EP)*, $V_{\text{eff}}(\xi; \eta)$, is given by

$$V_{\text{eff}}(\xi; \eta) = V_{00}(\xi) + \hat{V}(\xi; \eta) , \quad \hat{V}(\xi; \eta) \psi_0(\xi) = \int_{\Omega_\xi} d\xi' V(\xi, \xi'; \eta) \psi_0(\xi') , \tag{10}$$

$$V(\xi, \xi'; \eta) = \sum_{n,i} \frac{V_{0n}(\xi) \psi_{ni}^0(\xi) V_{n0}(\xi') \psi_{ni}^{0*}(\xi')}{\eta - \eta_{ni}^0 - \varepsilon_{n0}} , \quad \varepsilon_{n0} \equiv \varepsilon_n - \varepsilon_0 , \tag{11}$$

and $\{\psi_{ni}^0(\xi)\}$, $\{\eta_{ni}^0\}$ are complete sets of eigenfunctions and eigenvalues of a *truncated* system of equations:

$$[h_0(\xi) + V_{nn}(\xi)] \psi_n(\xi) + \sum_{n' \neq n} V_{nn'}(\xi) \psi_{n'}(\xi) = \eta_n \psi_n(\xi) . \tag{12}$$

Since the unreduced EP (10)–(11) depends essentially on the eigen-solutions to be found, the problem remains "nonintegrable" and formally equivalent to the initial formulation (1),(2),(5). However, it is the effective version of a problem that reveals the nontrivial properties of its unreduced solution. The most important property of the unreduced interaction result (9)–(12) is its *dynamic multivaluedness* meaning that one has a *redundant* number of different but individually complete, and therefore *mutually incompatible*, problem solutions describing *equally real* system configurations. We therefore call each of them *realisation* of the system and problem. Plurality of system realisations follows from the *dynamically nonlinear* EP dependence on the solutions to be found, reflecting the evident plurality of interacting eigen-mode combinations [13–26].

It is important that dynamic multivaluedness emerges only in the unreduced problem formulation, whereas the standard theory, including usual EP method applications (see e.g. [27]) and the scholar "science of complexity" (theory of chaos, self-organisation, etc.), resorts invariably to one or another version of *perturbation theory*, whose "mean-field" approximation, providing an "exact", closed-form solution, totally kills dynamic redundance by eliminating the non-linear dynamical links in (9)–(11) and retaining *only one*, "averaged" solution, usually expressing but small deviations from *imposed* system configuration:

$$\left[h_0\left(\xi\right) + V_{nn}\left(\xi\right) + \tilde{V}_n\left(\xi\right)\right]\psi_n\left(\xi\right) = \eta_n\psi_n\left(\xi\right) , \qquad (13)$$

where $|V_0\left(\xi\right)| < \left|\tilde{V}_n\left(\xi\right)\right| < \left|\sum_{n'} V_{nn'}\left(\xi\right)\right|$. General problem solution is then obtained as an essentially linear *superposition* of eigen-solutions of (13) similar to (4). This *dynamically single-valued*, or *unitary*, problem reduction forms the basis of the whole canonical science paradigm.

The *unreduced*, truly complete *general solution* to a problem emerges as a *dynamically probabilistic* sum of *redundant* system *realisations*, each of them being roughly equivalent to the whole "general solution" of usual theory:

$$\rho\left(\xi, Q\right) = \sum_{r=1}^{N_{\Re}}{}^{\oplus}\rho_r\left(\xi, Q\right) , \qquad (14)$$

where the observed (generalised) density, $\rho\left(\xi, Q\right)$, is obtained as the state-function squared modulus, $\rho\left(\xi, Q\right) = |\Psi\left(\xi, Q\right)|^2$ (for "wave-like" complexity levels), or as the state-function itself, $\rho\left(\xi, Q\right) = \Psi\left(\xi, Q\right)$ (for "particle-like" structures), index r enumerates system realisations, $N_{\Re}$ is realisation number (its maximum value is equal to the number of system components, $N_{\Re} = N$), and the sign $\oplus$ designates the special, dynamically probabilistic meaning of the sum. The latter implies that incompatible system realisations are forced, by the *same* driving interaction, to *permanently replace each other* in a *causally (dynamically) random order* thus consistently defined. The r-th realisation state-function, $\Psi_r\left(\xi, Q\right)$, in the unreduced general solution (14) is obtained as

$$\Psi_r\left(\xi, Q\right) = \sum_i c_i^r\left[\Phi_0\left(Q\right)\psi_{0i}^r\left(\xi\right) + \right.$$

$$\left. + \sum_{n,i'} \frac{\Phi_n\left(Q\right)\psi_{ni'}^0\left(\xi\right) \int_{\Omega_\xi} d\xi' \psi_{ni'}^{0*}\left(\xi'\right) V_{n0}\left(\xi'\right)\psi_{0i}^r\left(\xi'\right)}{\eta_i^r - \eta_{ni'}^0 - \varepsilon_{n0}}\right] , \qquad (15)$$

where $\{\psi_{0i}^r(\xi), \eta_i^r\}$ are r-th realisation eigen-solutions of the unreduced EP equation (9) and the coefficients c_i^r should be found from the state-function matching conditions at the boundary where interaction effectively vanishes. The corresponding r-th realisation EP takes the form (derived from (10)–(11)):

$$V_{\text{eff}}(\xi; \eta_i^r)\,\psi_{0i}^r(\xi) = V_{00}(\xi)\,\psi_{0i}^r(\xi) +$$

$$+ \sum_{n,i'} \frac{V_{0n}(\xi)\,\psi_{ni'}^0(\xi)\,\int_{\Omega_\xi} d\xi'\,\psi_{ni'}^{0*}(\xi')\,V_{n0}(\xi')\,\psi_{0i}^r(\xi')}{\eta_i^r - \eta_{ni'}^0 - \varepsilon_{n0}}. \tag{16}$$

Equations (14)–(16) reveal, in particular, *dynamic localisation* of a system in any its normal, "regular" realisation around its characteristic eigenvalue and configuration (due to the resonance denominator) and reverse delocalisation during *transition* between regular realisations, occurring though a special, *intermediate* realisation of the *wavefunction* [13, 17, 20, 23, 28] (see also below).

Direct comparison between the unreduced (9),(12),(14)–(16) and reduced (13) problem solutions reveals the exact dynamic origin and huge scale of difference between the real system complexity and its model simplification in the unitary theory. In particular, the unreduced solution (14) implies that any measured value is *intrinsically unstable* and *will* unpredictably change to another one, corresponding to another, *randomly* chosen realisation. Such kind of behaviour is readily observed in nature and actually explains the living organism behaviour [13, 16–18], but is thoroughly avoided in the unitary approach and technological systems (including ICT systems), where it is correctly associated with linear "noncomputability" and technical failure (we shall consider below that *limiting* regime of complex dynamics). Therefore the universal dynamic multivaluedness revealed by rigorous problem solution forms the fundamental basis for the transition to "bio-inspired" and "intelligent" kind of operation in artificial, technological and communication systems, where causal randomness can be transformed from an obstacle to a qualitative advantage (Sect. 3).

The rigorously derived randomness of the generalised EP formalism (14)-(16) is accompanied by the *dynamic definition of probability*. As elementary realisations are equivalent in their "right to appear", the dynamically obtained, *a priori probability*, α_r, of elementary realisation emergence is given by

$$\alpha_r = \frac{1}{N_{\Re}}, \quad \sum_r \alpha_r = 1. \tag{17}$$

However, a real observation may resolve only uneven groups of elementary realisations. The dynamic probability of such general, compound realisation is determined by the number, N_r, of elementary realisations it contains:

$$\alpha_r(N_r) = \frac{N_r}{N_{\Re}} \quad \left(N_r = 1, ..., N_{\Re}; \sum_r N_r = N_{\Re}\right), \quad \sum_r \alpha_r = 1. \tag{18}$$

An expression for *expectation value*, $\rho_{\exp}(\xi, Q)$, follows from (14),(17)–(18) for statistically long observation periods:

$$\rho_{\exp}(\xi, Q) = \sum_r \alpha_r \rho_r (\xi, Q) \ . \tag{19}$$

It is important, however, that our *dynamically* derived randomness and probability need not rely on such "statistical", empirically based result, so that the basic expressions (14)–(18) remain valid even for a *single* event of realisation emergence and *before* any event happens at all.

Realisation probability distribution can be obtained in another way, involving *generalised wavefunction* and *Born's probability rule* [13, 15, 17, 20, 23, 28]. The wavefunction describes system state during its transition between "regular", localised realisations and constitutes a particular, "intermediate" realisation with extended and "loose" (chaotically changing) structure, where system components transiently disentangle before forming the next "regular" realisation. The intermediate, or "main", realisation is *explicitly obtained* in the unreduced EP formalism as the single, *exceptional* one for which the nonintegrable terms of the general EP (11),(16) become indeed small and it is reduced to a separable version of perturbative, "mean-field" type (13) [13, 15, 17, 20, 23, 28]. This special realisation provides, in particular, the *causal, realistic* version of the *quantum-mechanical wavefunction* at the *lowest*, quantum levels of complexity. The "Born probability rule", now causally derived and extended to any level of world dynamics, states that realisation probability α_r is determined by wavefunction value (its squared modulus for "wave-like" complexity levels) for the respective system configuration X_r: $\alpha_r = |\Psi(X_r)|^2$. The generalised wavefunction (or distribution function) $\Psi(x)$ satisfies the *universal Schrödinger equation* (Sect. 2.2), rigorously *derived* by *causal quantisation* of complex dynamics, while Born's probability rule follows from the above *dynamic* "matching conditions" for the state-function (15), which are satisfied during transitions from regular realisations to the wavefunction and back [13, 15, 17, 20, 23, 28]. It is *only* this "averaged", weak-interaction state of the wavefunction, or "main" realisation, that remains in the *single-valued* model and paradigm of unitary science, which explains both its partial success and basic limitations.

Closely related to dynamic redundance is *dynamic entanglement* of interacting components, described in (15) by the weighted products of state-function elements depending on various degrees of freedom (ξ, Q). It is a *rigorous* expression of the tangible *quality* of the emerging system structure, absent in unitary models. The obtained *dynamically multivalued entanglement* describes a "living" structure, permanently changing and probabilistically *adapting* its configuration, which endows "bio-inspired" and "autonomic" technologies with a *well-specified basis*. The properties of dynamically multivalued entanglement and adaptability are amplified due to *probabilistic fractality* of the unreduced problem solution [13, 16–18, 20], essentially extending usual, single-valued fractality and obtained by application of the same EP method to solution of the truncated system of equations (12) used in the first-level EP expression (11),(16).

We can now consistently and *universally* define the unreduced *dynamic complexity*, C, of *any* real system (or interaction process) as arbitrary growing function of the total number, $N_{\Re}$, of *explicitly obtained* system realisations or the rate of their change, $C = C(N_\Re)$, $dC/dN_\Re > 0$, equal to zero for the *unrealistic* case of only one system realisation, $C(1) = 0$. Suitable examples are provided by $C(N_\Re) = C_0 \ln N_\Re$, generalised energy/mass (temporal rate of realisation change), and momentum (spatial rate of realisation emergence) [13–25]. It becomes clear now that the *whole* dynamically single-valued paradigm and results of the canonical theory (including its versions of "complexity" and e.g. "multi-stability") correspond to exactly *zero* value of the unreduced dynamic complexity, which is equivalent to the effectively zero-dimensional, point-like projection of reality from the "exact-solution" perspective (cf. [9–12]).

Correspondingly, *any* dynamically single-valued "model" is *strictly regular* and *cannot* possess any true, intrinsic randomness (chaoticity), which can only be introduced artificially, e.g. as a *regular* "amplification" of a "random" (by convention) *external* "noise". By contrast, our unreduced dynamic complexity is practically synonymous to the equally universal and intrinsic *chaoticity*, since *multiple* system realisations appearing and disappearing in the *real* space (and thus *forming* its tangible, changing structure) are *redundant* (mutually *incompatible*), which is the origin of *both* complexity and chaoticity. The genuine dynamical chaos thus obtained has a complicated internal structure (contrary to ill-defined unitary "stochasticity") and *always* contains *partial regularity*, which is dynamically, inseparably entangled with truly random elements.

The universal dynamic complexity, chaoticity, and related properties involve the *essential, or dynamic, nonlinearity* of the unreduced problem solution and system behaviour. It is provided by dynamical links of the developing interaction process, as they are expressed in EP dependence on the eigen-solutions to be found (see (9)–(11),(16)). It is the *dynamically emerging* and *irreducible* nonlinearity, since it appears inevitably even for a "linear" initial problem expression (1)–(2),(5), whereas usual, mechanistic "nonlinearity" is but an *imposed*, dispensable *imitation* of the essential EP nonlinearity. Essential nonlinearity leads to the omnipresent *dynamic instability* of any system state (realisation), since both are determined by the same dynamic feedback mechanism.

Universality of our description leads, in particular, to the unified understanding of the whole diversity of dynamical regimes and structures [13,14,17,19–22]. One standard, limiting case of complex (multivalued) dynamics, called *uniform, or global, chaos*, is characterised by essentially different realisations with a homogeneous probability distribution ($N_r \approx 1$, $\alpha_r \approx 1/N_\Re$ for all r in (18)) and occurs when major parameters of interacting entities (suitably represented by frequencies) have close values (which leads to a strong "conflict of interests" and resulting "deep disorder"). The complementary limiting regime of *multivalued self-organisation, or self-organised criticality (SOC)* emerges for sufficiently different parameters of interaction components, so that a small number of relatively rigid, low-frequency components "enslave" a hierarchy of high-frequency and rapidly changing, but configurationally similar, realisations (i.e. $N_r \sim N_\Re$ and realisation probability distribution is highly uneven). The difference of this extended, multivalued self-organisation (and SOC) from usual, unitary version is essential: despite the rigid *external* shape of system configuration in this regime, it contains the intense "internal life" and *chaos* of *permanently* changing "enslaved" realisations (which are *not* superposable unitary "modes"). In this sense the generalised SOC structure, and with it the whole unreduced complexity, can be described as *confined chaos*, where global chaos has the lowest and quasi-regular SOC the highest degree of chaos confinement.

Another advance with respect to unitary "science of complexity" is that the unreduced, multivalued self-organisation *unifies* the *essentially extended* versions of a whole series of separated unitary "models", including "self-organisation", "synergetics", SOC, any "synchronisation", "control of chaos", "attractors", and "mode locking". All intermediate dynamic regimes between those two limiting cases of uniform chaos and quasi-regular SOC, as well as their multi-level combinations, are obtained for respective parameter values.

The point of transition to the strong chaos is expressed by the *universal criterion of global chaos onset*:

$$\kappa \equiv \frac{\Delta\eta_i}{\Delta\eta_n} = \frac{\omega_\xi}{\omega_q} \cong 1 \ , \tag{20}$$

where κ is the introduced *chaoticity* parameter, $\Delta\eta_i$, ω_ξ and $\Delta\eta_n \sim \Delta\varepsilon$, ω_q are energy-level separations and frequencies for inter-component and intra-component motions, respectively. At $\kappa \ll 1$ one has an externally regular multivalued SOC regime, which degenerates into global chaos as κ grows from 0 to 1, and maximum irregularity at $\kappa \approx 1$ is again transformed into a SOC kind of structure (but with a "reversed" configuration) at $\kappa \gg 1$.

One can compare this transparent and universal picture with the existing diversity of separated and incomplete unitary criteria of chaos and regularity. Only the former provide a real possibility of understanding and control of ICT systems of arbitrary complexity, where more regular, SOC regimes can serve for (loose) control of system dynamics, while less regular ones can also play a *positive* role of efficient search and adaptation means. This combination forms the basis of any "biological" and "intelligent" kind of behaviour [13, 16–18, 20–22] and therefore can constitute the essence of *intelligent ICT paradigm* supposed to extend the now realised (quasi-) regular kind of operation in the uttermost limit of SOC ($\kappa \to 0$). While the latter *inevitably* becomes inefficient with growing system sophistication (where the chaos-bringing resonances of (20) *cannot* be avoided), it definitely lacks the "intelligent power" of unreduced complex dynamics to generate meaning and adaptable structure development.

2.2 Huge Efficiency of Unreduced Complex Dynamics and Universal Symmetry of Complexity

Dynamically probabilistic fractality is the intrinsic property of unreduced interaction development [13, 16–18, 20]. It is obtained by application of the same EP method (9)–(11) to the truncated system of equations (12), then to the next truncated system, etc., which gives the irregular and *probabilistically adapting* hierarchy of realisations showing the intermittent mixture of global chaos and regularity, or *confined randomness* (Sect. 2.1). The total realisation number $N_{\Re}$, and thus *operation power*, of this autonomously branching interaction process with a *dynamically parallel* structure grows *exponentially* within any time period. It can be estimated in the following way [17–21].

If our system of inter-connected elements contains N_{unit} "processing units", or "junctions", and if each of them has n_{conn} real or "virtual" (possible) links, then the total number of interaction links is $N = n_{\text{conn}} N_{\text{unit}}$. In most important cases N is a huge number: for both human brain and genome interactions N is greater than 10^{12}, and being much more variable for communication/software systems, it can easily grow to similar "astronomical" ranges. The key property of *unreduced, complex* interaction dynamics, distinguishing it from any unitary version, is that the maximum number $N_{\Re}$ of realisations taken by the system (also per time unit) and determining its real "power" P_{real} (of search, memory, cognition, etc.) is given by the number of *all possible combinations of links*, i.e.

$$P_{\text{real}} \propto N_{\Re} = N! \to \sqrt{2\pi N}\left(\frac{N}{e}\right)^N \sim N^N \ggg N \ . \tag{21}$$

Any unitary, sequential model of the same system (including its *mechanistically* "parallel" and "complex" modes) would give $P_{\text{reg}} \sim N^\beta$, with $\beta \sim 1$, so that

$$P_{\text{real}} \sim (P_{\text{reg}})^N \ggg P_{\text{reg}} \sim N^\beta \ . \tag{22}$$

Thus, for $N \sim 10^{12}$ we have $P_{\text{real}} \gg 10^{10^{13}} \gg 10^{10^{12}} \sim 10^N \to \infty$, which is a "practical infinity", also with respect to the unitary power of $N^\beta \sim 10^{12}$.

These estimates demonstrate the true power of complex (multivalued) communication dynamics that remains suppressed within the now dominating unitary, quasi-regular operation mode. Huge power of complex-dynamical interaction correlate with the new *quality* emergence, such as *intelligence* and *consciousness* (at higher levels of complexity) [17, 20], in direct relation to our *intelligent* communication paradigm meaning that such properties as *sensible*, context-related information processing, personalised *understanding* and autonomous *creativity* (useful self-development), desired for the new ICT systems, are *inevitable* qualitative manifestations of the above "infinite" power.

Everything comes at a price, however, and a price to pay for the above qualitative advantages is rigorously specified as *irreducible dynamic randomness* and thus unpredictability of operation details of complex information-processing systems. We rigorously confirm here an evident idea that *autonomous* adaptability and genuine *creativity* exclude any detailed, regular programming in principle. But then what can serve as a guiding principle and practical construction strategy for those qualitatively new communications networks and their intelligent elements? We show that guiding rules and strategy are determined by a general law of real dynamics, the *universal symmetry, or conservation, of complexity* [13, 15–18, 20–24]. This universal "order of nature" unifies the extended versions of all usual (correct) laws, symmetries, and principles (now *causally derived* and *realistically* interpreted). Contrary to any unitary symmetry, the universal symmetry of complexity is *irregular* in its structure, but always *exact* (never "broken"). Its "horizontal" manifestation (at a given complexity level) implies *dynamic transformation* of the system between its changing realisations, as opposed to *abstract* "symmetry operator" idea. Therefore the symmetry of system complexity totally determines its dynamics and expresses the deep connection between often visibly dissimilar and chaotically changing configurations.

Another, "vertical" manifestation of the symmetry of complexity determines emergence and development of *different* complexity levels of a real interaction. System "potentiality", or *real* power to create *new* structure is universally described by a form of complexity called *dynamic information* and generalising usual "potential energy" [13, 15, 17, 20, 24]. This potential, latent complexity is transformed, during interaction development, into explicit, "unfolded" form of *dynamic entropy* (generalising kinetic, or heat, energy). Universal *conservation of complexity* means that this important transformation, determining every system dynamics and evolution, *preserves* the *sum* of dynamic information and entropy, or *total complexity* (for a given system or process). This universal formulation of the symmetry of complexity includes its above "horizontal" manifestation and, for example, extended and *unified* versions of the first and second laws of thermodynamics (i.e. conservation of energy *by* its *permanent* degradation). It also helps to eliminate persisting series of confusions around information, entropy, and complexity in the unitary theory (thus, any real, useful "information" is expressed rather by our dynamic entropy [13,17]).

It is not difficult to show [13,15,17,20,23,24] that a universal measure of dynamic information is provided by action $\mathcal{A}$ known from classical mechanics, but now acquiring a universal, essentially nonlinear and causally complete meaning. One obtains then the universal expression of complexity conservation law in the form of generalised Hamilton-Jacobi equation for $\mathcal{A} = \mathcal{A}(x,t)$:

$$\frac{\Delta \mathcal{A}}{\Delta t}\Big|_{x=\text{const}} + H\left(x, \frac{\Delta \mathcal{A}}{\Delta x}\Big|_{t=\text{const}}, t\right) = 0 , \tag{23}$$

where the *Hamiltonian*, $H = H(x,p,t)$, considered as a function of *emerging* space coordinate x, momentum $p = (\Delta\mathcal{A}/\Delta x)|_{t=\text{const}}$, and time t, expresses the unfolded, entropy-like form of differential complexity, $H = (\Delta S/\Delta t)|_{x=\text{const}}$ (note that discrete, rather than continuous, versions of derivatives here reflect the *quantised* character of unreduced complex dynamics [13, 15, 17, 20, 23, 24]). As in the naturally *dualistic* multivalued dynamics every localised, "regular" realisation is transformed into the extended wavefunction and back (Sect. 2.1), one obtains also the universal Schrödinger equation for the generalised wavefunction (or distribution function) $\Psi(x,t)$ by applying causal quantisation procedure [13,15,17,20,23,24] to the Hamilton-Jacobi equation (23):

$$\mathcal{A}_0 \frac{\partial \Psi}{\partial t} = \hat{H}\left(x, \frac{\partial}{\partial x}, t\right) \Psi , \tag{24}$$

where $\mathcal{A}_0$ is a characteristic action value (equal to Planck's constant at the lowest, quantum levels of complexity) and the Hamiltonian operator, $\hat{H}$, is obtained from the Hamiltonian function $H = H(x, p, t)$ of equation (23) with the help of causal quantisation (we put continuous derivatives here for simplicity).

Equations (23)–(24) represent the universal differential expression of the symmetry of complexity showing how it determines dynamics and evolution of any system or interaction process (they also justify our use of the Hamiltonian form for the starting existence equation (1)–(2)). This universally applicable Hamilton-Schrödinger formalism can be useful for rigorous description of any complex interaction network, provided we find its *truly complete* (dynamically multivalued) solution with the help of unreduced EP method (Sect. 2.1).

3 Unified Science of Complex ICT Systems

3.1 Main Principles of Complex ICT System Operation and Design

The rigorously derived framework of the Universal Science of Complexity (Sect. 2) finds its further confirmation in numerous applications at different complexity levels, from fundamental physics and cosmology (Quantum Field Mechanics) [13,17,23–25,28] to living organism dynamics (causally specified genomics and nanobiotechnology) [13,16–19], ecological system development (realistic sustainability concept) [13,22], and theory of emergent true intelligence and consciousness [13,17,20] (see also Sect. 4). These results give a realistic hope for an equally successful application of the same complexity concept to the new generation of communication and software systems with "bio-inspired" and "intelligent" properties [2–7], which are actually *indispensable* for efficient work with the *critically emerging* real-system complexity from the above applications (Sect. 1). We provide here an outline of the *main principles* of expected behaviour and design of complex-dynamic communication networks and software as they follow from the universal complexity framework (Sect. 2).

The *single unifying principle* of complex system dynamics and evolution is provided by the *universal symmetry of complexity* describing complexity *conservation* by its *permanent transformation* from dynamic information into entropy as the *unified structure and purpose* of *any system evolution* (Sect. 2.2). While the very existence of such unified law is important for efficient analysis of generalised autonomic networks (Sect. 1), we can specify now the ensuing particular principles that can be especially useful for their practical design and control.

We start with the *complexity correspondence principle* that directly follows from the universal symmetry of complexity and takes various forms for different application tasks [13,17,20]. A general enough formulation maintains that any interaction between complex systems (e.g. within a "global" system) tend to have *maximum efficiency* for *comparable* values of interacting system complexities (see Sect. 2.1 for the universal complexity definition). Moreover, interaction components with higher complexity tend to "enslave", or control, those with lower complexity within a resulting SOC-type state (Sect. 2.1), while very close complexities of interacting components often give rise to global chaoticity.

It follows that in order to increase efficiency one should use tools of certain complexity for control of structures of *comparable and slightly lower* complexity. Lower-complexity tools *cannot* correctly control or *even simulate* higher-complexity behaviour in principle, while a *much* higher complexity tool will produce a lot of *unnecessary* activity during control of low-complexity structure. This "simple" rule has a *rigorous, reliable* basis and helps to avoid any inefficient solution (e.g. usual *unconditional,* "total" elimination of randomness).

Reproduction, or simulation, of a system behaviour by another, "computing" or controlling system can also be successful *only* if the simulating system has *superior* complexity, which immediately shows, for example, that any quantum device could at best simulate or compute only another quantum, but *not* classical, localised and deterministic behaviour, which provides a *rigorous* proof of *impossibility* of real quantum computation [13,17]. Losses produced by the dominating neglect of underlying hierarchy of complexity are evident and include a similar situation in nanotechnology (cf. [19]). Another use of complexity correspondence involves popular ideas of "context-based" information technologies, where the necessity of *unreduced dynamic complexity* in ICT systems becomes evident, as any *human* "context" has a high enough complexity.

The above rule of control (or "enslavement") of lower-complexity dynamics by a higher-complexity tool can be extended to a general *principle of complex-dynamical control.* Contrary to unitary control schemes (e.g. "control of chaos"), the *realistically* substantiated complex-dynamical control paradigm shows that any resulting, "controlled" dynamics *cannot* be regular, i.e. "totally controlled", as it is implied by the unitary control idea leading to unpredictably (and *inevitably*) emerging *catastrophic* failures of any technological systems with usual, "protective" control design. In reality one *always* obtains a *dynamically multivalued,* internally *chaotic* SOC state, and the *general purpose* of complex-dynamic, reality-based control is to ensure optimal, quasi-*free development of the global system complexity,* including gentle, "orienting" actions of control that cannot be separated from the controlled system dynamics and should be considered within a *unified, unreduced interaction analysis* (Sect. 2). In that way one can realistically obtain a *failure-proof, catastrophe-free systems* that will avoid *big* crashes by using *creative* power of *small,* interaction-driven irregularities, quite similar to *unreduced life dynamics,* now *causally* understood [13, 16–18].

This brings us to the principle of *huge creative power of unreduced complex dynamics* as it is described above (Sect. 2.2). It implies, practically, that designing truly autonomous and intelligent ICT systems, one should "liberate" them to go *freely,* by their own way, unpredictable in its *chaotically varying details,* to the *well-defined general purpose of maximum complexity-entropy* obtained at the expense of *inserted dynamical information* that replaces usual deterministic programme. One obtains thus the exponentially huge, practically infinite gain in efficiency with respect to unitary, sequential operation due to interactive adaptability of *probabilistic fractal* of *dynamically emerging* links [17–21] (Sect. 2.2). In exchange, one should accept the omnipresent, massive, unavoidable *uncertainty* of unreduced interaction dynamics. It can, however, be properly *confined* and *constructively* used by alternating uniformly chaotic (irregular, "searching") and SOC (regular, "fixing") states, whose separation is governed by our *unified chaoticity criterion* (20) in terms of major system resonances.

In conclusion of this outline of major principles of complex autonomic networks, it would be useful to return to the global framework of the symmetry of complexity that shows, in the above way, *what can happen* in the strongly interactive ICT system of *arbitrary complexity* and how one can efficiently design and control the unreduced interaction results by its *causally complete understanding*. The latter can certainly be properly specified and adapted, where necessary, to any particular case of reduced, mechanistic "complexity", but now with the underlying clear understanding of the performed actions (Sect. 5).

3.2 Complexity Transition in ICT Systems: Towards the New Era of Intelligent Communication Technology

The *qualitatively big* transition from unrealistic unitary models to the unreduced, multivalued dynamics of real, massively interactive ICT systems can be designated as *complexity transition*. It has a narrow meaning of transition from the uttermost limit of pseudo-regular SOC of usual ICT to the fractal dynamic hierarchy of various chaotic states, according to the chaoticity criterion (20). In a wider sense, one deals with a fundamentally based *change of concept* of modern technology (Sects. 1, 3.1, 5) and related *way of development*.

Unreduced complexity appearance should rather be tested first at the level of *software*. Using the results of complexity correspondence principle described in the previous section, we can suppose that complexity transition can be conveniently started within *context-based* technology, where complexity-bringing interaction involves essential, *structure-changing*, autonomic exchange between context-bearing elements. Their unreduced interaction should then be designed according to the principles of complex interaction dynamics (Sects. 2, 3.1).

As the unreduced interaction complexity forms a growing hierarchy of levels [13, 17, 20], one obtains eventually a whole series of system transitions to ever growing complexity. Software version of initial complexity emergence will later involve *hardware* elements into structure-changing interaction processes. Communication network or its respective parts operate in that case as a single, *holistic* process of "generalised quantum beat" (chaotic realisation change). Transition to a *high enough* complexity level will bring about first elements of genuine network *intelligence* and then *consciousness*, as both these properties can be consistently explained as high enough levels of unreduced interaction complexity [13, 17, 20]. One can designate then *intelligence and consciousness transitions* as sufficiently high-level complexity transitions involving unreduced soft- and hardware interaction. Whereas lower-level complexity transitions can be limited to separate network parts and operation layers, such higher-level features as intelligence and (machine) consciousness will progressively involve the *whole* network dynamics, which is the evident *highest* level of communication network *autonomy*. Whereas already the lowest complexity transition involves context-bearing elements of human complexity, intelligence transition marks the beginning of *inseparable entanglement* of machine *and* human complexity development that can be the *unique* real way of progressive development of "natural" intelligence and consciousness [20, 21].

4 New Mathematics of Complexity and Its Applications

After having outlined, in the previous section, practically oriented principles of ICT applications of the unreduced complexity, let us now summarise purely mathematical, rigorously expressed novelties of the unreduced interaction analysis to be used in the new kind of knowledge (see also the end of paper [18]).

The *new mathematics of complexity* is represented by the *unified, single structure* of *dynamically probabilistic fractal* obtained as the *unreduced solution* of *real* interaction problem (Sect. 2.1). All its properties, describing the *exact* world structure and dynamics, are unified within the single, never broken *symmetry, or conservation, of complexity* including its *unceasing transformation* from complexity-information to complexity-entropy (Sect. 2.2).

One can emphasize several features of this unified structure and law of the new mathematics, distinguishing it essentially from unitary mathematics:

(i) *Non*uniqueness of any real (interaction) problem solution taking the form of its *dynamic multivaluedness (redundance)*. Exclusively *complex-dynamic* (multivalued, internally *chaotic*) existence of any real system (cf. conventional "existence and uniqueness" theorems).

(ii) Omnipresent, explicit *emergence* of *qualitatively new* structure and *dynamic origin of time* (change) and *events*: $a \neq a$ for *any* structure/element a in the new mathematics *and* reality, while $a = a$ (self-identity postulate) in the *whole* usual mathematics, which thus *excludes any real change* in principle.

(iii) Fractally structured *dynamic entanglement* of unreduced problem solution (interaction-driven structure weaving within any single realisation): *rigorous* expression of *material quality* in mathematics (as opposed to "immaterial", qualitatively "neutral", "dead" structures of usual mathematics).

(iv) Basic *irrelevance* of perturbation theory and "exact solution" paradigm: the unreduced problem solution is *dynamically random* (permanently, chaotically changing), *dynamically entangled* (internally textured and "living") and *fractal* (hierarchically structured). *Unified dynamic origin* and *causally specified* meaning of *nonintegrability, nonseparability, noncomputability, randomness, uncertainty (indeterminacy), undecidability, "broken symmetry"*, etc. Real interaction problem is nonintegrable and nonseparable *but* solvable. Realistic mathematics of complexity is *well defined* (*certain, unified* and *complete*), but its structures are intrinsically "fuzzy" (dynamically *indeterminate*) and properly *diverse* (*not* reduced to numbers or geometry).

(v) *Dynamic discreteness (causal quantisation)* of the unreduced interaction products (realisations): *qualitative* inhomogeneity, or *nonunitarity*, of any system structure and evolution, *dynamic* origin of (fractally structured) *space*. Qualitative *irrelevance* of usual unitarity, continuity *and* discontinuity, calculus, and *all* major structures (evolution operators, symmetry operators, *any* unitary operators, Lyapunov exponents, path integrals, etc.).

Let us recall now how these *fundamental* novelties of the universal science of complexity help to solve consistently *real-world problems* [13–26, 28] that accumulate and remain *unsolvable* within the unitary science paradigm:

(1) In *particle and quantum physics* one obtains *causal, unified* origin and structure of *elementary particles, all* their *properties* ("intrinsic", quantum, relativistic), and fundamental *interactions* [13, 17, 23, 24, 28]. *Complex-dynamic origin of mass* avoids any additional, abstract entities (Higgs bosons, zero-point field, extra dimensions, etc.). *Renormalised Planckian units* provide consistent *mass spectrum* and other problem solution. *Complex-dynamic cosmology* resolves the dark mass and energy problems without "invisible" entities, together with other old and new problems of unitary cosmology.

(2) At a higher complexity sublevel of *interacting particles* [13, 17, 23, 25, 26] one obtains *genuine, purely dynamic quantum chaos* for Hamiltonian (nondissipative) dynamics and *correct correspondence principle*. A slightly dissipative interaction dynamics leads to the *causally complete* understanding of *quantum measurement* in terms of *quantum* dynamics. *Intrinsic classicality* emerges as a *higher complexity level* in a *closed*, bound system, like atom.

(3) *Realistic, causally complete* foundation of *nanobiotechnology* is provided by *rigorous* description of *arbitrary* nanoscale interaction, revealing the *irreducible* role of *chaoticity* [17, 19]. *Exponentially huge power* of unreduced, complex nanobiosystem dynamics explains the *essential properties of life* and has direct relation to complex ICT system development (Sect. 2.2).

(4) *Causally complete* description of *unreduced genomic interactions* leads to *reliable, rigorously substantiated genetics* and consistent understanding of related *evolutionary processes* [16, 18].

(5) Higher-complexity applications include *general many-body problem solution* and related description of "difficult" cases in *solid-state physics*, unreduced dynamics and evolution of *living organisms, integral medicine*, emergent (genuine) *intelligence* and *consciousness, complex ICT system dynamics, creative ecology* and practically efficient *sustainable development concept*, rigorously specified *ethics* and *aesthetics* [13, 16–18, 20–22].

Note that only the unreduced, universal concept of complexity can be useful for real problem solution culminating in creation of complex, autonomic and intelligent ICT systems, which in their turn form a *consistent*, necessary basis for further control and development of real interaction complexity.

5 Conclusion and Perspectives

We have presented a rigorously specified, working prototype of the unified science of complex ICT systems demonstrating its necessity, feasibility and practical application efficiency. One obtains thus a new, intrinsically unified and realistic kind of knowledge with extended possibilities of consistent understanding and progressive development of real-world complexity.

Application of the universal science of complexity to autonomic communication and information systems has a *special importance* among other applications, since it is the *first* case of totally *artificial*, man-made systems that can possess *unreduced complexity* features comparable to those of natural systems and remaining irrational "mysteries" within the unitary science framework (starting from "quantum mysteries" [13,17,23–26,28]). Successful realisation of unreduced ICT complexity will open the way to a much larger, unlimited and now *reliable* complexity design becoming so necessary today because of the rapid *empirical* technology progress (Sect. 1). Those major purposes *cannot* be attained within unitary *imitations* of communication and software complexity (e.g. [4,8]), since they avoid the *unreduced*, network-wide interaction analysis and use *essentially simplified* models even for separate component description (in particular, they cannot describe the emerging genuine chaoticity [13,17]).

It is difficult to have serious doubts about basic consistency of a unified complexity framework based on the unreduced problem solution and confirmed by a variety of applications (Sects. 2, 4). Understanding of unreduced interaction complexity is indispensable for efficient design of even regular, but mechanically "complicated" systems. It is evident that all increasingly popular "bio-inspired", autonomic and "intelligent" *imitations* of natural complexity will be much more successful with the help of *consistent understanding* of the *unreduced* versions and properties of life, intelligence, etc. In this sense one can say that application of the universal science of complexity will certainly provide *consistent* clarification of what is possible *or* impossible in *artificial complexity design*, whereupon further development of ICT applications of unreduced complexity analysis can produce *only positive* (and urgently needed) result.

References

1. M. Rees, *Our Final Hour: A Scientist's Warning: How Terror, Error, and Environmental Disaster Threaten Humankind's Future in This Century — On Earth and Beyond* (Basic Books, New York, 2003).
2. The First International Workshop on Autonomic Communication (WAC 2004), http://www.autonomic-communication.org/wac/wac2004/program.html. Proceedings are being published as LNCS No. 3457, Springer Verlag (2005).
3. European Commission FP6, FET Situated and Autonomic Communications, http://www.cordis.lu/ist/fet/comms.htm. Links to other related FET initiatives can be found at http://www.cordis.lu/ist/fet/areas.htm.

4. S. Bullock and D. Cliff, Complexity and Emergent Behaviour in ICT Systems, Foresight Intelligent Infrastructure Systems Project, UK Office of Science and Technology (2004), http://www.foresight.gov.uk/ Intelligent_Infrastructure_Systems/Complexity_and_Emergent_Behaviour.html.

5. G. Di Marzo Serugendo, A. Karageorgos, O.F. Rana, and F. Zambonelli (Eds.), *Engineering Self-Organising Systems: Nature Inspired Approaches to Software Engineering*, LNCS No. 2977 (Springer Verlag, Berlin, 2004).

6. T. Berners-Lee, K. Hendler, and O. Lassila, The Semantic Web, *Scientific American*, May (2001) 35–43.

7. ManyOne Networks, http://www.manyone.net/; Digital Universe Foundation, http://www.digitaluniverse.net/.

8. L. Kocarev and G. Vattay (Eds.), *Complex Dynamics in Communication Networks* (Springer Verlag, Berlin, 2005).

9. J. Horgan, From Complexity to Perplexity, *Scientific American*, June (1995) 74–79.

10. J. Horgan, *The End of Science. Facing the Limits of Knowledge in the Twilight of the Scientific Age* (Addison-Wesley, Helix, 1996).

11. G.F.R. Ellis, Physics, Complexity and Causality, *Nature* **435** (2005) 743.

12. G.F.R. Ellis, Physics and the Real World, *Physics Today*, July (2005) 49–54.

13. A.P. Kirilyuk, *Universal Concept of Complexity by the Dynamic Redundance Paradigm: Causal Randomness, Complete Wave Mechanics, and the Ultimate Unification of Knowledge* (Naukova Dumka, Kyiv, 1997). For a non-technical overview see also Physics/9806002 at http://arXiv.org.

14. A.P. Kirilyuk, Dynamically Multivalued Self-Organisation and Probabilistic Structure Formation Processes, *Solid State Phenomena* **97–98** (2004) 21–26. Physics/0405063 at http://arXiv.org.

15. A.P. Kirilyuk, Universal Symmetry of Complexity and Its Manifestations at Different Levels of World Dynamics, *Proceedings of Institute of Mathematics of NAS of Ukraine* **50** (2004) 821–828. Physics/0404006 at http://arXiv.org.

16. A.P. Kirilyuk, The Universal Dynamic Complexity as Extended Dynamic Fractality: Causally Complete Understanding of Living Systems Emergence and Operation, in: *Fractals in Biology and Medicine. Vol. III*, edited by G.A. Losa, D. Merlini, T.F. Nonnenmacher, and E.R. Weibel (Birkhäuser, Basel, 2002), pp. 271–284. Physics/0305119 at http://arXiv.org.

17. A.P. Kirilyuk, Dynamically Multivalued, Not Unitary or Stochastic, Operation of Real Quantum, Classical and Hybrid Micro-Machines, Physics/0211071 at http://arXiv.org.

18. A.P. Kirilyuk, Complex-Dynamical Extension of the Fractal Paradigm and Its Applications in Life Sciences, in: *Fractals in Biology and Medicine. Vol. IV*, edited by G.A. Losa, D. Merlini, T.F. Nonnenmacher, and E.R. Weibel (Birkhäuser, Basel, 2005), pp. 233–244. Physics/0502133 at http://arXiv.org.

19. A.P. Kirilyuk, Complex Dynamics of Real Nanosystems: Fundamental Paradigm for Nanoscience and Nanotechnology, *Nanosystems, Nanomaterials, Nanotechnologies* **2** (2004) 1085–1090. Physics/0412097 at http://arXiv.org.

20. A.P. Kirilyuk, Emerging Consciousness as a Result of Complex-Dynamical Interaction Process, Report at the EXYSTENCE workshop Machine Consciousness: Complexity Aspects (Turin, 29 Sep – 1 Oct 2003). Physics/0409140 at http://arXiv.org.

21. A.P. Kirilyuk, Complex Dynamics of Autonomous Communication Networks and the Intelligent Communication Paradigm, Report at WAC 2004, see Ref. [2]. Physics/0412058 at http://arXiv.org.

22. A.P. Kirilyuk, Unreduced Dynamic Complexity, Causally Complete Ecology, and Realistic Transition to the Superior Level of Life, Report at the conference "Nature, Society and History" (Vienna, 30 Sep – 2 Oct 1999), see http://hal.ccsd.cnrs.fr/ccsd-00004214.

23. A.P. Kirilyuk, Quantum Field Mechanics: Complex-Dynamical Completion of Fundamental Physics and Its Experimental Implications, Physics/0401164 at http://arXiv.org.

24. A.P. Kirilyuk, Complex-Dynamic Cosmology and Emergent World Structure, Report at the International Workshop on Frontiers of Particle Astrophysics (Kiev, 21–24 June 2004). Physics/0408027 at http://arXiv.org.

25. A.P. Kirilyuk, Quantum Chaos and Fundamental Multivaluedness of Dynamical Functions, *Annales de la Fondation Louis de Broglie* **21** (1996) 455–480. Quant-ph/9511034–36 at http://arXiv.org.

26. A.P. Kirilyuk, Theory of Charged Particle Scattering in Crystals by the Generalized Optical Potential Method, *Nucl. Instr. and Meth. B* **69** (1992) 200–231.

27. P.H. Dederichs, Dynamical Diffraction Theory by Optical Potential Methods, in: *Solid State Physics: Advances in Research and Applications*, Vol. 27, edited by H. Ehrenreich, F. Seitz, and D. Turnbull (Academic Press, New York, 1972), pp. 136–237.

28. A.P. Kirilyuk, 75 Years of the Wavefunction: Complex-Dynamical Extension of the Original Wave Realism and the Universal Schrödinger Equation, Quant-ph/0101129 at http://arXiv.org.

Predictive Mobility Support with Secure Context Management for Vehicular Users*

Minsoo Lee[1], Gwanyeon Kim[1], Sehyun Park[1†], Ohyoung Song[1] and Sungik Jun[2]

1 School of Electrical and Electronics Engineering,
Chung-Ang University, 221, Heukseok-dong, Dongjak-gu, Seoul, Korea
{lemins, cityhero}@wm.cau.ac.kr, {shpark, song}@cau.ac.kr
2 Electronics and Telecommunications Research Institute
161 Gajeong-dong, Yuseong-gu, Daejeon, 305-350, Korea
sijun@etri.re.kr

Abstract. This paper presents a predictive mobility management framework with the secure context management in mobile networks. We devised the authentication method for seamless handovers that exploit the knowledge of the mobility prediction. Previous Access Router (AR) forwards the pre-established context information to the new AR in the predicted target wireless cell where MN might move in the near future. Therefore the context for autonomous services is available in the right place at right time.

1 Introduction

In the vision of 4G networks the demand for telematics applications in smart vehicles will rise steeply over the next few years with navigation services, emergency call, real-time multimedia services, and becoming increasingly popular choices among motorists [1]. Seamless security, mobility and QoS management are therefore required for mobile users in vehicles, often equipped with several wireless network technologies, for example, wireless local area networks (WLANs), 3G cellular networks and wireless metropolitan area networks (WMANs).

The ability to provide seamless security QoS is the key to the success of autonomous services in 4G networks and ubiquitous computing. There has been a considerable amount of QoS research recently. However, the main part of this research has been in the context of individual architectural components, and much

* This research was supported by the MIC(Ministry of Information and Communication), Korea, under the Chung-Ang University HNRC(Home Network Research Center)-ITRC support program supervised by the IITA(Institute of Information Technology Assessment)
† The corresponding author

Please use the following format when citing this chapter:

Lee, M., Kim, G., Park, S., Song, O. and Jun, S., 2007, in IFIP International Federation for Information Processing, Volume 229, Network Control and Engineering for QoS, Security, and Mobility, IV, ed. Gaïti, D., (Boston: Springer), pp. 21–28.

less progress has been made in addressing the issue of an overall QoS architecture for the mobile Internet [2].

Another major challenge for seamless mobility is the creation of a secure vertical handover protocol: a secure handover protocol for users that move between different types of networks [3].

The seamless communication environments require a variety of context such as user identity, time of day, date or season, current physical location, mobility patterns and whether the user is driving or walking. However, the context information is difficult to manage, because the amount of the context information can be enormous and location dependent.

When the handover occurs in the most of mobile networks, the Mobile Node (MN) and the access router (AR) need to exchange security information. This process is time-consuming and creates a significant amount of signaling. To minimize the conversation over the wireless link, context transfer mechanism could be one solution [4, 5, 6, 7, 8].

This paper presents a secure context management scheme minimizing the signaling overhead. Previous AR forwards the pre-established AAA information to the new AR in the predicted target wireless cell where MN might move in the near future. Therefore the context for autonomous services is available in the right place at right time. We also designed the detailed context transfer procedure for secure telematics applications.

The rest of this paper is organized as follow. Section 2 describes the fast handover with the predictive mobility support in mobile networks. Section 3 suggests our secure context management framework for vehicular users in mobile networks. Section 4 describes the performance analysis of our framework through a closed queuing network model. Section 5 concludes this paper.

2 Mobility-aware Fast Handover with Context Transfer in Mobile Networks

Primary motivation of context transfer protocol with mobility prediction is to quickly re-establish context transfer candidate services without requiring the MN to explicitly perform all protocol flows for seamless security services.

However, context transfer may not always be the best solution for re-establishing services on a new subnet. There are some issues as following:

* Router compatibility: Context transfer between two routers is possible only if the receiving router supports the same context transfer-candidate services as the sending router. This does not mean that the two nodes are identical in their implementation, nor does it even imply that they must have identical capabilities.

* Requirement to re-initialize a service from scratch: There may be situations where either the device or the access network would prefer to reestablish or re-negotiate the level of service.

* Suitability for the particular service: Context transfer assumes that it is faster to establish the service by context transfer rather than from scratch.

These limitations should be taken into account in the design considerations of seamless mobility solutions.

As the predictive mobility support for vehicular users we designed Location Predictor (LP). LP performs mobility prediction both for micro movement in a cell and for macro movement between cells (Figure 1). LP request current time, destination information and movement patterns of the user from the Location History DB. For the micro movement prediction, LP performs the local prediction using location history of the user and the current user mobility. As the macro movement prediction, LP sets cell sequence and the next context transfer zones using road segments, road sequence and handover segments.

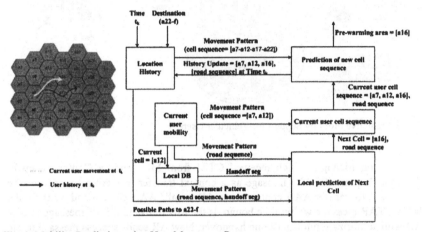

Fig. 1. Mobility Prediction using User Movement Patterns

3 Mobility-aware Security Context Management Framework for Autonomous Services

Figure 2 shows our predictive mobility management with secure context management for vehicular users. MN performs full authentication for initial login in core network (CN) where stores registration data for users after network selection procedure.

At this time, mobile user may configure user specific information such as destination, user applications and downloaded telematics services. After that, AAA context including cipher key is installed in current AR and MN gets GPS-based real-time location information and receives handover road segments and its coordination periodically from Location Manager. Mobile user who moves by car predicts next cell(s) through Mobile Manager inside the vehicle or within the mobile terminal, and transmits the next Context Transfer Zones Indication (CTZI) to Location Manager at appropriate time.

Minsoo Lee1, Gwanyeon Kim1, Sehyun Park1 , Ohyoung Song1 and Sungik Jun2

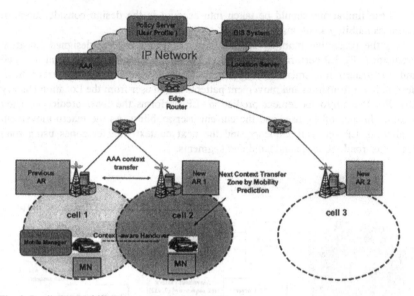

Fig. 2. Predictive Mobility Support for Vehicular Users

Location Manager which received CTZI from MN sends a Context Transfer Activate Request (CTAR) message as a context transfer triggering that causes the current AR to transfer AAA context. New AR installs AAA context and waits for the MN's CTAR message within time bound. If the MN transfers CTAR message to new AR with authorization token during handover, New AR sends success message to the MN if token verification is successful.

Mobile Manager may be built inside a vehicle typically. It predicts next cell(s) using real-time location data and mobility prediction application, and determines the next context transfer zones at appropriate time. Location Manager plays a role of context transfer trigger in the proposed architecture. It also monitors all MN's movements and maintains handover road segments and their coordination in its local DB. While a Location Manager interoperates all MNs in an administrative domain, it mediates AAA context transfer among ARs.

If the mobility prediction is correct, MN performs secure context-aware handover procedure. However, if it is failure, the MN can complete the handover using general context transfer.

4 Performance Analysis

We analyzed the performance of our context-aware handover scheme in the simulation environment as shown in Figure 3. We assumed that each router guarantees router compatibilities for context transfer and context transfer between two routers is possible only if the receiving router supports the same context transfer-candidate services as the sending router.

In the scenario of Figure 3, the context-aware handover procedure has three job classes; the context transfer zone setup step and two main steps according as it is successful or failure. If mobility prediction is successful, MN performs context-aware handover procedure. However, if the mobility prediction is failure, it is possible to use general context transfer protocol. We have modeled and tried to solve our architecture as a closed queuing system for the proposed protocol as in Figure 3 and Table 1.

We analyzed of approximate Mean Value Analysis (MVA) as described in [9, 10]. $r_{im,jn}$ means the probability that a class m job moves to class n at node j after completing service at node i. p represents a probability of the mobility prediction accuracy.

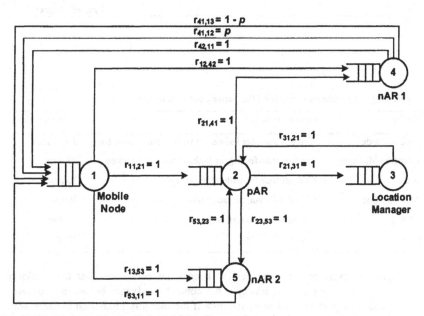

Fig. 3. The Testbed of the Predictive Mobility Support Scenario

Table 2 summarizes the basic parameter settings underlying the performance experiments. Location Manager and ARs used Solaris 8 machine with Pentium III 933 MHz, 512 MB RAM. MN used Pentium III 800 MHz, 256MB RAM, Windows XP operating system with Lucent Orinoco IEEE 802.11b wireless LAN card. The cryptographic library was OpenSSL 0.9.7c [11], and data size was 1KB in token verification and 10 KB in context transfer.

Minsoo Lee1, Gwanyeon Kim1, Sehyun Park1 , Ohyoung Song1
and Sungik Jun2

Table 1. The number of operations at each queue and class

Class	Pre-warming step (class 1)	Location-aware step (class 2)	Context-transfer step (class 3)
Mobile node (node 1)	1 location prediction indication	1 CTAR	1 CTAR
pAR (node 2)	2 forwarding (indication, context)	0	1 token verification 1 forwarding (context)
Location Manager (node 3)	1 forwarding (CT Trigger)	0	0
nAR 1 (node 4)	1 install context	1 token verification	0
nAR 2 (node 5)	0	0	1 CT-Req forwarding 1 install context

Table 2. Basic parameters for setting the queuing network model

Entity	Operation in scenario	Performance
Mobile Node	Context Transfer Indication with authorization token	30.34 ms
Location Manager	Context transfer trigger with authorization token	27.4 ms
pAR	Context transfer with token parameter	30 ms
Mobile Node	CTAR with authorization token	30 ms
nAR 2	CT-Req with authorization token	27.4 ms
pAR	Context transfer	30 ms

Figure 4 describes the authentication latency for each case after the handover events at layer 2. Our method sets up AAA context in advance before the handover events and only performs token verification if the mobility prediction is successful. Therefore, MN experiences low latency relatively when it uses our secure context-aware handover protocol with high mobility prediction accuracy.

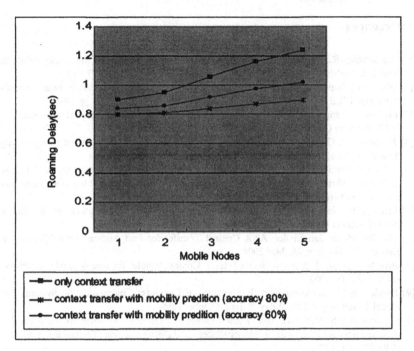

Fig. 4. Authentication delay of context-aware handover

5 Conclusions

In this paper, we proposed a mobility-aware handover scheme to minimize the signaling overhead during the handover procedure in the future mobile networks. We designed a Mobile Manager to effectively provide the seamless mobile services with the context transfer and the mobility prediction for fast re-authentication. To minimize the signaling overhead after the handover events at layer 2, we propose an efficient context transfer mechanism between Mobile Managers, providing the context is available in the right place at right time. Previous AR forwards the AAA pre-established information to the new AR of the predicted wireless cell where MN might move in the near future. Simulations of our context-aware handover performance gave a good insight into the current excitation. The proposed mobility-aware mechanism is being integrated with secure Web Services infrastructure [12] and the new interworking systems [13, 14].

References

[1] Leelaratne, R., Langley, R.: Multiband PIFA vehicle telematics antennas. Vehicular Technology,IEEE Transactions on, vol. 54, issue 2, March 2005 pp.477-485.

[2] Xio Gao, GangWu, Miki, T.: End-to-end QoS provisioning in mobile heterogeneous networks. IEEE Wireless Communications, vol. 11, issue 3, June 2004 pp.24-34.

[3] McNair, J., Fang Zhu: Vertical handovers in fourth-generation multinetwork environments. IEEE Wireless Communications, vol. 11, issue 3, June 2004 pp:8-15.

[4] J. Loughney: Context Transfer Protocol. Seamoby Working Group, Internet Engineering Task Force, draft-ietf-seamoby-ctp-11.txt

[5] Christos Politis, Kar Ann Chew, Nadeem Akhtar, Michael Georgiades and Rahim Tafazolli: Hybrid Multilayer mobility management with AAA context transfer capabilities for All-IP networks. IEEE Wireless Communications, Aug 2004

[6] J.Kempf: Problem Description: Reasons For Performing Context Transfers Between Nodes in an IP Access Network. RFC 3374, Internet Engineering Task Force.

[7] Tim Ruckforth, Jan Linder: AAA Context Transfer for Fast Authenticated Interdomain Handover. Swisscom SA, Mar 2004

[8] Juan M. Oyoqui, J. Antonio Garcia-Macias: Context transfer for seamless micromobility. IEEE ENC' 03, 2003

[9] Boudewijn R. Haverkort John: Performance of Computer Communication Systems : A Model-Based Approach' , Wiley & Sons, October 1999.

[10] Gunter Bolch, Stefan Greiner, Kishor Trevedi: A Generalized Analysis technique for queueing networks with mixed priority strategy and class switching. Technical Report TR-I4-95-08, Oct. 1995.

[11] OpenSSL, http://www.openssl.org

[12] Minsoo Lee, Jintaek Kim, Sehyun Park, Jaeil Lee and Seoklae Lee, "A Secure Web Services for Location Based Services in Wireless Networks," Lecture Notes in Computer Science, vol. 3042. May 2004, pp. 332-344.

[13] Minsoo Lee, Jintaek Kim, Sehyun Park, Ohyoung Song and Sungik Jun, A Location-Aware Secure Interworking Architecture Between 3GPP and WLAN Systems, Lecture Notes in Computer Science, vol. 3506, May 2005, pp. 394-406.

[14] Minsoo Lee, Gwanyeon Kim, and Sehyun Park: Seamless and Secure Mobility Management with Location Aware Service (LAS) Broker for Future Mobile Interworking Networks, JOURNAL of COMMUNICATIONS and NETWORKS, vol. 7, no. 2, JUNE 2005, pp. 207-221.

A Token Based Key Distribution Protocol for Closed Group Meetings

Fuwen Liu, Hartmut Koenig
Brandenburg University of Technology Cottbus
Department of Computer Science
PF 10 33 44, 03013 Cottbus, Germany
{lfw,koenig}@informatik.tu-cottbus.de

Abstract. Many emerging interactive and collaborative applications use the peer-to-peer paradigm nowadays. In every-day life peer-to-peer meetings of small groups are dominant, e.g. for business talks. Confidentiality is of primary concern in this context to provide group privacy. To assure confidentiality the partners have to agree upon a secret group key for encrypting their communication. This requires a secure distributed group key exchange protocol which assures that only active, uniquely authenticated group members know the current session key. In this paper we present a novel distributed key distribution protocol, called TKD, to efficiently support the key renewal in small dynamic peer groups. Performance comparisons show that TKD has a lower key refreshment delay compared to existing key exchange protocols.

1 Introduction

Nowadays modern group oriented applications tend to apply the peer-to-peer paradigm to be independent of a centralized group server representing a single point of failure. Decentralized managed groups are more flexible. They better support spontaneity and mobility to ad hoc set up meetings at varying locations. Such settings though make new demands on group security. Especially applications such as audio/video conferences have to provide group privacy and data integrity if they are deployed in business meetings.

In order to assure confidentiality in a meeting the partners have to agree upon a common secret key for encrypting their communication. It is intuitive that a decentralized key management protocol in which members themselves manage the group key should be deployed in peer-to-peer systems. In particular, real-time settings strongly require efficient decentralized key exchange protocols to minimize the interference period in group communication caused by the key refreshment, because in the asynchronous Internet hosts are usually unable to synchronously update their group key [1, 2].

Please use the following format when citing this chapter:

Liu, F. and Koenig, H., 2007, in IFIP International Federation for Information Processing, Volume 229, Network Control and Engineering for QoS, Security, and Mobility, IV, ed. Gaïti, D., (Boston: Springer), pp. 29–43.

In this paper we present a novel distributed key distribution protocol, called TKD (*token based key distribution*) to efficiently support the key renewal in small dynamic peer groups. We focus on closed dynamic peer groups of less than 100 participants here. The term *closed* indicates in this context that only current group members are allowed to send messages to the group. The entrance into the meeting is by invitation like oral or written invitations in every-day life. Many of these meetings such as business talks, project meetings, consultations, teleseminars, multi-party games, and others have usually only a small number of participants. Larger group meetings are usually managed in a hierarchical way rather than peer-to-peer [26]. However, small group peer-to-peer meetings are the dominant kind of meeting in every-day life. Simple and efficient features are required for their implementation on the Internet.

The paper is organized as follows. After addressing related work in Section 2 we describe the principle of the TKD protocol in Section 3. Next, Section 4 evaluates its performance compared to other key exchange protocols. In Section 5 we sketch how TKD fulfills the security demands. Some final remarks conclude the paper.

2   Related work

Group key management protocols can be generally classified into centralized and distributed protocols [3] depending on the fact whether the group key renewal is solely managed by a single entity (e.g. key server) or collaboratively performed by the group members themselves.

The *Group Key Management Protocol* (GKMP) is the simplest centralized approach used for the group key management [4]. The key server agrees upon a secret key with each group member. It delivers the new group key to each member encrypted with the corresponding secret key whenever required. This scheme is not efficient, because it requires $O(n)$ messages and $O(n)$ encryption cost for a rekeying event. Wong et al. proposed the *Logical Key Hierarchy* (LKH) protocol [5] which reduces the number of rekeying messages and the number of encryption from $O(n)$ in GKMP to $O(\log n)$. In this scheme the key server maintains a tree of keys so that for each group key refreshment the key server needs only to change the keys on the path from an affected leaf to the root. It is worth to mention that the rekeying efficiency of LKH mainly relies on a balanced key tree. After many rekeying operations the key tree may become imbalanced. To keep the efficiency of LKH it is necessary to rebalance the key tree [6].

Distributed group key management protocols can be divided into two groups: group key agreement and group key distribution protocols [7]. *Group key agreement protocols* are based on the original two-party Diffie-Hellman key exchange protocol [8]. Their basic idea is that each group member has to contribute a share to generate the group key. When the group membership changes, a group member is selected to compute new intermediate keys and distribute them to the group. Based on these intermediate keys and its own share each group member can independently compute the group key. Examples of such protocols are BD [9], CLIQUES [10], and TGDH [11]. The latter proved to be the most efficient one among these protocols related to computational and communication overhead [7]. For each group key renewal in TGDH, a defined group member, the so-called *sponsor*, generates the new intermediate keys and distributes them to the group over public channels. Each member computes the new group key using these intermediate keys and its own share.

In contrast to group key agreement protocols, *group key distribution protocols* dynamically select a group member to generate and distribute the new group key. Examples of such protocols are DTKM [12] and the proposal of Rodeh et al. [13]. The latter is more efficient than the DTKM protocol, because it only needs two communication rounds to complete the key renewal, while DTKM demands $log_2 n$ rounds. In the Rodeh protocol all used keys are arranged in a key tree. The leaves of the tree correspond to group members. The left-most leaf is defined as the *tree leader*. When renewing the key the tree leader generates the new group key and sends it to the subtree leaders over secure channels. The subtree leaders forward the new group key to their respective subtree members.

Key tree based protocols like LKH have been proven to be an appropriate solution for a centralized group key management, also for small groups [5]. Several distributed protocols like TGDH and the Rodeh protocol borrowed the key tree concept. Is the key tree based protocol an appropriate approach for small groups? In the sequel we propose an alternative approach for small dynamic peer groups and show that it is more efficient than key tree based one.

3 TKD Protocol

In this section we give an overview of the basic principle of the TKD approach. First we introduce the system architecture assumed for TKD.

System architecture. TKD assumes a three-layer architecture which consists of an application layer, a security layer, and a group communication layer (see Figure 1).

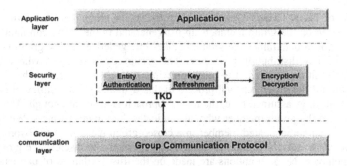

Fig. 1. System architecture

The *application layer* is not further specified here. We assume that it contains the control modules of the given application such as QoS management or floor control modules.

The *security layer* consists of two parts: the encryption/decryption module for data and media exchange, and the TKD protocol which distributes the group key used in the encryption/decryption function and authenticates joining members. The security layer is closely connected with the group communication layer which assures the consistency of the group data.

The *group communication layer* forms the basis for reliable, collaborative peer-to-peer applications. In our model we assume that the group communication layer indicates all changes in the group composition (join, leave, or failure of peers) to the upper layers to equally keep the membership consistent. Thus all peers have the same view on the actual group state and can uniquely decide all group related issues by themselves, e.g. QoS parameter settings, floor assignment, or key refreshment. To achieve this goal the group communication protocol should provide virtual synchrony [14] which assures that all recipients of the same group membership reliably receive messages in the same order as they are sent. This requires that a group communication protocol should be *reliable* to ensure that no data is lost, *ordered* to ensure that data are delivered in the order as they are sent, and *atomic* to ensure that all peers are updated equally. There are several protocols which meet these requirements like RMP [15], the Totem Protocol [16], Ensemble [17], Spread [18], and GCP [19]. Decentralized key management protocols heavily depend on the virtual synchrony property of the group communication protocol for refreshing the group key [9, 5, 11]. If this property is not provided, members may have a different view on the group membership when a key renewal is required. This may lead to confusions in the group key renewal process, since more than one member may be selected to generate the group or intermediate keys, respectively. Therefore, we assume like other decentralized key management protocols that a group communication protocol with virtual synchrony is applied in the communication layer.

We further assume that the group management, which executes the invitation procedure, is contained in this layer. Furthermore, all participants belong to an identical trust infrastructure or namespace. The group is set up by an initiator which invites the partners. Later further partners can join the group if desired. The decision to invite new partners is based on social agreement of all partners.

Principle of TKD. TKD is a token based protocol. The group members form a logical ring based on the group membership list generated in the group communication layer. The token determines the group member that generates a new group key and initiates the key distribution procedure. The group key is renewed whenever the group composition changes. The token principle was chosen to select the member responsible for the group renewal process in this dynamic group configuration. For smaller groups, as assumed here, the token approach is efficient enough. The token holder is also the group member who authenticates the joining partners. We further assume that an authenticated member in a closed group meeting is trustworthy, i.e. he/she does not actively attempt to disturb the system and to disclose the group key to non-members. No assumptions are made on the trustworthiness of partners after leaving. These assumptions correspond to practical security applications. Other decentralized group key protocols as discussed above rely on similar assumptions. The initiator of the group creates the first token. After renewing the group key the token holder hands the token over to the next group member in the ring. The token shift is part of the rekeying message which is multicast to the whole group. Thus each group member knows the current token holder at any time. The reliable delivering of the rekeying message is guaranteed by the underlying group communication layer as discussed above.

The group key renewal is based on the Diffie-Hellman (DH) key exchange principle [8]. After generating a new group key the token holder establishes temporary secure channels to all members to deliver the key. For this, it uses the shared DH secrets, which are shared with each other member, and a nonce, which is only valid for this group key renewal cycle. The details are given for the join and the leave procedure next.

Join procedure. The join procedure consists of two steps: (1) the authentication phase in which the invitee and the token holder mutually authenticate and (2) the proper join phase causing the group key refreshment (see Figure 2). Five messages or rounds, respectively, are needed for the join procedure: four rounds for authentication and one for the key refreshment.

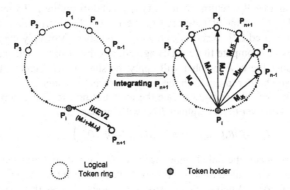

Fig. 2. Join Procedure

Unlike most group key management protocols TKD introduces a **partner authentication**. It is supposed to assure that the group key is only delivered to an authenticated member and that the new member can be sure that the received key is in fact sent by the inviting group. We apply the newly proposed internet draft standard IKEv2 [21] due to its increased efficiency, security, flexibility and robustness compared to the predecessor IKE [20]. Let us assume that P_{n+1} is invited to join a group of n participants: $P_1 \dots P_n$ (see Figure 2). The token holder is P_i. The group members including the token holder P_i are informed of the acceptance of the invitation by the underlying group communication protocol. Note that the token holder is not necessarily identical with the inviting participant. Thus it is avoided that this participant invites people whom are not agreed upon. To accomplish the mutual authentication between P_i and P_{n+1} the four messages (M_{J1}-M_{J4}) have to be exchanged in accordance with IKEv2.

$$M_{J1}(P_i \rightarrow P_{n+1}) : HDR, KE_i, SA_i, NA_i$$
$$M_{J2}(P_{n+1} \rightarrow P_i) : HDR, KE_{n+1}, SA_{n+1}, NA_{n+1}$$
$$M_{J3}(P_i \rightarrow P_{n+1}) : HDR, SK\{ID_i, CERT_i, SIG_i, ID_1, ID_2 \dots ID_n, g^{r1}, g^{r2} \dots g^m\}$$
$$M_{J4}(P_{n+1} \rightarrow P_i) : HDR, SK\{ID_{n+1}, CERT_{n+1}, SIG_{n+1}, g^{m+1}\}$$

With the exchange of messages M_{J1} and M_{J2}, the token holder and the invitee negotiate the security association SA which specifies the cryptography parameters used for the messages M_{J3} and M_{J4}. *Further* they generate the shared keys SK and $SK^{\hat{}}$ on the basis of the exchanged public DH values KE_i and KE_{n+1} as well as a nonce NA. The shared keys are used to protect the subsequent messages M_{J3} and M_{J4}. To avoid a reflection attack, separate session key SK and $SK^{\hat{}}$ are used for each direction [21]. SK (and also SK') consists of the encryption key Sk_e and the authentication key SK_a which are generated according to the IKEv2 draft [21].To adapt to the group communication scenario some message components was added to messages M_{J3} and M_{J4} to exchange information between the token holder and the invitee. The token holder delivers the group information to the new member in message M_{J3} including all members' identities (ID_1, ID_2,..., ID_n) and the respective public DH values (g^{r_1}, g^{r_2},...g^{r_n}). The invitee P_{n+1} returns its identity ID_{n+1} and its public DH value $g^{r_{n+1}}$ with message M_{J4}. Upon receipt of message M_{J3} the invitee P_{n+1} performs n DH agreements to get the shared DH secrets with the other members. Virtually the new member does not have to compute these n DH agreements in real-time. This can be done "off-line", because the new member will apply the shared DH secrets only when it becomes the token holder to establish the temporal secure channels.

If the token holder fails to authenticate the invitee it notifies the group about this and hands the token over to its neighbor ID_{i+1} with message M_{Jf}:

$$M_{Jf}(P_i \rightarrow P_1, P_2...P_n) : HDR, GK_{old}\{Token, VT, ID_{i+1}, Authf, ID_{n+1}\}$$

where *Authf* indicates the failed authentication, ID_{n+1} is the new member's identity. The token version VT is used to prevent replay attacks. It is increased by 1 each time the token is forwarded. When receiving M_{Jf} each member knows that the new member failed to join the group and who is the new token holder. All members keep the group key unchanged.

After successfully authenticating the invitee the token holder P_i starts the **group key renewal**. The new key GK_{new} is randomly generated and thus independent of previously used keys. The token holder multicasts the new key GK_{new} together with the token in the rekeying message M_{J5} to the new partner P_{n+1} and the other members (see Figure 2). For the latter, temporal secure channels are established as described below. Message M_{J5} has the following format:

$$M_{J5}(P_i \rightarrow P_1, P_2...P_{n+1}) : HDR, GK_{old}\{ID_i, N_i\}, K_{i1}\{VK, GK_{new}\}$$
$$,..., K_{in}\{VK, GK_{new}\}, SK\{GK_{new}, VK, GSA, ID_i\}, GK_{new}\{Token, VT, ID_{i+1}, g^{r_{n+1}}, ID_{n+1},\}$$

The message consists of four parts which serve different purposes. The first part of message M_{J5} contains token holder's identity ID_i and a nonce N_i used to construct the temporal secure channels between the token holder and the other members. This part is encrypted with the old group key GK_{old}. The second part of message M_{J5} contains the new group key GK_{new} and the group key version VK. The group key version distinguishes old group keys from the new one and is used to counter replay attacks. VK is increased by 1 each time the group key is renewed. These data are separately encrypted for each group member using its temporal channel keys K_{ij} ($j=1, 2,...n$ and $j\neq i$) between the token holder P_i and the other group members. The token holder P_i

creates a temporary secure channel K_{ij} with each group member using the shared secrets with them and the nonce N_i. The secure channels are established as follows:

$$K_{ij-e} = HMAC(g^{n_i r_j}, g^{n_i r_j} N_i\ ID_i\ ID_j\ 0) \tag{1}$$

$$K_{ij-a} = HMAC(g^{n_i r_j}, g^{n_i r_j}|N_i|ID_i|ID_j|1) \quad (j=1, 2,....n \text{ and } j \neq i) \tag{2}$$

N_i and ID_i are the nonce and token holder's identity contained in the first part of message M_{J5}. ID_j is the group members' identity and $g^{n_i r_j}$ the secret key stored at both sides. $HMAC(k,m)$ [22] is a pseudorandom function which hashes a message m using key k. The symbol "|" means concatenation. K_{ij-e} is the encryption key, while K_{ij-a} is used for message authentication. The third part of message M_{J5} for the new member contains the new group key GK_{new}, its version, the group key association GSA, which specifies the cryptographic algorithms and the security policies currently deployed for group communication, and the token holders' identity. These data are encrypted with the shared key SK determined during the authentication phase (see above). The fourth part contains the token, the token version VT, the neighbor's identity ID_{i+1}, the new members' identity ID_{n+1}, and its public DH value $g^{r_{n+1}}$. This part is protected under the new group key GK_{new}.

After having received M_{J5} the old group members can decrypt ID_i and N_i with the old group key GK_{old}. They can determine the channel key according to formula (1) and (2) and decrypt the new group key GK_{new}. The new group member decrypts the new group key using the shared key SK. Now all group members including the new participant P_{n+1} possess the new group key, the public DH values of the other members as well as their shared secrets. They are all in the same state so that the new token holder can refresh the group key when required.

Leave procedure. When a participant leaves the group the underlying group communication protocol informs the remaining members about the leaving. After that the token holder starts the key refreshment procedure. Figure 3 shows an example.

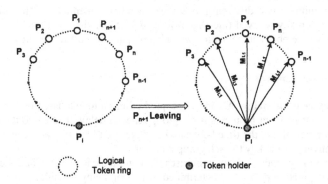

Fig. 3. Leave Procedure

We assume that participant P_{n+1} is leaving a group of $n+1$ members $P_1 \ldots P_{n+1}$. The token holder P_i generates a new group key GK_{new} and multicasts it in the leaving message M_{L1} to the remaining group members. M_{L1} has a similar structure like the join message M_{J5}:

$$M_{L1}(P_i \rightarrow P_1, P_2...P_n): HDR, GK_{old}\{ID_i, N_i\}, K_{i1}\{VK, GK_{new}\},..., K_{in}\{VK, GK_{new}\}, GK_{new}\{Token, VT, ID_{i+1}\}$$

It first encrypts the identity of the token holder ID_i together with a newly generated nonce N_i with the old group key. The new key GK_{new} and the actual key version VK are encrypted with the temporary channel keys for each remaining group member. These keys are derived according to formula (1) and (2). The token, the token version, and neighbor's identity ID_{i+1} are protected by the new group key. The leaving participant cannot take possession of GK_{new}, because it cannot reconstruct any of the temporary secure channels K_{i1}, K_{i2}...K_{in} without knowing the shared secrets $g^{r_ir_1}, g^{r_ir_2}, ...g^{r_ir_n}$ between the token holder P_i and the remaining members P_1, P_2,... P_j,...P_n ($j \neq i$). When receiving message M_{L1} the remaining group members can decrypt the new group key in the same way as described above for message M_{J5}. The group key refreshment is completed.

When the token holder leaves the group it first forwards the token to its neighbor and then starts the leave procedure. A host failure including that of the token holder is indicated by the underlying group communication layer. The group members equally update the group composition. In case of a member crash the token holder simply refreshes the group key. If the token holder crashes the neighbor in order is the next token holder by rule. It starts the leave procedure.

4   Performance analysis

This section evaluates the performance of TKD in comparison with other decentralized group key exchange protocols. We consider the key distribution protocol of Rodeh et al. and TGDH which are considered the most efficient group key distribution and agreement protocol, respectively. For the comparison, we apply the benchmarks of cryptographic algorithms from [23] to calculate the performance. The benchmarks are summarized in *Appendix*.

TKD comprises two different procedures: member authentication (message M_{J1}~ M_{J4}) and group key renewal (message M_{J5} or M_{L1}). Since the other two protocols do not possess a member authentication we only compare the cost for the key renewal.

4.1 Group key renewal

Group key renewal delay. A widely accepted criterion to evaluate the efficiency of group key management protocols is the group renewal delay. It refers to the duration of the key renewal, i.e. the time between the triggering of the procedure and the successful delivery of the key to each group member.

The group key renewal delay comprises the communication delay and the cryptographic computation delay. It is determined by the following formula:

$$D_{gkr} = \max(\ D_{cs} + D_{com} + D_{cr}\ ) \tag{3}$$

where D_{gkr} is the group key renewal delay, D_{cs} the cryptographic computation delay of the sender, D_{com} the communication delay, and D_{cr} the cryptographic computation delay of the receiver. Here the sender stands for the *tree leader* in Rodeh's protocol, the *sponsor* in TGDH, and the *token holder* in TKD, respectively. The receiver corresponds to the participants including the new member and the subtree leader in the Rodeh protocol, and the participants including the new member in TGDH and TKD.

The **cryptographic computation delay** directly depends on the computation cost of the protocol. Table 1 summarizes the computation cost of the considered protocols by indicating the number of cryptographic operations they carry out. The comparison shows that the protocols use asymmetric and symmetric cryptographic operations differently. TGDH at the one edge applies more intensively asymmetric cryptographic computations while TKD at the other edge uses mainly symmetric operations. Since asymmetric cryptographic computations, as known, are much slower than the symmetric operations, the resulting total computation cost of TKD is lower than that of the other two protocols. For example, the computation cost of one DH agreement corresponds to approximately 5500 hash and symmetric encryptions of the group key (16 byte size) based on the benchmarks of cryptographic algorithms of [23]. Assuming a group size of 100 members, only about 400 hash and symmetric encryptions are required to renew the group key in TKD.

Table 1. Computation cost for the group key renewal

Protocols	Operation	Members	Computation cost				
			Asymmetric operations			Symmetric operations	
			DH agreement	RSA signature[2]	RSA verification[2]	Hash and encryption (16 Byte)	Hash and decryption (16 Byte)
Rodeh	Join	Tree leader	1	-	-	2	-
		New member	1	-	-	-	1
		Participants	-	-	-	-	1
	Leave	Tree leader	$\log_2 n$[1]	-	-	$\log_2 n$	-
		Subtree leader	1	-	-	-	1
		Participants	-	-	-	-	1
TGDH	Join	Sponsor	$2\log_2 n$	1	-	-	-
		New member	$2\log_2 n$	-	1	-	-
		Participants	$1...2\log_2 n$	-	1	-	-
	Leave	Sponsor	$2\log_2 n$	1	-	-	-
		Participants	$1...2\log_2 n$	-	1	-	-
TKD	Join	Token holder	-	-	-	$2n+3$	-
		New member	-	-	-	-	2
		Participants	1	-	-	-	3
	Leave	Token holder	-	-	-	$2n+2$	-
		Participants	-	-	-	-	2

Note: 1) n is the number of group members.
2) RSA signature in TGDH is used to support message authentication rather than member authentication [5].
3) The computation costs of Rodeh and TGDH listed in the table are their best case when the key tree is balanced. For an imbalanced key tree Rodeh and TGDH need more computation for a rekeying event.

Applying the benchmarks of the cryptographic algorithms from [23] to Table 1 we can now compute the cryptographic computation delay for the three protocols, i.e. $max(D_{cs}+D_{cr})$. The results are listed in Table 2. It shows that TKD causes less computation delay than the other two protocols for the join and leave procedure.

Table 2 Computation delay for group key renewal (ms)

	Rodeh	TGDH	TKD
Join	7.72	$4.93+15.44 *\log_2 n^{1)}$	$3.86+(2n+6)* 7*10^{-4}$
Leave	$3.86*(\log_2 n+1)+(\log_2 n+1)*7*10^{-4}$	$4.93+15.44 *\log_2 n$	$(2n+4)*7*10^{-4}$

Note: 1) n is the number of group members.

The **communication delay** for a group key renewal depends on the number of communication rounds needed to complete the renewal procedure and on the duration of the communication rounds. For a fair comparison, we assume here that the three protocols run on top of the group communication protocol GCP [19]. According to [24] the delay D_{c1} for one communication round in a LAN setting can be estimated as follows:

$$D_{c1} = 8.71n-8.63+0.0015b \qquad (4)$$

where n is the number of group members and b the size of the rekeying message in bytes. TKD and TGDH require only one communication round to accomplish the group key renewal for joining and leaving, whereas the Rodeh protocol needs two communication rounds each.

Group key renewal delay. Based on Table 2 and formula (4), we can now determine the group renewal delay using formula (3). The resulting delays for the join and the leave procedures are depicted in Figure 4 and 5.

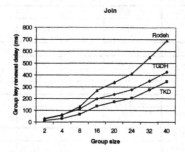

Fig. 4. Group key refreshment delay comparison for joining

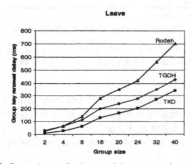

Fig. 5. Group key refreshment delay comparison for leaving

Inferred from formula (4) and the cited benchmarks of asymmetric algorithms in the appendix, the communication delay plays a larger role than the cryptographic computation delay in determining the group key refreshment delay. It is worth to mention that a reverse conclusion may be drawn, if the comparisons are based on lower computation power devices (e.g. PDAs, mobile phones) rather than on a modern computer platform (such as Pentium 4 platform used in our comparison). The lower the power of a device the larger the computation delays required by the asymmetric algorithms.

The comparison shows that TKD has a lower group key refreshment delay for both procedures than the Rodeh key distribution protocol and the most efficient key agreement protocol TGDH. The reason is that TKD needs less computation rounds and mostly uses symmetric cryptographic computations. The Rodeh protocol is the most expensive one, because it demands two communication rounds to accomplish the group key refreshment. Although also requiring only one communication round like TKD the TGDH protocol is the second expensive one, because it requires a lot of asymmetric cryptographic operations to generate the new group key for each member.

4.2 Communication overhead

The communication overhead depends on the message size of the protocol, i.e. how many bandwidth a protocol consumes. Many centralized group key distribution protocols such as LKH [5] apply a key tree structure, so that the group key server can update the group key using a message size of $O(log_2 n)$ symmetric keys. This is of particular significance for very large groups (e.g. one million members). Thus the rekeying message can be delivered in one packet. Some decentralized group key distribution protocols like Rodeh and TGDH follow the same principle to achieve a small rekeying message size, $O(log_2 n)$ symmetric keys for Rodeh and $O(log_2 n)$ asymmetric keys for TGDH. This is, however, achieved at the cost of two communication rounds in the Rodeh protocol and of $O(log_2 n)$ asymmetric cryptographic computations in TGDH. This is reason why they are slower than our scheme. In TKD the rekeying message size is $O(n)$ symmetric keys. For a group of 100 member peers, these are about 4 Kbyte. This can be transmitted without any problem in one UDP packet. Therefore bandwidth consumption for key renewal is not an issue for small group settings at all. In contrast, the group key renewal delay is the critical point for real-time applications.

4.3 Theoretical upper bounds of the group size

Finally we estimate the theoretical upper bounds of the group size of TKD. This estimation is made on two conditions: (1) the key renewal delay of TKD should fall below that of the compared protocols and (2) TKD accomplishes the group key renewal in one communication round.

The group key renewal delay of TKD, TGDH, and the Rodeh protocol can be determined based on Table 2 and formula (4) as follows:

$$D_{TKD} = 3.86 + (2n+6)*7*10^{-4} + 8.71n - 6.83 + 0.0015*36*n \tag{5}$$

$$D_{TGDH} = 4.93 + 15.44*\log_2 n + 8.71n - 6.83 + 0.0015*128*\log_2 n \tag{6}$$

$$D_{Rodeh} = 7.72 + 2*(8.71n - 6.83 + 0.0015*36*\log_2 n) \tag{7}$$

Condition (1) can be expressed through the following two formulas:

$$D_{TKD} \leq D_{TGDH} \tag{8}$$

$$D_{TKD} \leq D_{Rodeh} \tag{9}$$

These formulas can be now used to determine the upper limit of the TKD group size. The solution for formula (8) is $n=3420$, whereas formula (9) remains true for any group size, i.e. TKD is always more efficient than the Rodeh protocol if TKD completes the key renewal in one communication round. Condition (2) means that the size of the rekeying messages is always less than the maximum size of an UDP packet (65536 bytes). Thus the upper bounds of group size can be determined by the following formula:

$$(n+1)*(sk+h)+ak \leq 65536 \tag{10}$$

where n is the number of group members, while sk, h, and ak correspond to the size of the symmetric key, the hash value and the asymmetric key, respectively. Their corresponding typical values are 16 bytes, 20 bytes and 128 bytes. Formula (10) holds as long as n is smaller than 1815.

To sum up, TKD is more efficient related to the key renewal delay than other key exchange protocols as long as the group size does not exceed 1815 members.

5 Security demands

TKD fulfills important security demands. Due to space limitation we cannot give a detailed analysis of the security properties of TKD here. We sketch the most important aspects.

The protocol has to assure that nobody outside the group acquires the group key (*key authentication*). TKD assures this, because each invitee must be authenticated by a group member. Only if this authentication is successful, the invitee can join the group and obtain the group key. On the other hand, the invitee can convince itself by receiving their identities and public DH values with message M_{J3} that the received group key is of the expected group.

It has to be assured that earlier leaving members cannot access to any key generated later to further decrypt data exchanged (*forward confidentiality*). According to the leaving procedure described above the leaving participant can never access to the temporary secret channels, because they rely on the shared secrets between the token holder and the remaining members which are not accessible for him/her. Vice versa, a later joining member should never have access to any older key to decrypt previously exchanged data (*backward confidentiality*). This is achieved by never delivering the old group key to the joining member. The parts of message M_{J5} that can be decrypted by the new member do not contain the old key.

The protocol has further to assure that members after leaving a session are not being able to deduce the current key using their former keys (*collusion freedom*). TKD assures this by randomly generating new group keys each time the group composition changes, which do not depend of each other. A further desirable feature is to avoid that a compromised group key can lead to the disclosure of past keys (*perfect forward secrecy*). TKD achieves this by never using long-term credentials for encrypting the keys and avoiding any access to keys and key material of former sessions. Finally the protocol should not allow that a disclosure of past session keys could be used to compromise the current group key (*resistance to known key attacks*). TKD prevents such attack by never transmitting the shared DH secrets via the network so that an attacker is unable to access the temporary secrete channels used for the group key delivery.

Compared with the other mentioned key management protocols TKD is the only one which fulfills all these security requirements.

6 Final remarks

In this paper we have presented the group key distribution protocol TKD to support confidential meetings of small dynamic peer groups in the Internet, e.g. for business talks. The protocol approach is simple and straightforward using a token mechanism and mainly symmetric cryptographic operations for the group key renewal. This leads to a significantly lower key renewal delay compared to existing key distribution and key agreement protocols. It is especially appropriate for applications which except key management and encryption/decryption simultaneously run other time and resource consuming procedures such as media data decompression like in a peer-to-peer multiparty video conference. In addition, TKD introduces in contrast to others key management protocol an authentication based on IKEv2. TKD requires an underlying group communication protocol that supports virtual synchrony for group data consistency as well as dynamic group composition. There are several protocols proposed in literature which possess these properties.

We showed in the paper that a simple straightforward distribution approach is more efficient for small groups than a key tree based one. It provides a stable performance and needs less effort for its maintenance. Key tree based schemes like TGDH and the Rodeh protocol possess a fluctuating performance after many rekeying operations due to the unbalance of the key tree. To maintain a balanced key tree rebalance algorithms have to be applied which makes the protocols more complex and less practical.

TKD further fulfills important security demands like key authentication, forward and backward confidentiality, collusion freedom, and others. It is based on the well-studied protocol IKEv2 for member authentication and the well-known Diffie-Hellman problem (i.e. discrete logarithm problem) for the construction of the temporary secure channels. The security of TKD is achieved by carefully paying attention that group key material can be only accessed by current authenticated group members and by generating keys which do not depend of each other.

42   Fuwen Liu, Hartmut Koenig

We are currently introducing TKD into the security architecture of the peer-to-peer multiparty video conference system BRAVIS [25] to allow confidential talks of closed group meetings in the Internet.

References

1. P. McDaniel, A. Prakash, and P. Honeyman: Antigone: A Flexible Framework for Secure Group Communication, CITI Technical Report 99-2, University of Michigan.
2. P. S. Kruus: A survey of multicast security issues and architectures. In: Proc. of the 21st National Information Systems Security Conference (NISSC), Oct. 1998.
3. S. Rafaeli and D. Hutchison: A Survey of Key Management for Secure Group Communication. ACM Computing Surveys 35 (2003) 3: 309-329.
4. H. Harney and C. Muckenhirn: Group Key Management Protocol (GKMP) Specification, July 1997, RFC 2094.
5. C. Wong, M. Gouda, and S. Lam: Secure group communication using key graphs. IEEE/ACM Transactions on Networking 8 (2000)1: 16-30.
6. M. J. Moyer, J. R. Rao and P. Rohatgi: Maintaining balanced key trees for secure multicast. Technical report, IETF, June 1999. draft-irtf-smug-key-tree-balance-00.txt.
7. Y. Kim, A. Perrig, and G. Tsudik: Tree-based Group Key Agreement. ACM Transactions on Information Systems Security (TISSEC) 7(2004)1: 60-96.
8. E. Rescorla: Diffie-Hellman Key Agreement Method. RFC 2631, June 1999.
9. M. Burmester and Y. Desmedt: A secure and efficient conference key distribution system. In Advances in Cryptology (EUROCRYPT'94), Springer LNCS 950, 1995, pp. 275-286.
10. M. Steiner, G. Tsudik, and M. Waidner: CLIQUES: A new approach to group key agreement. IEEE ICDCS, 1998, pp. 380-397.
11. Y. Kim, A. Perrig, and G. Tsudik: Simple and fault-tolerant key agreement for dynamic collaborative groups. In: S. Jajodia (ed.): 7th ACM Conference on Computer and Communications Security, Athens, Greece, Nov. 2000, ACM Press, pp. 235-244.
12 L. Dondeti, S. Mukherjee, and A. Samal: Disec: A distributed framework for scalable secure many-to-many communication. In: Proc. of the 5th IEEE Symposium on Computers and Communications (ISCC), July 2000.
13. O. Rodeh, K. P. Birman, D. Dolev: Optimized Group Rekey for Group Communication Systems. In Symposium Network and Distributed System Security (NDSS), San Diego, California, Feb. 2000, pp. 39-48.
14. G. V. Chockler, I. Keidar, and R. Vitenberg: Group communication specifications: A comprehensive study. ACM Computing Surveys 4 (2001): 427-469.
15. B. Whetten, T. Montgomery, and S. Kaplan: A High Performance Totally Ordered Multicast Protocol. International Workshop on Theory and Practice in Distributed Systems, Springer LNCS 938, pp. 33-57, 1994.
16. D. A. Agarwal: Totem: A Reliable Ordered Delivery Protocol for Interconnected Local Area Networks, Ph.D Thesis, University of Santa Barbara, Dec 1994.
17. K. Birman, R. Constable, M. Hayden, C. Kreitz, O. Rodeh, R. Van Renesse, W. Vogels: The Horus and Ensemble Projects: Accomplishments and Limitations. In: Proc. of the DARPA Information Survivability Conference & Exposition (DISCEX '00), Hilton Head, South Carolina, 2000.
18. Y. Amir, C. Danilov, and J. Stanton: A low latency, loss tolerant architecture and protocol for wide area group communication. In: Proc. 30th IEEE FTCS, June 2000.

19. M. Zuehlke, and H. Koenig: A Signaling Protocol for Small Closed Dynamic Multi-peer Groups. In Z. Mammeri and P. Lorenz (eds.): High Speed Networks and Multimedia Communications (HSNMC 2004). Springer-Verlag, Berlin, Heidelberg 2004, pp. 973 – 984

20. D. Harkins and D. Carrel: The Internet Key Exchange (IKE), RFC 2409, Nov. 1998.

21. C. Kaufman, Internet Key Exchange (IKEv2) Protocol, draft-ietf-ipsec-ikev2-17.txt, September 2004.

22. H. Krawczyk, M. Bellare, and R. Canetti: HMAC: Keyed-Hashing for Message Authentication, RFC 2104, February 1997.

23. Crypto++ 5.2.1 Benchmarks. http://www.eskimo.com/~weidai/benchmarks.html

24. M. Zuehlke: Distributed organized multiparty video conference for closed group in the Internet. Ph.D thesis, Brandenburg University of Technology Cottbus, Department of Computer Science, May 2004.

25. The BRAVIS video conference system. http://www.bravis.tu-cottbus.de.

26. S. Chanson, A. Hui, E. Siu, I.Beier, H. Koenig, and M. Zuehlke: OCTOPUS-A Scalable Global Multiparty Video Conferencing System. In: Proc. of the 8th International IEEE Conference on Computer Communications and Networks (IC3N'99), Boston, 1999, pp.97-102

Appendix: Benchmarks of crypto operations

The speed benchmarks for the cryptographic algorithms used in this paper are listed in the following table which is adopted from [23]. These results are achieved on a Pentium 4 2.1 GHz processor under Windows XP.

Algo-rithms	Symmetric crypto operations		Asymmetric crypto operations		
	SHA-1	AES (128-bit key)	RSA 1024 Signature	RSA 1024 Verification	DH 1024 key Agreement
Speed	68 Mbyte/s	61 Mbyte/s	4.75 ms/operation	0.18 ms/operation	3.86 ms/operation

Upgrading PPP security by Quantum Key Distribution*

Solange Ghernaouti-Hélie and Mohamed Ali Sfaxi

Inforge-HEC
university of Lausanne, Switzerland
{sgh@unil.ch, MohamedAli.Sfaxi@unil.ch}

Abstract. Quantum cryptography could be integrated in various existing concepts and protocols to secure communications that require very high level of security. The aim of this paper is to analyse the use of quantum cryptography within PPP. We introduce basic concepts of the Point to Point Protocol; we propose a solution that integrates quantum key distribution into PPP. An example is given to demonstrate the operational feasibility of this solution

Keywords. PPP, Quantum Key Distribution (QKD) within PPP, unconditional security transmission, data-link layer security, enhance PPP security, feasibility study, application domain

1 Introduction

Cryptography is largely used to increase security level of ICT infrastructures. However the enciphering mechanisms currently deployed are based on mathematical concepts whose robustness is not proven. Nowadays, with the sight of new discoveries in cryptanalysis, technology empowerment, new generations of computers and architectures (GRID computing...), trust, security dependability and resilience cannot be satisfied any more by a classical approach of cryptography. Since few years ago, the progress of quantum physics allowed mastering photons which can be used for informational ends (information coding, transport...). These technological progresses can also be applied to cryptography (quantum cryptography). Quantum cryptography could be integrated in already existing algorithms and protocols to secure networks. For instance, IP Security protocol (IPSEC) [RFC2401] can support the use of quantum cryptography [11]. Another kind of protocols could take benefits of the quantum cryptography concepts to optimise and to enhance security in link layer (OSI layer 2 protocols) such as the Point to Point Protocol (PPP) [RFC1661].

---

* This work has been done within the framework of the European research project : SECOQC - www.secoqc.net

---

Please use the following format when citing this chapter:

Ghernaouti-Hélie, S. and Sfaxi, M.A., 2007, in IFIP International Federation for Information Processing, Volume 229, Network Control and Engineering for QoS, Security, and Mobility, IV, ed. Gaïti, D., (Boston: Springer), pp. 45–59.

2   The importance of OSI layer 2 security

Securing layer 2 transactions is fundamental because this layer is common to all kinds of nodes' connections. The security processing is made transparently to the users and to the other protocols. Securing this layer is more optimised than securing the above OSI layer since neither additional encapsulation nor header is required.

The Point to Point Protocol [RFC1661] is a layer 2 protocol. It is widely used to connect two sets of nodes. This protocol was published in 1994 and natively the only security is done by additional authentication protocols. The confidentiality is not implemented in the original protocol but it was introduced by the Encryption Control Protocol [RFC1968]. This protocol uses the classical cryptography (algorithms such as DES or 3DES). Since, traditional cryptography is not based on "unconditional" evidence of security in term of information theory, but on not proven mathematical conjectures. It rests thus on what one calls the "computational" assumptions, i.e. on the idea that certain problems are difficult to solve and that one can control the lower limit of time necessary to the resolution of these problems [1]. In this context, security cannot be guaranteed. It is a crucial problem for an effective protection of sensible data, critical infrastructures and services. Using quantum cryptography concepts, the sender and the receiver could exchange secret keys. This exchange is proved to be unconditionally secure. Quantum key distribution with the One Time Pad [27] brings an unconditional security aspect to the communication upon the layer 2.

3   Brief presentation of PPP [RFC1661]

This section describes the PPP concept to point out the operating mode and the security issues in this protocol. The point to point protocol is a data-layer protocol ensuring a reliable data exchange over a point to point link. When the connection is established and configured, the PPP allows the data transfer of many protocols (IP, IPX, AppleTalk). That's why; PPP is widely used in Internet environment.

3.1   PPP components

The PPP protocol consists of three elements:

- a link control protocol (LCP): this element carry on the establishment, the configuration, the test of data link connection;
- a set of network control protocols (NCP) to communicate (and configure if needed) with network layer protocols (NP);
- An encapsulation protocol: The packets or datagram are encapsulated in PPP frame. The protocols encapsulated in the frame are identified by protocol field.

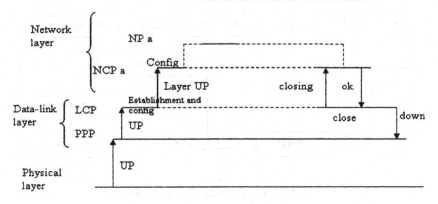

Fig. 1. PPP components connections (adapted from Labouret96)

The data-link layer is informed that the physical layer is "UP" and ready to be used (Figure 1). The LCP establishes and configure the PPP connection. After that, the network protocols could be encapsulated in PPP frame. In the figure 1, "NP a" is a network protocol related to the network control protocol "NCP a".

3.2   PPP connection

To establish a PPP connection, many steps have to be done before sending user's data. Following these steps, a reliable communication is possible between two linked nodes. These steps are presented in figure 2.

Dead status:
This status means that the link is not ready to receive any data. Every connection starts with this status. By receiving an "Up" event (carrier detection for instance), PPP goes to the "establishment" phase.

Establishment phase:
During the establishment phase, the Link Control Protocol (LCP) is used to establish and configure the connection.

Authentication phase:
The authentication phase is optional. If the use of an authentication protocol (PAP [RFC1334], CHAP [RFC1994], EAP [RFC2284],) has been required during the LCP negotiation, the authentication protocol is applied to authenticate

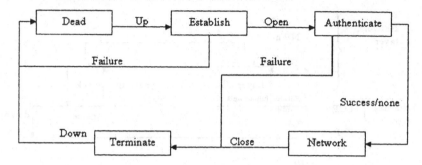

Fig. 2. PPP connection steps (RFC1661)

users. If the authentication fails, a "Down" event occurs.

Network phase:
After the establishment of the link connection by LCP, one or many NCPs have to be configured to let the corresponding network protocols to send their data by encapsulating it into PPP frame. As early as a NCP reaches the open status, the corresponding network protocol can transfer data until the closing of its NCP.

Terminate phase:
To close the connection, an LCP "Terminate frames" is sent. The LCP informs the network protocols that the connection will be closed.

3.3   The Link Control Protocol

The LCP transmits data using PPP; a LCP packet is encapsulated in PPP frame, in the PPP information field (Figure 3). The Link Control Protocol number is 0xC021. A LCP packet consists of 4 fields (Figure 4): The code field indicates the type of the LCP packet. There are 3 types of LCP packets:

- The configuration packets (Configure-Request, Configure-Ack, Configure-Nak, Configure-Reject). If a machine wants to establish a connection, it must start by transmitting a configuration packet (configure-request). The data field of this packet contains the desired configuration or modification.
- Termination packets (Terminate-Request and Terminate-Ack). These packets are sent if a machine wants to close a connection or if the identification fails.
- Maintenance packets (Code-Reject, Protocol-reject, Echo-Request, Echo-Reply, Discard-Request). These packets are used to test and to determine the performance of the link.

```
+-----------+-----------+-----------+-------------+--------------+
|   Flag    |  Adress   |  Control  |  Protocol   | Information  |
| 01111110  | 11111111  | 00000011  | 8/16 bits   |      *       |
+-----------+-----------+-----------+-------------+--------------+


+-----------+-------------+-----------+----------------------------
| Padding   |    FCS      |   Flag    |   Inter-frame Fill
|    *      | 16/32 bits  | 01111110  |
+-----------+-------------+-----------+----------------------------
```

Fig. 3. PPP frame

```
+-----------+------------+-----------+----------------------------
|   Code    | Identifier |  Length   |         Data...
|  8 bits   |   8 bits   | 16 bits   |
+-----------+------------+-----------+----------------------------
```

Fig. 4. a LCP packet

3.4   The security level in PPP

The unique security of PPP [RFC1661] is limited in the authentication phase. The two nodes use an authentication protocol such as Password Authentication Protocol (PAP) or Challenge Handshake Authentication Protocol (CHAP). In 1996, Meyer published an additional security protocol for PPP called ECP (Encryption Control Protocol) [RFC1968]. This protocol allows the use of the encryption in PPP frame. The ECP gives the possibility to select the encryption algorithm and its parameters. This ensures the confidentiality and the integrity of the PPP frame. The weakness of this use resides in the way of generating and exchanging the encryption key. In fact, for all the encryption algorithms the secret key is assumed to be already shared between the communicating parties.

4   Enhancing PPP security by Quantum Key Distribution (QKD)

4.1   The use of (QKD) to secure PPP (Q3P)

As we have seen previously, the key exchange is not considered in the common use of the encryption algorithms. This fact leads to a misuse of cryptography in PPP. A possible key exchange method is Diffie-Hellman key agreement protocol [26]. This protocol allows two users to exchange a secret key over an insecure medium without any prior secrets. However, the Diffie-Hellman key agreement protocol can be compared to the discrete logarithm problem for its security. This

is not unconditional secure (i.e. secure independently of the computation power
or the time) and can be broken. The Quantum Key Distribution is scientifically
proven to be unconditional secure. That's why we propose to use the QKD to
exchange the secret key between two nodes.

4.2   Key distribution using quantum concepts

Quantum cryptography is the only method allowing the distribution of a secret
key between two distant parties, the emitter and the receiver with provable
absolute security [2, 10]. Both parties encode the key on elementary quantum
systems, such as photons, which they exchange over a quantum channel, such
as an optical fiber. The security of this method comes from the well-known fact
that the measurement of an unknown quantum state modifies the state itself: a
spy eavesdropping on the quantum channel cannot get information on the key
without introducing errors in the key exchanged between the emitter and the
receiver. In equivalent terms, quantum cryptography is secure because of the no-
cloning theorem of quantum mechanics: a spy cannot duplicate the transmitted
quantum system and forward a perfect copy to the receiver [29].

4.3   Encryption Control Protocol (ECP) for Quantum Key
         Distribution (QKD)

The Encryption Control Protocol (ECP) defines the negotiation of the encryption over PPP links. After using LCP to establish and configure the data link,
the encryption options and mechanisms could be negotiated. The ECP packets
exchange mechanism is nearly the same as the LCP mechanism. The ECP packets are encapsulating into PPP frame (a packet per frame). The type is 0x8053
to indicate the Encryption Control Protocol. Two additional messages are added
to the code field: the Reset-Request and Reset-Ack message. These two messages
are used to restart the encryption negotiation. An encrypted packet is encapsulated in the PPP information field where the PPP protocol field indicates type
0x0053 (encrypted datagram). The ECP packet is presented in figure 5. In the

Fig. 5. an ECP packet

ECP packet, the type represents the encryption protocol option to be negotiated
(for instance type 1 is DES encryption). The number of octets in the packet is

contained in the length field. The values field gives additional data or option needed for the encryption protocol. Up to now, there are only 4 encryption algorithms (type 0 = OUI, type 1 = DES, type 2 = 3DES, type 3 = DES modified) that could be used [16].

5   Integrating QKD in PPP: QKD-PPP (Q3P)

In order to exchange the encryption key, a key exchange protocol is necessary. In this section, we present how to integrate QKD in PPP

5.1   Q3P requirements

Some requirements must satisfied to integrate quantum cryptography within PPP.

a- An optical channel: the optical channel is the physical link between two adjacent nodes. Nowadays, there are two means able to carry a quantum cryptography transmission: the optical fibber or the free space (the air) [14]. As the quantum cryptography uses photons to encode the information no other channel could be used up to now. However, as the quantum physics are experimenting the use of atoms and electrons as a quantum particle [28, 17] maybe other kind of channel could be used in the future.

b- A Q3P modem: this modem has to polarize, send and detect photons; it has to include a photon detector and a laser with a single photon emitter and photon polariser. The source and the detector are widely commercialised and many techniques are employed[1]. However, these devices are used to exchange the quantum key but could also used to send and receive simple data depending on how encoding the information. The modem in this case is a simple optical fiber modem.

c- QKD protocol: in order to establish an unconditional secure key, a quantum key distribution protocol is needed. This protocol must be implemented in the Q3P modem. The protocol will deliver a secure key after distilling the key and error correction [10]. The key is stored in a flash buffer memory and used when enciphering the data. The QKD protocols BB84 and B92 [2, 3] are nowadays the quantum cryptographic protocols widely used. These protocols are securely proven and largely experimented [13].

5.2   ECP-QKD format

To establish and configure the quantum key distribution between the two nodes, it is necessary to exchange some data between them. We propose a specific ECP packet format to carry QKD parameters (Figure 6):
Type field:

---

[1] Idquantique : www.idquantique.com
magiQ www.magiqtech.com
CNRS France : http://www2.cnrs.fr/presse/journal/1979.htm

Fig. 6. ECP packet carrying a QKD protocol

As in the ECP standard packet the type field gives information about the option of encryption protocol negotiated. For this case, we will use an unassigned number for the QKD protocol. The selected QKD protocol is BB84 and the request to obtain an assigned number for this protocol is on going in IANA organisation [16].

Length field:
The length is number of octets in the packet and it is more than "5" octets (1 octet for the type, 1 octet for the packet length, 2 octets for the key length and one octet for the TTL and the T field).

Key-length field:
This field indicates the length of the encryption key. It is encoded on 16 bits and represents the size of the key in octet. The key size is comprised between 1 to 65535 octets. The size can be viewed as huge but we consider the possibility to use the One Time Pad function as the encryption algorithm. In this case, the key size must be equal to the PPP-data size [27].

TTL field:
This field can represent either the number of messages or the amount of time (in second) where a key could be used in the encryption mechanism. When the max number of messages is reached or the deadline expires, the QKD starts.

T field:
The T field specifies if the TTL field concerns the number of messages or the amount of time. If the value is "1", the TTL field corresponds to the amount of time in second. If it is "0", the TTL is the number of messages per key.

5.3 The Q3P operating mode

We adapt PPP connection steps [RFC1661] to integrate QKD process as shown Figure 7. The three first steps of Q3P are identical with PPP (phase 1 to 3). After authenticating the two nodes, the negotiation of the encryption parameters starts. In this phase, the encryption algorithm with its parameters is negotiated. If the two nodes do not need to use encryption, then the network phase starts. Else, if an encryption key is required, a QKD phase begins.

For Encryption negotiation (4) the nodes negotiate the key length and the TTL by sending an adequate ECP packet. After that (in 5), a quantum cryptography

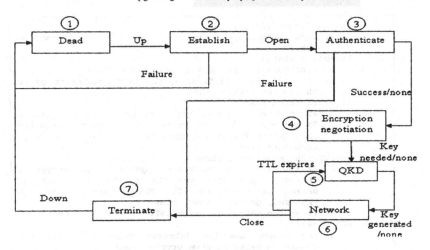

Fig. 7. Proposed Q3P steps and operating mode

exchange starts. At the end of the quantum key distribution phase, both nodes share a secret key, the encryption algorithm and the TTL of the key. This key is used in the network phase (6) while sending data. The data is enciphered thanks to the encryption key and the algorithm. When the TTL is expired, a new QKD phase starts. The end of the communication is the same as the PPP. The Figure 8 gives more details about Q3P operating mode. The modification (in bold in the figure 8) are little so that the adaptation of the PPP operating mode is easy to realise.

6   Advantages of Q3P solution

There many solutions dealing with the use of the quantum cryptography. Some of them are implementing on the layer 3 of the OSI model (network layer) [11]. Many issues rose when using the quantum key distribution in the network layer, such as the distance, the trust points, etc. Applying quantum cryptography in the layer two of the OSI model solves many issues and offers many advantages:

1. By using the link layer to carry on the quantum cryptography, the routing problem is avoided. In fact, as the network packets are encapsulated in a secure PPP frame and then transmitted, the routing issue is resolved as in a standard network. The encryption is transparent not only to the user but also to the whole network.

2. Implementing this solution do not need to built or invent any new quantum equipments. The only new device is the Q3P modem which is composed of

```
1- Initial state (Dead):
     a. When detecting an Up event then go the Establish
        phase
2- Establish phase:
     a. Configuration packets are exchanged (LCP)
     b. When finishing configuring the link connection go to
        the Authentication phase
3- Authentication phase:
     a. If required, the peer has to authenticate himself.
     b. If the authentication succeed or it is not required
        then go to Encryption negotiation phase else go to
        terminate phase
4- Encryption Negotiation phase:
     a. If required, the two nodes negotiate the encryption
        protocol parameters and the quantum key exchange
        parameters (such as TTL, Key length).     If not
        required, go the Network phase
     b. After the end of the negotiation, go to QKD phase
5- QKD phase:
     a. The source and the detector share a secret key
        exchanged using quantum cryptography
     b. When the secret key is ready go to Network phase
6- Network phase:
     a. The two node exchange data
     b. When the encryption TTL expires go to QKD phase
     c. If the communication is finished, go to terminate
        phase (a close event is generated)
7- Terminate phase:
     a. Terminate messages are exchange, when finish go to
        Dead state
```

Fig. 8. The Q3P algorithm

standard and already existing components such as the photon detector, the single photon source, etc.

3. Finally, the unconditional security could be reached with a very low price. In fact, many organisations and companies are already using optical fiber. So, organisations can use the existing infrastructure to exchange quantum key distribution. The Q3P modems are the most expensive equipments in these scenarios (approximately 100KEuros per pair[2]) however, according to specialist; it will become cheaper in the future.

7   Example of Q3P application - feasibility study

This section presents an example of using QKD-PPP to prove the functional feasibility. We assume that we have two LAN network connected via Q3P modems with optical fiber (Figure 9). We only apply protocols available nowadays with the QKD assigned number. We focus on the specific point of communication

---

[2] Source IdQuantique. www.idquantique.com

between the two modems (Figure 9).

Phase 1: The two modems are in the initial state. When the Q3P modems are on and connected via the optical fiber, an Up event is generated and the establishment phase starts.

Phase 2: The PPP configuration begins with the exchange of the LCP configura-

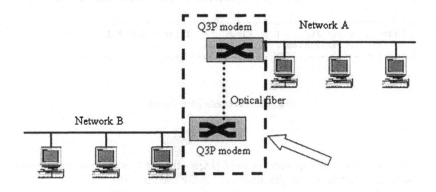

Fig. 9. An example of using Q3P

tion packets. In this example, we will select the authentication protocol CHAP from the list of the PPP authentication protocols. The identification of CHAP is 0xC223. So, the modem sends a LCP packet type3[3] for the authentication negotiation and the identification of authentication protocol is in the data field of the LCP packet (Figure 10). The Figure 11 shows the whole PPP frame for this exchange.

Phase 3: The modem sends a LCP packet type 4 to negotiate the quality proto-

Fig. 10. the data of the LCP authentication packet

---

[3] The most common LCP types are: type 1 for the maximum receive unit, type 2 for asynchronous control character map, type 3 for the authentication protocol, type 4 for the quality protocol, type 5 for magic number see RFCs 1661, 1570.

```
+-----------+-----------+-----------+-----------+-----------+
|  Flag     |  Adress   |  Control  | Protocol=|  LCP code |
| 01111110  | 11111111  | 00000011  |C021 (LCP)|   = 1     |
+-----------+-----------+-----------+-----------+-----------+


+-----------+-----------+-----------+-----------+-----------+-----------+
|Identifier| Length     |                    PPP Data...                |
| 10111101 | 16 bits    | Type =3   | Length=4 |       Values=C223      |
+-----------+-----------+-----------+-----------+-----------+-----------+


+----****-+-----------+-----------+--------------------------
| Padding  |    FCS    |   Flag    |  Inter-frame Fill
|   ***    | 16/32 bits| 01111110  |
+----****--+-----------+-----------+--------------------------
```

Fig. 11. the whole PPP frame

col. We choose the link quality protocol (LQP - 0xC025) as the quality protocol. In fact, the LQP is the quality protocol mostly used in PPP.

Phase 4: Then, the authentication phase starts. The CHAP packets are encapsulated in PPP frame.

Phase 5: When the authentication succeeds, the encryption negotiation begins. In our example, we use the triple DES encryption algorithm (ECP type 2)[4]. In fact, triple DES is the most secure algorithm usable in PPP. So the two nodes exchange ECP packets to negotiate the parameters of this protocol. The secret key shared by QKD protocol (we assumed that the IANA associates it to type 5), the length of the packet is 5 octets, the key length is 21 octets (168 bits), and we choose the TTL randomly say 100 messages so the T field is zero (Figure 12).

When, the network phase could start. For instance, we use Internet protocol as

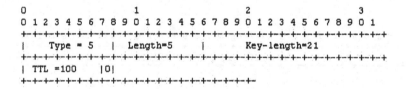

```
0                   1                   2                   3
0 1 2 3 4 5 6 7 8 9 0 1 2 3 4 5 6 7 8 9 0 1 2 3 4 5 6 7 8 9 0 1
+-+-+-+-+-+-+-+-+-+-+-+-+-+-+-+-+-+-+-+-+-+-+-+-+-+-+-+-+-+-+-+-+
|    Type = 5   |  Length=5        |       Key-length=21         |
+-+-+-+-+-+-+-+-+-+-+-+-+-+-+-+-+-+-+-+-+-+-+-+-+-+-+-+-+-+-+-+-+
|  TTL =100     |0|
+-+-+-+-+-+-+-+-+-+-+-+-+-+-+-+-+-+-+-
```

Fig. 12. ECP packet with QKD protocol negotiation

---

[4] The ECP types available nowadays are: 0 for OUI, 1 for DES, 2 for 3DES, 3 for DES modified. See [16] for more details.

the network protocol so we need to use the IPCP as a NCP in the Point to Point Protocol (Figure 13). After sending 100 messages, an ECP reset-request packet is sent to the peer node. Then, when receiving the reset-ack, a QKD phase starts. If one of the two nodes wants to close to communication, a terminate packet is sent.

Hypothesis:

- The authentication protocol : CHAP
- the encryption algorithm : 3DES
- the quality protocol : LQP
- the encryption Key length : 168 bits
- the TTL : 100 messages
- the network protocol : IP

Fig. 13. Q3P application hypothesis

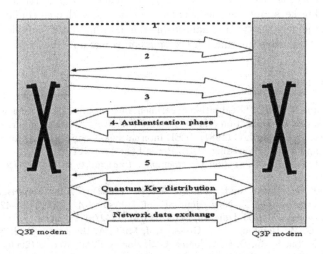

Fig. 14. type of messages exchanged between two quantum modems

8 Conclusion

Classical cryptography algorithms are based on mathematical functions. The robustness of a given cryptosystem is based essentially on the secrecy of its (private) key and the difficulty with which the inverse of its one-way function(s) can be calculated. Unfortunately, there is no mathematical proof that will establish whether it is not possible to find the inverse of a given one-way function. On the contrary, quantum cryptography is a method for sharing secret keys, whose security can be formally demonstrated. The use of quantum cryptography will enforce safety, dependability and security of ICT infrastructures and critical infrastructures. The enciphering mechanisms rely on classical cryptography which we know the limits. To enhance the security level of protocols, we studied the possibility to integrate quantum key distribution into already existing protocols. It is important to have the option to secure efficiently the data transmission between two adjacent nodes. Using quantum cryptography in conjunction with PPP offer a better level of security in transmission. Our study points out the adaptation of the PPP protocol to integrate quantum key exchange (Q3P). The modifications to PPP are identified (packet format and operating mode). A data exchange example illustrates the operational feasibility of the proposed solution. Applying quantum key exchange and one-time-pad function at the layer 2, communication is not only possible but will upgrade considerably, with a low cost and less effort (modification, performances,), the security level of a communication between 2 adjacent nodes. The unconditional security could be effective for transmission. We recommend the use of quantum key distribution to share enciphering keys and the one-time-pad function to exchange confidential data. By using jointly the two mechanisms at the data-link layer, confidentiality and integrity of sensible information transmission is maximised.

References

1. Alléaume R (2004). "Réalisation expérimentale de sources de photons uniques, caractérisation et application à la cryptographie quantique" (Secoqc partner)
2. Bennet, C; Brassard, G (1984). IEEE International Conference on Computers, Systems, and Signal Processing. IEEE Press, LOS ALAMITOS
3. Bennet, (1992). *C Quantum Cryptography: Uncertainty in the Service of Privacy.* Science 257.
4. Donald S.Bethune and William P.Risk (2002). "*AutoCompensating quantum cryptography*". New journal of physics 4 (2002)42.1-42.15 URL: http://www.iop.org/EJ/article/1367-2630/4/1/342/nj2142.html
5. Clark, C. W; Bienfang, J. C; Gross, A. J; Mink, A; Hershman, B. J; Nakassis, A; Tang, X; Lu, R; Su, D. H; Williams, C. J; Hagley E. W; Wen, J (2000). "*Quantum key distribution with 1.25 Gbps clock synchronization*", Optics Express.
6. Crypto-Gram (March 2005). "SHA-1 Broken".Schneier, B. March 15th 2005.
7. Artur Ekert (1991). "*Quantum Cryptography based on Bell's Theorem*". Physical Review Letters. URL: http://prola.aps.org/abstract/PRL/v67/i6/p661_1
8. Elliott, C (2002). "*Building the quantum network*". New Journal of Physics 4 (46.1-46.12)

9. Elliott, C; Pearson, D; Troxel, G (2003). *"Quantum Cryptography in Practice"*.
10. Gisin, N; Ribordy, G; Tittel, W; Zbinden, H. (2002). *"Quantum Cryptography"*. Reviews of Modern Physics 74 (2002): http://arxiv.org/PS_cache/quant-ph/pdf/0101/0101098.pdf
11. Ghernaouti Hélie, S; Sfaxi, M.A; Ribordy, G; Gay, O (2005). "Using Quantum Key Distribution within IPSEC to secure MAN communications". MAN 2005 conference.
12. Grosshans,Van Assche, Wenger,Brouri,Cerf,Grangier (2003). *"Quantum key distribution using gaussian-modulated coherent states"* Letter to nature. URL: http://www.mpq.mpg.de/Theorygroup/CIRAC-/people/grosshans/papers/Nat421_238.pdf
13. Guenther, C (2003) "The Relevance of Quantum Cryptography in Modern Cryptographic Systems". GSEC Partical Requirements (v1.4b). http://www.giac.org/practical/GSEC/Christoph_Guenther_GSEC.pdf
14. R.Hughes,J.Nordholt,D.Derkacs,C.Peterson, (2002). *"Practical free-space quantum key distribution over 10km in daylight and at night"*. New journal of physics 4 (2002)43.1-43.14.URL: http://www.iop.org/EJ/abstract/1367-2630/4/1/343/
15. IdQuantique (2004) "A Quantum Leap for Cryptography". http://www.idquantique.com/files/introduction.pdf
16. Internet Assigned Numbers Authority - IANA (2005). http://www.iana.org/numbers.html
17. Knight, P (2005). "Manipulating cold atoms for quantum information processing". QUPON conference Vienna 2005.
18. Labouret, G (2000). "IPSEC: présentation technique". Hervé Schauer Consultants (HSC). URL : www.hsc.fr
19. Le journal Le monde (march 2005). "Menace sur la signature lcronique". march the 5th 2005.
20. Lo, H.K; Chau, H.F. (1999). *"Unconditional security of quantum key distribution over arbitrarily long distances"*. Science 283: http://arxiv.org/PS_cache/quant-ph/9803/9803006.pdf
21. Magic Technologies (2004). "Quantum Information Solutions for real world". http://www.magiqtech.com/products/index.php
22. Mayers, D (1998). *"Unconditionnal Security in Quantum Cryptography"*. J. Assoc. Comput. Math. 48, 351
23. Paterson, K.G; Piper, f; Schack, R (2004). *"Why Quantum Cryptography?"*. http://eprint.iacr.org/2004/156.pdf
24. Riguidel, M; Dang-Minh, D; Le-Quoc, C; Nguyen-Toan, L; Nguyen-Thanh, M (2004). "Quantum crypt- Work Package I". ENST/EEC/QC.04.06.WP1B. (Secoqc partner)
25. Rivest, R.L; Shamir, A; Adleman, L.M (1978). *"A Method of Obtaining Digital Signature and Public-Key Cryptosystems"*. Communication of the ACM 21 no. 2 1978.
26. Schneier, B (1996). "Applied Cryptography" Second Edition. New York: John Wiley & Sons, 1996
27. Shannon, C.E (1949). "Communication theory of secrecy systems". Bell System Technical Journal 28-4. URL: http://www.cs.ucla.edu/jkong/research/security/shannon.html
28. Tonomura, A (2005). "Quantum phenomena observed using electrons". QUPON conference Vienna 2005.
29. Wootters, W.K; Zurek, W.H (1982). *"A single quantum cannot be cloned"*. Nature, 299, 802
30. Zemor, G (2001) "Cours de cryptographie", Editeur: Cassini

Fast and secure handoffs for 802.11 Infrastructure Networks

Mohamed Kassab[1], Abdelfettah Belghith[1], Jean-Marie Bonnin[2], Sahbi Sassi[1]

[1] CRISTAL Laboratory, Ecole Nationale des Sciences de l'Informatique, ENSI, Tunisia
{Mohamed.kassab,Abdelfattah.belghith,
sahbi.sassi}@ensi.rnu.tn
[2] Ecole Nationale Supérieure de Télécommunications de Bretagne, ENSTB, France
Jmb.bonnin@enst-bretagne.fr

Abstract. User mobility in IEEE 802.11 wireless LANs is ever increasing due to wireless technological advances, the recent popularity of portable devices and the desire for voice and multimedia applications. These applications, however, require very fast and secure handoffs among base stations to maintain the quality of the connections. Re-authentication during handoff procedures causes a long handoff latency which affects the fluidity and service quality of interactive real-time multimedia applications such as VoIP. Minimizing the re-authentication latency is crucial in order to support real-time multimedia applications on public wireless IP network. In this paper, we propose two fast re-authentication methods based on the predictive authentication mechanism defined by IEEE 802.11i security group. We compare our proposed methods to already existing ones. We have implemented these methods in an experimental test-bed using freeware and commodity 802.11 hardware. Conducted measurements show significant latency reductions compared to other proposed solutions.

1 Introduction

With the ever falling cost and power consumption wireless LAN chipsets and software, wireless public LAN systems based on IEEE 802.11 are becoming popular in hot spot areas. Public wireless LAN systems provide a high-speed Internet connectivity of up to 11Mbit/s, yet they should support different user mobility patterns. User authentication and handoff support between access points (APs) are therefore among the most important issues to be considered in the design of public wireless LAN systems. Generally, since a mobile station need to be authenticated during and after a handoff, a mobile station upon a handoff should perform a new authentication procedure and receive new data encryption keys. This authentication procedure requires the exchange of more than a dozen of messages and therefore impacts on the network performance. What is required is both a fast handoff technique coupled with a fast predictive authentication procedure.

Fast handoff management procedures have been proposed and studied by many researchers [1, 2, 3, 5, 7, 8, 13, 16 18, 19, 20] in order to minimize the handoff latency

Please use the following format when citing this chapter:

Kassab, M., Belghith, A., Bonnin, J.-M. and Sassi, S., 2007, in IFIP International Federation for Information Processing, Volume 229, Network Control and Engineering for QoS, Security, and Mobility, IV, ed. Gaïti, D., (Boston: Springer), pp. 61–74.

time, yet for real-time multimedia service such as VoIP, the problem of handoff latency still has to be shortened in order to satisfy the quality of service needed by such applications. Supporting voice and multimedia with continuous mobility implies that the total latency of a handoff must be adequately small [17]. Specifically, the overall latency should not exceed 50 ms to prevent excessive jitter [12].

Typically, a handoff can be divided into three phases: detection, search and execution. The detection phase corresponds to the time needed by a station to discover itself being out of range of its access point. At this point, the station launches the search phase for potential new access points. The execution phase corresponds to messages exchange allowing the station to re-associate and re-authenticate with the new chosen AP. Many previous works have studied and proposed fast handoff procedures. In [7], the authors aim to reduce the detection phase time. A station starts the search phase whenever a frame and its two consecutive retransmissions fail, the station can conclude that the frame failure is caused by the station's movement (i.e., further handoff process (search phase) is required) rather than a collision. As described in [1], the scanning latency is the dominant latency component. To reduce this scanning latency, a new scheme was proposed in [16]. Such a scheme reduces the total number of scanned channels as well as the total time spent waiting on each channel. Specifically, two algorithms were introduced: NG (neighbor graph) algorithm and NG-pruning algorithm. The NG algorithm uses the neighbor graph whereas the NG-pruning algorithm further improves the channel discovery process by using a non overlapping graph. In [18] and [19], the authors proposed a fast Inter-AP handoff scheme based on the predictive authentication method defined in IEEE 802.11i [10]. To predict the mobility pattern, the frequent handoff region (FHR) was introduced. The FHR is formed by APs having the highest probabilities to be next visited by a station upon handoff. A mobile station pre-authenticates according to the IEEE 802.1x [11] model with only APs given by the FHR. Authors in [3] proposed a pre-authentication method based on proactive key distribution following the recent and predominant wireless network authentication method amended by the IEEE 802.11i security group [10] (the predictive authentication procedure). They introduced a data structure called the Neighbor Graph which dynamically captures the ever changing topology of the network, and hence tracks the potential APs to which a station may handoff to in the near future.

The complete IEEE 802.11i authenticated handoff latency is brought to about 70 ms, a latency still above the required 50 ms target for the proper operation of interactive real-time multimedia applications such as voice. In fact, latency due to the detection and search phases has been reduced from around 500 ms to about 20 ms [1, 2, 5, 13, 8]. Fast re-authentication methods, based on the predictive authentication mechanism, reduce re-authentication from around 1.1s to about 50 ms [3]. However, it is rather interesting to note that neither the implementation nor the conducted measurements as reported in [3] do respect the exchanges specified in IEEE 802.11i and yet they do not take into account the load conditions of the network.

In this paper, we propose two new pre-authentication methods called: «Proactive Key Distribution (PKD) with anticipated 4-way-Handshake" and "PKD with IAPP caching". Our aim is to reduce the authentication exchanges between the station and the network to its minimum while guarantying conformity with the IEEE 802.11i security proposal. These two methods present a clear improvement over the method of pre-authentication suggested in [3] at any given network load. We show these improvements via measurements conducted on an actual test bed.

2 Background

2.1 The 802.11i standard

The IEEE 802.11i standard specifies the use of the IEEE 802.1X protocol [11] which offers a general framework to build an authentication service and keys distribution. This protocol uses EAP (Extensible Authentication Protocol) layer, standardized by the IETF (Internet Engineering Task Force), for the support of authentication methods [4]. One of the methods which correspond to the specification of IEEE 802.11i is EAP/TLS [10].

The IEEE 802.1X standard provides an architectural structure, basing on the «Controlled/Uncontrolled Port " concept, for controlling access to the network on link layer. It provides a skeleton of security by defining three entities: Supplicant, Authenticator and the Authentication Server. A client is an entity who wishes to use a service (MAC connectivity) offered via the controlled port. This client authenticates himself to an Authentication Server through authenticator. In case of success, the server orders authenticator to allow the service.

IEEE 802.1X uses Extensible Authentication Protocol (EAP) to define how messages are exchanged between network entities: Supplicant, Authenticator and Authentication Server. EAP has defined a standard exchange of messages between entities using an agreed authentication protocol. The most known authentication protocols supported by EAP are: EAP-MD5 (Message Digest 5), EAP-TTLS and in our case the EAP-TLS (Transport Security Level). Figure 1 portrays the authentication protocols stack.

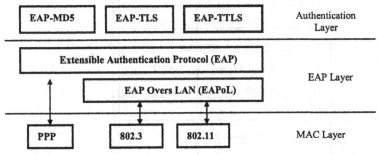

Fig. 1. Authentication Protocols

EAP does not specify the routing of the messages [4]. That's why, EAP messages must be encapsulated during their transfers. Thus, IEEE 802.1X defines the EAP over LAN (EAPoL) protocol to encapsulate the messages between Supplicant and Authenticator. The Authenticator relays authentication packets between

Authentication Server and Supplicant. In fact, Authenticator extracts EAP packets from IEEE 802.11 MPDUs and transmits them to Authentication Server.

In an IEEE 802.11i exchange using EAP/TLS, supplicant and Authentication Server start a mutual authentication. Authentication messages are exchanged between suppliant and Authentication Server over the access point (Authenticator) through the uncontrolled port.

Supplicant and Authentication Server generate separately a key named Master Key (MK). A second key is derived from the latter: Pairwise Master Key (PMK). Authentication Server sends this new key to the access point (Authenticator). Thus, the supplicant and the access point prove the possession of the same PMK, through an exchange of EAPOL-Key messages. This exchange is called the 4-Way-Handshake.

A second class of keys, « Group Transient Key » (GTK), is also defined for the broadcast traffic. Every Authenticator generates its own key and distributes it to associated stations.

4-Way-Handshake is an exchange of four EAPOL-Key packets between access point and Supplicant. It is initiated by the access point to:
- Prove that the pair has same key PMK.
- Derive a new key: Pairwise Transient Key (PTK) from the PMK.
- Install at the pair encryption key and control of integrity key.

GTK is sent by authenticator to the supplicant through the Group-Key-Handshake exchange who is composed of two EAPOL-Key messages.

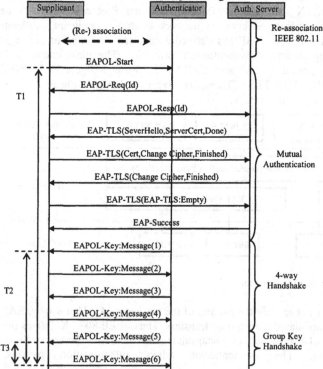

Fig. 2. EAP/TLS Authentication exchange

2.2 The Proactive Key Distribution

The PKD (Proactive Key Distribution) method defines a proactive key distribution between a mobile station and access points and thus establishes authentication keys before even the re-association. Upon handoff, authentication exchange between station and access point is reduced to 4-way-handshake and Group Key Handshake during the re-association. This method is based on an Accounting Server responsible to manage a Neighbor Graph for all network access points [3]. We will consider that the functionalities of authentication and Accounting will be gathered in a single AAA Server (Authentication, Authorization, and Accounting Server).

In contrast to IEEE 802.11i, PMK are derived through the following recursive equation:

$$PMK_0 = PRF(MK, \text{'client EAP Encryption'} \mid clientHello.random \mid \quad (1)$$
$$ServerHello.random)$$

$$PMK_n = PRF(MK, PMKn\text{-}1 \mid APmac \mid STAmac)$$

Where n represents the nth station re-association.

After the first mutual authentication between the station and AAA server, the access point sends to the AAA Server an Accounting-Request (Start). Consequently, the AAA informs the corresponding neighbor access points about a possible handoff of the station through a Notify-Request. At this point, every neighbor responds to the AAA Server through a Notify-Response message to initiate PMK_n generation based on equation (1). AAA Server sends the keys to neighbor's access points through an ACCESS-ACCEPT message [1]. Figure 3 portrays the exchange carried out with just one of the station AP neighbors.

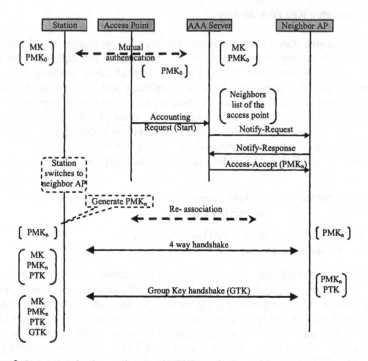

Fig. 3. Pre-authentication exchange with PKD method

Upon a handoff to a new access point, the station calculates a new PMK_n that is based on the generation parameters used and which corresponds to the key already sent by the AAA to the access point. All what is needed to check for liveness and freshness of the corresponding keys, is to perform a 4 way handshake and a group key handshake as shown in figure 4 below.

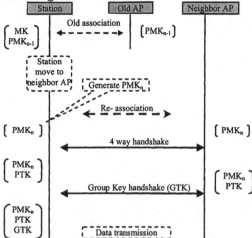

Fig. 4. Re-authentication exchange with PKD

3   Enhanced Pre-authentication Methods

A full IEEE 802.11i exchange, as already portrayed on figure 2 above, requires 14 messages requiring an authentication time denoted T1 and evaluated to 1.1s according to [3]. This time value further increases the handoff latency, and by itself represents an unacceptable value for multimedia and interactive applications. To decrease the authentication latency upon handoffs, previous works [19] and [3] restrict authentication phase exchange to only the messages exchanged between the station and the access point and anticipate exchange between station and authentication server (i.e., pre-authentication).

PKD method restricts the re-authentication exchange to the 4 Way Handshake and the Group key Handshake (a total of 6 messages) and consequently limits authentication time to only T2 (see figure 2). This method was evaluated experimentally in [3] where measurements estimated T2 to 50 ms. While this result indicates a significant reduction in authentication time as compared to a complete IEEE 802.11i (1.1 ms), their implementation performs only two messages exchange between station and access point instead of the complete 4-way-handshake and doesn't give any indication on Group-Key-Handshake. Moreover, network conditions such as the actual network load are not taken into account. As a part of our tested, we implemented the PKD method and indeed found different results as a function of the network load.

In this work, we aim to reduce the exchange between the station and its new access point to its minimum. This is done by anticipating the 4 Way Handshake and restrict re-authentication to just the Group key Handshake (2 messages) which reduces latency time to T3 as shown on figure 2. Two re-authentication methods: "PKD with IAPP caching" and "PKD with anticipated 4-way Handshake" are proposed, implemented and evaluated.

3.1   PKD with IAPP caching

In this approach, we propose to combine PKD keys pre-distribution with the use of the cache mechanism of the Inter Access Point Protocol (IAPP).

IAPP protocol [9] is a mechanism allowing to transfer mobile station contexts between access points. It defines a cache mechanism which allows access points to exchange information about moving stations before re-association. Cache management is based on a neighbor graph maintained at every access point. This graph contains the list of AP neighbors to which the access point must relay the contexts of its associated stations. Upon a station association, the access point transfers the station context to its neighbors through a CACHE-notify message. Each neighbor answers by a CACHE-response message in order to confirm his cache update. To secure IAPP exchanges between access points, IEEE 802.11f define the use of the RADIUS protocol. In fact, RADIUS ensures access point's authentication and context confidentiality through exchanges on the distribution system [9].

In addition to PMKs pre-distribution defined in the PKD method, IAPP allows PTKs keys pre-distribution. These keys will be used by the station to temporarily re associate with a new access point through a simple Group-Key-Handshake. Pre-distributed PTKs are calculated by the current access point. The key corresponding to neighbor X is calculated by the following equation:

$$PTK_X = PRF (PMK, PTKinit | STAmac|APmac) \qquad (2)$$

A mobile station will be able to calculate the key corresponding to its new access point. A PTK allows it to be authenticated with this access point through a Group-Key- Handshake. This is a temporary authentication. Indeed, the station engages immediately a PKD authentication with its new access point while continuing its data transmission. We define TIMER_AUTH to be the time limit within which the station must perform a complete authentication.

Steps of the method are defined below:
- Upon a station authentication, the access point consults its neighbor graph and starts IAPP exchange to update neighbor's cache. The station context transferred by the access point contains: a PTK key and the TIMER_AUTH value.
- The current access point informs the AAA server about this station association in order to start the PMKs generation used to complete the predictive authentication procedure.

Figure 5 shows messages implied by these two exchanges with a given neighbor access point.

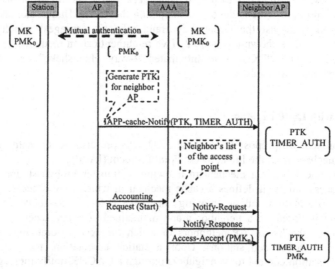

Fig. 5. Pre-authentication exchange with « PKD with IAPP caching » method

Let's take an example of an ESS with 3 neighbor access point A, B and C. The access point A send keys and timer corresponding to a station associated with it to neighbors B and C through IAPP messages. Access point B, for example, add PTK_B key and TIMER_AUTH timer to its IAPP cache and will use it in a future station re-authentication.

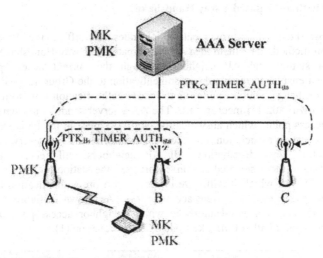

Fig. 6. Distribution of PTKs Keys with IAPP exchanges

- As shown in figure 7 below, when the station moves to a neighbor access point, it starts Group-Key-Handshake using the PTK and will then be able to transmit data. Then, the access point starts a timer while waiting for a 4-way Handshake with PMK_n. The value of this timer will not have to exceed the $TIMER\_AUTH_{sta}$
- Throughout data transmissions, and before timer expiration, station starts 4-way Handshake in order to calculate a new permanent PTK.

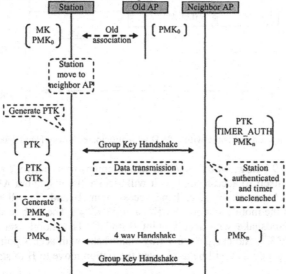

Fig. 7. Re-authentication exchange with « PKD with IAPP caching » method

3.2 PKD with anticipated 4-way Handshake

We propose here an improvement which does not affect the Proactive Key Distribution method. The main idea is to anticipate the 4-way-Handshake exchanges between a station and AP neighbors through the current access point. This improvement enables to restrict the re-authentication to the Group-Key-Handshake (2 messages) exchange, which enables us to reduce authentication time to its minimum (within the IEEE 802.11i mechanism). The AAA server sends to the station a list of neighbor access points which answered the Notify-Request in the PKD exchange (cf. 4.1).Upon a station association, its access point informs the AAA server in order to start proactive keys distribution. All AP neighbors will receive PMK keys corresponding to the associated station. Moreover, the station receives a neighbor's list (List_AP) with which it will have to carry out a pre-authentication through the distribution system (via its current access point). As shown in figure 8 below, the station carries out a 4-way-Handshake with a neighbor access point through its current access point with a PMK_n key calculated by equation (1).

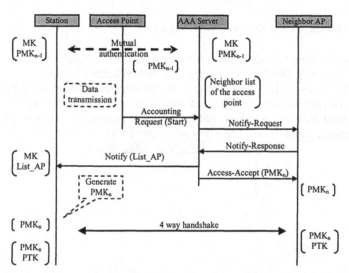

Fig. 8. Pre-authentication exchange with « PKD with anticipated 4-way Handshake » method

In the Figure 9 below, when a mobile station enter to the network and associate and authenticate itself to access point A, it will receive the neighbors AP list (B and C) from the AAA server. In other hand access point B and C, will receive keys corresponding to the mobile station (PMK^B_n and PMK^C_n). The mobile station would start a 4-way Handshake with access point B and C. The mobile station generate separately the PMK^B_n and carry out a 4-way Handshake with access point B in order to establish a PTK key that will be used, even the station move to B to start a Group-Key-Handshake.

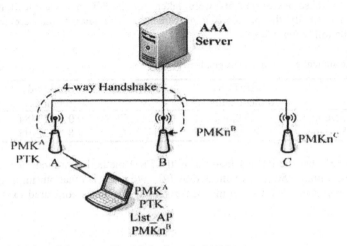

Fig. 9. Anticipation of the 4-way Handshake through the DS

When the station moves towards a neighbor access point two cases could happen:
- The station already has calculated the PTK through the pre-authentication and thus it only carries out a Group-Key-Handshake to be authenticated,
- Or, the station has not yet completed the pre-authentication, and thus it carries out a 4-Way-Handshake and Group Key Handshake corresponding to the full PKD method.

4 Implementation and performance evaluation

In a previous work, we described an IAPP implementation integrating a context transfer through IEEE 802.11 access points [15]. This implementation is based on Hostap software [14]. We have enhanced our test-bed with the support of secure fast handoffs by integrating the PKD method as well as our two improvements «PKD with 4-way anticipated Handshake» and «PKD with IAPP caching ". We use EAP/TLS and RADIUS server respectively as an authentication method and authentication server.

FreeRadius [6] was used to install RADIUS server. We modified this software in order to deal with Accounting Server functionalities (neighbors graph handling and the key pre-distribution). Authenticators are software access points based on the Hostap to which IAPP protocol was added. Hostap and wpa_supplicant allow setting up an IEEE 802.11i authentication [14]

We have evaluated the re authentication time for each one of the three methods and a full EAP/TLS authentication, in order to show the contribution of our two improvements " PKD with IAPP caching " and " PKD with anticipated 4-way Handshake ".

We considered two access points and a mobile station (MS). This station carries out handovers from AP-1 to AP-2. The re-authentication time is measured based on

AP-2 logs. These measurements were taken for EAP/TLS authentication, PKD methods and finally the proposed improvements. The latency measurements are given in the following table:

Table 1. Re authentication time in an empty network

	EAP/TLS Authentication	PKD	Proposed methods
Average	1,52532562	0,07344857	0,016413484
Variance	0,08018446	0,00022073	2,87917E-05

We remark that the latency induced by the PKD method is around 73 ms which exceeds the value of 50 ms as indicated by [9]. We note also that our improvements reduce latency time down to 16 ms, hence gaining 55 ms as compared to the PKD method.

5   Qualitative Comparison

The two enhancements proposed in this work restrict the re-authentication exchange to just the Group Key Handshake and they present the same performance in terms of handoff latency. However, they operate in very different ways during the pre authentication phase.

Firstly, the "PKD with anticipated 4-way Handshake" method anticipates the PTK generation (figure 7) via the current access point. The traffic generated for this PTK generation depends on the number of AP neighbours and on the actual handoff frequency. On the other hand in the "PKD with IAPP caching" method, the current access point distributes PTKs keys using the IAPP context transfer functionality using the distributed system infrastructure, hence not affecting the wireless media. Consequently, the two methods will be affected differently as a function of the network load. Moreover, under a high workload, using the "PKD with anticipated 4-way Handshake" method, a station may not be able to complete properly the pre authentication exchange and establish the needed keys. With the "PKD with IAPP caching", the cell load does not interfere with keys establishment (exchanged through the distribution system).

Secondly, the handoff frequency can also influence differently the performance of the two methods. In fact, with PKD with anticipated 4-way Handshake" a station must generate separately pre authentication keys for each neighbour AP and therefore the time needed for pre authentication is longer than for the "PKD with IAPP caching" where the keys are distributed by current access point. Consequently, for a fast moving station switching quickly between neighbours APs, it is most probable to have a key miss with the first method.

Thirdly, there may be a certain security concern with the "PKD with IAPP caching" since in the IEEE 802.11i, an AP is not supposed to know PTKs used by another APs.

But assuming confidence for the current AP and since such PTKs are only used during a short time between the first Group Key Handshake and the 4-way Handshake (less than TIMER_AUTH), the security is not really compromised.

6 Conclusion

In this paper, we proposed new re-authentication methods: "PKD with IAPP caching" and "PKD with anticipated 4-way Handshake". These two methods present a clear improvement over the PKD method suggested in [3] at all feasible network load. A test-bed is developed that supports secure fast handoffs integrating the PKD method as well as our proposed methods. Experiments conduced over this test-bed proved the clear superiority of our methods. Re-authentication latency is then reduced down to approximately 16 ms, a value much under the targeted 50 ms and achievement that makes it possible for real time applications to sustain fast secure handoffs. Our measurements are conducted under very light workload conditions. More measurements are underway to further evaluate the proposed methods for different scenarios and under different workload conditions.

References

1. A. Mishra, M. Shin and W. Arbaugh: An Empirical Analysis of the IEEE 802.11 MAC Layer Handoff Process. ACM SIGCOMM Computer Communications Review, Vol. 33, No. 2 (April 2003).
2. A. Mishra M. Shin and W. Arbaugh.: Context Caching using Neighbor Graphs for Fast Handoffs in a Wireless Network. IEEE INFOCOM conference, Hong Kong (March 2004).
3. A. Mishra, M. Shin and W. Arbaugh. : Pro-active Key Distribution using Neighbor Graphs. IEEE Wireless Communications, vol. 11 (February 2004) 26-36.
4. Blunk Larry and John Vollbrecht, "PPP Extensible Authentication Protocol (EAP)", IETF RFC 2284 (March 1998).
5. C. L. Tan et al.: A fast handoff scheme for wireless network. Proc of the 2 nd ACM Intl Workshop on Wireless Mobile Multimedia, Seattle. (August 1999).
6. FreeRadius: The FreeRadius Server Project. URL: http://www.freeradius.org (March 2004).
7. H. Velayos and G. Karlsson, "Techniques to Reduce IEEE 802.11b MAC Layer Handover Time" Proc. IEEE ICC (June 2004).
8. Hye-Soo Kim, Sang-Hee Park, Chun-Su Park and al. .: Selective Channel Scanning for Fast Handoff in Wireless LAN using NeighborGraph. The 2004 International Technical Conference on Circuits/Systems Computers and Communications (ITC-CSCC2004) Japan (July 2004).
9. IEEE 802.11f: IEEE Trial-Use Recommended Practice for Multi-Vendor Access Point Interoperability via an Inter-Access Point Protocol Across Distribution Systems Supporting IEEE 802.11 Operation. IEEE (July 2003).
10. IEEE 802.11i: Amendment 6: Medium Access Control (MAC) Security Enhancements. IEEE Computer Society (April 2004).
11. IEEE 802.1x: IEEE Standards for Local and Metropolitan Area Networks: Port based Network Access Control. IEEE (June 2001).

12. International Telecommunication Union: General Characteristics of International Telephone Connections and International Telephone Circuits. ITU-TG.114 (1988).
13. Ishwar Ramani and al.: SyncScan: Practical Fast Handoff for 802.11 Infrastructure Networks. Proceedings of the IEEE INFOCOM Conference, Miami (March 2005).
14. Jouni Malinen: Host AP driver for Intersil Prism.URL:http://hostap.epitest.fi/(March 2004).
15. M.Kassab, A.Belghith, J.M.Bonnin and H.Idoudi: Réalisation d'un point d'accès logiciel 802.11b .SETIT 2004, Tunisia (March 2004).
16. M. Shin, A. Mishra, and W. Arbaugh: Improving the Latency of 802.11 Hand-offs using Neighbor Graphs. Proc. ACM Mobisys (September 2004).
17. T. Henriksson: Hardware architecture for 802.11b based h.323 voice and image ip telephony terminal. Swedish system-onchip conference2001, Proceedings of the SSoCC, Sweden (March 2001).
18. Sangheon Pack and Yanghee Choi: Fast Inter-AP Handoff using Predictive-Authentication Scheme in a Public Wireless LAN. IEEE Networks (August 2002).
19. Sangheon Pack and Yanghee Choi: Pre-Authenticated Fast Handoff in a Public Wireless LAN based on IEEE 802.1x Model. IFIP TC6 Personal Wireless Communications (October 2002).
20. S. Pack, H. Jung, T. Kwon and al.: SNC: A Selective Neighbor Caching Scheme for Fast Handoff in IEEE 802.11 Wireless Networks. ACM SIGMOBILE Mobile Computing and Communications Review (February 2004).
21. Stefano Avallone and al.: D-ITG, Distributed Internet Traffic Generator. URL: http://www.grid.unina.it/software/ITG/ (May 2005).

The OpenEapSmartcard platform

Pascal Urien[1], Mesmin Dandjinou[2]

[1]ENST 36/38 rue Dareau 75014 Paris France,
[2]Université Polytechnique de Bobo-Dioulasso, Burkina Faso
Pascal.Urien@enst.fr, Mesmin.Dandjinou@voila.fr

Abstract. This paper presents the first javacard platform dedicated to IP (Wireless) LAN security issues. We have defined an open architecture that processes Extensible Authentication Protocol (*EAP*) in smartcards, which is the standard defined by IETF[1] and IEEE-802[2] committees for users' authentication in various network environments like *Wi-Fi, WiMax,* or *IPSEC.*[3] These tamper resistant devices are generally considered as the most trusted computing platforms. They have been selected by the DoD[4] for military ID cards, by the Belgium government for citizen ID cards, and they will be included in US and European passports. Although secure, javacards are cheap and manufactured in many companies. We present and analyze results obtained with five different smartcards, for two authentication scenari. The first works with an asymmetric algorithm (EAP-TLS, a transparent transport of the well known SSL[5] standard), the second uses a pre-share key scheme (EAP-PSK) based on the AES algorithm and the One-Key CBC MAC function (OMAC), which is under consideration by NIST[6] for standardization. We demonstrate that this open and flexible approach, is working with existing components, although performances enhancement is necessary.

KEYWORDS: Security, WLAN, smartcards, javacards

1 Introduction

Wireless IP networks, e.g. cheaper 802.11 technologies, follow an exponential growth. Everyday more and more people use wireless IP services at home, at office or in the city. However security issues still remain the Achilles' heel of these emerging ubiquitous networks [10], [11]. Even when Wi-Fi accesses are free, wireless clients need privacy, and organizations providing wireless infrastructures must control and manage network accesses.

---

[1] Internet Engineering Task Force.
[2] Institute of Electrical and Electronics Engineers, IEEE 802 LAN/MAN Standards Committee.
[3] IP Security Protocol.
[4] United State Department Of Defense.
[5] Secure Sockets Layer.
[6] National Institute of Standards and Technology.

Please use the following format when citing this chapter:

Urien, P. and Dandjinou, M., 2007, in IFIP International Federation for Information Processing, Volume 229, Network Control and Engineering for QoS, Security, and Mobility, IV, ed. Gaïti, D., (Boston: Springer), pp. 75–86.

After five years of efforts, standardization committees have built a secure architecture based on standards like WEP [8] (Wireless Equivalent Privacy), IEEE 802.1x [12], IEEE 802.11i [18] and Extensible Authentication Protocol [19]. The network user (*Supplicant*) is authenticated (via the EAP protocol) by a remote (*RADIUS*) server. Upon success of this operation, a master key is computed by these two entities, from which are deduced all parameters required by radio security protocols (WEP, TKIP, 802.11i), in order to provide privacy (encryption) and data integrity services.

This paper presents the first open architecture for processing the EAP protocol in JAVA smartcards (supplicant side). The basic idea is to define a framework suitable for organizations that intend to independently manage their wireless network security, according to symmetric (shared secret) or asymmetric (RSA keys and certificates) infrastructures.

Section one discusses about smartcard benefits for wireless security management. Section two presents basic technical constraints and the *OpenEapSmartcard* platform. Section three analyses experimental results obtained for EAP-TLS method [6] (SSL based authentication method) with various smartcards. Section four comments results observed for EAP-PSK method [22], based on the AES algorithm [12] that has been recently proposed as RFC at the IETF committee.

1.1   Smartcard benefits for wireless network security management

Reliable and cheap 802.11 technologies make it possible for companies, administrations, or cities to deploy wireless networks supporting data (WEB, email) or multimedia (voice, images) services. There is a need to control network accesses for confidentiality purposes (if wireless resources are restricted to authorized staff) or for legal issues (if some behaviors are forbidden in open networks).

The basic choice for user's authentication is using password or not. A good password is difficult to memorize, although it can be easily duplicated or stolen.

Smartcard is an alternative to passwords. It's a secure and cheap silicon slice [26], whose area is about 25 mm^2. It includes a CPU (8 to 50 MHz clock), ROM (up to 256 KB), non volatile memory (128 KB of E^{2}PROM or up to one MB of FLASH) and RAM (from 4 to 8 KB). Information is exchange via a serial link, whose throughput ranges between 9600 and 230,000 bit/s.

About one billion of SIM smartcards are manufactured each year[7]. SIM module [4] manages subscriber' authentication in GSM networks; it stores its

---

[7] Source, www.eurosmart.com

identity (IMSI) and computes a symmetric algorithm (A3/A8) associated to a secret key (Ki). Almost every SIM embeds a Java Virtual Machine (JVM); according to its price, a crypto processor supports additional cryptographic facilities like RSA or triple DES. Because it's possible to download applets in such components [5], which may process complex cryptographic protocols, we believe that they are very well adapted for wireless security issues.

Smartcards are generally considered as the most secure computing environment [23]. They have been selected by the DoD for military ID cards [24], by the Belgium government for citizen ID cards [25], and they will be included in US and European passports. Hundred of millions people used cash cards including tamper resistant chips running payment standards like BO' or EMV. Generally smartcard is unblocked by a *Personal Identification Number* (PIN) code whose size is 4 digits; the system is frozen after three wrong tries. Furthermore it is already possible to get components working with fingerprint recognition [13].

2 OpenEapSmartcard

Contrary to mobile phone operators that manage worldwide networks, we believe that IP wireless infrastructures could look like a constellation of "small" domains hold by public authorities (cities, campus...), private companies or individuals. It's likely than each of them will control network accesses, according to specific mechanisms and policies. As an illustration more than fifty EAP type, e.g. different authentication methods are already registered by the IANA[8].

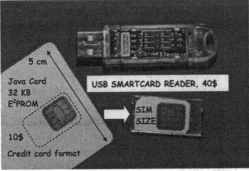

Figure 1: illustration of smartcard form factors and prices

The first requirement for *OpenEapSmartcard* initiative is *flexibility*. In the past many security threats were discovered for GSM (COMP 128-1 crack) or

---

[8] Internet Assigned Numbers Authority.

802.11 (WEP crack). Open code is a good security principle that enables code reviewing; it facilitates study of multiple security architectures; it allows evaluation of deployment costs induced by smartcards price or infrastructure management (secret key management, certificates management, communication reliability,...).

The second requirement is *feasibility*. In EAP context an authentication is a suite of requests sent to supplicant (the smartcard in our proposal) that produces responses. As specified in [12] the default return time trip (RTT) must be less than 30s. Another constraint is the complexity of authentication protocols; code byte is limited by non volatile memory capacities that currently range between 32 and 128 KBytes; hopefully this size could quickly evolve toward the MByte

The last requirement is **low costs** and **multi form factors**. Figure 1 illustrates this point, Javacard costs less than 10$ per unit, and USB readers are available for less than 40$.

As we will show it later, complex methods like EAP-TLS [6] or EAP-PSK [22] need about 20 KB of E^2PROM, and may work with RTT less than 30s with an authentication time comprised between 10s and 45s.

2.1   About java card platforms

They are two kinds of Javacard platforms.

First class, that we refer as general purpose devices, implements APIs [9] defined by the Javacard forum[9] whose current version are JC2.1 and JC2.2. All these releases support cryptographic facilities like RSA, MD5, SHA1 and random number generators (RNG). AES algorithm is only available beyond version 2.2.

Second class is based on SIM chips, and is described by the TS 03.19 standard [5]. It supports JC2.x classes and additional APIs that access to files embedded in these components.

From a functional point of view these two environments are quite similar. Although the GSM platform is widely available and cheap, it doesn't usually embed asymmetric cryptographic facilities that are not used in GSM networks.

2.2   Software architecture

The software architecture mainly comprises four java components
- The *EapEngine* which implements the *EAP core*, and acts as a router that sends and receives packets to/from authentication methods

---

[9]www.javacardforum.org

- An *Authentication* interface that defines all services offered by EAP methods
- A *Credential* object which stores information needed for method initialization.
- One or more *Methods* that instantiate authentication scenari like EAP-TLS or EAP-PSK.

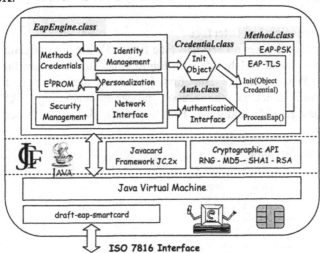

Figure 2. OpenEapSmartcard software architecture

2.2.1 EapEngine

Four services are offered by this module

- *Network interface.* Incoming EAP requests are checked and forwarded to the appropriate method. At the end of authentication process, each method computes a master cryptographic key (PMK) which is read by the supplicant operating system.
- *Identity management.* Smartcard manages several methods and/or multiple instances of the same one. An identities list stores credentials (EAP-ID, X509 certificates, RSA keys, shared secrets) required by embedded methods. This service allows to browse available identities and to select one of them.
- *Security management.* Smart card is protected by two PIN codes, one for its issuer and the other for its holder. In future versions this service could manage fingerprint recognition.
- *Personalization management.* Identity items and PIN codes are controlled and set by smartcard issuers. Some authentication methods like EAP-TLS or EAP-PSK create a secure channel. This protected link may be used for remote

management, which could modify *"over the air"* parameters embedded in tamper resistant chip. This model is closed to standard TS 03.48, which is widely deployed in GSM network for SIM card update purposes.

The ISO 7816 standard [1] defines logical structures of commands (*APDUs*) and responses exchanged with smartcards. APDUs understood by the *EapEngine* are described and explained by an internet draft [21].

2.2.2   Authentication Interface

This component defines all services (see figure 3) that are mandatory in EAP methods, in order to collaborate with *EapEngine*. The two main functions are *Init()* and *Process-Eap()*. The first initializes method and returns an Authentication interface; the second processes incoming EAP packets. Methods may provide additional facilities (fct()) dedicated to performances evaluations.

Interface auth	
void	`fct`(javacard.framework.APDU apdu, byte[] in, short inlength) Method functions apdu: incoming APDU in: buffer associated to the incoming APDU inlength: P3 value
byte[]	`Get_Fct_Buffer`() Returns a function buffer
short	`Get_Fct_Length`() Returns a function buffer length
short	`Get_Fct_Offset`() Returns a function buffer offset
byte[]	`Get_Out_Buffer`() Returns the response buffer
short	`Get_Out_Length`() Returns the response buffer length
short	`Get_Out_Offset`() Returns the response buffer offset
auth	`Init`(java.lang.Object credentials) Method Initialization
boolean	`IsFragmented`() Fragmentation in progress
boolean	`IsLongFct`() Indicates that the response of a function is stored in a private buffer
boolean	`IsLongResponse`() Indicates that the response of the method is stored in a private buffer
short	`process_eap`(byte[] in, short inlength) Method Processing in: incoming APDU buffer inlength: length of the incoming APDU Returns -length of the response -negative value if an error occurred
void	`reset`() Resets the method
short	`status`() Gets the method status

Figure 3. Authentication Interface

2.2.3   Credential object

Each method is associated to a *Credential* Object (see figure 3, *Init()*) that encapsulates all information required for processing a given authentication scenario.

2.2.4   Method

Each authentication scenario is processed by a specific Method class. Once initialized, it analyses each incoming EAP request and delivers corresponding response. The number of embedded methods is limited by the smartcard non volatile memory (E^2PROM) size.

2.3   Integration to terminals

Some operating systems, like win32, already support the EAP protocol for wired and wireless networks. A given EAP authentication scenario is processed by a particular dynamic library (DLL) named EAP-Provider [17]. A *generic* library that uses PC/SC [2] services (plug and play support for smartcard readers), forwards incoming EAP requests to EAP smartcard that computes corresponding responses.

3   EAP-TLS smartcard

The EAP-TLS authentication scenario [6] works with the IETF version of the well known SSL protocol. Additional cryptographic features that are not supported in JC2.x framework are written in java, like HMAC [3], RC4, TLS PRF ([7] *Pseudo Random Function*) and X509 certificate parser.

We have implemented two modes for EAP-TLS. The first is asymmetric and works with a mutual authentication based on RSA keys and X509 certificates. The second called session resume mode [7], is symmetric and is based on Session-ID and Master-Secret parameters computed during a previous (full and asymmetric) session. This last mode may be useful for SIM javacards that don't include RSA crypto-processor.

3.1   Experimental results

Tests were performed on four smartcards, equipped with 8 bits processors (8 MHz clock), issued by different manufacturers. Devices A, C and D are general purpose javacards, component B is a SIM module. Two of them that have RTT times less than 30s and may be used for authentication in existing 802.11 wireless infrastructures.

3.1.1   TLS "full mode"

During the authentication scenario about 2,500 bytes are sent and received. The time consumed by this operation ranges between 2 and 5 seconds. This parameter is dependant on three constraints; physical throughput,

performances of embedded JVM, and time required for writing operations in
E²PROM.

RSA resources, provided by crypto-processor, are used three times. Public
key operations need around 200ms, and encryption with private key is rather
fast, and consumes less than 500 ms.

According to the TLS specification, three dual digests (MD5 + SHA1) are
performed on these exchanged data, e.g. about 7500 bytes (120 blocs of 512
bits). We observe (see table1, Dual Hash column) average computing times
(per bloc) ranging between 3,7 ms (900ms/240) and 24 ms (5700ms/240)

Five occurrences of pseudo random function (PRF), imply the calculation
of 31 HMAC-MD5 and 31 HMAC-SHA1 procedures [3], which process 140
MD5 blocs and 140 SHA1 blocs. Each HMAC computes 2 digests, whose
average size is about 2, 25 blocs. We notice (table 1) an important overhead,
induced by our java implementation, excepted for the device D.

RC4 algorithm is fully written in java, observed performances clearly
illustrate various behaviors of multiple embedded virtual machines.

Device	RTT MAX	Total Authentica tion Time	Data Transfer 2500 bytes	Dual Hash 2x120 blocs	PRF 2x140 blocs	RC4 2 x 32 bytes	OTHER
A	52,3s	78,1s	2,3s 2,9%	5,7s 7,3%	42,4s 54,2%	14,7s 18,9%	13,0s 16,6%
B	21,0s	34,3s	4,3s 12,5%	4,5s 13,2%	19,7s 57,3%	2,3s 6,7%	3,5s 10,2%
C	22,3s	33,3s	4,9s 14,7%	3,5s 10,4%	13,3s 40,0%	2,8s 8,4%	8,8s 26,5%
D	5,2s	9,3s	1,6s 17,2%	0,9s 9,7%	4,5s 48,4%	0,7s 7,5%	1,6s 17,2%

Table 1. Measured authentication time for four smartcards, TLS full mode

Device	RSA 1024 bits Public Key Initialization	RSA 1024 bits Encryption	RSA(Verify Data) 1024 bits Private Key Encryption
A	0,21s	0,16s	0,33s
B	-	-	< 0,80s
C	0,31s	0,38s	0,43s
D	-	0,02s	0,11s

Table 2. RSA performances for four smartcards

3.2   Resume mode

In this mode around 250 bytes are exchanged, a previously computed master-secret is re-used, and no RSA resources are necessary. Two dual digests (MD5 + SHA1) are performed on about 2x150 bytes (6 blocs of 512 bits)

Four occurrences of the PRF functions imply the calculation of 15 HMAC-MD5 and 15 HMAC-SHA1 procedures which process 108 MD5 blocs and 108 SHA1 blocs. Each HMAC computes 2 digests, whose average size is about 3,6 blocs.

In summary (see table 3) the resume mode is quicker than the normal one, it may be useful for fast user's re-authentication.

Device	Total Authentication Time	Data Transfer 230 bytes	Dual Hash 2x6 blocs	PRF 2x108 blocs	RC4 2x32 bytes	OTHER
A	49,5s	0,9s 1,9%	0,3s 0,6%	32,5s 65,6%	14,7s 29,7%	1,1s 2,2%
B	18,7s	1,0s 5,4%	0,2s 1,0%	15,2s 81,3%	2,3s 12,3%	0,0s 0%
D	5,5s	0,2s 3,6%	0,0s 0%	3,5s 63,7	0,7s 12,7%	1,1s 20,0%

Table 3. Measured authentication time for three smartcards, TLS resume mode

3.3   Performances limits

	Full Mode					Session Resume Mode			
	Total Time	Data Transfer (2500 bytes)	Dual Hash 2x120 blocs	PRF 2x140 blocs	RSA	Total Time	Data Transfer (250 bytes)	Dual Hash 2x 6 blocs	PRF 2x108 blocs
A	15,6	2,3	5,7	6,7	<0,9	6,4	<1,0	0,3	5,1
B	16,5	4,3	4,5	5,3	<2,4	5,4	<1,0	0,3	4,1
C	14,0	4,9	3,5	4,1	<1,5	4,0	<1,0	0,2	2,8
D	3,7s	1,6	0,9	1,0	<0,2	1,0	<0,2	0,0	0,8

Table 4. TLS computing time estimation, obtained by neglecting java overhead, for PRF and RC4 calculation

Table 4 estimates ultimate authentication times for full and resume modes, by neglecting the java overhead. Scenario duration is only dependent on data transfer, number of digest operations, and RSA calculations. It clearly appears that performances are strongly linked to digest computing; although IO throughput can't be neglected for full mode operation.

4   The EAP-PSK smartcard.

The EAP-PSK method [22] is a symmetric authentication scenario, recently proposed at the IETF committee, and based on AES algorithm. We are going to briefly analyze its behavior. Server and client use a (secret) pre share key (PSK, 128 bits), from which are deduced two AES (128 bits) keys: AK (Authentication Key) and KDK (Key-Derivation Key).

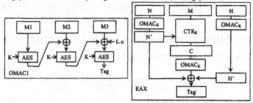

Figure 4: OMAC1 (left part) and EAX (right part) principles; K represents an AES key.

   These two entities exchange random values (RAND_P, RAND_S) which are associated to MAC (128 bits) values (MAC_P, MAC_S) computed according to the OMAC [15] algorithm, which is under consideration by NIST for standardization. This algorithm splits incoming messages in blocs (128 bits) encrypted by AK key and mixed with EXOR operations (see figure 4).

   A *Modified Counter Mode* [14] (MCM) algorithm computes from the RAND_P field and the KDK key, the *Transient EAP Key* (TEK) and the IEEE 802.1x *Pairwise Master Key* (PMK).

   EAX [20] is a block-cipher mode of operation, for solving the problem of authenticated encryption with associated header. It works with a nonce N, a message M, and a header H. It is used by EAP-PSK to provide a secure channel (S_CHANNEL), protected by the TEK key that transports at least, an encrypted and tagged *status byte*. EAX required three OMAC instances (for the nonce, the header and tag, see figure 4) and a counter mode encryption (*CTR* mode) for message ciphering.

Device	AES SET KEY	AES CIPHER (T_{AES})	OMAC 25 bytes 3xAES $T=n_{AES}(T_{AES}+p)$	OMAC 49 bytes 5xAES $T=n_{AES}(T_{AES}+p)$	AEX (N=16 bytes, H=5 bytes, M=1 byte) 10xAES
E	0,018s	0,011s	0,114s	0,170s	1,022s
C	2,6s	0,39s	1,30s	2,24s	5,13s

Table 5. Basic parameters for EAP-PSK

   Most of today available Javacards implement the JC2.1 standard, which doesn't support the AES algorithm, but hopefully it is included in JC2.2 smartcards. Consequently our tests deal with two kinds of AES instances, full

Java (device C) or native implementation (device E). As illustrated by table 5 the pure software version is rather slow (0,4s per block encryption), specially when it's necessary to initialize a key (1.3s). Additional cryptographic resources (AEX, OMAC, ...) are provided by java classes.

Operation	Number of AES Encrypted blocs (n)	Device E		Device C	
		Computing time CT	Estimated Java overhead CT-n.T_{AES}	Computing time CT	Estimated Java overhead CT-n.T_{AES}
First Request					
SET_KEY(AK)		0,018		2,60	
OMAC (49 bytes)	5	0,170	0,110	2,24	0,29
Second Request					
OMAC (25 bytes)	3	0,114	0,079	1,30	0,13
SET-KEY(KDK)		0,018		2,60	
MCM	6	0,070		2,34	
SET-KEY(TEK)		0,018		2,60	
AEX(N=16,H=5,M=1)	10	1,022	0,906	5,13	1,23
AEX(N=16,H=5,M=1)	10	1,022	0,906	5,13	1,23
TOTAL	34	2,45s	2,00s	23,90s	2,90s

Table 6. EAP-PSK computing time

We (not surprisingly) observe (see table 5) that computing time of OMAC increases proportionally to the number of (AES) blocs. The (Java) penalty per bloc (p, table 5) is about 20ms for device E and 50ms for device C. The EAX procedure is more complex and induces further Java additional computing times whose values are 0,9s for device D and 1,2s for device B. We finally notice for device E, that total computing time (2,45s) is mainly due to Java overhead because the AES penalty (34 x 0,011) is not the predominant factor.

Table 6 details observed computing times, and clearly illustrates that EAP-PSK is faster than EAP-TLS resume mode.

5 Conclusion

In this paper we have presented an open, modular and flexible approach for controlling network accesses in WLAN environment. We have demonstrated that this proposal is realistic, even with cheap smartcards that are not specially designed for that purpose. We have published [27] these source codes and we plan to develop an open library that will cover more scenari.

6 References

[1]   International Organization for Standardization (ISO) "Identification cards - Integrated circuit(s) card with contact" ISO/IEC 7816.

[2]   PC/SC (1996), Interoperability Specification for ICCs and Personal Computer Systems, © 1996 CP8 Transac, HP, Microsoft, Schlumberger, Siemens Nixdorf.
[3]   H. Krawczyk, M. Bellare, R. Canetti, "HMAC: Keyed-Hashing for Message Authentication", RFC 2104, September 1997.
[4]   ETSI - GSM 11.11 "Digital cellular telecommunications system (Phase2+); Specification of the Subscriber Interface Identity Module – Mobile Equipment (SIM_ME) interface".
[5]   ETSI GSM 11.19, "Digital cellular telecommunications system (Phase 2+); GSM API for SIM toolkit stage 2"
[6]   B. Aboba, D. Simon, "PPP EAP TLS Authentication Protocol", RFC 2716, October 1999.
[7]   T. Dierks, C. Allen, , "The TLS Protocol Version 1.0", RFC 2246, January 1999
[8]   Institute of Electrical and Electronics Engineers, "Standard for Telecommunications and Information Exchange Between Systems   - LAN/MAN Specific Requirements - Part 11: Wireless LAN Medium Access Control (MAC) and Physical Layer (PHY) Specifications", IEEE Standard 802.11, 1999.
[9]   Zhiqun Chen, "Java Card Technology for Smart Cards: Architecture and Programmer's Guide", SUN book, 2000
[10]   N. Borisov, I.GoldBerg, D.Wagner, Intercepting Mobile Communications: The Insecurity of 802.11, Proceeding of the Eleventh Annual International Conference on Mobile Computing And Network, p180, July 16-21, 2001.
[11]   S.Fluhrer, I.Mantin, A.Shamir, Weakness in the key scheduling algorithm of RC4, 8th Annual Workshop on Selected Areas in Cryptography, August 2001.
[12]   National Institute of Standards and Technology, "Specification for the Advanced Encryption Standard (AES)", Federal Information Processing Standards (FIPS) 197, November 2001.
        Institute of Electrical and Electronics Engineers, "Local and Metropolitan Area Networks: Port-Based Network Access Control", IEEE Standard 802.1X, September 2001.
[13]   Struif, B.; Scheuermann, D, "Smartcards with biometric user verification", Multimedia and Expo, 2002. ICME '02. Proceedings. 2002 IEEE International Conference on , Volume: 2 , 26-29 Aug. 2002 Pages:589 - 592 vol.2
[14]   Gilbert, H., "The Security of One-Block-to-Many Modes of Operation", FSE 03, Springer-Verlag LNCS 2287, 2003.
[15]   Iwata, T. and K. Kurosawa, "OMAC: One-Key CBC MAC", FSE 03, Springer-Verlag LNCS 2887, 2003.
[16]   M.Loutrel, P.Urien, G.Pujolle, "A smartcard for authentication in WLANs", Proceedings of the 2003 IFIP/ACM Latin America conference on Towards a Latin American agenda for network research, La Paz, Bolivia, October 2003
[17]   P.Urien, M.Loutrel,"The EAP smartcard. A tamper resistant device dedicated to 802.11 wireless networks", 3rd Worshop on applications and Services in Wireless Networks, Berne, Switzerland, July2-4, 2003.
[18]   Institute of Electrical and Electronics Engineers, "Approved Draft Supplement to Standard for Telecommunications and Information Exchange Between Systems-LAN/MAN Specific Requirements - Part 11: Wireless LAN Medium Access Control (MAC) and Physical Layer (PHY) Specifications: Specification for Enhanced Security", IEEE 802.11i-2004, 2004.
[19]   Aboba, B., Blunk, L., Vollbrecht, J., Carlson, J. and H.Levkowetz, "Extensible Authentication Protocol (EAP)", RFC 3748, June 2004.
[20]   Bellare, M., Rogaway, P. and D. Wagner, "The EAX mode of operation", FSE 04, Springer-Verlag LNCS 3017, 2004
[21]   Urien P, Farrugia F, Groot M, Abellan J, "EAP-Support in Smartcard", draft-urien-eap-smartcard-08.txt , 2005
[22]   Bersani.F, "The EAP-PSK Protocol: a Pre-Shared Key EAP Method", IETF draft, draft-bersani-eap-psk-06, 2004
[23]   Renaudin, M.; Bouesse, F.; Proust, Ph.; Tual, J.P.; Sourgen, L.; Germain, F.; "High security smartcards", Design, Automation and Test in Europe Conference and Exhibition, 2004. Proceedings , Volume: 1 , 16-20 Feb. 2004
[24]   R.Brandewie, "Smart cards:world passport to security -identity solutions for a complex world." e-Smart 2004, Sept 22-24, 2004, Sophia Antipolis, Nice, France
[25]   "Belgium electronic identity card (eID)". http://eid.belgium.be
[26]   Timothy M. Jurgensen, Scott B. Guthery, "Smart Cards: The Developer's Toolkit", PRENTICE HALL
[27]   OpenEapSmartcard WEB site, http://www.infres.enst.fr/~urien/openeapsmartcard

End to End Quality of Service over Heterogeneous Networks
EuQoS

O. Dugeon1, D. Morris2, E. Monteiro3, W. Burakowski4, M. Diaz5
1 – France Telecom R&D
2, Avenue Pierre Marzin, F-22300 Lannion – France
Olivier.Dugeon@francetelecom.com
2 – RedZinc Ltd
3 – University of Coimbra
4 – Warsaw University of Technology
5- LAAS-CNRS

Abstract: In this paper, the EuQoS Consortium offers its first architecture release in order to provide an initial view on how end to end QoS is provided over multiple and heterogeneous networks. The EuQoS end to end Architecture has two views; a network deployment view across a number of autonomous systems (AS) domains and a software view within an AS. It was funded on a division of the end to end QoS paradigm along a vertical axis - Service, Control and Transport plane – and an horizontal axis – network division between the various technology especially Core and Access networks. The solution is based on the concept of end to end path build, used and managed by three processes: Provisioning, Invocation and Operating Maintenance (OAM).

1 Introduction

End to End quality of service support for multiple applications is required for the next major growth spurt in the telecommunications industry. With the increasing shift to the Internet Protocol for many networks and the desire by the telecommunications service providers to offer new value to their customers the need exists to finally coordinate the delivery of end to end quality of service so that providers may offer new services to support their customer's applications. The

Please use the following format when citing this chapter:

Dugeon, O. Morris, D., Monteiro, E., Burakowski, W. and Diaz, M., 2007, in IFIP International Federation for Information Processing, Volume 229, Network Control and Engineering for QoS, Security, and Mobility, IV, ed. Gaïti, D., (Boston: Springer), pp. 87–101.

EuQoS [1] Consortium[1] offers its first architecture release in order to provide an initial view on *how this application-network-software* coordination might happen.

We provide an overview of the EuQoS architecture in Section 2 below. In Section 3 we describe the network view of the architecture by means of end to end path concept. And in Section 4, we detail the architecture of the various modules which compose the control plane of the EuQoS system.

2   EuQoS Architecture Overview

The EuQoS end-to-end architecture has two views; a network deployment view across a number of autonomous systems (AS) domains and a software view within an AS. The basic network deployment view is shown in figure below.

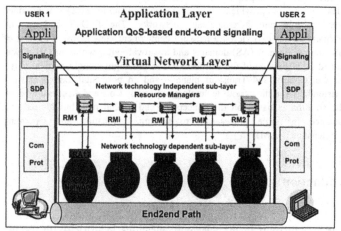

Fig. 1. EuQoS End to End Network Architecture

The EuQoS architecture approach to the scale challenge is the standard divide and conquers approach of separating the size of problem by splitting it into smaller parts. From the horizontal view, i.e. the different planes, this implies a clear separation between the Service (application layer) and Control Plane from the Transfer Plane which could be found in [2]. Again, the Control plane is sliced between a technology independent layer control by a Resource Manager (RM) and a

---

[1] EuQoS is a consortium of organizations whose main objective is to research, develop, integrate, test, validate and demonstrate end-to-end QoS technologies to support advanced QoS aware applications – voice, video-conferencing, video-streaming, tele-engineering, educational and medical applications – over multiple, heterogeneous scientific, industrial and national research network infrastructure for real life users.

technology dependent layer control by a Resource Allocator (RA). From the vertical view i.e. the different network partitions, this divide and conquer implies a clear separation between the various access technology and the different core network involved in the end-to-end connection.

The other ideas which govern our solution come from the synchronisation between service and control. Indeed, the control plane is solicited when an application needs some network resources. The aim of EuQoS architecture is not to provide end-to-end QoS for all applications, which is a significant challenge for large scale. But, it is rather to provide QoS for only applications which need them and only when they are needed. For this feature, the EuQoS system is based on session. First of all, application setups a session which triggers the corresponding network QoS setup. This has the advantage to perfectly synchronize the QoS requirement / setup and the usage of the QoS by the application. One other hard problem solved by the session concept is the *"graceful start release"* which allows synchronizing the end of the application and the release of network resources. Even if the application or the server crash, as soon as the session stops, or crashes, the QoS is released. In addition to the session setup, an application must be registered in the EuQoS AAA system. This allows the control of the application and the possibility to provide information to bill the end user. For this purpose, the EuQoS system used an enhanced version of SIP [3] which allows the QoS negotiation within the session establishment named EQ-SIP. The QoS request is simply transport in an extension of the SDP field, named EQ-SDP, of the SIP protocol. A dedicated SIP proxy handles this EQ-SDP and sends them to the Control.

In the same order, and after divided the problem by level and network partitioning, the EuQoS system divides and conquers the time scale. The architecture is based on three processes which are aligned with [4] and [5]:

- The provisioning process, whose function is to provision resources amongst the different AS, runs in background. It is the first process which starts the EuQoS system.
- The invocation process, whose role is mostly to perform admission control (CAC) of new connection, runs only when an application requests some QoS. It could be execute only when the provisioning process as finished its work.
- The Operating and Maintenance (OAM) process, whose function is to measure and monitor the EuQoS system, runs also in background. It provides the fault management sub-system. It interacts with the provisioning process in order to adjust or repair resources and with the invocation process in case of failure to notify the application.

Each process runs on a level (service and network) and for a given network partition or for the whole network (end-to-end).

3   End-to-end QoS path – EQ-path

3.1   Definition

The purpose of the EuQoS System is to build, use and monitor end-to-end QoS paths, named EQ-paths, with underlying QoS guarantees across multiple AS. The purpose of these EQ-paths is to support quality guarantees to applications on an end-to-end basis. Each EQ-path corresponds to a given set of QoS parameters and, in particular, of Classes of Service (CoS). If the number of CoS in a EuQoS system is under the control of the operators, it seems that a small number of different CoS will be sufficient for a wide range of application. For the EuQoS system, we have decided to based our CoS selection on the ITU-T Y.1541 recommendation [6].

EQ-paths have several properties which serve both the QoS guarantee and the scalability requirement. Indeed, building dedicated path on a per flow basis (a.k.a Intserv) is not scalable. At the opposite, just setup big trunk (a.k.a DiffServ) to carry a large amount of flow doesn't guarantee any individual or strict QoS for a given flow. The EQ-path notion tries to combine advantage of DiffServ and IntServ while excluding their disadvantages. The EQ-paths follow the requirement of the EuQoS system. They are built, used and monitored by the control plane in the transfer plane, in order to address QoS needed by the service plane. In the same way, they are built to handle the Autonomous Systems (AS) paths with the clear separation between a wide variety of technology and network. The EuQoS system is responsible for choosing and joining each piece of network/technology path to form the EQ-path. Finally, the three different processes act as follows:

- The provisioning process is in charge to build the EQ-paths across network partition at both independent and dependent network level,
- The invocation process use the EQ-paths by selecting the most appropriate one and perform CAC to protect EQ-paths from overflows,
- The OAM process protects EQ-paths from failure and inter-act with provisioning and invocation processes to repair EQ-paths if needed.

3.2   Building the EQ-path (Provisioning)

Two main options could be considered in building an EQ-path: The multi-domain option and the per domain option. For the multi-domain option, an EQ-path is built from a source Access Network to a destination Access Network. For the per-domain option, the EQ-path is the result of the sequence of BR-to-BR path (where BR is a Border Router). The strengths and weakness of both are summarised below. The EuQoS architecture is based on the per domain option because it gives more freedom.

In addition to the per-domain path, EuQoS system enables aggregation and merging from one AS to another. This also allows a better scalability while setup fine paths and tune resources in the Access Network. The EQ-path could be view as a sum and concatenation of individual path setup in the different network partition. This avoids setup a partial or full mesh of EQ-path across all AS.

Table 1. Per domain versus Multi-domain EQ-path

Multi domain	**Strength**: No need of Border Router (BR) configuration via a resource allocator, just the Access/Core router, in source and destination Access network, need configuration. Per flow CAC is done only in the access since the end to end path is well-known. **Weakness**: Need cooperation between all operators to build the EQ-path. Scalability is an issue since you must setup a full or partial full mesh of EQ-path. This is hard to maintain since it's difficult to provide a full backup path.
Per domain	**Strength**: Scalability is given since you can merge and aggregate traffic from one path to another. Flexibility is given too because each operator can setup its BR-to-BR paths independently, and it is easy to maintain by providing backup BR-to-BR path. **Weakness**: per flow CAC need to be performed by each domain Resource Manager (RM) to verify the traffic entering in each BR-to-BR path. The BR needs to be configured in each AS to connect the BR-to-BR path to form an EQ-path

Since EQ-paths are end to end path, they cross several Autonomous System (AS). Because the Internet used BGP to connect Autonomous Systems, it is natural for EuQoS system to use it. The border routers creates a complex structure when building an AS path. Each AS may have multiple connections, some of which may be redundant connections to the same AS. The path determined by BGP-4 may not be the optimum path from a QoS or business point of view. Furthermore BGP-4 does not propagate QoS information, such as available bandwidth, AS delay or cumulative delay, packet loss, jitter. Such information is needed by the EuQoS system to determine the best AS path which could provide the requested QoS. The qBGP [7] scheme proposed by the IST/project Tequila [7] and developed by the IST/project Mescal [8] offers advantages as it propagates QoS information.

The principle of BGP is to convey information suitable to compute the AS path by means of NLRI (Network Layer Reachability Information). qBGP simply uses this NLRI field to convey information related to QoS From this new NLRI information, the AS path computation algorithm could determine an AS path based on QoS. In fact, qBGP just guarantee the continuity of a given Per Hop Behaviour (PHB) along an AS path.

If some of CoS satisfies a simple continuity of PHB, some others need strict QoS guarantees. These two models are well-know as the "*loose*" and "*hard*" model. The EuQoS architecture can be deployed in a loose model where the data path is determined by routing protocol on a hop by hop basis or in a hard model where the data path is established, a priori, by MPLS-TE in complement to q-BGP.

The key ingredients in building the data path are: qBGP, a Resource Manager (RM) which computes a set of QoS NRLI and qBGP enabled router.

- For the loose model the RM computes the QoS NLRI and configures the border router in order to convey this NLRI by the qBGP protocol. The RM and BR router, after exchanging their QoS NLRI capabilities, compute the best AS path and update their routing table.
- For the hard model the RM computes the QoS NLRI capabilities and exchanges them via qBGP. When each RM received all QoS NLRI, it computes the best AS path and enforces the route by means of MPLS-TE tunnel via the RA.

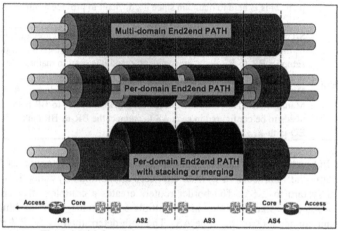

Fig. 2. Multi-domain versus per-domain option of EQ-path

3.3   Using the EQ-path (Invocation)

Once the EQ-paths have been built for each Class of Service, using either the hard or loose model, the invocation process can occur. A QoS request, which includes a CoS, is sent from the service plane to the first RM under the form of an SLS (Service Level Specification) during the SIP session establishment. The first RM corresponds to the one, in the chain, which is asked by the service plane and not by another RM. This first RM, which is responsible of the end to end QoS commitment, checks if it exists a suitable EQ-path regarding the requested CoS. This action in only done by the first RM since the EQ-path is selected once at the beginning of the path. At this point, the EuQoS system, in fact the RM, knows if there is a suitable EQ-path capable of deliver the requested QoS in term of CoS.

The remaining part of the invocation process consist of verifying, that there is sufficient QoS resources in all AS, claim by the SLS, along this EQ-path. At this moment, each RM performs the same actions:

1. Perform resources checking for its own part of the EQ-path
2. Forward the remaining part of QoS request and the selected EQ-path to the next RM.

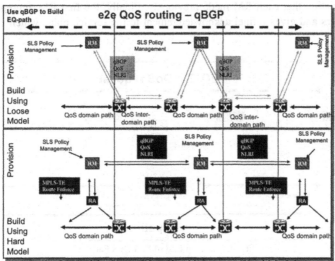

Fig. 3. Provisioning an EQ-path with Loose or Hard Model

The next RM is automatically retrieves from the EQ-path information. Indeed, each RM manages its own database which, at least, stores all information around the EQ-path. This includes the next RM. So, hop by hop, each RM checks the resources availability along the given EQ-path. If the QoS could be meeting, QoS enforcement information is sent by the RM to the device nodes it controls (only those which need to be configured) through the Resource Allocator.

As describe in chapter 2, the EuQoS system is split between an independent and dependent network technology layer. The RM, which represents the independent network technology layer, performs its CAC on database information related to the route, bandwidth availability ... Even if this information are linked to the reality, they are not the real state of the network. There are estimated, measured and/or computed resources, which for certain case is sufficient. So, at this step, the RA could also perform a CAC based on network technology dependent which represents the reality. Not only network resources are taking into account, but also constraints to enforce the QoS. When RA finishes its CAC and QoS enforcement, it sends an ACK or NACK message back to the RM. Then, the QoS request continues its trip to the next RM.

When the last RM on the EQ-path receives the QoS request, it checks the resources and start sending a final acknowledge message to the previous RM. Again, hop by hop, each RM confirms the reservation for the previous one up to the first one. At this point, the QoS request has been transformed into a QoS reservation, stored in each RM database, and enforces in the needed device through the Resource Allocator. If one RM on the EQ-path failed to reserve resource, the reservation process stop and a NACK message is sent back. This has for effect to remove the pre-reservation that each RM made previously. Finally, the first RM aggregates all the answers and gives a final acknowledgement to the service plane which requests the SLS.

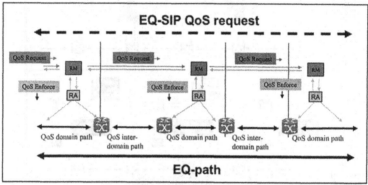

Fig. 4. Using an End to End QoS Path

3.4   Monitoring the EQ-path

In order to guarantee the QoS commitment, the EuQoS system performs two actions: the first is the admission control given above, and the second is the monitoring of EQ-path. This is held by the OAM process. Monitoring is done by means of measurement and fault management. The measurement sub-system allows the EuQoS system to verify that EQ-paths are not overflow and used like expected i.e. the measured bandwidth corresponds, more or less, to the sum of reserved bandwidth. Fault management sub-system allows verifying the EQ-path continuity and takes care of device node and link failure. These two sub-systems interact with the invocation process, in fact the CAC, to adjust the admission control threshold, and the provisioning process in order to re-compute EQ-path in case of node or link failure. This path protection could also be improved by setting up some backup path when EQ-path is build with the hard model.

4   Control Layer Architecture view

First of all, the QoS request is exchanged at the Service plane by means of EQ-SIP messages which carry the QoS request inside the EQ-SDP blocks. The EQ-SDP message is setup by the ASIG module which resides in the application or in a signalling proxy and process by the A-SSN module which reside in the proxy server (see figure below). A detail description of the service plane could be found in [10] and [11].

4.1   The Resource Manager

The RM contains a set of modules articulated around a common database, named RM-DB, which store all pertinent information from the various modules which composed the RM. This includes the different SLS manipulated by the RM as well as topology and policy information. Three QoS and 2 signalling modules composed the RM as follow:

- CAC modules
- The Traffic Engineering and Route Optimization (TERO) modules
- Monitoring, Measurement and Fault Management (MMFM) modules
- RM-SSN which manages the signalling between the RM
- RA-SSN which manages the signalling with the Resource Allocator

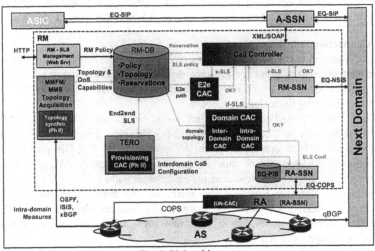

Fig. 5. RM architecture

4.1.1 Signalling blocks

NSIS [12] is used by the RM-SSN module. It was chosen as it is the natural upcoming IETF new signalization for IP. It is named EQ-NSIS because a new NSLP layer has been designed to carry EuQoS system message. This protocol suite will be used for resource reservation between the initiator and the receiver EuQoS systems, using the hop-by-hop paradigm of NSIS. NSIS will be the basis for signalling interactions between RM. Despite its relatively immature state in the standards bodies, the basic NSIS functionality is defined, which allows the development of a simplified version and adoption in the EuQoS architecture. But it is especially its path-coupled nature which decided to select NSIS because the RM must be in touch with the data path.

In EuQoS, EQ-NSIS takes care of all NSIS protocol interactions between peer RM-SSN modules; the main purpose of these interactions is the support of resource reservation and management along the data path across the various QoS domains. Decisions on resource reservation itself will be performed by the Call Controller module of the RM, which will interact with the various CAC functions for the purpose of its operation.

Because COPS was chosen as the protocol between the RA and device nodes for the configuration, this protocol was also chosen for the communication between the RA and the RM. Indeed, the RM pushed configuration into the device through the RA. These types of configurations are technology independent, but remain similar to those carried by COPS [13]. So, the RA-SSN acts as a PDP for the RA which implement a PEP function regarding the link with the RM. The RA also implements a PDP regarding the device nodes. An EQ-PIB database which contains the Policy send by the RM to the RA is also managed by the RA-SSN function.

4.1.2 Connection Admission Control (CAC)

The CAC function in the EuQoS system is probably the most difficult to design as it is here that the crunch point for resource distribution in the network occurs. The main goal of CAC is to check availability of resources. Different CAC are considered regarding the technology levels:

- Inter-Domain, Intra-Domain and End-to-End which are independent of the network technology. The resources availability checking is performed on the part of EQ-path which crosses a given AS domain. The RM-DB contains the resources associated to each path (EQ-path and domain path). CAC algorithm is a simple counting of QoS resources on the different paths.
- Underlying Network which is dependent on the network technology. The resources availability checking is performed by complex algorithms depending on the technology, from simple case, like LAN, xDSL, to complex one for UMTS, Satellite and WiFi.

In addition, and because CAC manipulates QoS parameters at different level under the form of SLS, a certain number of SLS have been defined:

- *SLS* : the QoS parameters give by the service plane to the RM
- *e-SLS* : the QoS parameters corresponding to the end to end part
- *i-SLS* : the QoS parameters of the inter-domain part

- *d-SLS* : the QoS parameters belongs to the domain own by the RM
- *r-SLS* : the QoS parameters give to the next RM
  From this division, the CAC module was slice into four sub-modules:
- A coordinator named Call Controller which implements the CAC state machine and controls all CAC sub-modules.
- One devoted to the end to end, named e2e-CAC, in charge to select the EQ-path corresponding to the CoS contain in QoS parameters.
- One devoted to the domain, named domain CAC. This sub-module includes both the control of the intra-domain part and the inter-domain part by checking resources availability on the peer link.
- One devoted to the underlying network, named UN CAC. This sub-module is located in the Resource Allocator because it is dependent on the network technology like all sub-modules include in the RA.

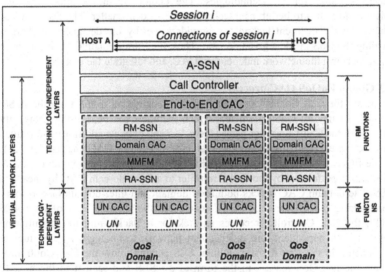

Fig. 6. EuQoS CAC Functions

End to end CAC is defined by checking if there is an EQ-path to the destination. Of course, this EQ-path is derived from the qBGP routing protocol. There might be a possibility that there is no EQ-path that meets the QoS requirements (the CoS part of the QoS). This can happen from different reasons, i.e. if all possible EQ-path have too much delay, jitter or losses regarding all parameters describing the QoS objectives. One example is when the application requires strong interactivity and when there is only a satellite link available to reach the remote site.

Inter-domain CAC. Even if an EQ-path exists, may be there is no enough resources available to ensure this QoS request along the EQ-path. Note that when an

EQ-path exists, it could be thought to be sufficient to also check that the requested bandwidth exists at that time in this EQ-path; nevertheless, this is not acceptable, as this capability implicitly means that there is a (end-to-end) tunnel from the sending domain to the receiving domain. Such EQ-path could be setup by means of end to end MPLS-TE. In the general case, we cannot assume that such a end-to-end tunnels with assigned bandwidth will exist, because keeping end-to-end tunnels does not solve the scalability problems (too many tunnels are needed and multiplexing gain is lost). As a consequence, in the general case, when QoS paths exist, their capabilities along the paths can be quite different: the existence of the requested resources along the path, in the consecutive inter-domain links has to be dynamically checked for the requests.

Intra-domain CAC is different for each domain. Intra-domain CAC can apply to QoS domains or AS constituted either by only an access network or by both an access network and a related core network. It is quite difficult to define a generic efficient solution for all technologies. The choice of the solution and of its implementation has to be left as a technology dependent matter. The decision has to be taken by the different technology providers, i.e. by the designers in charge of providing the QoS inside a given domain. Thus, the Intra-domain CAC has to trigger the RA, perform the network independent CAC, and integrate the results.

4.1.3 Global EuQoS CAC process
First of all, the Call Controller of the first RM receives an *a-SLS* from the A-SSN. This *a-SLS* carry all QoS parameters which include CoS, bandwidth, delay, jitter, loss… Then the Call Controller parses the *a-SLS* and extracts all information suitable to invoke the e2e-CAC by sending to it an *e-SLS*. The e2e-CAC checks if it exists a suitable EQ-path and sends it to the Call Controller. Again a parsing and extraction of the SLS is performed by the Call Controller to ask the domain CAC by means of a *d-SLS*. The domain CAC checks both intra-domain and inter-domain QoS resources before asking the different UN CAC located in the suitable RAs of its domain. Finally, the Call Controller receives an Ack (or a Nack) from its domain which embraces both dependent and independent network technology. At this moment, QoS is setup in the first domain. A final SLS parsing allow the Call Controller to produce the last QoS request in the form of a r-SLS and send it to the next RM through the RM-SSN signalling module. The SLS splitting follow the rules:

$$r\text{-}SLS(i+1) = r\text{-}SLS(i) - i\text{-}SLS(i)$$

where r-SLS(1) = a-SLS and i designs the ith RM.

In subsequent RM, the Call Controller receives the *r-SLS* and start to interrogate only its domain CAC with the computed *i-SLS*. The e2e-CAC is no longer solicited by the subsequent RM since the EQ-path is selected once by the first RM. The process stops when *r-SLS = NULL* i.e. when we reach the destination domain.

At this step, the last Call Controller starts sending back the global acknowledge message. If a domain CAC failed, the process stops and a NACK message is immediately returned. The Call Controller removes the on-going QoS reservation or confirms it by storing it in the RM-DB.

So, the EuQoS system end to end CAC is based on a three level process as shown in figure below: a distributed end to end CAC performed by the e2e-CAC and the inter-domain checking of each domain CAC, an intra-domain performed by the domain CAC and a technology CAC performed by the each solicited UN CAC. The Call Controller, the e2e and domain CAC sub-modules use the RM-DB to store and manage the SLS and all suitable information suitable to check resources availability.

4.1.4 Traffic Engineering and Resource Optimization

Note that, in order to setup end to end path, we have to select an adequate set of QoS-related network reachability information (QoS NLRI) parameters values for defining this EQ-path. In particular, this QoS NLRI parameter value or values should not be too limited statically by some not powerful AS in the routes existing between the different domains, and should not be too large to loose bandwidth. Tuning these QoS NLRI parameters is a hard work and could give to EuQoS system a success or a failure.

So, inside the RM, and in the provisioning process, the TERO module is responsible to build the EQ-path in the best possible way. Its main objective is to control and optimize the routing process, so as to steer the traffic through the network in the most effective way, thus optimising the available resources when it builds the EQ-path. At the technology independent layer, traffic routes to be identified are between network domains (i.e., different Autonomous Systems), with the objective of optimising the inter-domain routing process based on QoS requirements. To perform this activity TERO interacts with qBGP router protocol in order to better configure it by giving them the most appropriate QoS NLRI.

It is assumed that this function does not directly control inter-domain or intra-domain resources, i.e. direct configuration of border and/or internal routers, but rather it provides a network administrator with the necessary information, hereafter called (with intentional generality) *policies*, to configure inter-domain traffic routes, which it carries out by means of the specific network technology dependent mechanism. Depending on the specific underlying network technology, the output of this function may also affect the intra–domain routing within the respective domain. In such a case, these policies can be provided also as input to intra-domain traffic engineering, whenever requested by a specific underlying network technology.

As a consequence, TERO works in background during the provisioning process (i.e. offline) with respect to the EuQoS system operation, its timeframe being that of *network engineering cycles* (i.e. hours, days or weeks) rather than the session lifetime, or round trip time.

4.1.5 Monitoring, Measurement and Fault Management (MMFM)

The goal of this function is to manage network measurement in order to monitor the network resource and discover the network topology to support CAC and TERO functions. It also performs fault management and QoS classes and SLA/SLS monitoring. To achieve these objectives, the MMFM architecture contains the following components:

- A test and a measurement subsystem to manage tests in a scheduled environment.
- A Web services in charge of starting the subsystems, in order to check the delivered end-to-end QoS.
- A set of probes in the network to collect test data.

As a first step in the function specification, the MMFM module:

- monitors the current status of the network in order to support the CAC decisions to accept/reject new session QoS requests,
- provides feedback to the TERO function,
- supports fault detection by monitoring the network elements and measuring their parameters in order to identify faults,
- notifies the service plane of any fault that can force a QoS level failure,
- monitors the level of QoS supported and delivered for determining if SLA/SLS requirements are met.

The network technology independent sub-layer of the Resource Managers defines what parameters must be measured. So, that the technology-specific Resource Managers are able to map these parameters to the technological specific ones, and vice versa.

5 Conclusion

End to End QoS is a difficult problem as the various QoS mechanisms for packet networks are being developed over ten years ago. The main reasons they have not been widely deployed is the absence of general architecture coordination, synchronisation with applications and business models.

Here we set out what is our first release of the architecture. We believe it is a most advanced result at this time but we do believe that we need to increase its maturity level to deal with the open issues, to incorporate feedback from the trials and in order to continue to simplify the system in order to minimise complexity and cost.

A first implementation – with Wifi and Ethernet as access network - has been released and show during the Communicating European Research (CER'2005) event in Brussels in November 2005. Next steps will refine and detail the architecture, in particular the "hard model". Attention will be pay to scalability, IMS interoperability and performance. New implementations, including full MMFM support and first pan-European deployment, over 9 testbeds and 5 access network technology (Ethernet, Wifi, xDSL, UMTS, GMPLS) will be achieve during 2006 year.

6 Acknowledgements

The information drawn from this document is drawn from the EuQoS Consortium and individual contributors are too many to list. Particular thanks are due to people involved in CAC within the EuQoS consortium who edited much of the EuQoS material from which this paper comes from. A full version of this paper could be found in [11]

7 Bibliography

[1] FP6-IST/EuQoS project, (September 1, 2004 – August 31, 2007) ; http://www.euqos.org

[2] O. Dugeon & A. Diaconescu, *"From SLA to SLS up to QoS control: The CADENUS framework"*, WTC 2002, September 2002.

[3] S. Salsano,*"SIP Extensions for QoS support"*, draft-veltri-sip-qsip-01.txt.

[4] O. Dugeon and all, *"D6.2: Service Provisioning in Premium IP: Recommendations to Telecom Operators and ISPs"*, CADENUS, EU IST Project IST-1999-11017.

[5] *"eTOM Solution Suite"*; http://www.tmforum.org

[6] ITU-T Recommendation Y.1541, *"Network performance objectives for IP-based services"*, ITU, May 2002.

[7] M. Boucadair, *"QoS-Enhanced Border Gateway Protocol"*, draft-boucadair-qos-bgp-spec-01.txt.

[8] FP5-IST/Tequila project (2001-2003); http://www.ist-tequila.org

[9] FP5-IST/Mescal project (2003-2005); http://www.mescal.org

[10] EuQoS Consortium, Deliverable D3.1.1, *"Extended QoS API and Middleware layer for phase 1 application use-cases"*, (not yet published), August, 2005.

[11] EuQoS Consortium, Deliverable D1.1.3, *"Business models and system design specification"*, (not yet published), August 2005.

[12] R. Hancock and all, *"Next Steps in Signalling (NSIS): Framework"*, RFC4080, IETF, June 2005.

[13] Durham, Ed., J. Boyle, R. Cohen, S. Herzog, R. Rajan, A. Sastry, *"The COPS (Common Open Policy Service) Protocol"*, RFC 2748, IETF, January 2000.

QoS management for mobile users

Badr Benmammar, Francine Krief

LaBRI Laboratory, Bordeaux1 University, 33400 Talence, France
{badr.benmammar,francine.krief}@labri.fr
WWW home page: http://w5.labri.fr/

Abstract: The major challenge in wireless environment is the provision of quality of service (QoS) guarantees that different applications demand considering the highly dynamic nature of these environments. In this context, provide to mobile users the QoS required is a very important field of research. Our approach to improve the QoS in the wireless network is based on the user mobility profile, after the determination of this profile, an advance resources reservation is made for the mobile terminal solely in the locations where it can visit. The determination of this location is made after an observation phase during which the user is new and his mobility profile is unknown for the system. During the observation phase, the system can't make advance resources reservation for the user. In this case, we use Agent technology in order to improve the QoS for this user.

1 Introduction

The IETF has launched in 2002, the Next Steps In signaling working group (NSIS), the initial objective of this group was to unify all the existing solutions of IP signaling or to make them coexist.

Initially, the NSIS working group aimed the QoS, and proposed the QoS NSLP [1] signaling application. In order to reduce the impact of the handover on the user quality of service, we propose to use the QoS NSLP messages in order to make resources reservation in advance. This reservation is based on an object called MSpec (Mobility Specification) that determines the future locations of the mobile terminal. The MSpec object is a part of a user mobility profile, which is determined by the mobile terminal. We propose a format for this object, which will be included in the QoS NSLP messages. In order to minimize signaling in the network, we use HMIPv6 architecture for the application of this mechanism. The MAP (Mobility Anchor Point) plays a significant role to reserve the resources in advance on behalf of the mobile terminal.

The determination of the MSpec is made after an observation phase during which the user is new and his user mobility profile is unknown for the system. During the

Please use the following format when citing this chapter:

Benmammar, B. and Krief, F., 2007, in IFIP International Federation for Information Processing, Volume 229, Network Control and Engineering for QoS, Security, and Mobility, IV, ed. Gaïti, D., (Boston: Springer), pp. 103–115.

observation phase, the system can't make advance resources reservation for the user. In this case, we use Agent technology in order to improve the QoS for this user.

This paper is organized as follows. First, we present the protocol approach with a synthesis of research relating to resources reservation in a wireless environment, the QoS NSLP signaling application, the user mobility profile which includes the MSpec object, as well as the procedure of resources reservation in advance using the QoS NSLP signaling application and the handover procedure. Then, we present the Agent approach; we describe the main principles of the agent technology, our approach which use Agent technology without resources reservation. Finally, we present the validation of the Agent approach with Petri net tools and the first simulation results for the protocol approach.

2   Protocol approach with advance resource reservation

2.1   Advance resource reservation and mobility profile

Recent researches are interested in advance resource reservation to provide the necessary QoS to the mobile terminals. In the integrated services networks, the majority of research is interested in extending the RSVP protocol in a mobile environment. User mobility prediction also represents a key factor for providing a seamless delivery of multimedia applications over wireless networks.

The authors in [2] proposed a new protocol of resource reservation in mobile environment called MRSVP (Mobile RSVP). In this model of reservation, the mobile terminal can make advance reservations in a set of cells named MSPEC (Mobility Specification). The MSPEC is not very clear, it only indicates the future locations of the mobile terminal but the MSPEC is not described. Authors proposed other RSVP messages in order to treat the user's mobility. This technique requires additional classes of service, major changes of RSVP, and a lot of signaling.

Min-Sun Kim and al [3] proposed a resource reservation protocol in a mobile environment. The proposed protocol introduces the *RSVP agent* concept in order to guarantee the necessary QoS through an anticipation of the resource reservation. In this protocol, there are 3 classes of resource reservation to obtain a better use of resources:

- *The Free class:* it represents the resources used in Best Effort.
- *The Reserved class:* it represents the reserved resources for a specific flow, which are currently used.
- *The Prepared class:* it represents the reserved resources for a specific flow, which are not currently used.

Another way to obtain a better use of resources is to determine the future locations of the mobile terminal. Authors in [4] present the architecture of a mobility prediction agent (MPA) that accurately performs mobility prediction using the knowledge of user's preferences, goals, and spatial information without imposing any assumptions about the availability of his movement's history. Using concepts of evidential reasoning of Dempster-Shafer's theory, the MPA captures the uncertainty of the user's navigation behaviour by gathering pieces of evidence concerning different groups of candidate future locations. These groups are then refined to predict the user's future location when evidence accumulates using Dempster rule of combination.

2.2 Advance resource reservation with QoS NSLP

2.2.1 The QoS NSLP signaling application

The QoS NSLP signaling application makes it possible to generate a signaling in order to provide certain level of QoS.
QoS NSLP generates 4 messages types:

- *Reserve*: the only message, which handles the reservation state (refresh, create, remove).
- *Response:* using this message, a response is sent to a message received.
- *Query:* this message is used to require information concerning the nodes, which are on the data path, for example: the available resources.
- *Notify*: using this message, it possible to inform a node without preliminary request.

2.2.2 Mobility profile

The user's mobility profile is built on the basis of its behaviour / movement after **m** associations with the system. The goal of this profile is to build a user's behaviour model. The system model is based on the Continuous Time Markov Chain (CTMC).
Our system can evolve between N states defined by the following set:
$C = (C_1, C_2, ... C_i .... C_n)$.
The system is in the state i = the terminal mobile is in the cell C_i.
P_{ij}: the probability of transition from the cell C_i to the cell C_j.
$P_i(t_r)$: the probability, which defines the location of the mobile terminal in the cell C_i at the time t_r.
The user's mobility profile contains the following information:

- User's identifier: User_ID
- $M = [P_{ij}] [N*N]$: The Matrix of transition, which contains the P_{ij}.

We note:
    t [i, j]: the number of transition from the cell i to the cell j during the **m** associations with the system.
    g (i): the number of transition outgoing from the cell i during the **m** associations with the system. We calculate it as follows: $g(i) = \sum_{j=1}^{n} t[i, j]$.

After the **m** associations, the probability of transition from the cell i to the cell j is calculated as follows: $P_{ij} = t[i, j] / g(i)$.

- $V = [P_i(t_0)] [N]$

$P_i(t_0)$: this probability defines the location of the mobile terminal in the cell C_i at the time t_0.

k (i): the number of associations with the cell i during the **m** associations at the time t_o. We have: $\sum_{i=1}^{n}$ k (i) = m and $P_i(t_o)$ = k (i) / m.

- The MSpec (Mobility Specification): it determines the future locations of the mobile terminal. The proposed format for the MSpec is as follows: MSpec = <MSpec ID> <Duration> <Cell ID>.

Where:

- *MSpec ID* is the identifier of the MSpec.
- *Duration* is the interval of time (< start time>, <end time >) during which the future locations of the mobile terminal can be determined.
- *Cell ID* : <cell ID1>, <cell ID2>, <cell ID3>, ..., <cell IDn> is a set of cells identifiers. We suppose that each cell is identified by a single identifier.

We use the Continuous Time Markov Chain (CTMC) in order to determine the MSpec.

$P_j(t_{r+1})$: the probability of the mobile terminal's location in the cell C_j at the time t_{r+1}.

We can calculate this probability by the following formula:

$$P_j(t_{r+1}) = \sum_{i=1}^{n} P_i(t_r) * P_{ij}.$$

We define θ ($0 \leq \theta \leq 1$), a threshold which is used to select the cells according to their probabilities. The MSpec is defined as follows: MSpec (t_r) = {C_j / $P_j(t_{r+1}) \geq \theta$ }.

Before the **m** associations, the system do not calculate the MSpec because the user is new and the system has not the necessary information to calculate the MSpec; it has no information concerning the M Matrix and the V Vector (observation phase).

2.2.3 MQoS NSLP

We name MQoS NSLP, the procedure of resources reservation in advance using the QoS NSLP messages in a mobile environment. This procedure of reservation is applied in HMIPv6 architecture.

In the following, we present a scenario of communication between two mobile terminals where the MH1 is the entity, which generates the flow and which initiates the reservation.

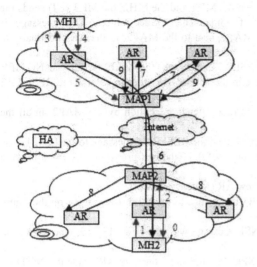

Fig. 1. Advance resource reservation procedure

We note MSpec1 and MSpec2 respectively, the set of future locations of MH1 and MH2 during the communication.

The procedure of advance resources reservation using QoS NSLP is as follows (the registration can start with the MH1 or the MH2, the following scenario considers that the MH2 is the first mobile, which makes the registration):

0: The AR informs the MH2 with the message *Router Advertisement* of the availability of resources. For that, we propose to add a bit Q in this message. If Q = 0 then the AR does not have resources and in this case the MH2 can be connected in BE.

1: During the registration, the MH2 asks its AR for a certain QoS. In this case, we propose to add the MSpec2 object to the *registration request* message. (Here, we are interested only in the interactions between MIPv6 and the QoS NSLP messages, other MIPv6 messages are necessary in order to continue the registration).

2: After the registration with the MH2, the AR sends the QoS request to the MAP2. For that, we use the NOTIFY message with the MSpec2 object included in it. After the reception of the NOTIFY message, the MAP2 analyses the MSpec2 object.

3: The AR informs the MH1 with the *Router Advertisement* message of the availability of resources using the bit Q. If Q = 0 then the AR has not resources and in this case the MH2 can only be connected in BE.

4: during the registration, the MH1 asks its AR for a certain QoS. The MSpec1 object is added to the *registration request* message.

5: After the registration with the MH1, the AR sends the QoS request to the MAP1, for that we use NOTIFY message and the MSpec1 object. After the reception of the NOTIFY message, the MAP1 analyses the MSpec1 object.

6: To reserve the resources between the MH1 and the MH2, the MH1 (NI) sends the RESERVE message, which must contain the QSpec object. This message is transported by GIMPS until the MAP1, sent to the MAP2, to the AR and finally to the MH2 (NR).

7: After the reception of the RESERVE message, the MAP1 sends the NOTIFY message to all the ARs, which are in the MSpec1 in order to receive the RESERVE message.

8: the RESERVE message is forwarded after its reception by the MAP2, in all the ARs, which are in the MSpec2.

9: the ARs, which are in the MSpec1 send the RESERVE message to the MAP1.

The Handover procedure. The stages of the handover procedure are the following (Figure 2):

- Registration of MH2 with its new AR (MIPv6 protocol).
- The new AR sends the RESERVE message to the MH2, (message 1 on the figure 2).
- The MH2 sends the RESPONSE message with the new MSpec2, (message 2 on the figure 2).
- After the reception of the RESPONSE message, the new AR sends the NOTIFY message to the MAP2 with the new MSpec2 (message 3 on the figure 2).
- The MAP2 analyses the new MSpec2, and performs the following actions: (message 4 on the figure 2):
- It keeps the reservation for the old cells, which belong to the new MSpec2.
- It makes advance reservations in the new cells, which do not belong to the old MSpec2.
- It removes the reservation for the old cells, which do not belong to the new MSpec2, except for the current cell.
- Registration of MH1 with its new AR (MIPv6 protocol).
- The MH1 sends the RESERVE message to the new AR with the new MSpec1, it will be forwarded to the MAP1 (message 5 on the figure 2).
- The MAP1 includes the old and the new MSpec1 in a NOTIFY message. Then, it sends this message to all the ARs whose identification is in the new and the old MSpec1 (message 6 on the figure 2).
- Each AR analyses the two MSpec1 objects and performs the following actions (message 7 on the figure 2):
- The old AR keeps the reservation for the old cells, which belong to the new MSpec1.
- Each new AR makes advance reservations in the new cells, which do not belong to the old MSpec1.
- Each old AR removes the reservation for the old cells, which do not belong to the new MSpec1, except for the current cell.

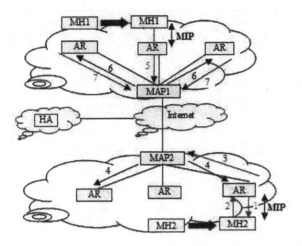

Fig. 2. The Handover procedure

3   Agent approach without resource reservation

3.1   Agent technology

In the case of a new user, the system cannot make advance resources reservation because the user mobility profile is unknown and the MSpec cannot be calculated, without resources reservation, we use Agent technology in order to improve the quality of service for the mobile user.

In a Wi-Fi environment, the strategy of changing the access point is static i.e. neither the service provider nor the customer can change the selection of the access point. However this selection can be bad in certain cases. In figure 3, the Mobile Host 5 (MH5) on which the user starts an application requiring a high level of QoS (a video application for example), receives the best signal of AP2; however, the cell 2 is very loaded and consequently QoS necessary for MH5 cannot be assured. A dynamic strategy consists in guiding the MH5 towards cell 1 which is empty and which can provide the necessary QoS.

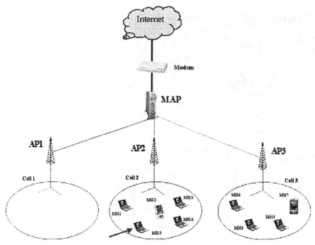

Fig. 3. Example of Wi-Fi network

If all the cells are filled, the user must be able to use another access technology at his disposal which corresponds to his needs. In this example, it is the UMTS technology which will be used; the great number of users on the spot prevents the Wi-Fi from fulfilling the requirements of QoS for the required application. As soon as the user activates another less critical application in term of QoS or that the performance of Wi-Fi becomes acceptable for the application, the user must also be able to reconsider Wi-Fi technology (because of the high cost of the UMTS for example). Different vertical handover must be carried out in a completely transparent way for the user according to the applicative constraints and the user profile.

To provide quality of service on a Wi-Fi network, it is necessary to respect 3 principles [5]:
- The number of hosts authorized to use the channel must be limited;
- The geographical area inside which the users communicate must be limited so that all of them can use the highest throughput;
- The sources must be limited by configuring the conditioners of traffic in the equipment.

In order to provide necessary QoS to a multimedia application, we will respect these three principles and we'll make three assumptions:
- From a certain number of users (N), gathered in the same cell, QoS necessary for a multimedia application will not be ensured any more and the cell will be considered as filled.
- Each access point contains a single "identifier of location".
- According to the work which was realized in [6], an estimate of the position of the MH is made and an application which gives the distribution of the cells in each room of the university (conference room, library...) is downloadable from the server.

3.2   Agent approach

The multi-agent system contains 3 agents:
- *Application agent:* This agent is located on the MH, its role is to associates an application profile to the user, in a first phase, the *Application agent* determines the application type launched by the user.
- *Terminal Agent:* This agent is located on the MH, it establishes the connection between the user and the system, and it communicates with another agent on the access point in order to find the state of the cell and the states of the cells in the neighborhood. It asks for the deployment of another access technology if necessary.
- *State Agent:* This agent is located on the access point; it determines the state of the cell and the state of the neighbouring cells. From N users gathered in the cell, the state of the cell will be regarded as filled. To know the state of the neighboring cells, the State agent contacts the same agents on the neighboring cells, and thus it can recover their states.

Figure 4 represents the modelling of interactions between agents by the AUML model. In this example, the user is in the cell number 2 of the conference room. He consults his emails or makes a transfer file. At the launching of a multimedia application, the Application agent actives the Terminal agent (message m1), the Terminal agent is activated and sends a message (m2) to the State agent in order to know the state of the current cell; the State agent compares the number of users in the cell with the number N. If it is lower or equal to the number of users in the cell, it sends a message (m3) to the Terminal agent to indicate to it that the current cell is filled. At the same time the State agent contacts the same agents on the neighboring access points (messages m4 and m5) in order to know the state of the neighboring cells. Each agent answers by a message which contains the state of the cell or the number of users in the cell with the location identifier of the cell (messages m6 and m7).

The State agent in the current cell makes a comparison between the numbers of users in the neighbouring cells or between their states. If there is at least a cell which is not filled, it sends the location identifier of the chosen cell to the Terminal agent (m8), and it sends an ACK message (m9) to the State agent in the chosen cell. At present, the Terminal agent sends a request to the server in order to download the application which will enable the user to know the place of the concerned cell in the room.

On the other hand, if all the cells are filled, the State agent contacts the Terminal agent (message m10) which will require the deployment of the UMTS.

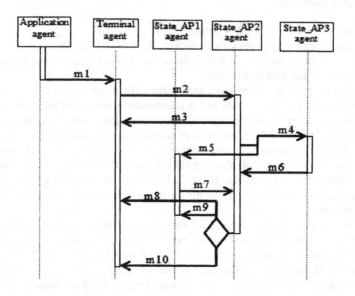

Fig. 4. The modelling of interactions between agents by the AUML model

4 Simulation

4.1 Validation of the Protocol Approach

The validation of the protocol approach is done on two stages; the first stage consists in seeking the good value of θ, for this, we use the MATLAB Mathematical Software. The second stage consists in comparing our approach of advance resources reservation with a model without resources reservation, for this, we use the OMNeT++ simulation tools.

For the second stage, we have chosen two parameters which are:

• The resources reservation time in the new cell.
• The packet loss before the resources reservation in the new cell.

The two parameters are based on the MSpec failure rate.

For the first stage, we suppose that the user's neighbourhood contains 10 cells and the value of **m** is 40 (the number of associations with the system).

During theses 40 associations, we will follow the different locations of the mobile terminal in order to determine the M Matrix and the V Vector.

The system calculates the vector $V_1 = V * M$ in order to determine the MSpec1 for the 1st handover. For the second handover, the system calculates the vector $V_2 = V_1 * M$ in order to determine the MSpec2 and so on.

After 6 handover, we have the following results:

$V_1 = [0.2712 \quad 0.0700 \quad 0.1350 \quad 0.0665 \quad 0.1900 \quad 0 \quad 0.1440 \quad 0 \quad 0.0920 \quad 0.0313]$.

$V_2 = [0.2015 \quad 0.1193 \quad 0.1089 \quad 0.1558 \quad 0.0504 \quad 0.1404 \quad 0.0271 \quad 0.0940 \quad 0.0343 \quad 0.0683]$.

$V_3 = [0.2217 \quad 0.1119 \quad 0.1531 \quad 0.0873 \quad 0.1308 \quad 0.0406 \quad 0.0876 \quad 0.0331 \quad 0.0791 \quad 0.0548]$.

$V_4 = [0.2147 \quad 0.1275 \quad 0.1263 \quad 0.1350 \quad 0.0689 \quad 0.0941 \quad 0.0433 \quad 0.0693 \quad 0.0500 \quad 0.0709]$.

$V_5 = [0.2176 \quad 0.1225 \quad 0.1509 \quad 0.1022 \quad 0.1064 \quad 0.0543 \quad 0.0684 \quad 0.0446 \quad 0.0696 \quad 0.0635]$.

$V_6 = [0.2159 \quad 0.1296 \quad 0.1361 \quad 0.1250 \quad 0.0792 \quad 0.0777 \quad 0.0501 \quad 0.0597 \quad 0.0569 \quad 0.0698]$.

The following graph shows the impact of θ on the determination time of the MSpec (The time is calculated in millisecond).

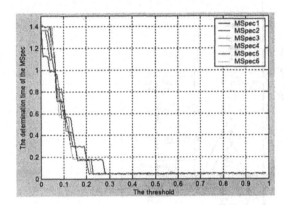

The second graph shows the impact of θ on the MSpec size.

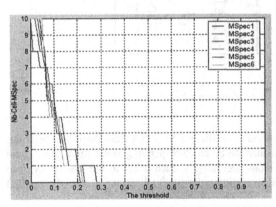

If $θ \geq 0.28$, the MSpec is empty, we remark that $θ = 0.1$ is a good value for the simulation.

With $θ = 0.1$, we have the following results: MSpec 1 = $\{C_1, C_3, C_5, C_7\}$, MSpec 2 = $\{C_1, C_2, C_3, C_4, C_6\}$, MSpec 3 = $\{C_1, C_2, C_3, C_5\}$, MSpec 4 = $\{C_1, C_2, C_3, C_4\}$, MSpec 5 = $\{C_1, C_2, C_3, C_4, C_5\}$, MSpec 6 = $\{C_1, C_2, C_3, C_4\}$.

Currently, we simulate the system with OMNet++ in order to validate the second stage.

4.2 Validation of the Agent approach by Petri nets tools

Implementing Agent technology in a wireless environment is a heavy task. So, for the validation of the Agent approach, we use Petri nets tools.

The following figure represents the modelling of interactions between agents by Petri nets tools.

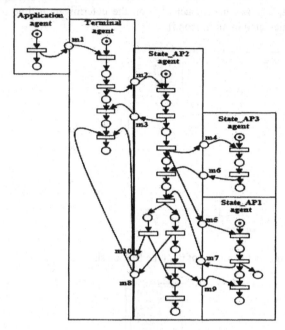

Fig. 5. The modelling of interactions between agents by Petri nets tools

A simple manual verification is sufficient to verify the Petri net describes previously, it is necessary to launch the token corresponding to the Application agent and to cross successive transitions according to each event in the system. We can verify that the Petri net contains neither the blockage situation nor the conflict situation.

5 Conclusion

We have presented in this paper a mobility profile management based approach for advance resource reservation in wireless networks.

This reservation is made according to the MSpec object which determines the future locations of the mobile terminal. Our objective through this approach is to minimize the degradation of services during the handover. The determination of the

MSpec is made after an observation phase during which the user is new and his mobility profile is unknown for the system. During the observation phase, the system can't make advance resources reservation for the user. In this case, we use Agent technology in order to improve the QoS for this user. The validation of the Agent approach is based on the Petri nets tools. Currently, we simulate the system with OMNet++ in order to validate the protocol approach.

References

1. J. Manner, S. Van den Bosch, G. Karagiannis, A. McDonald, NSLP for Quality-of-Service signaling <draft-ietf-nsis-qos-nslp- 08.txt> (2005).
2. A. K. Talukdar, B. R. Badrinath, A. Acharya, MRSVP: A resource reservation protocol for an integrated services network with mobile hosts. ACM Journal of Wireless Networks, vol. 7 (2001).
3. K. Min-Sun, S. Young-Joo, K. Young-Jae, C. Young, A Resource Reservation Protocol in Wireless Mobile Networks". ICPP Workshops (Valencia, Spain, 2001).
4. N. Samaan, A. Karmouch, An Evidence-Based Mobility Prediction Agent Architecture. MATA 2003, pp. 230_239 (Berlin, 2003).
5. J.A. García-Macías, F. Rousseau, G. Berger-Sabbatel, L. Toumi, A. Duda, Différenciation des services sur les réseaux sans-fil 802.1. Proc. French-speaking conference on the ingeniery of the protocols (Montreal, Canada, 2002).
6. M. McGuir, K. N. Plataniotis, A. N. Venetsanopoulos, Estimating position of mobile terminal from path loss measurements with survey data, Wireless Communications & Mobile Computing, vol. 3, pp. 51-62 (2003).

A Differentiated Services API for Adaptive QoS Management in IP Networks

Gérard Nguengang[1], Dominique Gaiti[2], and Miguel F. de Castro[3]

[1]LIP6, Université Pierre et Marie Curie, R&D Ginkgo-Networks
g.nguengang@ginkgo-networks.com
[2]ISTIT, Université de Technologie de Troyes
gaiti@utt.fr
[3]DC, Universidade Federal do Ceará
miguel@ufc.br

The introduction of quality of service in IP Networks brings solutions to real time applications requirements over Internet. Because of its simplicity, Differentiated Services architecture proposed by the Internet Engineering Task Force (IETF) is becoming the most employed solution for providing end-to-end QoS (Quality of Service) to network based applications. However, tuning QoS parameters in edge and core routers of a DiffServ domain for efficient resource utilization and stable network behavior is not an easy task. Because of the unpredictable and dynamic behavior of the Internet traffic, network entities need to take fast decisions and perform fast adaptations for the provision of adequate end-to-end QoS. This paper proposes an Application Programming Interface for near real time bandwidth allocation and parameters tuning of DiffServ queues in Cisco routers as a first step to address to the aforementioned problem.

1 Introduction

Due to the emergence of real time voice and video applications over Internet which are delay and jitter sensitive, the classic IP best-effort service is no longer sufficient. These multimedia applications have high bandwidth requirements as well as delay constraints and just adding links capacity is

Please use the following format when citing this chapter:

Nguengang, G., Gaïti, D. and de Castro, M.F., 2007, in IFIP International Federation for Information Processing, Volume 229, Network Control and Engineering for QoS, Security, and Mobility, IV, ed. Gaïti, D., (Boston: Springer), pp. 117–129.

not a rational solution. That is why, in recent years, there has been considerable research focused on extending the Internet architecture to allow Quality of Service. The Internet Engineering Task Force (IETF) has proposed two architectures for providing end-to-end QoS in the Internet: Integrated Services (IntServ) and Differentiated Services (DiffServ).

IntServ [4] architecture is based on reserving network resources for individual flows by the means of the Resource Reservation Protocol (RSVP) [5]. This raises two important deployment issues. First, all the routers along an end-to-end network path must be RSVP-capable in order to realize IntServ benefits. Second, a router has to manage per-flow state and perform per-flow processing. This is why IntServ is not a scalable solution for providing end-to-end QoS. It ensures absolute guarantees for each flow crossing the network but requires too much memory resource to maintain per-flow state since there may potentially be thousands of flows composing the Internet traffic.

In the DiffServ [3] architecture, traffic flows that are similar in terms of QoS requirements, are aggregated and identified as classes. Packets are classified based on contracted parameters according to their service requirements and are marked to receive particular per-hop behavior. Typically, different traffic streams that belong to the same traffic aggregate receive the same treatment when crossing the network. The Differentiated Services Code Point (DSCP) field in the IP header is used to carry the marking information. Since the number of DiffServ traffic classes is expected to be far fewer than the number of flows in IntServ, DiffServ is seen as the emerging technology to support QoS in IP backbone networks in a scalable fashion. However, tuning QoS parameters for edge and core routers of a DiffServ domain for efficient resource utilization and stable network behavior is not an easy task. The following quote from a router manual highlights the problem: "When first implementing WRED on the router, we recommend that you initially use the default values for min-threshold, max-threshold, the weighting constant, and the probability denominator. If you begin to experience congestion or if congestion continues (especially with TCP traffic), try adjusting WRED by making small changes to the various parameters (one at a time) and observing the effect on congestion" [13]. To overcome it, the network must be able to recognize and adapt itself to the running traffic fluctuations to enhance service performance. The unpredictable and dynamic behavior of network traffic requires a real-time operation to take fast decisions and to perform fast adaptations [15]. There is also a need for cooperation between network devices to define a global QoS policy for network stability and efficient end-to-end QoS in each traffic class. Our approach for solving this problem is to find a way to dynamically act on a router in order to perform effective

QoS parameters tuning. Hence, the aim of this paper is to better understand the provision of Quality of Service in market's routers and provide a Java library for DiffServ queues monitoring and scheduling configuration. The API is Cisco-specific but can be easily extended to other vendors.

This paper proposes a DiffServ based API for the monitoring and the configuration of QoS features in Cisco QoS routers. It is organized as follows. A brief description of the QoS features on a Cisco router is presented in Section 2. Afterwards in Section 3, we make reasoning about how to implement Differentiated Services with Cisco Internetworking Operating System (IOS). The developed API is described in Section 4. In Section 5, we present some experiments performed to check and validate the API's functionalities. Finally, we present our conclusion and outline some future works.

2   QoS features in Cisco routers

In order to provide end-to-end QoS, Cisco Systems has implemented a set of features for packets classification and marking, congestion management / avoidance and traffic policing /shaping.

2.1 Packet classification and marking

Classification comprises using a traffic descriptor to categorize a packet within a specific group, to assign that packet and make it accessible for QoS handling on the network. Once the packets are classified, they are marked to signal to core routers the QoS policy which must be applied to them. Cisco IOS (Internetworking Operating System) provide three main features for packets classification:

2.1.1 Policy Based Routing (PBR)

PBR [7] allows for the traffic classification based on Access Control List (ACL). ACLs establish the match criteria and define how packets have to be classified. ACLs classify packets based on port number, source and destination address (e.g., all traffic between two sites) or Mac address. PBR also provides a mechanism for setting the IP Precedence or DiffServ code point (DSCP) enabling the network to differentiate classes of service. IP Precedence employs the three precedence bits in the IP version 4 header's Type of Service (ToS) field to specify class of service for each packet [1]. Six classes of service may be assigned. The remaining two classes are reserved for future use. The DSCP [3] replaces the ToS in IP version 6 and can be used to specify 1 of 64 classes for a packet. PBR finally provides a mechanism for routing packets through traffic-engineered paths. The Border Gateway Protocol (BGP) [14] is used to propagate policy information between routers. Policy propagation allows packet classification based on ACL's or router table source or destination address entry use with IP Precedence [7].

2.1.2 Committed Access Rate (CAR)

CAR [7] implements both classification and policing functions. Classification is done by the setting of the IP Precedence for packets entering the network. CAR provides the ability to classify and reclassify packets based on physical port, source or destination IP or MAC address, application port or IP protocol type, as specified in the ACL [1].

2.1.3 Network Based Application Recognition (NBAR)

NBAR [7] is a classification engine that recognizes a wide variety of applications, including web-based and other difficult-to-classify protocols that employ dynamic TCP/UDP port assignments. When an application is recognized and classified by NBAR, a network can invoke services for that specific application. Hence, NBAR adds intelligent network classification to network infrastructure.

2.2 Congestion management

Congestion management allows congestion control by determining the order in which packets are forwarded out of an interface based on priorities assigned to those packets. It entails the creation of queues, assignment of packets to the respective queues based on their classification, and scheduling of the packets in a single queue for transmission. Cisco IOS provides four queuing and scheduling schemes:

2.2.1 First In Fist Out (FIFO)

FIFO is the default queuing mechanism. There is only one queue and all packets are treated equally and served in a first come first serve fashion. FIFO is the fastest of Cisco's queuing and scheduling schemes.

2.2.2 Priority Queuing (PQ)

Cisco PQ [1] provides four queues with assigned priority: high, medium, normal, and low. Packets are classified to queues based on protocol, incoming interface, packet size, or ACL criteria. Scheduling is determined by absolute priority. All packets queued in a higher priority queue are transmitted before a lower priority queue is served. Normal priority is the default if no priority is assigned when packets are classified.

2.2.3 Weighted Fair Queuing (WFQ)

WFQ [8] offers dynamic scheduling algorithm that shares bandwidth among queues based on their weights. There are two main types of WFQ: Flow Based WFQ (FBWFQ) and Class-Based WFQ (CBWFQ). FBWFQ provides priority management grained by individual traffic flows. It breaks up the sequence of packets within a conversation to ensure that bandwidth is fairly shared among individual conversations and that low-volume traffic is transferred in a timely fashion. The traffic is classified into different flows, based on packet header fields, including characteristics such as source and destination network or MAC address, protocol, source and destination ports, session socket numbers of the session, Frame Relay datalink connection identifier (DLCI) value, and ToS value. CBWFQ extends the standard WFQ functionality to provide support for user-defined traffic classes. For CBWFQ, traffic classes are defined based on match criteria including protocols, Access Control Lists (ACLs), and input interfaces. Packets satisfying the match criteria for a class constitute the traffic for that class. A FIFO queue is reserved for each class, and traffic belonging to a class is forwarded to the queue assigned for that class. In order to characterize a class, on can assign bandwidth, weight, and queue limit. The bandwidth assigned to a class is the guaranteed bandwidth delivered to the class during congestion. The queue limit is the maximum number of packets allowed to accumulate in the queue for a class. After a queue has reached its configured queue limit, enqueuing of additional packets to the class enables the queue management (Tail Drop or WRED) depending on how the class policy is configured. CBWFQ finally provides a mechanism called Low Latency Queuing (LLQ). LLQ [8] enables the use of a single, strict priority queue within CBWFQ at the class level, allowing low jitter for delay-sensitive data.

2.2.4 Custom Queuing (CQ)

Cisco CQ [8] discipline reserves a percentage of an interface's available bandwidth for each selected traffic type. If a particular type of traffic is not using its available bandwidth, then another type may consume it. CQ is composed by 17 queues numbered from 0 to 16. Queue 0 is a system queue reserved for the mechanism and therefore cannot be set by the user. For each queue, the byte count parameter has to be fixed. The router forwards packets from a particular queue until the byte count is exceeded. Once the byte count value is exceeded, the packet that is currently being served will be completely sent. Therefore, if the byte count is set to 100 bytes and the packet size of your protocol is 1024 bytes, then every time this queue is served, 1024 bytes will be sent, not 100 bytes. The bandwidth that a custom queue will receive is given by the following formula:

$$BW_i = \frac{BC_i}{\sum BC} \times TBW$$

where BC_i stands for the byte count of for queue i and TBW means the bandwidth capacity for the ouput link minus the bandwidth for prioritary queues.

2.3 Congestion avoidance

Congestion avoidance techniques are used to monitor the network traffic loads in an effort to identify the initial stages of congestion and proactively avoid it. Cisco IOS provides two features for congestion avoidance: Tail Drop and Weighted Random Early Detection (WRED). Tail Drop [9] is Cisco's default congestion avoidance behavior. Tail Drop treats all traffic equally and does not differentiate classes of service. Queues are filled during periods of congestion. When the output queue is completely full, packets are dropped. This process continues until the congestion is eliminated. WRED is IOS' implementation of RED. WRED combines the features of the RED algorithm with IP Precedence to provide for preferential traffic handling for higher priority packets [9]. When the average queue size is above the minimum threshold, WRED starts dropping packets. WRED drops packets selectively based on IP Precedence. Packets with higher IP Precedence are less likely to be dropped than packets with a lower precedence. WRED treats non-IP traffic as precedence 0 making them the most likely to be dropped. WRED can be configured to behave as RED by explicitly ignoring IP Precedence during WRED configuration [1].

2.4 Traffic Policing and Shaping

Cisco IOS QoS offers two kinds of traffic regulation mechanisms [10]: Policing that typically consists in dropping packets when a traffic contract is violate and shaping which role is to delay excess traffic when the data rate of the source is higher than expected. Policing is realized by employing the rate-limiting feature of Committed Access Rate (CAR). The parameters for CAR configuration are those of a token bucket completed with the action to apply if the incoming traffic is conform or exceeds the bucket filling rate. For shaping functionality, IOS provides two main components: the Generic Traffic Shaping (GTS), which shapes traffic by reducing outbound traffic flow to avoid congestion by means of a token bucket mechanism and Frame Relay Traffic Shaping which is a Frame Relay implementation of GTS.

3 DiffServ implementation in Cisco routers

The purpose of this section is to show how it is possible to combine some of the previous Cisco features for DiffServ implementation. Combining such features within a Cisco router can be easily perform thanks to the Cisco Modular QoS Command Line Interface (CLI) which is a kind of script language for rapid QoS configuration. Using Modular CLI, there are three steps [11] to perform for enabling services differentiation in the router:

3.1 Creating a traffic class

A traffic class specifies a set of match criteria to which an incoming and/or outgoing traffic must match to belong to that class. The classification is done based on the match criteria.

3.2 Creating a traffic policy

The next step to implement a Differentiated Service Domain using Cisco is to create traffic policies which are used:

- To collect Traffic Classes together in one object called Traffic Policy. It is more practical to associate a Traffic Policy with an object because in this way, it can be manipulate with flexibility.
- To apply to each Traffic Class component the PHB (Per-Hop Behavior) corresponding to it (bandwidth, queue limit, policing, shaping, congestion avoidance queue behaviour, etc.)
- To mark or re-mark packets belonging to a selected Traffic Class before they are forwarding to their next hop.

By default, scheduling among the traffic classes is done in a Class-Based WFQ manner. It is possible to enable LLQ for one of the traffic classes.

3.3 Attaching the traffic policy to an interface

Once that a traffic policy is built up, the last step consists in assigning it to one or more interfaces of the Cisco router in such a way that the definitions implemented in the object, i.e., the traffic policy, will be applied to traffic crossing the router through the selected interface(s).

4   The API architecture

In Cisco routers, the DiffServ Quality of Service policy is enabled only when congestion occurs. There is no resource allocation during non-congested periods. The available bandwidth is then used for all the incoming traffic. However, when congestion occurs, the QoS policy in charge of QoS management in the router cannot adapt itself to the unpredictable, bursty nature of network traffic. Moreover, QoS parameters turning for global efficient resources utilization and stable network behavior needs their adaptation in a real-time fashion. Since Cisco routers are closed proprietary systems, the DiffServ API provides an interface to control and configure DiffServ QoS features.

The API has to achieve the following goals:

- The continuous monitoring of the DiffServ queues;
- The adjustment of queuing and scheduling parameters for a possible automatic reconfiguration of the QoS features aiming a better optimization of network resources and effective end-to-end QoS.

4.1 DiffServ queues monitoring

Since Cisco routers are closed systems, it is impossible to add new modules on the IOS. Queues monitoring can only be done using the external methods offers by the router. Simple Network Management Protocol (SNMP) is a powerful protocol to retrieve data from Management Information Base (MIB) on network devices. Cisco provides a private QoS MIB called CISCO-CLASS-BASED-QOS-MIB [12]. This MIB allows read-only access to QoS configuration information and QoS statistics based on the modular QoS CLI. Statistics on the various queues are available in **cbQosQueueingStats** table. In order to achieve queues controlling of to evaluate the congestion risk on them, we focus our attention on the following objects of the table:

- **CbQosQueueingCurrentQDepth,** which represent the current depth of the queue.
- **CbQosQueueingMaxQDepth,** which represent the maximum depth of the queue.

Once the current queue depth is known, the API has to provide features for adjusting QoS parameters.

4.2 Configuration of the queuing and scheduling parameters

SNMP provides the ability to configure routers by means of its "snmp-set" command. But since the CISCO-CLASS-BASED-QOS-MIB is in read access only, the configuration of Cisco QoS features can uniquely be done in the Command Line Interface (CLI) mode. As seen previously, in a Diff-Serv context, only the following parameters are configurable when a policy is defined: bandwidth, queue limit for Tail Drop queues, max-threshold, min-threshold and probability denominator for WRED [11] queues. Cisco also provides a telnet server for entering CLI mode in a remote fashion.

4.3 The architecture

In the proposed API, the SNMP functions are realized thanks to the AdventNet SNMP API (ASA). The ASA [2] offers a comprehensive development toolkit for SNMP-based network management applications. AdventNet's SNMP stack comprises a set of Java SNMP library to build real-time applications for monitoring and tracking network elements that are reliable, scalable, and OS independent.

In addition to SNMP functionalities, a Telnet TCP module enables a telnet connection to the router and, consequently, to the CLI. The telnet con-
nexion consists of the creation of a Java TCP Socket aiming the port 23 of
the router. A parser is defined to translate the router responses. Figure 1 illustrates our DiffServ API architecture.

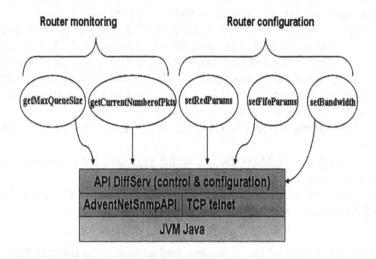

Fig. 1. API Architecture

Five methods are implemented:
- **getMaxQueueSize**: this method retrieves the maximum length of the
  traffic class specified in argument.
- **getCurrentQueueSize**: this method gets the queue's current depth of
  the traffic class specified in argument.
- **setRedParams**: it enables the assignment of WRED active queue
  management parameters.
- **setFifoParams**: this method enables the setting of the tail drop queue
  given in argument.
- **setBandwitdth**: this method is for the bandwidth setting of a traffic
  class.

Hence, using the API, it is possible to query the Cisco QoS MIB and get
the current and the maximum queue size in terms of number of packets
from a given traffic class. It is also possible to modify the allocated bandwidth for a class, to fix the values of a WRED queue parameters and the
depth of a Drop Tail queue.

5 Experiments

A test has been carried out to check the proper working of Cisco DiffServ API. Figure 2 shows the main test characteristics and the scenario. The test bed is made up with two routers running in DiffServ mode: a Cisco 1751 router and a Linux based router. Cisco IOS version 12.2(8) T5 is installed on the Cisco router. All the interfaces used on the test-bed have 10Mbps link speed. The IOS allows the commitment of 7.5 Mbps from the 10 Mbps link capacity for user data. The rest of bandwidth is automatically allocated to network signalization and routing protocols exchanges.

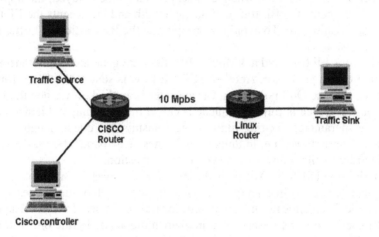

Fig. 2. Scenario Test

A policy named **diffserv** is defined with three traffic classes: a best effort traffic class with a DSCP equal to 0 attached to a Tail Drop queue, an Assured Forwarding (AF) traffic class with a DSCP equal to 10 (AF11) served by a WRED queue and an Expedited Forwarding (EF) traffic class with a DSCP equal to 46 also attached to a Tail Drop queue. The available bandwidth is allocated as follows:

Traffic classes	Bandwidth allocation
Class EF	3000 Kbps
Class AF	3000 Kbps
Class BE	1500 Kbps

JTG (Jugi's Traffic Generator) is used to generate traffic and the Cisco controller runs an application built using the API. The following rule defines the router behavior:

While EF queue_length is more than 10 packets
Do
   BE_bandwidth = BE_bandwidth - 1Mbps
   EF_bandwidth = EF_bandwidth + 1Mbps
   BE_queueSize = BE_queueSize + 10 packets
Until BE_bandwidth = 1 Mbps

In period of congestion, when EF packets start to be delayed, the application decrements the BE traffic class bandwidth and increments the EF traffic class bandwidth. To avoid the dropping of the BE traffic, the buffer size is increased.

A 3 Mbps EF flow and a 4 Mbps AF11 flow are generated simultaneously by the traffic generator. Another TCP BE flow is sent to the Cisco router. Notice that the QoS policy in a Cisco router is applied only when the level 2 transmit queue is full. This queue is called transmit ring and it size is set by the parameter "tx-ring-limit". The transmission queue length is expressed in particles, i.e. in units of 512 bytes. This parameter was fixed to 1 in order to allow fast occurrence of the congestion.

Using the DiffServ API tools during the test, it was possible to read the number of packets in each queue, to modify the length of the queues and to dynamically reallocate the bandwidth for traffic classes. In a first stage of the experiments, we observe that implementing a simple rule on the top of the API allows rapid adjustment of the EF class bandwidth according to his queue length. This propitiates a reduction on the number of packets in the queue and consequently, the avoidance of packets dropping.

6   Conclusion and future works

In this paper, we present an API for the monitoring and configuring Cisco QoS features with the aim to provide the tools for an adaptive QoS management. Now that it is possible to interface external software with a router and modify its QoS parameters "on-the-fly", the next step for this work is to design an intelligent agent on top of this API, whose purpose will be to enhance network performance by allowing automatic adaptation on network devices according to traffic fluctuations. We also intend to extend the experiments by measuring the impacts of continuous router reconfiguration on the network stability and performance.

References

1. Adams K, Nguyen T Router Support for Quality of Service
2. Advent   Net.   AdventNet   SNMP   API   online   site http://snmp.adventnet.com/
3. Blake S, Black D, Carlson M, Davies E, Wang Z, Weiss W (1998) An Architecture for Differentiated Services. RFC 2475
4. Braden R, Clark D, Shenker S (1994) Integrated Services in the Internet architecture: An overview. RFC 1633
5. Braden R, Zhang L, Berson S, Herzog S, Jamin S (1997) Resource reSerVation Protocol RSVP. RFC 2205
6. Cisco Systems (2001) Cisco IOS 12 Documentation, Internetworking Technology Overview
7. Cisco Systems (2001) Cisco IOS 12 Documentation, Quality of Service Solutions Configuration Guide, Classification Overview
8. Cisco Systems (2001) Cisco IOS 12 Documentation, Quality of Service Solutions Configuration Guide, Congestion Management Overview
9. Cisco Systems. Cisco IOS 12 Documentation, Quality of Service Solutions Configuration Guide, Congestion Avoidance Overview, 2001
10. Cisco Systems (2001) Cisco IOS 12 Documentation, Quality of Service Solutions Configuration Guide, Policing and Shaping Overview
11. Cisco Systems (2001) Cisco IOS 12 Documentation, Quality of Service Solutions Configuration Guide, Quality of Service Solutions
12. Cisco   Systems.   Cisco   Class-based   MIB   online   description: ftp://ftp.cisco.com/pub/mibs/v2/CISCO-CLASS-BASED-QOS-MIB.my
13. Enterasys X-Pedition ER16 (2003) User Reference Manual
14. Lougheed K, Rekhter Y (1990) Border Gateway Protocol BGP. RFC 1163
15. Miguel Franklin de Castro (2004) Gestion programmable et adaptative de la qualité de service sur IP. INT Evry

A generic conceptual framework for self-managed environments

E. Lavinal, T. Desprats, and Y. Raynaud

IRIT, UMR 5505 - Paul Sabatier University
118 route de Narbonne, F-31062 Toulouse cedex 9
{lavinal, desprats, raynaud}@irit.fr

Abstract. The high complexity of existing managed environments has led to the need to increase the autonomy of network and service management solutions. This short article presents a generic multi-agent organizational framework dedicated to the management domain. This conceptual framework constitutes a first step towards the design of self-managed environments.

1 Introduction

The self-management concept is a vision of network and service management (NSM) which results from the evolution of management solutions facing the increasing complexity of the managed environment [1]. This vision of management consists in providing managed resources with a high degree of autonomy, allowing them to manage themselves according to high level objectives and to situations they observe in their environment. Due to its inherent autonomy property, the multi-agent system (MAS) paradigm seems a propitious candidate to support this self-management concept. Generally speaking, a MAS can be described as a large number of autonomous entities, called agents, in interaction with each other within a common environment.

In this short article, we briefly present an organizational multi-agent framework dedicated to NSM as a first step towards the conception of self-managed services and network resources. This conceptual framework consists of groups of management agents coupled with managed resources and endowed with specific management skills. Our objective is to keep this framework as generic as possible in order to be independent of the management functional domain (configuration, protection, etc.) as well as the target managed environment (physical or logical resources, atomic or compound, etc.). Moreover, we define a dedicated model of the managed environment which captures different types of relationships existing between managed elements. Within the multi-agent framework, this model is shared

Please use the following format when citing this chapter:

Lavinal, E., Desprats, T. and Raynaud, Y., 2007, in IFIP International Federation for Information Processing, Volume 229,
Network Control and Engineering for QoS, Security, and Mobility, IV, ed. Gaïti, D., (Boston: Springer), pp. 131–136.

by groups of management agents that can thus take management decisions according to their own managed resource as well as the rest of the managed environment.

2   A generic multi-agent management framework

Based on existing works emanating from the domain of multi-agent organizations [2], this section successively presents the different concepts of a multi-agent framework dedicated to self-management [3]. This specialization process of the MAS paradigm for the NSM domain has been achieved by adopting an organizational centered multi-agent design methodology (meaning that the stress is put on the relationships the agents have one with the other in a specific organization).

- Managed Element (ME). A ME corresponds to any real world resource that has to be managed. It can consist of either a hardware resource (e.g. modem), or software resource (e.g. service), or even an abstract resource (e.g. an administrative domain). Note that a ME may be either an atomic or compound resource, and that it may eventually depend on one or more other ME(s).
- Managed environment (MEnv). A set of one or more MEs – eventually interrelated – which constitutes an operational system that has to be self-managed.
- Manager Agent (MA). It is a specialization of the agent concept for the management domain. A certain number of management skills which act on one or many ME(s) are embedded into the MA. These management skills constitute the management functionalities an agent is able of accomplishing. Diagnosing faults or configuration actions are examples of management skills. Naturally, a MA also incorporates aptitudes inherent to the agent concept such as viability preservation, reactivity to environmental changes, or inter-agent interaction. We thus give the following definition: *a MA is an autonomous agent, part of a multi-agent system dedicated to self-management, endowed with specific management skills and coupled with one or many MEs.*
- MA-ME coupling. The coupling relationship allows the overall MAS to integrate itself to the existing managed environment. Individually, a MA-ME coupling relationship means that the MA can at least perceive the ME (i.e. it has read access to the resource) and eventually act on it (i.e. it has write access to the resource). In concrete terms, examples of this coupling relationship can consist of local system calls, web-based or SNMP messages. This relationship also implies that the MA should have in its knowledge base a logical representation of its coupled ME(s) (as a classical manager would have of the resource it is responsible for using a management information model).
- Generic Management Functionality (GMF). It can be one of the following: monitoring, configuration, healing, optimization and protection. These functionalities are generic enough to include most of the existing management functionalities. Other management functionalities, more explicit, can inherit from these GMF. For example, an access control functionality can be considered as an extension of the protection functionality. Notice also that these management

functionalities can be based on legacy code (e.g. wrapping an existing intrusion detection engine as a management skill).

− Role of a MA (MRole). Although many organization-centered multi-agent design methodologies have their own specificities on how to represent the role concept, they all agree on its general definition: a description of an abstract behavior of agents. In the management context, a role played by an agent is strongly related to a functional dimension of the system to design (what to do), but also to an environmental one (on whom). Both of these generic aspects should be included in the expression of a MA's role. A GMF is used to represent the functional part of the role while the coupling relationship MA-ME is used to represent the environmental component. A MA can thus have numerous roles for a same ME if it implements several management functionalities (e.g. a MA can simultaneously play a *configure firewall* role and an *optimize firewall* role).

− Group of MAs (GrpMA). Generally speaking, a group represents a set of agents that share some common characteristic. According to the approach we follow, MAs belonging to the same group should obey to two conditions: first, they should share a common representation of the managed environment (MEnv) and second, at least one of their coupled MEs should be included in this representation of the MEnv. Notice that although a MA has a representation of the overall MEnv of the group it belongs to, it can only perceive and act locally on the MEnv via its coupled ME(s).

This group definition allows a MA to belong to several groups if it has a representation of the MEnv for each group it belongs to (with eventually different representation languages for each group) and if it is coupled with a ME included in each of these MEnv.

The concepts we have just presented are illustrated in figure 1 through a UML class diagram. They constitute the core of an organizational multi-agent architecture dedicated to autonomous NSM solutions.

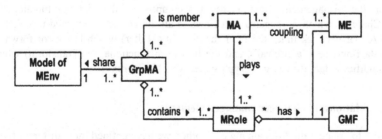

Fig. 1. Generic management multi-agent framework

At runtime, it should be essential for each MA to adapt its local and social behavior according both, to its coupled ME and to the relationships its ME has with the rest the MEnv. Within a group of MAs, to achieve this self-adaptation process, the existence of shared model representing the MEnv is primordial.

3   A dedicated model of the managed environment

One of the main factors of complexity of the managed environment resides in the interrelated nature of all the resources to be managed. Although a MA has a partial perception of the complete managed environment (i.e. its coupled MEs), a local management action on a ME can indirectly affect a large part of the rest of the managed environment. Therefore, in order for a MA to take locally the most appropriate management decision, the MA needs to be aware – as much as possible – of the nature of the existing relationships its coupled ME has with the rest of the MEnv. To capture these relationships, we have defined a dedicated model based on the definition of different types of MEs as well as different types of relationships between these MEs. The objective of this model is not to describe in details the characteristics of the MEs such as a classical management information model would do but rather to express the different types of relationships the resources have with each other within the managed environment. According to the nature of these relationships, the MAs will automatically adapt their local and social behavior, thus participating in the overall autonomy of the management multi-agent framework.

3.1   Expression of the managed elements

Currently we have restricted the expression of the MEs to three categories commonly found in the NSM domain. We will briefly describe each one of them.

– Service. This type of managed element is used to model any application service independently of its function (e.g. an email service or any business service).
– EndSystem. This type of managed element is used to model any kind of end system (e.g. a computer system) which hosts services.
– MidSystem. This type of managed element is used to represent any entity directly manipulating data flows such as in the Laborde's et al. specification language [4]. Three subtypes of this MidSystem entity can be defined depending on the management functionality it accomplishes: the channel functionality (Channel) which propagates data flows to all the entities connected to it (e.g. a LAN or network link), the filter functionality (Filter) which blocks or forwards data flows (e.g. a firewall), and the transform functionality (Transform) which modifies a data flow (e.g. a cryptosystem or a NAT proxy).

3.2   Relationships between managed elements

In order to connect the MEs among each other, we have defined three different types of relationships which constitute different operational dependencies. The identified relationships are the following:

– Service Dependency (SD). It is used to model a dependency between two application services, meaning that a service is dependent on another service to be fully operational (e.g. a web service using a directory service).

- Hosted Dependency (HD). It is applied to model the fact that a service is hosted on an end system (e.g. a directory service hosted on a server).
- Flow Dependency (FD). It represents a dependency at a network level between *EndSystems* and *MidSystems*. These MEs are connected to each other with this relationship in order to obtain a logical network topology.

The interest of these relationships is to allow MAs to deduce local and social behaviors according to their underlying semantic. Therefore, MAs will be able to achieve management actions according to the state of MEs with which they are not necessarily coupled with, but with which they may be related to.

4   Instance example of the conceptual framework

We illustrate here an instance example of the multi-agent conceptual framework we have presented previously. We consider a target managed environment composed of two networks separated by a firewall. Two services (one depending on the other) are hosted on different end-systems connected to each of these networks. This environment is specified by the model *M1* in figure 2.

Based on this managed environment, a group of MAs sharing this model can be created. This group is composed of different MAs which are coupled with one or more ME(s) included in the model M1. Each MA implements a specific GMF which, when associated with the coupled ME, assigns a specific role to the MA. For example, in figure 2, MA1 has a "protect end-system es1" role and MA4 has a "configure firewall fw1" role.

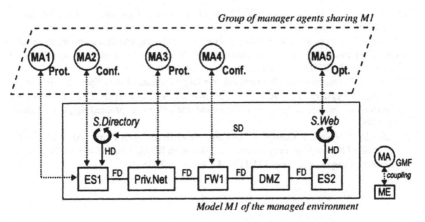

Fig. 2. Instance example of the multi-agent management framework

Currently, we are specifying several rules to analyze the managed environment model based on the different types of relationships the MEs have one with the other. The objective of these rules is to allow the MAs included in the same group to first, automatically adapt their local management behavior on their coupled ME while considering the rest of the managed environment and second, to deduce interactions with other MAs in order to accomplish management actions they could not achieve on their own. For example, in figure 2, by analyzing the managed environment M1, MA1 could deduce that protecting *es1* could result in adding an access control rule within *fw1* (i.e. MA1 interacting with MA3 in order to dynamically add a filtering rule on *fw1* which would allow MA1 to meet its management goal).

5   Conclusion

The approach we presented in this paper promotes the usage of the MAS paradigm to support autonomous management solutions. This approach results in the design of a generic conceptual framework which specializes existing multi-agent concepts for the management domain. Instances of this framework consist of multi-agent groups composed of manager agents playing management roles and interacting with each other to participate in the accomplishment of the global management objective on the underlying resources.

Current work address the automatic deduction of local and social behaviors between MAs based on the analysis of the shared managed environment. This dynamic adaptation will contribute to the self-organization of the MAs and therefore to the self-management of the overall environment.

References

1. J.O. Kephart and D.M. Chess. The Vision of Autonomic Computing. *IEEE Computer*, 36(1):41–50, January 2003.
2. J. Ferber, O. Gutknecht, and F. Michel. From agents to organizations: an organizational view of multi-agent systems. In *International Workshop on Agent-Oriented Software Engineering (AOSE'03)*, Melbourne, Australia, July 2003.
3. E. Lavinal, T. Desprats, and Y. Raynaud. An Organizational-driven Specialization of the Multi-Agent System Paradigm for Self-Management. In *IFIP/IEEE International Symposium on Integrated Network Management (IM'05)*, poster proceedings, Nice, France, May 2005.
4. R. Laborde, B. Nasser, F. Grasset, F. Barr'ere, and A. Benzekri. A Formal Approach for the Evaluation of Network Security Mechanisms Based on RBAC Policies. *Electronic Notes in Theoretical Computer Science*, 121:117–142, February 2005.

Modified Location-Aided Routing Protocols for Control Overhead Reduction in Mobile Ad Hoc Networks

Sidi-Mohammed Senouci and Tinku Mohamed Rasheed

France Telecom R&D

2 Avenue Pierre Marzin, 22307

Lannion, France

{ sidimohammed.senouci,
tinku.mohamedrasheed} @francetelecom.com

Abstract— In geographical ad hoc routing, each node has to be equipped with Global Positioning System (GPS). This requirement is quite realistic today as such devices are inexpensive and can provide reasonable precision. In this work, we are interested in the optimization of the geographical routing protocol, LAR (Location-Aided Routing) [1]. LAR is an on-demand routing protocol using geographical location information to limit the area for discovering a new route to a smaller "request zone". Instead of flooding the route requests into the whole network, only nodes in the request zone will forward them. Thus, the routing overhead is widely reduced. In this paper, we compare some optimization of LAR. The proposed optimizations use alternative definitions of request zone by intermediate nodes. The simulation results show that these algorithms lead to an improvement in terms of routing overhead.

Keywords – ad hoc routing; location; GPS; LAR.

1 Introduction

A Mobile Ad-Hoc Network (MANET) is a collection of wireless mobile nodes forming a temporary network without using any centralized access point, infrastructure, or centralized administration. The wireless mobile hosts communicate in a multi-hop fashion. A set of ad hoc routing protocols have been proposed in the IETF's MANET [2]group to ensure the network connectivity. In

Please use the following format when citing this chapter:

Senouci, S.-M. and Rasheed, T.M., 2007, in IFIP International Federation for Information Processing, Volume 229, Network Control and Engineering for QoS, Security, and Mobility, IV, ed. Gaïti, D., (Boston: Springer), pp. 137–146.

[3], the author classifies these protocols into three categories: (i) flat routing schemes, which are further classified into two classes: proactive and reactive; (ii) hierarchical routing; and (iii) geographic position assisted routing. Flat routing approaches (like OLSR, TBRPF, AODV and DSR) adopt a flat addressing scheme. Each node participating in routing plays an equal role. In contrast, hierarchical routing (like CGSR, HSR and ZRP) usually assigns different roles to the network nodes. Some protocols require a hierarchical addressing system. Routing with the assistance from geographic location information (like LAR, GeoCast and GPSR) requires each node to be equipped with Global Positioning System (GPS). This requirement is quite realistic today as such devices are inexpensive and can provide reasonable precision. The author gives a summary of the scalable features of protocols in the three categories and with some future research direction.

In this work, we are interested in the optimization of the geographical routing protocol, LAR (Location-Aided Routing) [1][4]. The remainder of this paper is organized as follows. After a brief description of the basic LAR protocol in section 2, we review the related work in section 3. In section 4, an overview of the optimization schemes of LAR are given. The methodology used for the performance evaluations is exposed in section 5. Finally, section 6 summarizes the main contributions of this work.

2 LAR Routing Protocol Basics

LAR is an on-demand routing protocol whose operation is similar to DSR (Dynamic Source Routing) [5]. In contrast to DSR, LAR protocol uses geographical location information to limit the area for discovering a new route to a smaller "request zone". Instead of flooding the route requests into the entire network, only those nodes in the request zone will forward them.

To determine the request zone, there are two schemes. In the first one, the source estimates a circular area (expected zone) in which the destination is expected to be found at the current time. The position and the size of the circle are calculated based on the location knowledge of the previous destination, the time instant associated with the previous location record and the average speed of the destination (see Fig.1). The request zone is the smallest rectangular region that includes the expected zone and the source. The coordinates of the four corners are included in the route request packet when initiating the route discovery process. RREQ broadcast is limited to this request zone. Thus, when the node in the request zone receives RREQ, it forwards the packet normally. However when a node which is not in the request zone receives an RREQ, it drops the packet. For example, in Fig1, if node I receives the route request from another node, node I forwards the request to its neighbors, because I determines that it is within the rectangular request zone. However, when node J receives the route request, it discards the request, as node J is not within the request zone.

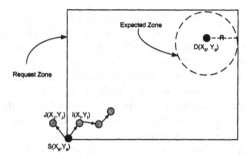

Fig. 1. Standard LAR scheme 1.

If source node S knows a previous location of destination node D at time t_0, if it also knows its average speed v and the current time t_1, then the expected zone at time t_1 is a circle around P with radius $R = v*(t_1 - t_0)$.

As soon as the destination D receives the route request packet, it sends back a route reply packet as in the flooding algorithms. Its reply differs by containing its current position, the actual time, and its average speed. Source node S is going to use this information for a route discovery in the future.

In the second scheme, the source calculates the distance to the destination based on the location of the destination. This distance, is included in the route request message and sent to neighbors. When an intermediate node receives the request, it calculates its distance to the destination. It will relay the request only if its distance to the destination is less than the distance included in the request message.

3 Related Work

Designing efficient routing protocols is an important research issue in mobile ad hoc networks. Many routing algorithms have been proposed to reduce route discovery overhead [6][7][8]. TORA (Temporally-Ordered Routing Algorithm) [6] is designed to reduce reaction to topological modification by localizing routing related messages to a smaller region near the change. On-Demand Multicast Routing Protocol (ODMRP) [7] is a multicast routing protocol based on a mesh topology and a forwarding group concept (i.e., only a subset of nodes forward the multicast packets). OLSR (Optimized Link State Routing) [8] reduces the control traffic overhead by using Multipoint Relays (MPR). An MPR is a node's one-hop neighbor which has been chosen to forward packets. Instead of pure flooding of the network, packets are just forwarded by a node's MPRs. This delimits the network overhead, thus being more efficient than pure link state routing protocols. Q-AOMDV (Q-routing for Ad hoc On-demand Multipath Distance Vector in ad hoc networks) [9] computes multiple paths in a single route discovery attempt. A new route discovery is required only when all paths to the destination break. Reviewing all these protocols is out of the scope in the present context.

Most of these MANET routing algorithms do not consider the physical location of a destination node. Recall that the principal goal of position-based routing protocols is to minimize the route discovery overhead by minimizing the number of forwarding nodes. For position-based routing protocols, if a source node wants to communicate with a destination node, it generally knows the position of its destination. Packets are forwarded to the next hop in the direction of the destination until they reach their destination. A set of position-based proposals, exploiting information about the geographic location of the mobile node, has emerged which improves the routing performances [10]. Among location-based routing protocols, we focus on the Location-Aided Routing (LAR) described in section 2. However, several optimizations are possible to achieve more efficient performance with the basic LAR protocols. In [1][4][11][12], some potential optimizations to the basic LAR algorithms have been suggested, for instance, alternative definitions of request zone or use of directional antenna, etc. In this section, we summarize them. Optimizations related to the definition of new request zones are detailed and evaluated in the following sections.

In [4], the authors propose an adapted request zone by intermediate nodes. Indeed, in standard LAR scheme 1, the requested zone is computed only by the source node. The adaptation of this zone by intermediate nodes, using more recent location information for destination host, can improve the probability of finding a route to the destination.

In [11] the authors suggest an approach where they suppose the existence of fixed hosts (or rarely moving hosts) in the network. If such fixed host, say node P (post), exists in the request zone defined in LAR algorithm, then the route request is performed in two steps. At first, source node S sends a route request to node P, and node P forwards the request to the destination node D. Thus, the size of the request zone is reduced which results in reducing the route request overhead.

In [12] the authors propose a modified-LAR algorithm and examine three variants of it. All of them are based on the idea of enlarging the request zone, in case of failure of the route discovery phase, instead of resorting to flooding.

4 Optimizations of LAR

We have seen in section 3, that several optimizations are possible to achieve more efficient performance of the basic LAR protocols. In this section, we deal with those related to alternative definitions of the request zone. These new schemes are evaluated in the next section.

As stated in section 2, an intermediate node will forward a route request packet, only if it belongs to the request zone. The request zone should contain the expected zone to reach the destination node D. In standard LAR scheme 1, the sides of the rectangle are always parallel to the X and Y axes.

Only this rectangular shaped request zone is implemented. However, other definitions may be used. For instance, it is possible to remove this restriction when defining the rectangular region: one side of the rectangle may be made parallel to the line connecting the location of source node S to the previous location of D (see Fig. 2).

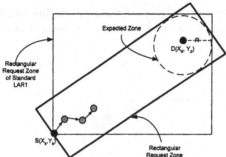

Fig. 2. Alternative definitions of request zone: tilted rectangular shaped.

In this scheme, the source node S determines the coordinates of the four request zone vertices. These coordinates are relative to the plane where the node S is the origin and the x-axis is parallel to the line connecting S and D. Afterwards, the source translates these coordinates (for the four vertices) to the real coordinates using these formulae:

$$x = x_1 \times (y_D - y_S)/l + y_1 \times (x_D - x_S)/l + x_S \qquad (1)$$

$$y = x_1 \times (x_s - x_d)/l + y_1 \times (y_D - y_S)/l + y_S \qquad (2)$$

Where (x_1, y_1) are the coordinates of the vertex in the first plane, and l is the distance between the source node S and the destination node D. Hence, the coordinates of the four vertices area computed. These coordinates are included in the route request packet when initiating the route discovery process. RREQ broadcast is limited to this rectangular request zone. Thus, a node I (x_I, y_I) forwards the RREQ packet only when it is in the request zone:

$$\begin{cases} x_I \geq RequestZone.topLeft.x, \text{ and} \\ x_I \leq RequestZone.bottomRight.x, \text{ and} \\ y_I \geq RequestZone.bottomLeft.y, \text{ and} \\ y_I \leq RequestZone.topRight.y \end{cases} \qquad (3)$$

As we can see in Fig. 3, the request zone can also be defined as a cone rooted at node S. When a node receives a route request, it discards the request if the node is not within the cone. A node J is within the cone if it is either in the expected zone or in the triangle formed by the three lines (Δ_1, Δ_2, and Δ_3):

$$\begin{cases} J \in Expected\ Zone : \sqrt{(l - x_J)^2 + y_J^2} \le R,\ or \\ J \in Triangle : y_J - l - R \le 0\ and\ y_J - x_J \times l\,/\,R \ge 0\ and\ y_J + x_J \times l\,/\,R \ge 0 \end{cases} \tag{4}$$

Where (x_J, y_J) are the coordinates of node J in the first plane (plane where the node S is the origin and the x-axis is parallel to the line connecting S and D).

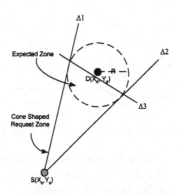

Fig. 3. Alternative definitions of request zone: cone shaped.

In contrast to the first scheme (titled rectangular shaped) where the source node S includes the coordinates of the vertices of the request zone within the route request message, in the second scheme (cone shaped) only the radius information is transmitted within the RREQ messages when initiating a route discovery.

We can easily notice that these two approaches would often result in a smaller request zone than the standard LAR scheme 1. Their performances are tested in section 5.

5 Experimental Results

The performances of our algorithms are evaluated using QualNet simulator [13]. QualNet is the commercial version of the GloMoSim [14]. It is a discrete event, parallel simulation environment implemented in PARSEC [15]. Number of nodes in the network is chosen to be 20, 30 and 50 for different simulation runs. The nodes are confined in a 1000x1000 m² area. Their initial locations are obtained using a uniform distribution. Individual nodes move following a random waypoint mobility model, and as in [1], each node moves continuously, without pausing at any location. We consider average speeds in the range of 1.5 to 22.5 m/s. A random connection is established using CBR traffic. As in [1], the source generates 10 data packets per second (on average), with a packet size of 64 bytes. In our simulations, standard IEEE 802.11 radios are adopted with channel rate as 2

Mbps and transmission range as 300 meters. Simulation results are averaged over 10 runs, each with a different mobility pattern (different mobility patterns were obtained by choosing different seeds for a random number generator).

The performance metric is the fraction of routing packets per data connection, as a function of average speed. This is calculated as the ratio of the number of routing packets, and the number of data packets received by the destination.

Fig. 4, shows the performance comparisons by varying the average speed with 50, 30, and 20 nodes. As the number of nodes increases, the performance improvement of modified LAR1 becomes larger especially when the number of nodes is greater.

As the speed of mobile nodes increases, the routing overhead accumulates for all the routing protocols. With higher speed, the frequency of route breaking increases, thereby increasing the routing overhead to discover new routes. However, modified LAR1 schemes provide a lower routing overhead than standard LAR1 especially for higher speed. This is due to reduction of the number of route requests by limiting route discovery to a smaller request zone. As can be seen from the graph, cone shaped optimization has the smallest number of routing packets per route discovery since it has the smallest request zone.

Besides, with lower speed, the new schemes do not perform much better than standard LAR1 especially for a low network density (20 nodes). In order to explain this, recall that the radius of the expected zone for these simulations is obtained using the average speed of the destination node. The size of this zone is very significant for LAR and especially for its two variants. Indeed, with lower node velocities, the request zones become smaller and the probability of finding a route becomes increasingly difficult. The case is more complicated with a sparsely dense ad hoc network where there are not enough nodes in the request zone. Here, the number of neighbors for each node decreases especially for the cone shaped scheme. This factor affects the probability of a route discovery within the timeout interval, using the initial request zone. Recall that, in this case, LAR schemes allow the sender to initiate a new route discovery using the flooding algorithm. We believe that this is the reason why modified LAR schemes do not perform too well when network density is small.

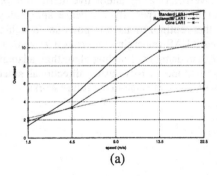

(a)

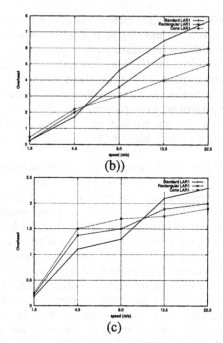

Fig. 4. Routing overhead versus average speed for: (a) 50 nodes, (b) 30 nodes, and (c) 20 nodes.

6 Conclusion

This paper describes how the basic LAR may be optimized to improve its performance. The proposed algorithms limit the request zone which results in reducing the route request overhead. Simulation results indicate that we can reduce the routing overhead using alternative definition of request zone as compared to LAR algorithm especially for dense and highly dynamic ad hoc networks. Several other optimizations are possible to achieve more efficient performance of the basic LAR (enlarging the request-zone area after the failure of a route-request rather than using the flooding algorithm, adaptation of the request-zone area according to node density, using directional antenna, etc.) and are intended to be dealt with and evaluated in the future works.

7 References

1   Y.-B. Ko and N. H. Vaidya, "Location-aided routing (LAR) in mobile ad hoc networks," in *ACM/IEEE International Conference on Mobile Computing and Networking (MobiCom'98)*, pp. 66-75, October 1998.

2   IETF MANET WG (Mobile Ad hoc NETwork), www.ietf.ora/html.charters/manet-charter.html.

3   X. Hong, K. Xu, and M. Gerla, "Scalable Routing Protocols for Mobile Ad Hoc Networks," *IEEE Network*, pp. 11-21, July/August 2002.

4   Y.-B. Ko and N. H. Vaidya, "Location-aided routing in mobile ad hoc networks," *Tech. Rep. 98-012*, CS Dept., Texas A&M University, June 1998.

5   D. B. Johnson, D. A. Maltz, Y.-C. Hu, "The Dynamic Source Routing Protocol for Mobile Ad Hoc Networks (DSR*)"*, *IETF Internet Draft*, draft-ietf-manet-dsr-09.txt.

6   V. D. Park and M. S. Corson, "Temporally Ordered routing algorithm (TORA) version1: functional specification", *IETF Internet-Draft*, August 1998.

7   M. Gerla, G. Pei, S. J, Lee, and C-C.Chiang, "On-Demand Multicast Routing protocol (ODMPR) for Ad hoc networks", *IETF Internet-Draft*, November 1998.

8   T. Clausen and P. Jacquet, "Optimized Link State Routing Protocol (OLSR), IETF, RFC 3626, October 2003.

9   S. Senouci, "Minimization of Energy Consumption in Ad Hoc Networks", Annals of telecommunications, vol. 60, n° 3-4, pp. 505-523, 2005.

10 M. Mauve, I. Widmer, H. Hartestein, "A Survey on Position-Based Rouitng in Mobile Ad Hoc Nehvorks", *IEEE Network*, November 2001.

11 J.-K. Jeong and J.-H. Kim, "Performance Improvement of Location-Aided Routing Using Fixed Post in Mobile Ad Hoc Networks", *PDPTA 2000*, Las Vegas, Nevada, USA, June 24-29, 2000.

12 F. De Rango, A. Iera, A. Molinaro, S. Marano, "A Modified Location-Aided Routing Protocol for the Reduction of Control Overhead in Ad-hoc Wireless Networks", *ICT'2003*, vol.2, pp.1033-1037, February 23 - March 1, 2003

13 QualNet by Scalable Networks Technologies, http://www.qualnet.com.

14 X. Zeng, R. Bagrodia, and M. Gerla, "GloMoSim: a Library for Parallel Simulation of Large-scale Wireless Networks", *In Proceedings of the 12th Workshop on Parallel and Distributed*

Simulations (PADS'98), Banff, Alberta, Canada, pp. 154-161, May 26-29, 1998.

15 R. Bagrodia, R. Meyer, M. Takai, Y. Chen, X. Zeng, J. Martin, and H.Y. Song, "PARSEC: A parallel simulation environment for complex system," *IEEE Computer Magazine*, vol. 31, no. 10, pp. 77-85, October 1998.

A Distributed Architecture
for Massively Multiplayer Online Services
with Peer-to-Peer Support

Keiichi Endo[1], Minoru Kawahara[2], and Yutaka Takahashi[3]

[1] Kyoto University, Kyoto 606-8501, Japan (endo@sys.i.kyoto-u.ac.jp)
[2] Ehime University, Matsuyama 790-8577, Japan (kawahara@cite.ehime-u.ac.jp)
[3] Kyoto University, Kyoto 606-8501, Japan (takahashi@i.kyoto-u.ac.jp)

Abstract. This paper deals with Massively Multiplayer Online Services, users of which communicate interactively with one another in real time. At present, this kind of services is generally provided in a Client-Server Model, in which users connect directly with a central server managed by a service provider. However, in this model, since a computational load and a communication load concentrate on the central server, high-performance server machines and high-speed data links are required. In this paper, we propose an architecture for distributing the loads by delegating part of the server's function to users' machines, which is based on a Peer-to-Peer Model.
When we adopt a Peer-to-Peer Model, we face a security problem. In our research, we let multiple machines of users manage the same data and apply a decision by majority rule. This mechanism adds robustness against halts of users' machines and data tampering by malicious users to the service.

Key words: peer-to-peer, cheat-proof, interactive, real-time applications

1 Introduction

In recent years, more and more people make use of those interactive services such as online games, online chats, online auctions, and online trades, users of which send and receive information in real time. In the services, many users connected to the Internet share the database. In this paper, this kind of services is called Massively Multiplayer Online (MMO) services.

At present, MMO services are generally provided in a Client-Server Model, in which users connect directly with a central server managed by a service provider. However, this model has a disadvantage that a computational load and a communication load concentrate on the central server. High-performance server machines and high-speed data links are required to provide an MMO service in the model. Therefore, many researchers have devised methods to provide the service in a Peer-to-Peer (P2P) Model. In a P2P Model, users contribute CPU cycles, memories, and bandwidths to the service, and the load

Please use the following format when citing this chapter:

Endo, K., Kawahara, M. and Takahashi, Y., 2007, in IFIP International Federation for Information Processing, Volume 229, Network Control and Engineering for QoS, Security, and Mobility, IV, ed. Gaïti, D., (Boston: Springer), pp. 147–158.

on the server machine is reduced. However, there are some problems to be solved for a practical use. First, the service must have robustness against halts of users' machines. That is, the service must not be stopped or lose data by user's sudden disconnection. Second, the service must overcome network congestion. Users' machines are apt to get communication interruption over several seconds. Finally, the service must not be influenced by cheating. Delegating part of the server's function to users' machines increases the opportunities for illegal acts such as data tampering.

In this paper, we try to solve the above-mentioned problems by letting multiple machines of users manage the same data and applying a decision by majority rule. We compare the proposed model with Client-Server Model and an existing P2P Model by performance analysis. We focus mainly on MMO role playing game services here, however, the model with appropriate modifications can be applied to other services such as online chats, online auctions, and online trades.

The rest of this paper is organized as follows. Section 2 presents related work. In Section 3, we discuss our model. Section 4 describes the detailed algorithms used in our system. Performance analysis is stated in Section 5. We conclude and discuss future work in Section 6.

2 Related Work

Bucket Synchronization [1] is a distributed synchronization mechanism which enables a P2P multiplayer game to maintain state consistency regardless of network delay. This mechanism divides time into fixed-length periods and a *bucket* is associated with each period. A user sends an action message to other users when he takes an action. Receiving the message, a user stores it in the bucket corresponding to the period during which it was sent. Actions in a bucket are executed to compute each user's local view some time after the end of the period for the bucket. The game *Age of Empires* is an example of real applications based on Bucket Synchronization. This mechanism has several problems about cheating. For instance, a user can unjustly gain an advantage by deciding his action after getting the information of what other users do for the current period, which is called *lookahead cheat*.

Lockstep Protocol [2] solves this problem by forcing each user to commit all the actions for the current period before the actions are revealed. In this protocol, each user at first sends a cryptographic hash of his action, instead of the content of the action. However under the protocol, *action delay*, i.e. time required for an action to be displayed on users' screen after the action is taken by a user, is longer than three times the latency of the slowest link between any two users. *Asynchronous synchronization* is also suggested to shorten the average of action delay, but it worsens *jitter* (how much action delay varies). This property is unfavorable especially for game applications.

Adaptive Pipeline Protocol [3] improves the jitter by adjusting its parameter to adapt to network conditions. However, the action delay under the protocol is still rather long.

Reference [4] proposes a way to make action delay shorter by permitting rollbacks when state data become inconsistent among users. However, displaying wrong information temporarily is not acceptable for many kinds of applications. Though it is possible to decrease the frequency that rollbacks are carried out at the cost of action delay [5], the delay becomes too long if we attempt to make the probability low enough because of network congestion.

NEO Protocol [6] achieves a shorter action delay without the need of rollbacks by letting each user accept an action message from another user if the majority of users receive it during a fixed-length period. Though this protocol realizes a high-performance and cheat-proof system on a fixed topology, cheat-proof processing methods of storing state data and user's moving into another *group* (what is called *site* in the next section) are not stated, and this problem is probably difficult to solve. Moreover, users with high-latency data links are not able to use the service. For those users, making use of the service with some disadvantages due to the slow link would be better than being refused to use the service. A service provider also would like to get as many users as possible, provided that slow users do not cause other users inconvenience (e.g. longer action delay).

In the architectures discussed above, each user manages state data which he needs to know, and directly receives action messages from other users. We call these *user-centric architectures* in this paper. The architecture has some drawbacks. One of those is that a user must receive an action message with a message header, which consists of an IP header etc., separately from each user. That is quite inefficient especially in a game application where users frequently send small packets to one another.

The following studies discuss *server-centric architectures*. In the architecture, only one user has an authority to update a certain portion of state data, which provides a consistent environment for all users.

Mercury [7] is a distributed publish-subscribe system for game applications. The routing algorithm in this architecture takes $O(n)$ hops on average, where n is the number of users. References [8] and [9] reduce required routing hops to $O(\log n)$ by the use of Distributed Hash Table. Reference [8] also achieves high durability of state data by replicating them. In all these architectures stated in this paragraph, each part of state data is exclusively managed by one user. Therefore, these architectures have cheating problems such as data tampering.

3 Proposed P2P Model

The P2P Model we propose is similar to server-centric architectures stated above, but differs in that *multiple* users manage each part of state data.

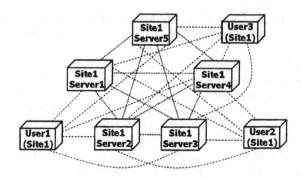

Fig. 1. Model of managing a site.

Although the MMO service has many simultaneous users, a user can always see a limited area, which is called a site in this paper. That is, there are some sites in the service, and each user belongs to one of them. A user can move from one site to another. User's action is made known in real time to only those users staying on the same site. This property makes it possible to transfer the service function of a site to users' machines. User's machine managing a site is called a Site Server.

Fig. 1 illustrates how Site Servers manage one site in our model. Each user is connected with all the Site Servers which manage the site where the user is. All the Site Servers managing the same site form a complete graph. When a user takes an action, the user sends a message to all the Site Servers in order to tell the action. Then, Site Servers update state data, which are classified into two types: those of a user and those of a site. For instance, in a role playing game service, the position of a user and information of items put on a map (site) correspond to state data of a user and those of a site, respectively. When updating state data, Site Servers synchronize processing order of users' actions to have the same state data as one another's. Finally, the Site Servers notify the users on the site of the update. For robustness against cheating, each user accepts the update which the majority of the Site Servers send.

4 Algorithms

4.1 User's Logging in

When a user starts using the MMO service, the first thing to do is to connect[1] with the Administration Server. Then the Administration Server authenticates the user.

---

[1] All connections in our system are TCP connections.

4.2 Transferring the Service Function of a Site

While there are only a few users, the MMO service is provided in a normal Client-Server Model, i.e., the service functions of all the sites are in the Administration Server. As the number of users increases, the load on the Administration Server becomes higher and higher. Therefore, the service function of a site is transferred to users' machines on a certain condition. For example, the transfer is carried out when the number of users on a site reaches a given parameter. By this mechanism, the users' machines, which are called "peers" in the following discussion, gradually form a (Hybrid) P2P Network.

When the Administration Server decides to transfer the service function of a site, it chooses N_{server} peers which the service function is delegated to, where N_{server} is a fixed positive odd number. Although the selection can be made on various strategies, currently we adopt a simple way, which is to make a random choice from all the peers not managing a site yet. In order to decrease the influence of cheating, the Administration Server also avoids selecting a user on the site whose service function is about to be transferred.

4.3 Handling Action Messages

When a user takes an action except logging in or out, the user makes an action message, which represents the user's behavior. If the user is on a site which is managed by the Administration Server, the user sends the message to the server. After receiving the message, the server immediately processes it and updates state data. The message can change not only state data of the user but also state data of the site and/or those of other users on the site. Then, by sending an update message to all the users on the site (or to users who have the necessity of knowing the state update), the server lets the change of conditions be known.

On the other hand, if the site is managed by Site Servers, the procedure stated in the rest of this subsection is carried out. The user sends the action message to all the Site Servers which manage the site. The message includes an action number for identification. After receiving the message, each of the Site Servers memorizes the user number, the content of the message, and the time when the message is received. The clocks of the Site Servers are synchronized in advance by a mechanism like NTP (Network Time Protocol) [10]. Unlike the case of an Administration Server, the Site Server does not process the message at this time. A mechanism which makes the processing order of action messages the same between the Site Servers is required. In our system, the processing order of action messages is determined using the median of the arrival time at each Site Server. The reason why a median time is used is to diminish the influence of cheat. The next paragraph shows the details.

At intervals of a fixed span $T_{timeslot}$, a Site Server sends a Timeslot Message to all the other Site Servers of the same site. The message consists of the site number, the transmission time (time stamp), and the sets of {user number, action number, arrival time} for all the action messages which are received after the last transmission of a Timeslot Message. When a Site Server receives a Timeslot Message, the server memorizes the message and updates state data in the algorithm shown below.

1. From actions such that the information of them is received from at least N_{majority} Site Servers including the server itself, the server picks out the actions whose N_{majority}-th earliest arrival times are older than any time stamp of the last Timeslot Message from each Site Server. N_{majority} is a minimum integer which is greater than the half of the number of Site Servers managing the same site, i.e.,

$$N_{\text{majority}} = \frac{N_{\text{server}} + 1}{2}. \tag{1}$$

This step means that the server singles out the actions whose median arrival times are determined. If there are not such actions, the update of state data is not done.

2. The Site Server updates state data by processing the action messages corresponding to the picked actions in the order of N_{majority}-th earliest arrival time. If there is an action message which the server has not received yet, the server waits for the arrival of the message from the user who has taken the action.

3. The server sends an update message to the users.

A user receives the same update messages in the same order from all the Site Servers of the site unless there are malicious users or network congestion. The user does not accept an update message until the user receives N_{majority} update messages with the same contents from different Site Servers for fear that the MMO service should be attacked by some cheaters. After the update message is accepted, the image on the screen is updated.

To reduce communication load, $(N_{\text{majority}} - 1)$ Site Servers actually sends only a hashed value computed from an update message.

4.4 Overcoming Network Congestion

The algorithm stated in the foregoing subsection needs to be improved because the action delay is strongly affected by network congestion. For instance, when Timeslot Messages from a Site Server to not less than N_{majority} Site Servers are delayed, the service function of the site is stopped. We solve this problem in the way stated below.

We let T_{timeout} be a fixed span which is longer than T_{timeslot}. If a Site Server has not received a Timeslot Message from another Site Server at T_{timeout} after the time stamp of the last Timeslot Message, the server sends a Timeslot Request Message (TRM) to all the other Site Servers of the same site except the server which the Timeslot Message has not come from. If a Site Server receives a

TRM, the server checks whether the server has received the requested Timeslot Message before. If it has, the server sends back the requested message.

If the server receives TRMs from all the Site Servers which the server has sent the TRM to, or if a given length $T_{req\_timeout}$ has passed since the transmission of the TRM, the server ignores the delayed Site Server for a period of T_{ignore}. Ignoring a Site Server means disregarding Timeslot Messages from the server and performing ordering of users' actions without the server when updating state data. In this algorithm, a Site Server which is ignored by one Site Server is ignored by all the other Site Servers of the same site, too. If the delayed message is not received within the period of T_{ignore}, the Administration Server is requested to choose an alternative Site Server. This mechanism adds robustness against halts of users' machines to the service.

4.5 Switching Sites

When a user moves to another site, the user gets the IP addresses of the Site Servers managing the site from the Administration Server. The Administration Server receives the state data (or the hashed value of the state data) of the user from all the Site Servers managing the current site. Then, after verifying the rightness of the state data by comparison, the Administration Server sends the data to all the Site Servers managing the destination site.

As already stated, it is undesirable for a site to be managed by a user on the site. Therefore, if a user moves to a site which is managed by the user, the Administration Server selects an alternative Site Server and orders the moving user to send all the data concerning the site to the new Site Server. The Administration Server also notifies the other Site Servers and all the users on the site that the Site Server has been changed.

4.6 User's Logging out

When a user finishes using the MMO service, the Administration Server stores the state data of the user. In case that Site Servers have the data, the Administration Server requests the Site Servers to send back the data and stores the majority of them. If the user has a service function of a site, the user sends all the data about the site to the Administration Server, and the Administration Server gives the data to a newly selected Site Server.

5 Performance Analysis

5.1 Communication Load

In terms of communication load, we compare the proposed P2P Model with Client-Server Model and NEO Protocol, which is considered to be one of the best user-centric architectures. If only unicast can be used, the total size of messages a user has to send for one action in each model is:

$$\text{Client-Server: } S_{\text{header}} + a, \qquad (2)$$

$$\text{NEO: } (n-1)\{S_{\text{header}} + a + \lceil (n-1)/8 \rceil + S_{\text{key}}\}, \qquad (3)$$

$$\text{Proposed: } N_{\text{server}}(S_{\text{header}} + a). \qquad (4)$$

In the above formula, a represents the size of an action message, and n denotes the number of users in the same site. S_{header} and S_{key} mean the sizes of a message header and a decryption key to prevent lookahead cheat, respectively.

The total size of messages a user must receive to know other users' respective actions in each model is:

$$\text{Client-Server: } S_{\text{header}} + na, \qquad (5)$$

$$\text{NEO: } (n-1)\{S_{\text{header}} + a + \lceil (n-1)/8 \rceil + S_{\text{key}}\}, \qquad (6)$$

$$\text{Proposed: } N_{\text{majority}}(S_{\text{header}} + na) + (N_{\text{server}} - N_{\text{majority}})(S_{\text{header}} + S_{\text{hash}}), \qquad (7)$$

where S_{hash} represents the size of a hashed value computed from an update message. In both P2P Models, we assume that each user sends an action message at the same rate as action messages are processed. For example, if T_{timeslot} equals 100 milliseconds in the proposed model, each user transmits an action message every 100 milliseconds. We also suppose that the size of an update message equals 'the number of users in the same site' times 'the size of an action message.' Under the substitution[2]

$$S_{\text{header}} = 66, \ S_{\text{hash}} = 16, \ S_{\text{key}} = 8, \ N_{\text{server}} = 5, \ n = 30, \qquad (8)$$

and $a = 10$ (this is enough for telling a user's move in most cases), the values of (5) – (7) are 366, 2552, and 1262, respectively. Under the condition (8), the proposed model achieves less communication load on users than NEO Protocol if $a \leq 31$. This is because of the advantage that a user can receive the result of multiple users' actions at the same time.

If a user has a service function of a site where n users are staying, he must bear additional load as follows:

$$\text{Send: } n(S_{\text{header}} + na) \qquad \text{(if he sends the content of an update message),} \qquad (9)$$

$$n(S_{\text{header}} + S_{\text{hash}}) \qquad \text{(if he sends the hash of an update message),} \qquad (10)$$

$$\text{Receive: } n(S_{\text{header}} + a). \qquad (11)$$

Moreover, the user and the Administration Server must exchange state data when a user logs in, logs out, and switches sites. However, this is not such a big problem since users who can not afford to manage a site do not have to do that.

---

[2] $S_{\text{header}} = 20$ *(TCP Header)* $+ 20$ *(IP Header)* $+ 26$ *(Ethernet Header)* $= 66$.

5.2 Action Delay

Average action delays in respective models can be approximated as follows:

$$\text{Client-Server: } 2l_{\text{cu}}, \tag{12}$$

$$\text{NEO: } 2l_{\text{uu}} + (T_{\text{arrival}}/2), \tag{13}$$

$$\text{Proposed: } 2l_{\text{su}} + l_{\text{ss}} + (T_{\text{timeslot}}/2), \tag{14}$$

where l_{cu}, l_{uu}, l_{su}, and l_{ss} denote one-way transfer latencies between a central server and a user, between two users, between a Site Server and a user, and between two Site Servers, respectively. T_{arrival} is what is called *arrival delay* in [6], which is similar to T_{timeslot}. T_{arrival} and T_{timeslot} can be reduced close to zero at the expense of communication load. The proposed model requires one more hop than NEO Protocol, but actually the difference is small since the latencies have the following relation if users with high-speed data links are selected as Site Servers:

$$l_{\text{uu}} > l_{\text{su}} > l_{\text{ss}}. \tag{15}$$

This is because not only users' geographical locations but also the performance of lines for connecting to the Internet has a big impact upon transfer latencies.

5.3 Robustness against Network Congestion

To investigate robustness against network congestion, we calculate the probability that a user fails to have his action processed under the condition that a link between two machines becomes temporarily unavailable with the probability p. The probability of the failure in each model is:

$$\text{Client-Server: } p, \tag{16}$$

$$\text{NEO: } \sum_{k=\lceil n/2 \rceil}^{n-1} \binom{n-1}{k} \cdot p^k (1-p)^{n-1-k}, \tag{17}$$

$$\text{Proposed: } \sum_{k=N_{\text{majority}}}^{N_{\text{server}}} \binom{N_{\text{server}}}{k} \cdot p^k (1-p)^{N_{\text{server}}-k}, \tag{18}$$

where

$$\binom{n}{k} = \frac{n!}{k!(n-k)!}. \tag{19}$$

In Client-Server Model an action message from a user is not processed if he can not transmit it to the central server, while in P2P Model an action message is successfully processed in most cases unless half of the destination nodes fail to receive it.

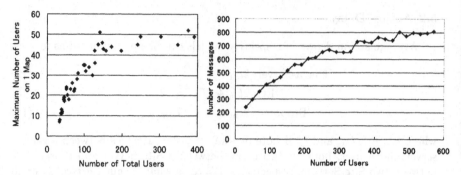

Fig. 2. (a) [left] Number of users on the most popular map. (b) [right] Number of messages sent to the most popular chat channel in an hour (averaged at intervals of 20 users).

5.4 Scalability

In this subsection, we consider what happens when the number of users increases.

Fig. 2(a) shows the relation between the number of total users and the number of users on the most popular *map* (what we call *site* in this paper). The sample data was collected on August 13, 2004 from a real MMO game service, which is provided in a Client-Server Model. In the game world there are 53 maps, which seem to be ample for 400 users. The number of users in a site seems to have a saturation point.

Fig. 2(b) illustrates the relation between the number of users and the number of messages sent to the most popular *chat channel* in an hour. We collected the sample data from the real MMO game service in January through May of 2004. A *chat channel* means a room where users can talk with one another. We can regard it as a site. In the service, users are able to create new chat channels whenever necessary. The maximum number of messages to one chat channel is almost independent of the number of users when lots of users are playing the game.

It is inferred from these data that the number of users on the most popular site is almost stable against the increase of total users when there are a lot of users. This is because gathering of too many users in one site makes the users uncomfortable in most cases. In conclusion, too much load is hardly ever put on Site Servers, provided that there are sufficient sites in the application (or users can make new sites freely). Putting a limit on the number of users in one site may be a good idea, because users in a too crowded site can not normally use the service anyway (e.g. slow drawing on users' screen).

The communication load on the Administration Server in the proposed P2P Model varies directly with the number of total users. However, the server can provide the service for much more users than Client-Server Model, because the

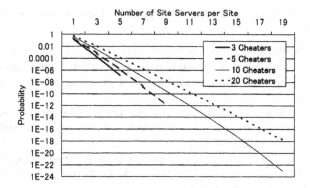

Fig. 3. Probability that colluding cheaters can affect the service.

amount of data sent or received is dramatically decreased by transferring the service function of a site to users' machines. It will also be possible to do away with the Administration Server and make the model completely scalable by the use of other technologies such as distributed storage system.

5.5 Robustness against Cheating

In the proposed P2P Model, multiple cheaters must collude to succeed in cheating (when $N_{server} > 1$). We let $C_i(N, c)$ represent the probability that there is at least one site where more than half of the Site Servers are controlled by malicious users when there are i sites, c colluding cheaters, and N users in total. Then the probability can be calculated by using the following recurrence equation:

$$C_i(N, c) = 1 - \sum_{k=0}^{N_{majority}-1} \frac{\binom{c}{k} \cdot \binom{N-c}{N_{server}-k}}{\binom{N}{N_{server}}} \cdot \{1 - C_{i-1}(N - N_{server}, c - k)\}$$

(20)

Fig. 3 illustrates how the probabilities $C_{250}(5000, 3)$, $C_{250}(5000, 5)$, $C_{250}(5000, 10)$, and $C_{250}(5000, 20)$ change with N_{server}. The probability that colluding cheaters can affect the service decreases exponentially with the number of Site Servers managing one site.

6 Conclusion

In this paper, we have proposed an architecture for distributing server's loads by delegating part of the server's function to users' machines.

The proposed architecture has the following characteristics compared with other studies.

1. We applied the method to the MMO service that the majority of multiple machines which manage the same data is accepted. It prevents data from being falsified or lost. Moreover, the service has robustness against network congestion.
2. The users whose machines manage a site are selected from those who are not on the site by an Administration Server. It reduces the benefit of cheat and makes conspiracy difficult.
3. The processing order of action messages is determined using the median of the arrival time at each Site Server. It leads to the tolerance for the alteration of time stamps on messages.
4. Not all of the users' machines manage sites. Therefore, if we properly determine the rule of transferring the service function of a site, users with narrow bandwidths, with low-performance machines, or behind firewalls (or NAT routers) can use the service.

As future work, we plan to consider the robustness against cheating in greater detail. We also have a plan to make a practical experiment using a real MMO game service.

References

1. C. Diot and L. Gautier, A Distributed Architecture for Multiplayer Interactive Applications on the Internet, *IEEE Network* **13**(4), 6–15 (1999).
2. N. E. Baughman and B. N. Levine, Cheat-Proof Playout for Centralized and Distributed Online Games, *Proceedings of Infocom 2001* (2001).
3. E. Cronin, B. Filstrup, and S. Jamin, Cheat-Proofing Dead Reckoned Multiplayer Games, *Proceedings of ADCOG 2003* (2003).
4. E. Cronin, A. R. Kurc, B. Filstrup, and S. Jamin, An Efficient Synchronization Mechanism for Mirrored Game Architectures, *Multimedia Tools and Applications* **23**(1), 7–30 (2004).
5. J. Brun, F. Safaei, and P. Boustead, Tailoring Local Lag for Improved Playability in Wide Distributed Network Games, *Proceedings of NSIM 2004* (2004).
6. C. GauthierDickey, D. Zappala, V. Lo, and J. Marr, Low Latency and Cheat-Proof Event Ordering for Peer-to-Peer Games, *Proceedings of NOSSDAV 2004* (2004).
7. A. R. Bharambe, S. Rao, and S. Seshan, Mercury: A Scalable Publish-Subscribe System for Internet Games, *Proceedings of NetGames 2002* (2002).
8. B. Knutsson, H. Lu, W. Xu, and B. Hopkins, Peer-to-Peer Support for Massively Multiplayer Games, *Proceedings of Infocom 2004* (2004).
9. T. Iimura, H. Hazeyama, and Y. Kadobayashi, Zoned Federation of Game Servers: a Peer-to-Peer Approach to Scalable Multi-Player Online Games, *Proceedings of NetGames 2004* (2004).
10. D. L. Mills, Network Time Protocol (Version 3) Specification, Implementation and Analysis, *RFC 1305* (1992).

The use of COPS and NSIS in the EuQoS Project

Edmundo Monteiro, Fernando Boavida, Paulo Simões, Jorge Sá Silva,
Marilia Curado, Luís Cordeiro, Romulo Ribeiro, Maxweel Carmo, Jian
Zhang
University of Coimbra
Laboratory of Communications and Telematics
CISUC-DEI
Pólo II, 3030-290 Coimbra – Portugal
{edmundo,boavida,psimoes,sasilva,marilia,cordeiro,romulo,maxweel}
@dei.uc.pt

Abstract. This paper discusses the use of the Policy Based Network paradigm, COPS (Common Open Policy Service) and NSIS (Next Steps In Signalling) frameworks being developed by the IETF, in the context of the European Project EuQoS (End-to-End Quality of Service over Heterogeneous Networks). An overview of the EuQoS architecture is provided followed by the analysis of the use of PBN/COPS and NSIS to support the Signalling and Service Negotiation (SSN) function. The implementation status and validation aspects are also discussed in the paper and some preliminary results are included.

1 Introduction

The motivation of the European Integrated Project EuQoS (End-to-end Quality of Service support over heterogeneous networks) [1] is to solve the outstanding design issues presently associated with the delivery of end to end QoS service across heterogeneous networks. It is necessary to resolve these issues and accordingly upgrade the infrastructures so that new applications can be supported by the Internet and new service packages can be offered by operators and service providers.

The key objective of EuQoS is to research, integrate, test, validate and demonstrate end-to-end QoS technologies to support the infrastructure upgrade for advanced QoS-aware applications over multiple, heterogeneous network domains, belonging to research, scientific and industrial communities. The project will deliver the EuQoS system which will support the delivery of end to end QoS. As QoS is primarily a challenge for the access network, the EuQoS system will be developed and tested on various types of research access networks with the GEANT [2] core providing Pan European support. This heterogeneous infrastructure, which models

Please use the following format when citing this chapter:

Monteiro, E., Boavida, F., Simões, P., Sá Silva, J., Curado, M., Cordeiro, L., Ribeiro, R., Carmo, M. and Zhang, J. 2007, in IFIP International Federation for Information Processing, Volume 229, Network Control and Engineering for QoS, Security, and Mobility, IV, ed. Gaïti, D., (Boston: Springer), pp. 159–171.

future production networks, requires a QoS technical solution that has not been synthesized to date.

The EuQoS project will propose and develop new QoS mechanisms build upon the state of the art and incorporate the following components: Monitoring and Measurement, Admission Control, Failure Management, Signalling & Service Negotiation, Security and AAA, Charging and Traffic Engineering and Resource Optimization. EuQoS will integrate state of the art protocols and technologies with new mechanisms to be developed in the project in order to build the above specified functions.

This paper addresses the use of the Policy Based Network (PBN) paradigm [3] and its support protocol, the Common Open Policy Service (COPS) [4] together with the NSIS (Next Steps in Signalling) IETF (Internet Engineering Task Force) framework [5] in order to support some of the EuQoS functionalities.

The remaining of the paper is structured as follows. The EuQoS architecture is briefly described in Section 2. Sections 3 and 4 provide some background about PBN and NSIS. Section 5 describes the proposed solution. Validation issues are discussed in Section 6. Finally, Section 7 concludes the paper and points out some directions for future work in the scope of the EuQoS project.

2   EuQoS Architecture

The EuQoS project aims at creating a flexible and secure QoS Assurance System (the EuQoS System) by developing new QoS mechanisms which build upon the state-of-the-art. The EuQoS System consists of two major research components: User and QoS aware Control Plane and QoS Protocol Stack, as shown in Figure 1. The QoS Protocol Stack will result in a new API over existing and new transport protocols that will provide variable levels of order and reliability.

The Control Plane will include a set of functions that might be supported in network elements such as routers and in end systems. To integrate the Control Plane of the EuQoS architecture six main functions were identified: Function 1 – Signalling and Service Negotiation (SSN); Function 2 – Connection Admission Control (CAC); Function 3 – Monitoring Measurement, Fault Management (MMFM); Function 4 – Traffic Engineering and Resource Optimization (TERO); Function 5 – Security and AAA (SAAA); Function 6 – Charging (CHAR).

The SSN function is responsible for the dynamic configuration of the communication system, in order to provide the requested level of QoS to applications. It covers the application connection setup, data transfer and teardown phases and is triggered by applications located at end systems, by application proxies or by network elements.

The EuQoS SSN function will be built over state-of-art signalling and service negotiation mechanisms complemented with new functionalities to be researched and developed in the EuQoS project. Among other proposals the PBN, COPS and NSIS will play an important role in EuQoS as will be described in the following sections.

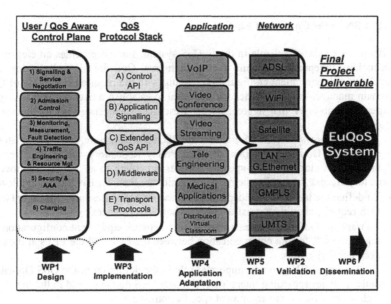

Fig. 1. The EuQoS system

3 PBN and COPS in EuQoS architecture

This section discusses the use of the Policy-Based Networking and the Common Open Policy Service in the EuQoS project context.

3.1 Policy-Based Networking Concepts

The PBN concept and architecture were developed by IETF's Policy Framework group [3]. The objective of PBN is to enable centralized network administration by supporting the definition of abstract rules, that is, by specifying what the network should do in a high-level language instead of specifying how to do it. This is done in a network-element-independent way, through a policy specification language.

The PBN architecture comprises four basic components: Management Console, Policy Repository (PR), Policy Decision Point (PDP) and Policy Enforcement Point (PEP). The Management Console provides an interface between the administrator and the policy management system. The PR stores the policies that are applicable to a given administration. Every policy database is structured as a Policy Information Base (PIB). PDPs translate high-level policies stored in the PR into lower level policy rules. PEPs receive rules from PDPs and deal with network elements accordingly, performing actions such as packet filtering and marking. The communication between PDPs and PEPs is achieved using a policy transfer protocol such as COPS protocol [4] or COPS-PR (COPS for Policy Provisioning) [6].

3.2 PBN in the Context of EuQoS

PBN plays an important role in the EuQoS system, since it provides an elegant and technology independent schema to map high-level QoS domain policies into low-level network equipment configuration, coping with the required autonomy of QoS-domain management boundaries and the need to establish a network technology independent sub-layer that aggregates the Resource Managers (RM) of the various QoS domains.

Figure 2 shows how COPS fits into the EuQoS architecture. Each administrative domain (QoS Domain) maintains its own Policy Repository and Policy Decision Point. The PR stores domain-specific policies according to an LDAP (Lightweight Directory Access Protocol) schema. The policies are then used at two distinct levels:

- To define the technology-independent behaviour of the Resource Manager (which QoS requests should be satisfied, under what circumstances);
- To translate QoS requirements into specific network equipment configuration, using COPS-PR for the communication between the PDP and the PEPs at the managed network nodes.

In this way, PBN plays an important role in the definition of the QoS Domain as a whole (policies regarding interaction with peer QoS domains) and in the translation of high-level policies into equipment specific configurations.

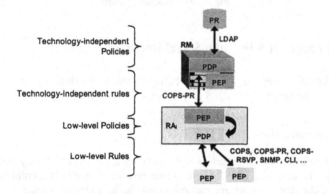

Fig. 2. PBN in the EuQoS context

4 NSIS in the EuQoS Context

This section discusses the use of the NSIS framework in the EuQoS project.

4.1 NSIS Concepts

The Next Steps in Signalling suite of protocols is being developed by the IETF NSIS working group [5]. The NSIS framework aims at providing signalling elements for the global Internet environment, to answer different needs (e.g. resource reservation, firewall transversal), without requiring a complete end-to-end deployment. Signalling protocol messages can take either the same path as the data path between end-points or a different path (on-path and off-path signalling).

The NSIS protocol stack is divided in two layers: a generic lower layer for signalling transportation and an upper layer specific to each signalling application. For the lower layer a General Internet Messaging Protocol for Signalling (GIMPS) [7] is currently being standardized. For the upper layer the NSIS working group is currently working in two protocols: the QoS NSIS Signalling Layer Protocol (QoS-NSLP) [8] for resource reservation and QoS support and the NAT/Firewall NSIS Signalling Layer Protocol (NAT/FW-NSLP) for firewall transversal [9].

4.2 NSIS in the context of EuQoS

The NSIS framework is well fitted for the EuQoS project architecture. GIMPS provides the signalling transport mechanism that can be used between RMs (off-path signalling) and also between routers and other network equipment (on-path signalling). This protocol also provides an abstraction layer that can be used for all the high-level signalling functions needed in the EuQoS framework. QoS-NSLP provides mechanisms to establish and maintain state at nodes along the path of a data flow in an end-to-end environment and can also be used for resource reservation between RMs, across network domains.

The main limitation for the adoption of the complete NSIS framework in the EuQoS context is its relative immaturity, affecting mainly the application signalling protocols like QoS-NSLP. To overcome this limitation, the use of NSIS in EuQoS started by GIMPS and will progressively include QoS-NSLP.

5 Putting it all together: the SSN Function

The Signalling and Service Negotiation function is responsible for the dynamic configuration of the communication system, in order to provide the requested level of QoS to applications.

5.1 General Overview of the SSN Function

There are four different "signalling levels" in the EuQoS architecture, as illustrated in Figure 3 by the various red arrows (Level 1 to Level 4).

Besides horizontal signalling interactions between peer entities, there are complementary signalling interactions that take place vertically between adjacent levels. These interactions are named "cross-layer signalling" and are identified by the vertical arrows in Figure 3.

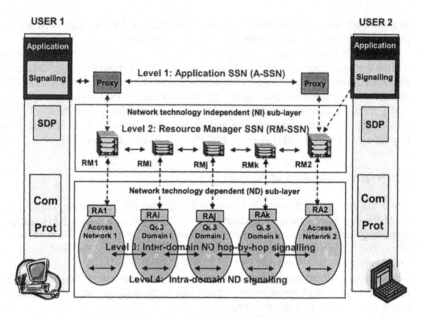

Fig. 3. Signalling levels in the EuQoS architecture

5.2   Level 1: A-SSN

The first signalling level pertains to applications and provides Application QoS-based Signalling and Service Negotiation (A-SSN). In order to establish, maintain and release sessions with the necessary QoS levels, applications must express their needs and interact with the communication system. The objectives of this interaction are to guarantee that the needs of the application will be fulfilled, and that it will adapt to network conditions under which the available resources don't allow the requested level of QoS. Furthermore, the interaction between applications and the communication system will be responsible for releasing the resources when sessions end. The main requirements of Level 1 signalling functions are:

- Identification of users, accounting and billing functions (AAA functions);
- Negotiation and definition of session characteristics between user terminals including the possibility of choice of QoS characteristics by the user;
- Prioritization of data-flows;
- Identification of QoS requirements for the communication system;
- Verification of the possibility to setup connections with the required (or available) quality requirements (by interacting with CAC functions);
- Set-up connections between user terminals with the required (or available) quality level (by interacting with RMs);
- Maintain the quality level during sessions or adapt to quality variation in the communication system (by interacting with RMs);
- Release communication system resources at the end of sessions;
- Provide information to users about the quality level and relevant session characteristics during session set-up, session life and at session tear-down.

Signalling interactions between applications and the communication system can be explicitly made in the control plane by using a signalling protocol like SIP [11], or they can be implicitly initiated by the inspection of the data path and detection of session activation and termination. When explicit signalling is used, Level 1 signalling can be direct end-to-end between the applications or mediated by proxy entities. If implicit signalling is used, the quality requirements of applications have to be defined a priori by some sort of mechanism (e.g. policy mechanisms defined at application and/or user level). The interaction between Level 1 signalling functions and RMs is achieved by the vertical interactions as depicted by the vertical arrows in Figure 3.

For the purpose of EuQoS, SIP QoS extensions will be used and named in the context of this document as EQ-SIP. The vertical interactions between RMs and RAs, and between RAs and network equipment can be supported, among others solutions, by the COPS protocol or by SNMP.

5.3 Level 2: RM-SSN

The Resource Managers Signalling and Service Negotiation (RM-SSN) is the most important and the most complex to be developed in the EuQoS architecture. The main objective of Level 2 signalling functions is to support resource reservation and management along the data path across the various network domains. The main requirements of Level 2 functions are:

- Activation of SLSs with adjacent domains (chosen by the TERO function) in reaction to local application needs (triggered by Level 1 signalling);
- Activation, renegotiation, reception and termination of SLSs with adjacent domains, in reaction to local application needs (triggered by Level 1 signalling) and quality level variations;
- Verification of the availability of resources to support the requested SLAs with the specified (or available) quality requirements (by interacting with CAC functions);
- Maintenance of SLSs with adjacent domains with the specified quality (and renegotiation of the SLAs when needed);
- Support SLS Monitoring and Measurement (interface with MMFM function), and support SLS optimization (interface with TERO function).
- To support inter-domain service negotiation, Level 2 signalling functions will perform hop-by-hop negotiation between RMs in the path starting in the local RM at the origin access network (Access Network 1 domain in Figure 3). Each RM interacts with the Traffic Engineering and Resource Optimization (TERO) function to find the next hop domain, install provisional reservations if resources are available (using the CAC function that, in turn, will use cross-layer signalling identified by the blue arrow in Figure 3 to interact with the RA of the domain), and then will start signalling with the next domain's RM, which will repeat the process until the last RM in the path is reached (Access Network 2 domain in Figure 3). When the remote RM is reached, signalling is sent in the opposite direction to confirm the provisional reservations made in the downstream direction. Alternatively to the use of the TERO function to find next hops between domains, this can be done in a static way at each RM. The options to support Level 2 signalling include the development of a specific solution for the EuQoS architecture, the use

of the SLS negotiation mechanism developed in the scope of the European IST project Mescal [12], the use of the COPS extension for SLS negotiation (COPS-SLS) [13], or the use of NSIS. Figure 4 shows the utilization of a simplified version of NSIS in the EuQoS project, named EQ-NSIS.

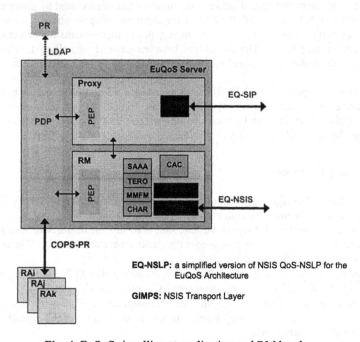

Fig. 4. EuQoS signalling at application and RM levels

5.4 Level 3: Inter-domain signalling

The third level of signalling in the EuQoS SSN Function is the network-technology-dependent hop-by-hop inter-domain signalling. At this level BGP (Border Gateway Protocol) is the most common solution currently used. BGP provides mechanisms for inter-domain traffic routing and enables the use of routing policies to control the exchange of routing information between different administrative domains (Autonomous Systems).

The BGP version currently in use supports only Best Effort traffic, but extensions, usually called BGP+, are being studied to deal with different traffic classes with different QoS requirements. The use of BGP+ enable high level RMs to rely on network level mechanisms for QoS support and network resilience.

The control of BGP+ routing policies can be made by RAs (and, indirectly, by RMs using cross-layer signalling interactions) to route specific traffic classes via specific intermediate domains according to QoS and business requirements. Traffic Engineering and Resource Optimization (TERO) and Monitoring Measurement, Fault Management (MMFM) functions can provide useful information about the state of the network to support the policy control decisions. Figure 5 illustrates the use of BGP+ inter-domain signalling, as well as intra-domain signalling interactions (discussed below).

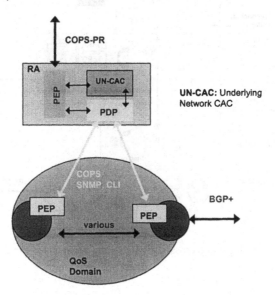

Fig. 5. Inter-domain ND hop-by-hop signalling in the EuQoS architecture

5.5 Level 4: Intra-domain signalling

The configuration of the resources of a domain is performed by RAs using solutions ranging from RSVP to specific access network mechanism like ADSL bandwidth management, 3GPP, and Ethernet and WIFI priorities. The path-coupled version of NSIS can also be used for this level of signalling. When these signalling mechanisms are not available, the RAs must have a detailed knowledge of the domain configuration and topology so they can act directly in the configuration of each network element along the path subject to QoS requirements, using cross-layer signalling interactions.

Figure 6 presents the overall EuQoS signalling picture, according to the description presented above.

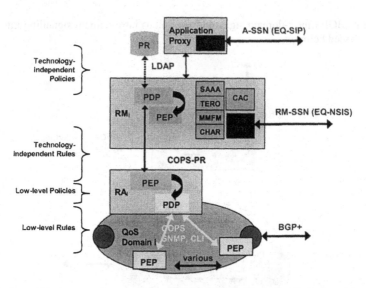

Fig. 6. Overall in-layer and cross-layer signalling protocols in the EuQoS architecture

6 Validation

The EuQoS system will be validated by simulation, in the NS-2 framework, and by trial evaluation in wide test scenarios including different user communities, applications and access technologies. The main objective of the experiments is to evaluate its capacity for delivering end-to-end QoS with special emphasis on the QoS mechanisms and algorithms developed in the scope of the project.

6.1 Simulation

In this section we present one of the studies that we made to evaluate the NSIS advantages in network scenarios, particularly by the use of the GIMPS layer specified in the NSIS framework, when it is necessary to implement a QoS signalling mechanism. For this purpose, we have developed a set of new modules for NS-2: 802.1p/Q and a NSIS package.

A simple NSLP has also been deployed to work on an Ethernet switch. Our NSLP interacts with the switch in order to configure prioritization levels, using the IEEE 802.1p and Q standards. The next figure presents the Small Office Home Office (SOHO) scenario used in the study.

For foreground traffic we decided to use VoIP G.711 sources without Voice Activity Detection (VAD), as described in Table 1.

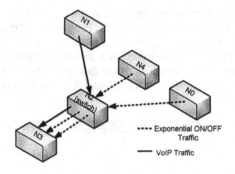

Fig. 7. Scenario #1

Table 1. Source parameters

Traffic Type	VoIP	Traffic1	Traffic1
Description	G711 without VAD	Packet Size 800	PacketSize 200
	Packet size 200 B	Burst_time 0.03	Burst_time 0.02
	Inter-arrival 0.02 s	Idle_time 0.03	Idle_time 0.02
		Rate 1000k	Rate 600k
		Exponential traffic	Exponential traffic

The purpose of this study was to evaluate the NSIS effect on the traffic and on the congestion level. In these simulations, the traffic between the nodes N1 and N3 was modelled as G.711 VoIP, requiring a high prioritization level. The background traffic (from N0 and N4) was modelled as exponential ON/OFF sources in order to overload the links. A NSIS agent was configured in each node.

Figure 8 shows the one way delay (OWD) experienced by each of the traffic flows, when no prioritization was performed in the switch. In this case, the switch had just two queues. As expected, all the traffic presented similar behaviour, experiencing high delays in the face of network congestion.

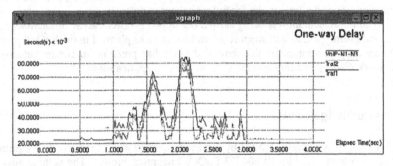

Fig. 8. Packet delay without traffic prioritization

Figure 9 shows the OWD when prioritization was introduced in the switch, activated by a NSIS signalling message. The switch was initially configured with 2 queues, and no prioritization mechanism was used. At 1.3 sec, the NSIS agent, located in N1, sent a path-message to node N3. The payload of this NSIS message contained the command to reconfigure the switch (N1 =>N2=>N3) with 7 virtual queues. Each NSIS agent initialized the peer discovery negotiations while the NSLP function reconfigured each switch along the data path. After that, traffic was sent between N1 and N3. As can be observed in figure 9, the VoIP delay remained low during all the simulation.

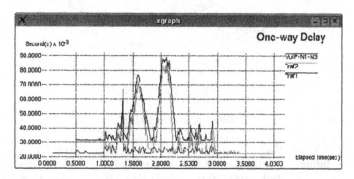

Fig. 9. Packet delay with traffic prioritization after the NSIS Message

These simulation tests demonstrated NSIS advantages when it is necessary to implement different classes of traffic. Different NSIS mechanisms can be built, extending the NSLP functionalities used in this example.

7 Conclusion

This paper discussed the use of the Policy Based Network paradigm, COPS and NSIS frameworks being developed by IETF, in the context of the European Project EuQoS. The analysis of the use of PBN/COPS and NSIS to support the SSN function revealed that these protocols can be used to provide a basis to support the desired functionality and a framework for further enhancements.

The implementation is being carried out in two parallel tracks: simulations models and prototype that will support the validation tasks planned in the EuQoS project. Preliminary simulation results show that NSIS has potential to control underlying network devices and improve the QoS provided to applications.

Acknowledgements

This work was partially funded by the European Union 6th Framework Programme under contract IST FP6 IP 004503 EuQoS Integrated Project. The authors also acknowledge the various comments and valuable suggestions received from the EuQoS project team.

References

1. EuQoS Project consortium, Integrated Project EuQoS End-to-end Quality of Service support over heterogeneous networks Annex I - DoW, May 2004.
2. The GÉANT project – http://www.geant.net
3. IETF Policy Framework Working Group (IETF-PG) – http://www.ietf.org/html.charters/policy-charter.html
4. Durham, Ed., J. Boyle, R. Cohen, S. Herzog, R. Rajan, A. Sastry, The COPS (Common Open Policy Service) Protocol, RFC 2748, IETF, January 2000.
5. R. Hancock G. Karagiannis J. Loughney S. van den Bosch, Next Steps in Signaling: Framework, Internet-Draft, IETF, 2005.
6. K. Chan, J. Seligson, D. Durham, S. Gai, K. McCloghrie, S. Herzog, F. Reichmeyer, R. Yavatkar, A. Smith, COPS Usage for Policy Provisioning (COPS-PR), RFC 3084, IETF, March 2001.
7. Schulzrinne, R. Hancock, GIMPS: General Internet Messaging Protocol for Signaling, Internet-Draft, IETF, 2004.
8. S. Van den Bosch, G. Karagiannis, A. McDonald, NSLP for Quality-of-Service signaling, Internet-Draft, IETF, 2004.
9. M. Stiemerling H. Tschofenig M. Martin, C. Aoun, NAT/Firewall NSIS Signaling Layer Protocol (NSLP), Internet-Draft, IETF, 2004.
10. R. Braden, L. Zhang, S. Berson, S. Herzog, S. Jamin, Resource ReSerVation Protocol (RSVP), RFC 2205, IETF, September 1997.
11. Handley, H. Schulzrinne, E. Schooler, J. Rosenberg, SIP: Session Initiation Protocol, MRFC 2543, March 1999
12. MESCAL Project, Management of End-to-end Quality of Service Across the Internet at Large - http://www.mescal.org/
13. T.M.T. Nguyen, G. Pujolle, N. Boukhatem, COPS Usage for SLS negotiation (COPS-SLS), Internet-Draft, IETF, June 2001.

New CAC Algorithm using Adaptive Modulation Control

Sung-Kee Noh[1], Young-Ha Hwang[1], Byung-Ho Ye[1], and Sang-Ha Kim[2]

[1] Electronics and Telecommunications Research Institutes, Daejon, Korea,
{sknoh,hyh,bhye}@etri.re.kr
[2] ChungNam National University, Daejon, Korea,
shkim@cnu.ac.kr

Abstract. Adaptive modulation control (AMC) has been proposed as the next generation modulation method for increasing network performance in cellular networks. Adaptive modulation is a powerful technique to improve the spectral efficiency in wireless transmission over fading channels. Similarly, it is possible to apply the adaptive modulation technique to Call Admission Control (CAC) scheme in order to enhance network performance and satisfy Quality of Service (QoS) requirements. In this paper, we investigate a novel call admission control (CAC) mechanism in the cellular networks using AMC. First, we build the system model in which takes into account to both CAC and AMC. Second, we verify that the CAC model can offer better performance by using adaptive modulation technique. Finally we prove our claim by numerical analysis.

1 Introduction

In multimedia wireless communication networks, the demand for high data rates and quality of service is growing at a rapid speed. In order to meet these needs, it is necessary to use more intelligent functions such as resource management, transmission technology, and network management. Thus, the proposed technology is Call Admission Control (CAC) with adaptive channel reservation (ACR) and adaptive modulation control(AMC).

The modulation method in communication systems have been introduced to meet finite frequency spectrum and efficient power control. The modem composed by the modulation method has power margin to satisfy time-based variable channel requests. The technique to transmit data efficiently using this power margin is called adaptive modulation, which is to enhance QoS and system throughput by changing the modulation method adaptively according to the instantaneous propagation conditions, interference scenarios, and traffic or data rate requirements. That is, adaptive modulation techniques do not require additional resources such as power and bandwidth according to variable traffic environment. Many previous adaptive modulation schemes have been suggested to maximize the data rate and match transmission parameters to time-varying channel conditions related to variable-power and variable-rate [1]-[6].

Please use the following format when citing this chapter:

Noh, S.-K., Hwang, Y.-H., Ye, B.-H. and Kim, S.-H., 2007, in IFIP International Federation for Information Processing, Volume 229, Network Control and Engineering for QoS, Security, and Mobility, IV, ed. Gaïti, D., (Boston: Springer), pp. 173–186.

A CAC scheme deals with the problem of whether or not a call is accepted into the network while taking QoS constraints into account in a given cell capacity. Thus, the objective of CAC scheme is to minimize handoff-call-dropping probability (CDP) and new-call-blocking probability (CBP), and to maximize the utilization of the assigned cell capacity at the same time. Generally, reserved guard channel schemes in which a certain number of channels from overall cell capacity have to be reserved solely for the use of handoff and new calls for different services have proposed to minimize CDP and CBP [7].

This paper evaluates the performance of new CAC algorithm using the advantages of practical AMC environments. Without AMC schemes, the system allocates new different frequency channel to user when the quality of the communications channel degrades. If the new channel belongs to the same base station, this is referred to as an intracell handoff. If we use AMC techniques, the system can reuse the same frequency channel under worse channel degradation. This leads to decreasing intracell handoff as well as increasing the utilization of system resources. In this paper, we analyze the joint effects of CAC and AMC techniques considering the user distance and signal strength.

The rest of this paper is organized as follows. We introduce the traffic model and user mobility characteristics in Section 2. We present an analytical procedure to solve the two-state markov chain in Section 3, and suggest the CAC algorithm and adaptive channel reservations policy in Section 4. Numerical results are discussed in Section5, and finally draw concluding remarks in Section 5.

2   System Model

2.1   Traffic Model

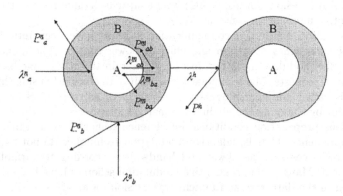

Fig. 1. System Model for a cell.

The base station architecture is illustrated in Fig. 1. The idea behind adaptive modulation is to select a modulation mode according to the instantaneous radio channel quality [8]. We assume that different modulation is expressed by virtual region in a cell. Namely, calls in region A use modulation A. We assume that each cell is equipped with same C channels. For each cell k, there are two types of calls sharing these channels: the calls in region A using modulation A and the calls in region B using modulation B. Region B call requires m bandwidths. Region A call requires one basic bandwidth. It is assumed that the new calls in A, B are arrived according to a Poisson process with mean arrival rate $\lambda_a^n = \lambda^n p_a$ and $\lambda_b^n = \lambda^n p_b$, respectively and that service time(call holding time) is exponentially distributed with mean service time of $1/\mu_a^n$ and $1/\mu_b^n$. Where, the probability $p_a(p_b)$ that a given call in a cell occurs in region $A(B)$ is

$$p_a = \frac{region\ A}{region\ A + region\ B} \quad and \quad p_b = 1 - p_a$$

When modulation mode switching is occurred, new channel should be allocated for the moving call in order to satisfy the Quality of Service (QoS) requirements. The intracell moving calls between A and B are generated with arrival rate λ_{ab}^m and λ_{ba}^m, respectively. In next section we will describe the algorithms to generate λ_{ab}^m and λ_{ba}^m. The intercell handoff occurs only in region B with arrival rate λ^h and that service time is exponentially distributed with mean service time of $1/\mu^h$. Furthermore, the time that calls stay in the cell before moving into other cells also follows an exponentially distribution with mean $1/h_a$ and $1/h_b$. We also describes that calls in region A and B calls are summed with arrival rates $\lambda_a(\lambda_a^n + \lambda_{ba}^m)$ and $\lambda_b(\lambda_b^n + \lambda_{ab}^m + \lambda^h)$, respectively. Moreover channel occupancy times for region A and B calls are summed with means $1/\mu_a(1/(\mu_a^n + \mu_{ba}^m + h_a))$ and $1/\mu_b(1/(\mu_b^n + \mu_{ab}^m + \mu^h + h_b))$, respectively. Let C be the total number of channels and G_a and G_b be the dedicated channels for region A and region B traffic, respectively. Then, the system can be modelled as a two dimensional Markov process shown in Fig. 2, characterized by $\{i, j\}$, where i and j are the numbers of calls in region A and B, respectively and the state space is represented by the set set $\{s(i,j)|0 \le i \le G_a, 0 \le j \le \lfloor(C - G_b)/m\rfloor$ and $G_b \le i \le C - G_a, 0 \le j \le \lfloor(C - i)/m\rfloor\}$. $\lfloor x \rfloor$ denotes the greatest integer smaller than or equal to x.

2.2 Handoff rate for Distance and Signal Strength

Generally, it is assumed that the new calls are arrived according to a Poisson process. However, the assumption of handoff or adaptive modulation change events being Poisson Process may no longer be practical. Some field studies [9], [10], [11] showed that the channel occupancy times having an influence on handoff or adaptive modulation change events are not exponentially distributed for cellular systems. Thus, handoff call traffic can be expressed as a arrival rate $\lambda^h = \lambda E[H]$, where $E[H]$ is the average number of handoff calls induced [12]. Handoff or adaptive modulation change events initiation may be based on the

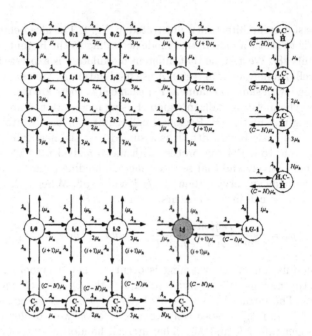

Fig. 2. The state diagram of call occupancy in region A and B.

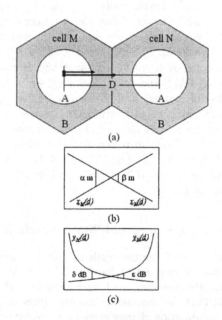

Fig. 3. Network model. (a) cellular layout (b) values of distance and (c) values of signal strength.

distance between the mobile station and surrounding base stations, and the signal strengths the mobile station receives from base stations.

Itoh [13]proposed handoff algorithm that take account into distance and signal strength at the same time. Using *Itoh* [13]'s algorithm, we consider a network of two base station M and N separated by distance D, and a mobile station that is moving from A to B in a straight line with constant velocity (Fig. 3(a)). The algorithm considered performs a moving from area A to B within cell M if both of the following conditions are met, as illustrated in Fig. 3(b).

1. if the measured signal strength from the adjacent area or base station exceeds that of the serving area or base station by a hysteresis level δ or ϵ (dB), respectively;
2. if the measured distance from the serving adjacent area or base station exceeds that of the adjacent area or station by a threshold distance α or β (m), respectively.

At a distance dm from base station M, the estimated distance from base stations M and N is given by

$$x_M(d) = d + n_M$$

and

$$x_N(d) = (D - d) + n_N. \qquad (1)$$

where n_M and n_N represent distance measurement error and are modeled as zero-mean independent white Gaussian processes with variance σ_N^2. The relative distance is defined as

$$x(d) = x_M(d) - x_N(d) = 2d - D + n. \qquad (2)$$

where $n = n_M - n_N$ is zero-mean white Gaussian process with variance $\sigma^2 = 2\sigma_n^2$.

The signal levels received from base station M and N, are given by

$$y_M(d) = -K log(d) + \mu(d)$$

and

$$y_N(d) = -K log(D - d) + \nu(d). \qquad (3)$$

Following the procedure used in [14], let $P_h(k)$ denote the probability that there is a handoff at interval k. $P_{MN}(k)$ denotes the probability of handoff from M to N, and vice versa for $P_{NM}(k)$. Then, if $P_M(k)$ and $P_N(k)$ denote the probability that the mobile is assigned to base station M or N at interval k, the following recursive relations hold:

$$P_h(k) = P_M(k-1)P_{MN}(k) + P_N(k-1)P_{NM}(k) \qquad (4)$$
$$P_M(k) = P_M(k-1)(1 - P_{MN}(k)) + P_N(k-1)P_{NM}(k) \qquad (5)$$

$$P_N(k) = P_M(k-1)P_{MN}(k) + P_N(k-1)(1 - P_{NM}(k)). \qquad (6)$$

It is clear that once we find a way to compute $P_{MN}(k)$ and $P_{NM}(k)$, the problem is solved.

$$
\begin{aligned}
P_{MN}(k) &= P\{N(k)|M(k-1)\} \\
&= P\{y_k < -\varepsilon, x_k > \beta | M(k-1)\} \\
&= P\{y_k < -\varepsilon | M(k-1)\} P\{x_k > \beta | M(k-1)\}.
\end{aligned} \tag{7}
$$

$P_{AB}(k)$, $P_{BA}(k)$ can be calculated in a similar fashion, i.e.,

$$
P_m(k) = P_A(k-1)P_{AB}(k) + P_B(k-1)P_{BA}(k) \tag{8}
$$
$$
P_A(k) = P_A(k-1)(1 - P_{AB}(k)) + P_B(k-1)P_{BA}(k) \tag{9}
$$
$$
P_B(k) = P_A(k-1)P_{AB}(k) + P_B(k-1)(1 - P_{BA}(k)). \tag{10}
$$

It is clear that once we find a way to compute $P_{AB}(k)$ and $P_{BA}(k)$, the problem is solved.

$$
\begin{aligned}
P_{AB}(k) &= P\{B(k)|A(k-1)\} \\
&= P\{y_k < -\varepsilon, x_k > \beta | A(k-1)\} \\
&= P\{y_k < -\varepsilon | A(k-1)\} P\{x_k > \beta | A(k-1)\}.
\end{aligned} \tag{11}
$$

Then, the handoff call attempt rate per cell is expressed as

$$
\lambda_{ab}^m = \lambda_a^n \cdot \sum k P_{AB}(k)
$$
$$
\lambda_{ba}^m = \lambda_b^n \cdot \sum k P_{BA}(k). \tag{12}
$$

3   Analysis with MMPP

The steady-state probability vector p is then partitioned as $p = (p_0, p_l, ...)$. The vector p is the solution of equations

$$
pQ = 0, \qquad pe = 1 \tag{13}
$$

Where e and 0 are vectors of all ones and zeros, respectively, and Q is the transi-tion rate matrix of the Markov process which will be obtained for each allocation strategy. we can obtain the transition rate matrix Q of the Markov process

$$
Q = \begin{bmatrix}
A_0 & D & & & \\
B_1 & A_1 & D & & \\
& B_2 & A_2 & D & \\
& & B_3 & A_3 & D \\
& & & \cdot & \cdot & \cdot \\
& & & & & \cdot
\end{bmatrix} \tag{14}
$$

Let $p_{i,-1} = 0$ for $0 \leq i \leq C - G_b$ and $p_{-1,j} = 0$ for $0 \leq j \leq \lfloor (C - G_a)/m \rfloor$. We show some balance equations as follows.

$$0 \leq i \leq G_a, 0 \leq j \leq \lfloor (C - G_a)/m \rfloor :$$
$$(\lambda_a + i\mu_a + \lambda_b + j\mu_b)p_{ij} = \lambda_a p_{i-1,j} + (i+1)\mu_a p_{i+1,j} +$$
$$\lambda_b p_{i,j-1} + (j+1)\mu_b p_{i,j+1}$$
$$0 \leq i \leq G_a - 1, \lfloor (C - G_a)/m \rfloor \leq j \leq \lfloor (C - G_a - 1)/m \rfloor :$$
$$(\lambda_a + i\mu_a + \lambda_b + \lfloor (C - G_a)/m \rfloor \mu_b)p_{ij} = \lambda_a p_{i-1,j} +$$
$$(i+1)\mu_a p_{i+1,j} + \lambda_b p_{i,j-1} + \lfloor (C - Gn)/m \rfloor \mu_b p_{i,j+1}$$
$$0 \leq i \leq G_a, j = \lfloor (C - G_a)/m \rfloor :$$
$$(\lambda_a + i\mu_a + \lfloor (C - G_a)/m \rfloor \mu_b)p_{ij} = \lambda_a p_{i-1,j} + (i+1)$$
$$\mu_a p_{i+1,j} + \lambda_b p_{i,j-1}. \tag{15}$$

Equations (15) maybe written concisely in matrix form. To do this define a set of $(C - G_a)$ elements row vector p_i.

$$p_i \equiv [p_{i0}, p_{i1}, p_{i2}, \ldots]. \tag{16}$$

From above equations (16), we can define submatrices for $i, j = 0, 1,, C - G_b, 0 \leq l \leq \lfloor (C - G_a)/m \rfloor$ by

$$A_l(i,j) = \begin{cases} \lambda_a & \text{if } i = j-1 \text{ and } (0 \leq i \leq G_a | i < C - l \cdot m) \\ j\mu_a & \text{if } i = j+1 \text{ and } i \leq C - l \cdot m \\ a_i(j) & \text{if } i = j \\ 0 & \text{otherwise.} \end{cases} \tag{17}$$

$$D(j,k) = \begin{cases} \lambda_w & \text{if } i = j \text{ and } i \leq C - l \cdot m \\ 0 & \text{otherwise.} \end{cases} \tag{18}$$

$$B_l(i,j) = \begin{cases} min(l, \lfloor (C-G_a)/m \rfloor, \lfloor (C-i)/m \rfloor) & \text{if } i = j \text{ and } i \leq C - l \cdot m \\ 0 & \text{otherwise.} \end{cases} \tag{19}$$

Where $a_i(j)$ is the value that makes the sum of the row element s of Q equal to zero.

4 The CAC Algorithm

Channels are divided by three sub-channels. Designed G_b and G_a channels are dedicated for region B traffic and region A traffic, respectively. The shared channels can be used by either type of traffic. When a new user arrives in a cell, the proposed CAC algorithm decides acceptance or rejection based on each call's current resource occupancy, reservation partition, and dynamic guide channels. A new region B call is admitted if the number of existing region B calls is less than the number of guard channels G_b for region B traffic. When the number of existing region B calls is greater than or equal to the number of guard channels

G_b for region A traffic, a new region B call is accepted when the total existing used channels are less than a predefined threshold. Hand-off region B calls are accepted as long as the channels are not full.

```
if region_B_new_call is requested
   if region_B_new_call is less than Gb
      Accept
   else if (existing used channels < Tb)
      Accept
   else
      Reject


if region_B_handoff_call is requested
   if (existing used channels < C) then
      Accept
   else
      Reject
```

5   The Adaptive Resource Management

In our CAC algorithm described in chapter VI, we should compute G_a, and G_b. In this section, we describe how to decide reservation partition for region A and region B calls. These reservation partitions play a very important role in admission control and resource utilization, so that it is very critical problem to set these values properly. Each service call reservation partition is allocated with traffic behavior as well as fairness level. Each reservation partition has minimum channel pool to guarantee minimum resource to each service. Using minimum channel pool, it prevents all resources from being occupied by one service so that it can help to make Call Blocking Probability (CBP) ratio balance and achieve fairness for resource usage.

5.1   Initialization

Initial reservation partition for each class is proportionally allocated with the offered load per cell, which is defined as call generation rate * required bandwidth units * average call staying time in a cell. So, the much resource is allocated to class with larger offered load than class with small offered load. The minimum channel pools for each class is set as the same as initial reservation partition. The computations are given by the following equations.

$$G_a = C * \frac{load\_region\_A}{\Sigma load\_region\_A, load\_region\_B} * \alpha$$

$$G_b = C * \frac{load\_region\_B}{\Sigma load\_region\_A, load\_region\_B} * \alpha$$

where, α has the value between 0 and 1.

5.2 Adjustment

Based on CBP_ratio, resource management algorithm works as follows. If CBP_ratio is greater than threshold, the reservation partition for underprivileged class is incremented up to sum of resource for expecting on-going calls over next term and required resources for CBP fairness. The former is calculated by call's departure rate and the latter is done by call's arrival rate. The required resource for CBP fairness are defined as calls_for_CBP_fairness * BU. The term calls_for_CBP_fairness means the relative number of calls, which should be admitted to make current unfair CBP fairness equal or similar. To compute these calls, at first current available resource is accomplished. This calculation is based on current occupied resource. Once calculating this resource, the remaining resources are partitioned depending on CBP fairness level and offered traffic load. That is, the CBP fairness level has a great important role in deciding call admission during next term. For example, if the CBP unfairness is serious, the bandwidths accommodating all expected calls are to be allocated. On the contrary, if the CBP unfairness is light, bandwidths for admitting several calls among all expected calls are to be demanded. As a result, it is very important to predict the number of calls for getting adequate resources for CBP fairness. Once completing estimation, system calculates how many calls should be admitted in order to lower CBP of unprivileged calls up to current CBP of privileged calls. The detail procedures for this computation are as follows. In order to make CBP fair, the calls_for_CBP_fairness are calculated by (1 - CBP of other service) * available_resource. This concept is based on biased coin method [15]. That is, the CBP restricts to the admitted calls over next terms. So, the CBP fairness can be gradually achievable. For better understand, we take an example. We assume that the CBP of service i is $1/5$ and CBP of service j is $1/4$. And, the available resources are 20 units where offered traffic load of each class is given as 1 and 2, respectively. According to our algorithm, the acceptance threshold of service i and j in next interval are set to $(1 - (1/4)) * 20 * 1/3 = 5$ and ($1 - (1/5)) * 20 * 2/3 = 11$, respectively. So, during next interval, 5 units are reserved for service i and 11 units are reserved for service j. The remaining 4 units are competed with two service class equally. Using this method, the CBP unfairness is gradually to be balanced.

```
If CBP_ratio > threshold  and Then
    a_r = C -  Ri
    Gi=Ri+(1-CBP_j)*a_r*o_load_i/o_load
    Gj=Rj+(1-CBP_i)*a_r*o_load_j/o_load
Else
    Nothing is done
```

6   Numerical Results

The objective of this numerical analysis is to verify the excellency of new CAC algorithm and adaptive channel allocation method in mobile network environment using adaptive modulation compared to using fixed modulation with respect to call dropping probability. The system parameters used in numerical analysis are show in Table 1.

Table 1. System Parameters.

Name	Value	Explanation
C	15	cell capacity
G_a	2	initial guard channel for A
G_b	4	initial guard channel for B
m	2	basic channel units for B
μ_a	1	channel occupancy times for A
μ_b	1	channel occupancy times for B
λ	0.1 - 3	new call arrival rate

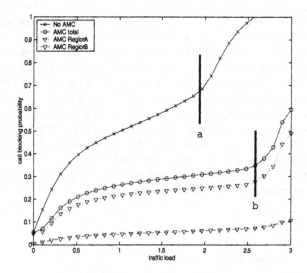

Fig. 4. Blocking probability (AMC vs No AMC.)

Fig. 4 shows the obvious distinction of call blocking probability between AMC and no AMC. Under fixed modulation (no AMC), it is clear that the new call

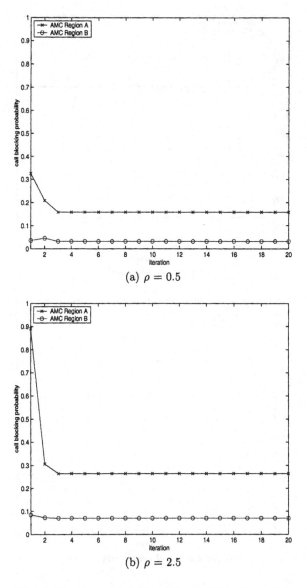

(a) $\rho = 0.5$

(b) $\rho = 2.5$

Fig. 5. Blocking probability with $\rho = 0.5$ and $\rho = 2.5$.

blocking probability (CBP) increases drastically over CBP_{th} (0.3) in proportion to increase of traffic load (ρ). On the contrary, under AMC environment, CBP is kept below CBP_{th} (0.3) until traffic load increase to the point of about 2.5. Fig. 5 shows that how our CAC scheme using adaptive resource management guarantees CBP_{th} after some iterations. The figure indicates that our scheme is

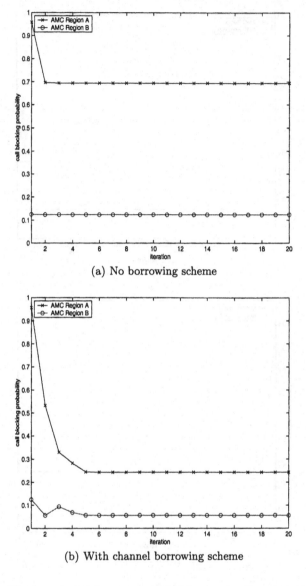

(a) No borrowing scheme

(b) With channel borrowing scheme

Fig. 6. Blocking probability using channel borrowing scheme with $\rho = 5$

more efficient under high traffic load. For examples, at the first step of our CAC scheme, we also can not guarantee $CBP_{th} = 0.3$, even in case of traffic load ($\rho = 0.5$) as show in Fig. 5(a), but after short iteration, CBP converges under CBP_{th}. Fig. 5(b) also reveals that CBP converges rapidly below CBP_{th} (0.3) with $\rho = 2.5$ after 4 iterations of our algorithm, while no AMC shows that CBP is over 0.9.

Fig. 6(a), however, shows that CBP of region A seems not to be converged within the CBP_{th} (0.3). It is because the traffic load is relatively higher than total channel capacity to handle input traffic. Namely, CBP for highly overloaded situation cannot be adjusted. Thus, we think that it is necessary to apply extra channel borrowing scheme from adjacent cells to solve this highly overload status. In Fig. 6(b), we increase the traffic parameters until the CBP satisfies the CBP_{th}. That is, we assume that cell capacity (C) increases from 15 to 21 by borrowing extra cell channels from adjacent cells because the available channels are absolutely deficient to meet CBP_{th}. Fig. 6(b) shows that CBP converges very well below CBP_{th} when channel borrowing scheme is used.

7 Conclusion

In this study we investigated the new CAC algorithm in wireless networks using adaptive modulation technique. The main concern of this work is to verify that the CAC model can offer better performance by using adaptive modulation technique that take into account user mobility property. The proposed method has been analyzed by conducting a two-dimensional Markov chain, and has been proven by using SOR solutions. Using numerical result, we demonstrated that our CAC scheme actually achieves resonable admitting probability regardless of traffic behavior. Adaptive modulation is a powerful technique to improve the spectral efficiency in wireless transmission over fading channels. Similarly, it is possible to apply the adaptive modulation technique to Call Admission Control (CAC) scheme in order to enhance network performance and satisfy Quality of Service (QoS) requirements.

References

1. J. S. Blogh, P. J. Cherriman, and L. Hanzo, "Dynamic Channel Allocation Techniques Using Adaptive Modulation and Adaptive Antennas," *IEEE J. Select. Areas Commun.*, vol. 19, no. 2, pp. 312-321, Feb. 2001.
2. S. F. Falahati, A. Svensson, T. Ekman, and M. Sternad, "Adaptive Modulation Systems for Predicted Wireless Channels," *IEEE Trans. Commun.*, vol. 52, no. 2, pp. 307-316, Feb. 2004.
3. B. Vucetic, "An adaptive coding scheme for time-varying channels," *IEEE Trans. Commun.*, vol. 39, pp. 653.663, May 1991.
4. S. M. Alamouti and S. Kallel, "Adaptive trellis-coded multiple phaseshift keying for Rayleigh fading channels," *IEEE Trans. Commun.*, vol. 42, pp. 2305.2314, June 1994.
5. M.-S. Alouini and A. J. Goldsmith, "Adaptive M-QAM modulation over Nakagami fading channels," in Proc. *IEEE Global Communications Conf.*, Phoenix, AZ, Nov. 1997, pp. 218.223.
6. A. J. Goldsmith and S. Chua, "Variable-rate variable-power M-QAM for fading channels," *IEEE Trans. Commun.*, vol. 45, pp. 1218.1230, Oct. 1997.

7. J. Y. Lee, "Realistic cell-oriented adaptive ad- mission control for QoS support in wireless multimedia networks," *IEEE Trans. Veh. Technol.*, vol. 52, no. 3, May 2003.

8. L. Hanzo, W. T. Webb, and T. Keller, *Single- and Multi-Carrier Quadrature Amplitude Modulation.* New York: Wiley/IEEE, 2000.

9. C. F. Barcelo and J. Jordan, "Channel Holding Time Distribution in Cellular Telephony," *Proc. Ninth Int'l Conf. Wireless Comm. (Wireless 97)*, vol. 1, pp. 125-134, Alberta, Canada, 9-11 July 1997.

10. C. Jedrzycki and V.C.M. Leung, "Probability Distribution of Channel Holding Time in Cellular Telephony Systems," *Proc. IEEE Vehicular Technology Conf. (VTC 96)*, pp. 247-251, 1996.

11. J. Jordan and F. Barcelo, "Statistical Modelling of Channel Occupancy in Trunked PAMR Systems," *Proc. 15th Intl Teletraffic Conf. (ITC 15)*, V. Ramaswami and P.E. Wirth, eds., pp. 1,169-1,178.

12. Y. Fang and Y. B. Lin, "Channel Occupancy Times and Handoff Rate for Mobile Computing and PCS Networks," *IEEE Trans. Computers*, vol. 47, no. 6, pp. 679-692, Jun. 1998.

13. K. I. Itoh, J. S. Shih, and T. Sato, "Performance of Handoff Algorithm Based on Distance and RSSI Measurements," *IEEE Trans. Vehicular Technology*, vol. 51, no. 6, pp. 1460-1468, Nov. 2002.

14. P. S. Kumar and J. Holtzman, "Aanlysis of Handoff Algorithms Using Both Bit Error Rate and Relative Signal Strength," in *Proc. 3rd Annu. Int. Conf. Universal Personal Communications*, 1994, pp. 1-5

15. L. J. Wei, "The Adaptive Biased Coin Design for Sequential Experiments," *Journal of Annals of Statistics*, Vol. 6, Jan. 1978, pp. 92 - 100.

DiffServ Management on Mobile IP Networks using COPS-PR

Edgard Jamhour, Mauro Fonseca, Andre Beller, Thiago Pereira
PUCPR, PPGIA, Imaculada Conceição 1155,
90815-901 Curitiba, Brazil
{jamhour, mauro.fonseca, a.beller, tmp}@ppgia.pucpr.br,
WWW home page: http://www.ppgia.pucpr.br/docentes.html#redes

Abstract. This paper describes and evaluates a framework for managing Differentiated Services (diffserv) configuration on Mobile IP-based networks. In the considered scenario, users can keep their QoS privileges while they move along through different access networks interconnected by a diffserv domain. In this case, the edge routers receive the diffserv configuration dynamically, according to the authentication events registered by the home agent during the mobile node's handoff. The proposed framework is based on the IETF standards concerning diffserv management. The device configuration is represented in terms of a diffserv PIB, which is distributed to the diffserv edge routers using the COPS-PR protocol. By exploring the COPS-PR facilities, we define an efficient strategy for updating the PIB information in the managed devices without generating excessive management traffic. We conclude that, by properly exploring the COPS-PR facilities, the latency introduced by the COPS-PR management is not significant when compared with the Mobile IP handoff latency.

1 Introduction

This paper describes and evaluates a framework for managing SLS assignments on Mobile IP-based networks. The Mobile Internet Protocol (MIP) is an IETF standard that defines a tunneling technique for permitting a mobile host to keep its IP address regardless its attachment point with a backbone network [1]. MIP can be employed in cellular networks technologies such as GPRS and EDGE. MIP can also be employed to provide seamless roaming between wireless local-area networks (WLANs), or even across different types of infrastructures (i.e., WLAN and cellular networks).

In the scenario considered in this paper, users can keep their QoS privileges (i.e. SLS assignments) while they move along through different access networks interconnected by a *diffserv* domain. According to the IETF terminology, a SLS

Please use the following format when citing this chapter:

Jamhour, E., Fonseca, M., Beller, A. and Pereira, T. 2007, in IFIP International Federation for Information Processing, Volume 229, Network Control and Engineering for QoS, Security, and Mobility, IV, ed. Gaïti, D., (Boston: Springer), pp. 187–198.

(Service Level Specification) represents a subset of a SLA (Service Level Agreement) that refers to traffic characterization and treatment [2]. In order to keep the SLS assignments of mobile nodes, the *diffserv* edge routers must receive their configuration dynamically, according to the authentication events related to the mobile node's handoff.

This paper addresses the problem of building a framework for supporting QoS provisioning in presence of mobility by exploring the IETF standards concerning *diffserv* management. The framework follows a PEP/PDP architecture, using a provisioning approach [2]. The PEP (Policy Enforcement Point) is responsible for representing a managed device and requesting the initial *diffserv* configuration from the PDP. The *diffserv* configuration is represented in terms of a *diffserv* PIB (Policy Information Base), which contains a vendor independent description of the configuration assigned to a network device [3]. The PEP is also responsible for interpreting the PIB and installing the configuration into the managed device. The PDP (Policy Decision Point) is responsible for generating the PIB with the configuration corresponding to the SLS assigned to the users. The PIB is transferred from the PDP to the PEP using the COPS-PR protocol [4].

In order to support the user's mobility, the PIB information must be updated and transferred from the PDP to the PEPs as a response of a handoff confirmation event. The COPS-PR protocol supports sending non-solicited PIB updates from the PDP to the PEP. However, an important aspect that must be addressed is how to preserve the user's QoS privileges in distinct access networks, where the network devices implement distinct QoS mechanisms and benefit from different levels of available bandwidth. This paper addressed this problem by proposing a three-layer policy model. A high level policy model (HLPM) is used for defining SLS assignments using rules that take into account the facilities in each access network. A configuration level policy model (CLPM) is used for defining the device configuration independently of the specific device capabilities. Finally, a *diffserv* PIB is generated by compiling the CLPM and by taking into account the specific device capabilities. This strategy is based on the work published on [5], but several modifications have in introduced in order to support mobility.

This paper is structured as follows. Section 2 reviews the concepts related to MIP and *diffserv*. Section 3 presents an overview of our framework for managing *diffserv* configuration in MIP-based networks and discusses the strategy for implementing the *diffserv* PIB updates. Section 4 presents the three-layer policy model adopted by the framework. Section 5 presents some results concerning the strategy defined in section 3. Section 6 reviews some related works, pointing the main difference of this paper with respect to other published works addressing the QoS management in mobile environments. Finally, the conclusion summarizes the main results of this work and points to future developments.

2   Mobile IP and Diffserv

The Mobile IP (MIP) standard [1] treats the problem that may arise when a host changes its IP address during a communication. A mobile host changes its IP address because the IP protocol assumes that each IP network identifier is related to a specific physical network. If a mobile node (e.g. a cellular device) connects to another physical network, it must change its IP address. Changing the IP address during a communication session will require restarting any application being executed in the mobile node.

MIP solves this problem by using a tunneling technique. Each mobile host has two IP addresses. One address is related to its "home network" (where the mobile host is registered), and does not change when the host changes its position. The second address is related to a "foreign network", and changes each time the host attaches to a different physical network (refer to Fig. 1). This second address is called CoA (Care-of Address). The router attached to the mobile host at the foreign network is called "foreign agent" (FA). The router at the home network is called "home agent" (HA). The home agent is a special router, responsible for authenticating the mobile host, and keeping an internal table mapping the CoA to the home IP address of every mobile host it serves. Mobile IP specifies that is up to the mobile host the responsibility of informing the home agent that it has changed its CoA. For doing this the mobile host sends a "binding update" message to the home agent each time it changes a CoA. The message is delivered to the home agent by the foreign agent. The binding update message contains a digital signature allowing the home agent to validate the binding request. From a non-mobile host viewpoint, a mobile host is identified by its home IP address. Packets from the Internet are delivered to the mobile host through a tunnel that follows the hosts while it changes its position and attaches to different networks. Depending on the preferred implementation, this tunnel can be created between the home agent and the foreign agent, or between the home agent and the mobile host. The tunnel is created by encapsulating the incoming packets from the Internet, addressing the mobile host by its home address, with an IP header that addresses the mobile host by its Care-Of Address (CoA). If the tunnel is created only up to the foreign agent, then all the mobile hosts served by the same foreign agent can share the same CoA. If the tunnel is created up to the mobile host, than every mobile host must have their own CoA. Please refer to [1] for more details about the Mobile IP standard terminology and operation. The work described in this paper assumes all the tunnels are created between the home agent and the foreign agent (i.e., the mobile nodes share the foreign agent CoA).

The *diffserv* QoS methodology defines two main entities: the edge router and the core router [6]. The *edge router* is responsible for policing and assigning an aggregated class to the packets transmitted by the hosts. According to the *diffserv* methodology, a *core router* does not differentiate individual flows. Instead, packets are handled according to the aggregated classes assigned by the edge routers. Fig. 1 illustrates how a MIP-based network could be adapted to the *diffserv* QoS methodology. For the sake of simplicity, we have assumed that the functions of foreign agent (FA) and home agent (HA) are accumulated by the edge routers.

The IETF defines fourteen aggregated classes for the core network (i.e., expedited forwarding - EF, 12 X assured forwarding - AF and best effort - BE). An edge router is responsible for policing the traffic and assigning an aggregated class according to the SLS assigned to the mobile host. Considering the MIP scenario, the edge router configuration must be updated when the mobile host moves from a FA domain to another. In this case, the mobile host's SLS configuration must be added to the FA in the incoming domain and removed from the FA in the previous domain.

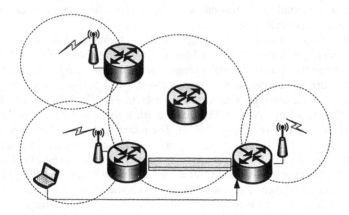

Fig. 1. Diffserv and MIP

3 Strategy for Updating the Foreign Agent Configuration

The framework described in this paper adopts the *diffserv* PIB standard for representing the distributing the edge router's configuration [3]. A PIB module is a named data structure described as a conceptual tree where the branches represent Provisioning Classes (PRCs) and the leaves represent Provisioning Instances (PRIs). The *diffserv* PIB PRCs model a Traffic Condition Block (TCB), which is formed by zero or more classifiers, meters, actions, drop algorithms, queues and (packet) schedulers.

As shown in Fig. 2, in the *diffserv* PIB, the functional elements (classifier, meter,...) and their parameters (IP filter, token-bucket parameters,...) are represented by distinct PRCs. The *"Specific"* attribute in the functional PRCs is used for associating a functional element to its parameters by using an *Object Identifier* (OID) pointer. The functional PRCs also include the *"Next"* attribute to indicate the sequence of *diffserv* treatment for the packets (Fig. 2 illustrates a possible sequence). Fig. 3 shows an example of how the packets from a user are classified (by the IPfilter) and receives a specific policing treatment (by the Meter, TBParam and AlgDrop) and specific marking action (DSCPMark). The marking action is responsible for assigning an aggregated core class to the packets generated by the user.

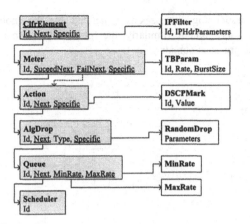

Fig. 2. Diffserv PIB overview

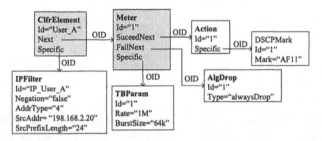

Fig. 3. Diffserv PIB configuration example

Considering the MIP scenario, a FA should contain the configuration of all possible mobile users that could be attached to its network. This approach, however, is understandably not practical. Therefore, the framework proposed in this paper adopts a dynamical configuration of the FAs, which is triggered by the authentication events generated by the HA. By analyzing the *diffserv* PIB structure, one observes that the configuration process can be significantly simplified if the PIB elements are classified into static and dynamic information. This approach, illustrated by Fig. 4, assumes that most users will share a small number of SLS definitions. The SLS definitions are represented by the "white PRCs" and are considered static information. The PRCs responsible for the SLS assignment (i.e., mapping a user to a SLS definition) are represented by the "dark PRCs" and are considered dynamic information. Because we have assumed that all tunnels are created between the FA and the HA, the mobile host is represented by its home address. The static information can be provisioned at the initialization of the FA. The dynamic information must be updated when mobile host moves from one FA domain to another. In this case, the FA in the incoming domain must receive the new filter information for associating the packets generated by the mobile host to the corresponding SLS assignment. Similarly, the filter information must be removed from the FA in the previous domain.

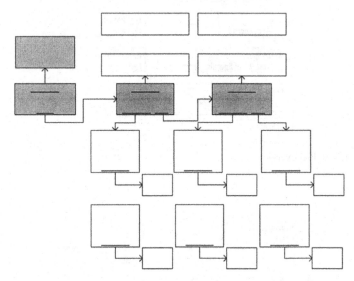

Fig. 4. Static and Dynamic PIB information

Fig. 5 illustrates how the PDP/PEP approach can be adapted to the MIP - *diffserv* environment. The *diffserv* routers are represented by the PEP agents. In a typical operation scenario, when the HA authenticates a binding request from a mobile host **(1)**, it sends a notification event to the PDP **(2)**. Then, by using the COPS-PR protocol, the PDP updates the configuration of the FA *diffserv* routers. In order to reduce the latency of the update process, a logical choice is to place the PDP in the same network as the HA.

The messages exchanged between the PDP and the PEPs are illustrated by Fig. 6. The first set of messages (1 to 5) corresponds to the initial provisioning process where a PEP requests the static PIB configuration. After this, the PDP sets the PIB's flag "FullState = False", informing the PEP that the subsequent DEC messages must be interpreted as updates (i.e., the PEP must not delete the previous PIB incarnation). The update process is implemented by a non-solicited decision message transmitted from the PDP to the PEP.

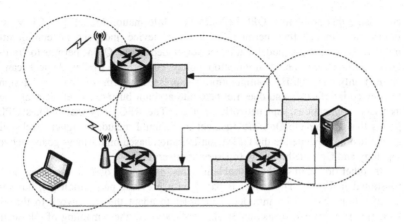

Fig. 5. Deployment Overview

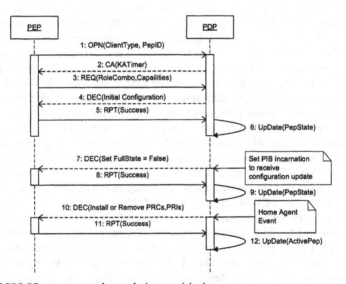

Fig. 6. COPS-PR messages exchange during provisioning process

4 Three-Layer Policy Model

An important problem that must be solved by a *diffserv* management framework is how to take into account the different QoS mechanisms implemented by the edge routers during the configuration process. An important IETF contribution for addressing this problem is QPIM (Policy QoS Information Model) [7]. QPIM is an information model that permits to describe device independent configuration policies. By defining a model that is not-device dependent, QPIM permits to "re-use" QoS configuration, i.e., configuration policy concerning similar devices can be defined only once. QPIM configuration is expressed in terms of "policies" assigned to "device interfaces", and does not take into account business level elements, such as users, applications, and network topology. The RFC 3644 that defines QPIM, points that a complete QoS management tool should include a higher level policy model that could generate the QPIM configuration based on business goals, network topology and QoS methodology (diffserv or intserv) [6].

In other to address these problems, this paper proposes a tree-layer model illustrated in Fig. 7. The model is based on a previous publication [5], but some modifications have been introduced in order to adapt the framework to the MIP scenario, as explained in section 3. The explanation in the remaining of this section follows the numbers in Fig. 7.

According with the strategy defined by the framework, an administrator defines a library of QPIM actions (1) corresponding to the SLS's that will be assigned to the users. In the high-level policy model (HLPM) (2), the administrator writes the business goals assigning SLSs (i.e., QPIM actions) to the customers in the managed environment. The HLPM extends the IETF PCIM/PCIMe model and supports the semantic: "User(s) accessing (an) Application(s) in (a) remote Server(s), from (an) access Network(s) receives a specific Service Level". Users, Applications and Network elements in a HLPM policy are expressed in terms of CIM objects (3) (see [2] for CIM and PCIM definitions). By using CIM associations, the HLPM defines also protocol and topology information, by assigning Users and Servers to IP addresses and Applications to protocols and transport layer ports.

The Translation Process (4) converts the high-level information into configuration policies, which are device independent (i.e. the configuration translates the desired QoS effect without specific mechanisms details, such as scheduler type or drop algorithm). For example, "The traffic with IPsrc=210.0.0.5 and port=21 receives BW=25%". The configuration-level policy model (CLPM) (5) is defined as a combination of PCIM/PCIMe and QPIM classes in order to support the representation of both elements in a device configuration: traffic identification (conditions) and traffic treatment (actions). Conditions are described in terms of IP header packet filters and actions are described in terms of QoS mechanisms, such as schedulers and drop algorithms. The CLPM includes also the mapping between the configuration policies and the device interface roles. This mapping is deduces from the topology information extracted from the HLPM. Both high-level and configuration model classes, as well as the translation process, are detailed in [5].

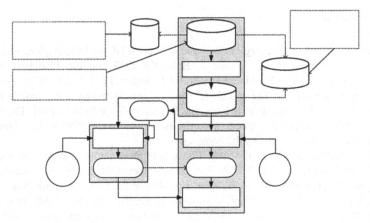

Fig. 7. Framework Overview

In the decision process **(6)**, the configuration policies are transformed to *diffserv* PIB instances **(7)**. This process is executed when the PDP receives a COPS-PR request message (REQ) **(5)** from the PEP asking for provisioning configuration. The REQ message includes two set of information that is used as input parameters in the decision process: (i) *RoleCombination*, which are labels associated to the managed device interfaces; (ii) *DeviceCapabilities*, describing the specific QoS mechanisms supported by the managed device. First the PDP uses *RoleCombination* for selecting the relevant policies for the managed device interface and second, the PDP converts the configuration policies into provisioning instances of the *diffserv* PIB, according to the set of *DeviceCapabilities*. The PIB information is generated from the QPIM configuration by a transformation process that takes into account the capabilities (i.e. supported QoS mechanisms) of the managed device.

In order to support mobility, the initial PIB provisioning generated by the REQ event **(5)** does not contain the filter definitions. Instead, it contains only the actions corresponding to the SLSs supported in a specific access network represented by the PEP. The filter definitions are generated as a response to a mobility event (i.e., an authentication event generated by the home agent [1]). An authentication event has two effects: First, it removes the corresponding filters entries from the PEP representing the previous network the user were registered. Second, it adds new filter entries to the PEP representing the new network the user has registered. A PIB can be partially updated by adding or removing PRIDs, which correspond to specific PIB information represented by unique identifies (OIDs).

Finally, the distribution process **(8)** consists in transmitting the *diffserv* PIB PRIDs using the COPS-PR protocol.

5 Evaluation

In order to evaluate the strategies discussed in Section IV, we have implemented the prototype illustrated in Fig. 5 and 7. Both, the PDP and the PEP have been implemented in Java and are hosted by an Intel Pentium IV, 1.5 GHz PC, running a Linux operating system. The Mobile IP software corresponding to the mobile host, foreign agent and home agent is based on the free code available on [8]. The code was modified in order to generate a notification event to the PDP when a binding update request is confirmed by the home agent.

As illustrated in Fig. 5, the same Linux host plays the role of *diffserv* router, mobile IP foreign agent and PEP. The diffserv mechanisms are implemented by using the "*linux traffic control*" facilities available on the Linux platform. Similarly, the host that implements the home agent also accumulates the role of *diffserv* router. The PDP is implemented on an independent machine, and communicates with the home agent through a socket interface. In the evaluation scenario, the MIP tunnel is created only between the home agent and the foreign agent. Tests have been implemented in order to evaluate the latency introduced by the diffserv PIB update process. Table 1 presents a summary of the average delay measured for the most important events related to the handoff process. The table results must be considered for comparison purposes only, since we have considered only a single hop between the FA and the HA, and Ethernet links of 10 Mbps for connecting the routers.

The messages in Table 1 have been captured at the home agent network. The only exception is the MIP advertisement messages, which have been captured at the mobile host. One observes that the total latency introduced from the moment the mobile node has its registration confirmed (4) to the moment the PEP reports that the PIB update have been installed into the device (6) is about 0.31 seconds. The most important latency is introduced by the MIP messages. According to the MIP standard [1], each mobile IP advertisement message has a lifetime field that defines for how long a foreign agent route must considered "active" in the absence of new advertisement messages. After a link layer handoff, the mobile host must wait for the previous foreign agent route lifetime expiration before starting the registration in the incoming network. The latency of 3.40 seconds between the handoff event and the registration request event is the result of a lifetime of 3 seconds (the default value in the MIP package implementation [8]). Considering that the lifetime field in the mobile IP advertisement messages is an integer number of seconds, the minimum expected lifetime is 1 second. The MIP standard defines that the mobile advertisement messages must be transmitted in intervals of 1/3 of the defined lifetime.

Table 1. Average time between the events related to the Mobile's IP handoff process

Event	Elapsed Time [s]	Message Size [bytes]
1. Network Layer Handoff	0.00	-
2. Third Mobile IP Advertisement Message	3.21	67
3. Mobile Registration Request (at HA)	3.40	236
4. Mobile Registration Reply (at HA)	3.42	275
5. COPS Decision (DEC) Message	3.49	538
6. COPS Report State (RPT) Message	3.73	90

6 Related Works

There are a growing number of significant works relating QoS management of mobile users. Generally speaking, these works can be classified into two major groups: those addressing micro-mobility and those addressing macro-mobility. Micro-mobility and macro-mobility are defined as changes of access point association (attachment) while a session is in progress. Micro-mobility is the simplest form of mobility. The subscriber is moving within a single domain, where, usually, mobility is handled at the link layer level. Macro-mobility involves moving between two domains, where the link layer facilities are not sufficient for keeping a transparent session to the subscriber. The work in this paper can be classified as addressing the Macro-mobility issue only.

While the work in this paper adopts a provisioning approach, some works address the QoS issue by proposing a signaling protocol for providing QoS on demand. The authors in [9] propose a new signaling protocol allowing mobile users to contact a differentiated bandwidth broker for QoS negotiation. The work presented in [10] proposes a mobility-aware QoS signaling architecture that integrates resource management with mobility management to provide the necessary QoS on demand in mobile wireless networks. It is based on a domain resource manager concept and support anticipated handover with pre-reservation of resources before the mobile node is attached to the new access point.

Our proposal adopts the *diffserv* QoS methodology. There are some proposals adopting a combination of *intserv* (Integrated Service) and *diffserv* methodologies. For example, to negotiate *QoS* specification in macro mobility, [11] proposes an end-to-end QoS provisioning architecture, combining both *diffserv* and *intserv* QoS methodologies. The BRAIN European project [12] and its successor the MIND [13] project proposed an access network that provides seamless mobility and QoS for different applications, ranging from best effort services to services with hard QoS requirements, such as IP telephony. The BRAIN QoS architecture is based on the *intserv* and *diffserv* architectures. The fundamental concept is to use *intserv* parameters and RSVP signaling to communicate application requirements to the connecting network, and to provide the actual service differentiation with the diffserv scheme. Extensions to the basic architecture have been designed to enable enhanced support for mobility and QoS, although lacking a SLA support.

7 Conclusion

This paper has presented framework for supporting the diffserv configuration in mobile IP based networks. The proposal is based on IETF standards, concerning diffserv configuration, where the most important elements are the PIB *diffserv* and the COPS-PR protocol. Our study shows that both, the PIB and COPS-PR offer enough flexibility for addressing the mobility problem without introducing new protocols or modification on the existing standards. Our work has proposed a strategy for updating the *diffserv* configuration by exploring the PIB structure, where the QoS action mechanisms are provisioned at the initialization of the *diffserv* edge routers and the filter definitions (i.e., SLS assignments) are updated dynamically as a response to the registration confirmation event generated by the home agent. The strategy is very simple to implement and introduce a relatively low latency in the configuration process, when compared with the latency introduced by the MIP handoff process. Future works will evaluate the strategy considering larger environments in order to estimate possible bottlenecks related to the PDP performance.

References

1. Perkins C (1996), ed, "IP Mobility Support", IETF RFC 2002.
2. Schnizlein J, Strassner J, Scherling M, Quinn B, Herzog S, Huynh A, Carlson M, Perry J, Waldbusser S (2001) "Terminology for Policy-Based Management", IETF RFC 3198.
3. Chan K, Sahita R, Hahn S, McCloghrie K (2003) "Differentiated Services Quality of Service Policy Information Base", IETF RFC 3317.
4. Chan K, Seligson J, Durham D, Gai S, McCloghrie K, Herzog S, Reichmeyer F, Yavatkar R, Smith A (2001) "COPS Usage for Policy Provisioning (COPS-PR)", IETF RFC 3084.
5. Beller A, Jamhour E, Pellenz M (2004) "Defining Reusable Business-Level QoS Policies for DiffServ", Proceedings of Distributed Systems Operations and Management WorkShop, pp 40-51.
6. Blake S, Black D, Carlson M (1998) "An Architecture for Differentiated Services", IETF RFC 2475.
7. Snir Y, Ramberg Y, Strassner J, Cohen R, Moore B (2003) "Policy Quality of Service (QoS) Information Model", IETF RFC 3644.
8. Andersson B, Malinen J, Forsberg D, Kari H, Hautio J, Mustonen K, Weckström T, "Dynamics Mobile IP", http://dynamics.sourceforge.net/.
9. Braun T, Stattenberger G (2001) "Providing Differentiated Services to Mobile IP Users", The 26th Annual IEEE Conference on Local Computer Networks (LCN'2001), Tampa, USA.
10. Bless R, Zitterbart M, Hillebrand J, Prehofer C (2003) "Quality-of-Service Signaling in Wireless IP-based Mobile Networks", VTC2003-Fall, Orlando, FL, USA.
11. Pack S, Choi Y (2001) "An End-to-End QoS Provisioning Architecture in Mobile Network", in Proc. International Symposium on Communications and Information Technologies (ISCIT) 2001, Chiangmai, Tailand.
12. IST-1999-10050 BRAIN, Broadband Radio Access for IP-based Networks, www.istbrain.org.
13. IST-2000-28584 MIND, Mobile IP-based Network Developments, www.ist-mind.org.

Towards a global autonomic management and integration of heterogeneous networks and multimedia services

Anasser Ag Rhissa and Adil Hassnaoui

GET INT, CNRS Samovar
Institut National des Télécoms, 9 Rue charles Fourier 91011 Evry (FRANCE)
anasser.ag-rhissa@int-evry.fr, adil.hassnaoui@int-evry.fr

Abstract. Traditionally, networks and systems are manually managed. It usually takes one or more human operators to manage all aspects of a dynamically evolving computing and communicating system. The operator is tightly integrated in this management process, and his tasks range from defining high-level policies to executing low-level system commands for immediate problem solving. Although this form of human-in-the-loop management was appropriate in the past, it has become increasingly unsuitable for modern networked computing systems and telecommunication. The potential advantage that autonomic computing brings is reducing the cost and complexity of managing Information and Communication Technology Infrastructure(ICT).

The objectives of this paper are to underline the characteristics of autonomic architectures and present an outline of our autonomic management architecture based on OGSA (Open Grid Services Architecture) and Peer-to-Peer model. The autonomic management architectures of CISCO and IBM are briefly described and compared with our autonomic management architecture.

Keywords : Autonomic Computing, Grid computing, OGSA, Self-management, Autonomic Management, Peer-to-Peer, Global QoS management.

1 Introduction

Autonomic computing is a new paradigm with a goal to give systems the ability to manage themselves and dynamically adapt to change in accordance with business policies and objectives. Self-managing systems can perform management activities based on situations they observe or sense in the ICT (Information and Communication Technology) environment.

Like their biological origins, autonomic systems will maintain and adjust their operations in the face of changing components, workloads, demands and hardware or software failures. The autonomic system might continually monitor its own use, check for component upgrades for example and reconfigure itself if necessary. When it detects errors, the system will revert to the older version

Please use the following format when citing this chapter:

Rhissa, A.A. and Hassnaoui, A., 2007, in IFIP International Federation for Information Processing, Volume 229, Network Control and Engineering for QoS, Security, and Mobility, IV, ed. Gaïti, D., (Boston: Springer), pp. 199–207.

while its automatic problem-determination algorithms try to isolate the source of the error.

Nowadays in most of management systems the adaptation to change situations in accordance with business policies are not autonomic, and they don't generally manage themselves. In order to do so, autonomic architectures are needed.

This paper is organized as follow. After an introduction, the second section introduces the characteristics of autonomic architectures and the link with OGSA. The third section introduces our autonomic management architecture based on Peer-to-Peer model. A comparison between our autonomic architecture, OGSA and the autonomic architectures of IBM and CISCO is made in the fourth section. Conclusion and perspectives are given in the last section.

2 Control loop and characteristics of autonomic architectures.

An autonomic system is made of a connected set of autonomic elements that contain resources and deliver services to humans and other autonomic elements. Autonomic elements will manage their internal behaviors and their relationships with other autonomic elements in accordance with policies that humans or other elements have established [7].

Autonomic architecture consists of a set of systems that are self-configuring (with autonomic configuration and adjustment), self-healing (with autonomic detection, diagnosis and repair of local problems), self-protecting (with autonomic protection and anticipation of problems) and self-optimizing (with autonomic improvement of performance and efficiency) [6].

The role of autonomic element consists on providing its services and managing its own behavior. To do so autonomic element monitors behavior through sensors, analyzes those data, then planes what action(s) should be taken, and executes that (those) action(s) through effectors. That creates a control loop [7] which allows to manage the systems (see figure 1).

The biggest challenge in an autonomic architecture is to build closed control loops, the most important concept of self-management.

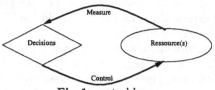

Fig. 1. control loop.

Autonomic computing proposes a solution for self-management system based on a service-oriented architectural approach such as Web services or OGSA infrastructure. OGSA combines web services and grid computing with open interfaces, it can be seen [5] as an extension and a refinement of the emerging Web Services architecture. By combining these two approaches (autonomic computing and OGSA), the autonomic computing profits from the advantages of OGSA such as computational capacity, virtualization, higher QoS, great availability and allows to integrate service mobility in management operations.

3   PARIS: our generic and autonomic management architecture

3.1   Overview of our architecture

At GET INT, the research works related to AGIRS [1] [2] [3] [4] has designed a generic architecture for the autonomic management of the heterogeneous networks and services, named PARIS (Platform for the autonomic Administration of netwoRks and Integration of multimedia Services). As depicted in figure 2, this architecture is divided into three generic classes.

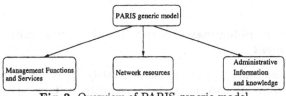

Fig. 2. Overview of PARIS generic model

The main components of PARIS are:

- *Administrative information :* This information shows the management resources use, like the services profile, the managers availability and the state of the managed resources. Therefore, this class helps the administrators to manage complex networks by providing strategic information to the organization and by defining management policies, in order to provide them a dynamic network management.
- *Management functions and services :* This class gathers all the necessary resources only for management.
- *Network resources :* This class represents the resources which are managed by the services of management system.

The components of PARIS are organized in three-layers. The bottom level represents physical devices such as switches, routers and hosts, as well as logical services such as VLANs, IP networks, file servers, and web services.

The medium level represents the autonomic management level which gathers all the necessary resources for autonomic management services. The top level is dedicated to SLS (Service Level Specification) and administrative information.

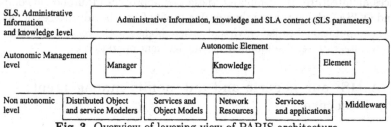

Fig. 3. Overview of layering view of PARIS architecture

In the bottom level (see figure 3), composed with non autonomic resources, services, applications and systems, we use OGSA for virtualisation, self-healing, computational and middleware capabilities. So, for the autonomic level (level 2) all the resources of layer 3 are considered as services and are transparents.

In order to deliver an integrated service to customers the different interconnected service providers must cooperate through their management domains using their business policies and objectives.

3.2   Global QoS policy based network and services autonomic management

Our QoS criterias are flexibility, scalability, safety, delay, jitter, mainly availability and survivability. According to the comparison (table 1) between P2P and hierarchical architectures, we have choosen an hybrid architecture for our autonomic management architecture.

Criterias / Architecture	P2P	Hierarchical
Response time	Slow/Medium	Fast
Survivability, Availability, Reliability	High	Low/medium
Scalability, Flexibility, Safety	High	low
Load for policy exchange	High	low
Manager between domains	No	Yes
Organization	Dynamic	Static

Table 1. Comparison between P2P and Hierarchical architectures.

The global QoS Policy management is based on a peer-to-peer approach (Peer-to-Peer QoS cooperation) between different operators' policy domains and a hierarchical approach in an operator's policy domain. An end-to-end QoS negotiation will take place to achieve the global business and policy goals.

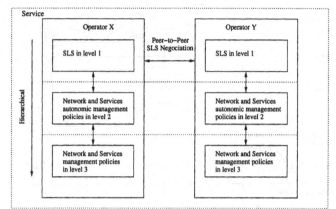

Fig. 4. Global QoS policy based services and network management.

The figure 4 shows an overview of the global QoS policy based services and network management. It represents the peer-to-peer and hierarchical approach management. The following figures will describe these approaches in more details. In an operator's domain, management functions are organized in three levels. The top level contains global management policy and SLS parameters to negotiate with other operators. Once the two operators agreed, The SLA is transmitted to the second level (autonomic level) for enforcement then to the third level (non-autonomic level).

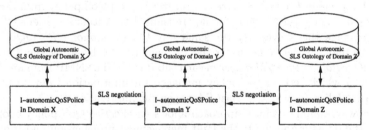

I-autonomicQoSPolice : Inter-domains autonomic QoS policy agent/manager.
Fig. 5. Peer-to-Peer QoS policy cooperation between different operators Domains.

The figure 5 highlights the QoS policy cooperation between the *Inter-domains-autonomicQoSPolicy Agents/Managers* of each operator domain : Each *I-autonomicQoSPolice* in one domain negotiates SLS parameters with other peer domains according to the global QoS Objectives.

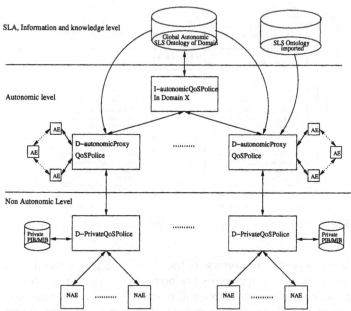

Fig. 6. Hierarchical QoS policy cooperation in an operator Domain.

In the hierarchical approach (see figure 6) we distinguish clearly the three levels of an operator's domain. The *I-autonomicQoSPolice* interacts with the SLS ontology in the Administrative information and SLS level to get the global QoS policy and manage the *Domains-AutonomicProxyQoSPolicy Agent/Manager*. Each *D-autonomicProxyQoSPolice* can recover its own QoS policy from the SLS ontology of the operator's domain and transmit it to Autonomic Element (AE) which manage themselves. By the same way the *D-autonomicProxyQoSpolice* allows to manage the Non-Autonomic Element (NAE) by using the *Domain-PrivateQoSPolicy Agent/Manager* of each sub-domain (i.e SNMP Domain, TMN Domain...) which recover the policy management information from its private PIB/MIB(Policy Information Base/Management Information Base).

This way, the hierarchical approach allows an effective QoS policy cooperation in the domain and limits the fault management propagation and topology changes.

3.3   Semantic negotiation using SLS ontology

In this scenario, we will consider a virtual web hosting, on our P2P architecture, in which clients negotiate their services parameters using a web services ontology (specification of the conceptualization as a hierarchy of concepts).

The web services ontology used contains a generic part about web services standard characteristics and a specific (local) one. For example, in the generic part, a web service belongs to a community service which is provided by a (or a set of) service provider(s). The QoS (Quality of Service) provided to the clients could be one or many of the following SLS parameters: availability, security, reliability,..., survivability. In the local part of this ontology, we have web hosting specific parameters such as operating system, transfer rate and storage disk space. A file SLAC(Service level Agrement Configuration) is used by the clients to negotiate their SLA contract using policies.

4 comparison between autonomic management architectures

In this section, we compare (see table 2) the autonomic computing Initiative (ACI) of IBM, the Adaptive Service Framework (ASF) of CISCO and the Open Grid Service Architecture (OGSA) with our architecture PARIS.

4.1 Comparison between ASF, ACI & OGSA.

The autonomic computing Initiative (ACI) of IBM is based on the control loop and the four area of self-management. Cisco and IBM, made the decision to collaborate on an Adaptive Services Framework (ASF) [8] based on the Adaptive Network Care (ANC) of CISCO and the Autonomic Computing Initiative(ACI) of IBM [7].

ASF is a set of proposed interfaces and formats that allow customers to interact with service providers.

The SSP (Support Service Provider) acts as a proxy (mediation gateway) to achieve the actions of the autonomic manager for integrating multiple vendors services.

ASF (CISCO/IBM) and ACI (IBM) architectures are based on service oriented architecture and they use similar standards to develop Web services. However the ASF framework proposes five levels of security (Authentication, Authorization, Encryption, Data Privacy, Signature) contrary to ACI and OGSA (which represents several gaps of security).

In table 2, it appears that our autonomic management architecture PARIS is more suitable to take into account business needs of ICT and telecom managers, in term of global governance of their information systems, to support semantic and autonomic negotiation of configuration and services parameters and to permit self-organization in an operator's peer domain by using shared administrative information, ontology and self-governing capabilities of autonomic elements.

Criterias / Architecture	OGSA(GGF)	ACI(IBM)	ASF(CISCO)	PARIS (INT/AGIRS)
Self-configuring	-	+	+	+
Self-healing	+	+	+	+
Self-protecting	-	+/-	+	+/-
Self-optimizing	-	+	+	+
Services oriented Architecture and virtualization	+	+	+	+
Taking into account business needs of ICT and telecom managers: Global governance	-	-	-	+
Taking into account mobility and nomadisme	+/-	+/-	+/-	+/-
Complete self-organization, dynamic and end-to-end Qos management	-	+/-	+/-	+/-
Interface with non autonomic environment and complete integration	+/-	-	+	+/-
Semantic and automatic negotiation of configuration and services parameters	-	-	-	+

Table 2. Comparison between OGSA and autonomic management architectures.

4.2   Advantages of our autonomic management architecture

The global P2P management architecture in our administrative information and SLS layer supports *concurrent* multi-manager control of network elements. The regrouping of manager-element roles improves *safety* by eliminating the state synchronization problem between managers and elements. The replacement of management agents by Autonomic Management Elements improves reliability through reductions in the size and complexity of implementing managed network services. The P2P management architecture also provides scalable monitoring and control of network elements. Management functions can be safely distributed across multiple managers due to the protection of transactional concurrency control. The unification of the manager and element roles in a peering relation enables the delegation of management functions, effectively distributing management load and supports *self-healing* in the face of local network failures.

This new peer-to-peer architecture benefits from the advantage of both approaches, autonomic computing and peer-to-peer, in order to allow an autonomic and dynamic management and to provide to the user a service with a satisfactory quality of service (availability).

5   Conclusion and Prospective work

Current network management functions will not be able to support the growing of networked devices and complex dependencies created by new web-based services architectures. The proposed peer-to-peer autonomic management architecture offers several advantages over the traditional manager-agent (client-server) architecture by creating a flexible, scalable, reliable and survivable environment supporting safe multi-manager access. The unification of the traditional roles of manager and element allows management functions to be distributed in different elements supporting autonomic behavior.

In the future we plane to highly distribute a P2P repository of our architecture to support scalable operations as well as recovery after failures. Future research will determine the granularity of distribution (service, node, Autonomic Element...), will extend the security and mobility management aspects and will details the complete integration of non-autonomic devices, such as hubs, switches, etc. The other points of our research will be to define exactly how autonomic elements interact between themselves to allow a cooperation and learning in autonomic environment and how to make possible a complete self-organization in autonomic environments of extended operators, virtual organizations and enterprises.

References

1. A. Ag Rhissa, AGIRS project, Web technologies and information systems, Scientific meeting of GET at ENST Paris, october 14, 2004.
2. A. Ag-Rhissa, A. Hassnaoui, Global self-management of network and telecommunication information systems and services. IEEE/SITIS'05, November 27th - December 1st, 2005.
3. F. Benayoune et L. Lancieri, Models of Co-operations in Peer-to-Peer Networks-A Survey , 3rd European Conference on Universal Multiservice Networks, Vol. 3262: 327-336, 2004.
4. F. Benayoune, Adaptive management of content services for new generations of mobile networks, ongoing work of PhD thesis, Directors of thesis: A. Ag Rhissa et P. Vincent, INT/AGIRS and France Télécom R&D Caen, 2004.
5. I. Foster and C. Kesselman and J. Nick and al., The Physiology of the Grid: An Open Grid Services Architecture for Distributed Systems Integration, Globus Project, 2002.
6. K. Herrmann, G. Muhl and K. Geihs, Self Management: The Solution to Complexity or Just Another Problem?, in the IEEE DISTRIBUTED SYSTEMS ONLINE, Vol. 6, No. 1, 2005.
7. J. Kephart and D.M. Chess., The vision of autonomic computing, in the IEEE Computer Journal, Vol. 36: 41-50, 2003.
8. T. Studwell and K. Sankar, Adaptive Services Framework, Wd-asf-1.00, 2003.

Towards an Adaptive and Intelligent MPLS Network

Rana Rahim-Amoud, Leila Merghem-Boulahia, and Dominique Gaiti
ISTIT, University of Technology of Troyes
12, rue Marie Curie, BP 2060, 10 010 TROYES CEDEX, FRANCE
{rana.amoud, leila.boulahia, dominique.gaiti}@utt.fr,
WWW home page: http://www.utt.fr/labos/LM2S/

Abstract. The Multi-Protocol Label Switching (MPLS) is an Internet Engineering Task Force (IETF) framework. It is a versatile solution to address the problems faced by present-day networks like speed, scalability and traffic engineering. However, the Quality of Service (QoS) management of MPLS is made by static methods. In this paper, we propose a solution based on Multi-Agent Systems (MAS) to manage the QoS into MPLS by adequate adaptive methods.

1 Introduction

The Multi-Protocol Label Switching (MPLS) [10] is a new technology that integrates the label-swapping paradigm with network-layer routing. This means that it uses labels, instead of IP addresses, to forward packets.

MPLS network provides more advantages than the traditional IP networks like the Traffic Engineering (TE) [3]. With the use of TE, MPLS provides a considerable efficient traffic control [11] more than the traditional OSPF or IS-IS. In addition, MPLS provides the Virtual Private Networks [5] which are currently the most selected by a wide range of costumers to provide private services, etc. Many protocols can be used to distribute labels, LDP (Label Distribution Protocol) [1], CR-LDP (Constraint based–LDP) [2] and RSVP-TE [4]. With these previous features, the MPLS management is not as simple as a traditional management function.

As network conditions frequently change, the network must be able to recognize and adapt itself to the running traffic conditions in order to choose the most appropriate algorithm to be used.

In line with this, recent researches showed the effectiveness of Multi-Agent System (MAS) for the dynamic management of distributed systems. This explains our tendency to use a Multi-Agent System to introduce some decision-making abilities in the complex network management tasks.

Please use the following format when citing this chapter:

Rahim-Amoud, R., Merghem-Boulahia, L. and Gaiti, D., 2007, in IFIP International Federation for Information Processing, Volume 229, Network Control and Engineering for QoS, Security, and Mobility, IV, ed. Gaïti, D., (Boston: Springer), pp. 209–214.

This paper is organized as follows. We first find the decision points into MPLS, and then we present our proposed architecture. Finally, we make a brief conclusion.

2   The actual weakness of MPLS

Currently, the actual weakness of MPLS resides in its inability to provide application-level routing intelligence, which is a fundamental component especially for voice delivery [9].

Voice over IP (VoIP) is a critical application that requires intelligent routing alternation on the call level to prevent latency, delay, packet loss and jitter and this cannot be provided by MPLS.

Adapting MPLS to VoIP traffic necessitates the distinction of different traffic types. Some solutions, which couple MPLS with DiffServ or RSVP, were proposed to solve MPLS limitations.

DiffServ over MPLS, according to [9], is able to provide end-to-end solution for MPLS only if the entire traversed path is controlled by a single entity. Most importantly, "DiffServ does nothing to solve the static route problem of MPLS" [9] while it introduces complexity into the architecture.

The implementation of RSVP with MPLS enables the reservation of bandwidth on a router for each LSP. In this way, it is possible to prevent an overbooking in the router from the start. However it does nothing to solve the fluctuating demands of VoIP.

Even with these proposed solutions, MPLS remains unable to guarantee the QoS of incoming traffic, so it is very essential to find another solution. Our proposition is based on the introduction of an MAS within the MPLS domain, to do that, we must first find the positions in which the intelligent agents will be introduced. These positions are the MPLS decision points.

3   MPLS Decision points

One of the most important steps of our research is to find the MPLS decision points. Once found, we can add our agents within these points.

3.1   The first MPLS decision point

Different types of traffic flows arrive to the entry of the MPLS domain. The classification of the packets is done just at the entry of the domain by the I-LSR (Ingress-Label Switch Router), by assigning a particular packet to a particular FEC (Forwarding Equivalence Class). Within the domain, there is no reclassification, packets are just switched.

Currently the most used criteria to build FEC is based on the prefix or the destination address, by taking advantage from the aggregation of flows that have the same destination. Aggregation may reduce the number of labels which are needed to handle a particular set of packets. However, it does not take into account the type of traffic, and degrades as a result the network performance.

We propose to introduce an intelligent agent on the level of each I-LSR router which is an efficient and a pertinent decision point. This agent will have as a role to examine the incoming flows and to create for each type of traffic a different FEC and consequently a different LSP, even for traffics which have the same destination.

As each E-LSR (Egress-LSR) is at the same time an I-LSR for the packets forwarded in the opposite direction, then our agent will be introduced on the level of each LER (Label Edge Router) within the MPLS domain, and consequently we obtain a Multi-Agent System (Fig .1).

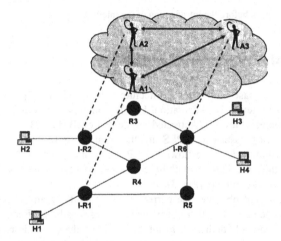

Fig. 1. Introducing an MAS in an MPLS domain

3.2   The second MPLS decision point

According to [6], an LSR is capable of label merging if it can receive two packets from different incoming interfaces, and/or with different labels, and send both packets on the same outgoing interface with the same label.

In the following example (Fig. 2), if LSR R6 was merge-capable, it simply would act as an E-LSR to upstream neighbors and as Merge LSR to downstream neighbors [6]. Then, it would perform aggregation of requests from upstream neighbors R1 and R2, reducing as a result the label consumption within the MPLS Network. To do the aggregation, flows must be in the same FEC.

Furthermore, label merging causes a small delay because it is designed for IP traffic and need not to be used for delay-sensitive traffic.

Our proposal is to introduce an agent on the level of the LSR R6 having for role to activate the merge-capable of R6 when traffic is not delay-sensitive and to deactivate it in other cases. As a consequence, the two LSP will be aggregated into only one LSP from their point of intersection.

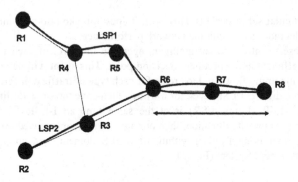

Fig. 2. LSP attribution before the introduction of the intelligent agent

4   MPLS Multi-Agent System Model

Our approach is based on the architecture developed in [7]. It is two-level architecture: The level 1 (Adaptation Level) contains the Master agent which monitors the agents of level 0 (Activated Protocols Level) (Fig. 3).

The most critical issues in MPLS are the creation of LSP, the aggregation of flows, the distribution of these flows to LSP taking into account their natures, etc. According to this, the level 0 will be composed of several agents: LSP Creator Agent, Aggregator Agent, etc (Fig. 3).

The Master Agent observes the current router conditions and chooses the most appropriate protocols to the other agents under its responsibility. Each agent of level 0 has a set of protocols dedicated to the task it is in charge of. For example, LSP Creator agent establishes some rules for selecting which label distribution protocol to use under which circumstances.

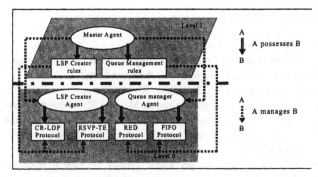

Fig. 3. Two-level MAS architecture

Each Master Agent possesses a set of rules allowing to select the appropriate protocols to activate, and therefore to select the best actions to execute. These rules respond to a set of events and trigger the actions which affect the protocols supervised by that Master Agent.

Their role is to manage a set of protocols in order to provide the best functioning of the node and to avoid incoherent decisions within the same node. These rules give the node the means to guarantee that the set of actions executed, at every moment, by its agents are coherent, in addition to be the most relevant to the current situation [8]. In order to minimize conflict situations, rules are organized in separate modules following the task they are interested in (Fig. 3 shows an example).

The Master Agent actions adapt the node's protocols and may consist in: letting the protocol running, modifying the internal functioning of the protocol, inhibiting the protocol, activating the protocol.

The actions undertaken by the node have local consequences but may influence the decisions of the other nodes. In fact, by sending messages bringing new information on the sender node's state, a receiver's Master Agent rule may be triggered. This can involve a change within the receiver node (the inhibition of an activated protocol, or the activation of another one, etc.). This change may have repercussions on other nodes, and so forth until the entire network becomes affected.

This dynamic process aims to adapt the network to new conditions and takes advantage of the agents' abilities to alleviate the global system. We argue that these agents will achieve an optimal adaptive management process because of the following two points: (1) each agent holds different processes (protocols and adaptive selection of these protocols) allowing to take the most relevant decision at every moment; (2) the agents are implicitly cooperative in the sense that they possess rules that take account of the neighbors' state in the process of protocols' selection.

5 Conclusions and future work

This paper presents the first step towards an adaptive and intelligent MPLS network. As QoS management configuration may not be suitable for all traffic scenarios, a solution is required in order to respond to this challenge, improve the network performance and satisfy users' requests. Our proposed solution is based on Multi-Agent Systems. Future work in this area should explicitly address the agents' rules in our two-level model improving as a result our architecture. Once defined we will move to make a testbed.

Finance: PhD research supported in part by "Conseil Régional Champage-Ardenne" (district grant) and the European Social Fund.

References

1. Anderson L, Doolan P, Feldman N, Fredette A, Thomas B (2001) LDP Specification. Network Working Group, RFC3036
2. Ash J, Girish M, Gray E, Jamoussi B, Wright G (2002) Applicability Statement for CR-LDP. Network Working Group, RFC3036

3. Awduche D O (1999) MPLS and traffic engineering in IP networks, IEEECommunications Magazine, vol. 37, no.12, pp. 42-47
4. Awduche D, Berger L, Gan D, Li T, Srinivaan V, Swallow G (2001) RSVP-TE Extensions to RSVP for LSP Tunnels. Network Working Group, RFC3209
5. Carter SF (2005) Quality of service in BT's MPLS-VPN platform. BT TECHNOLOGY JOURNAL 23 (2): pp. 61-72
6. Fredette A, White C, Andersson L, Doolan P (1997) Stream Aggregation. Work in progress, draft-fredette-mpls-aggregation-00.txt
7. Merghem L, Lecarpentier H (2002) Agents: A Solution for Telecommunication Network Simulation. NetCon'2002. Kluwer Academic publishers, pp.165-176. Paris, France.
8. Merghem, L., Gaïti, D., Pujolle, G.: On Using Agents in End to End Adaptive Monitoring. E2EMon Workshop, in conjunction with MMNS'2003. Lecture Notes in Computer Science, Vol. 2839. Belfast, Northern Ireland (2003) 422-435
9. PRIMEDIA Business Magazines & Media Inc., available at: http://infocus.telephonyonline.com/ar/telecom_questioning_mpls/ (2003)
10. Rosen E, Viswanathan A, Callon R (2001) Multiprotocol Label Switching Architecture. RFC3031, IETF
11. Xiao X., Hannan A., Bailey B. et Ni L., « Traffic engineering with MPLS in the Internet », IEEE Network Magazine, pp. 28-33, Mar. 2000.

MULTICAST GROUP AUTHENTICATION

Ritesh Mukherjee, J. William Atwood

Department of Computer Science and Software Engineering, Concordia University, Montreal, Canada

E-mail: mukherj@cse.concordia.ca, bill@cse.concordia.ca

Abstract.
Multicast is an attractive mechanism for delivering data to multiple receivers over the Internet as it saves bandwidth. However the delivery of copyrighted data over the Internet requires it to be encrypted to render the data useless for eavesdroppers or illegal users. Authentication is necessary to ensure that the received packet is sent by the actual sender. Message integrity is necessary to ensure that the packet was not changed by an attacker while in transit. The network must be able to perform these tasks even if packets are dropped, rearranged, changed or injected into the stream. This paper presents an efficient scheme for multicast authentication and to check multicast message integrity when asymmetric keys are used to protect the data. The proposal is validated using SPIN, which uses PROMELA to design the validation model.

1. INTRODUCTION

IP multicast is a bandwidth saving technology for the delivery of high bandwidth multimedia content over the Internet. Multicast replaces multiple packets over a shared link addressed to individual receivers with a single packet addressed to a group. This large saving in bandwidth makes multicast the desired choice of packet delivery when a large number of receivers are involved as is the case in applications such as pay-per-view TV, online games, stocks and news feeds, etc.

Please use the following format when citing this chapter:

Mukherjee, R. and Atwood, J.W., 2007, in IFIP International Federation for Information Processing, Volume 229, Network Control and Engineering for QoS, Security, and Mobility, IV, ed. Gaïti, D., (Boston: Springer), pp. 215–230.

For the delivery of copyrighted and confidential data it is necessary to encrypt packets. This makes it necessary to deliver a decryption key to a potentially large number of receivers. Solutions for multicast key management and distribution such as GKMP [1] [2], SKMD [3], IOLUS [4], Broadcast Encryption [5] and SIM-KM [6] [7] have been proposed.

In addition to the requirement to distribute keys securely, multicast authentication is necessary to ensure that
• the received packets actually originated from a legitimate sender.
• the received packets were not modified while in transit.
• packets sent by an adversary are not mistaken as legitimate packets.

Multicast authentication is important when receiving news feeds, stock quotes or when watching pay-per-view TV. These kinds of applications require low-cost, highly efficient packet authentication. Consider a TV station, such as ESPN broadcasting sporting events live. The TV station is broadcasting to thousands of receivers where people are logged in watching the telecast. The users would want to ensure that the broadcast is from ESPN rather than a malicious third party transmitting offensive material. Another scenario could be a different brokerage houses receiving stock quotes from the New York Stock Exchange (NYSE) for their agents and displaying it to their clients through their respective brokerage house websites. Also online newspapers could receive quotes from the stock exchange and display it on their websites for the general public. The brokerage house and newspapers around the world would like to ensure that the quotes they are receiving have not been tampered with. A host of other scenarios can be envisaged where multicast authentication is imperative such as online teaching, soft-ware updates, company broadcasts, etc. These services all have a one sender-multiple receiver model. In fact multicast has the maximum bandwidth saving ad-vantage when there are thousands of receivers and very few senders.

From a key multicast key management perspective, many of the key management schemes use the multicast protocol itself for re-keying and this requires that the key distribution packets be authenticated otherwise an adversary may sent bogus re-key packets and disrupt the service.

In this paper we present a technique for performing multicast packet authentication and a message integrity check when asymmetric keys are used to protect the data. As an example, we will show how our technique can provide group authentication when used with SIM-KM. Our method may also be used independently with any asymmetric key distribution scheme. It uses symmetric message authentication codes (MACs) to add data source authentication to secure group communication. Section 2 describes the related work that has been done in this area. Section 3 describes the challenges associated with multicast packet authentication. Section 4 gives an overview of SIM-KM. Section 5 presents our multicast authentication and message integrity check. Section 6 analyzes the protocol against known attacks. Section 7 compares the scheme to other available schemes. Section 8 discusses the construction of a validation model using PROMELA and the validation of this model using SPIN. Section 9 contains the concluding remarks.

2. RELATED WORK

There have been a few approaches to multicast authentication. In this section we present an overview of some of the approaches.

One approach is to use MACs where the group members share a secret key and a MAC is included in every packet. In this scheme any group member can spoof packets. To avoid this each receiver can be given a secret key and the sender can have all such keys. The sender now has to add a MAC for each receiver. This scheme is prone to collusion attacks and the size of each packet increases with the number of receivers resulting in enormous communication overhead. The Multiple MACs scheme [8] is not scalable and suffers from large communication overhead. Timed Efficient Stream Loss-tolerant Authentication (TESLA) [9] has low communication overhead but requires time synchronization between senders and receivers, which is difficult to maintain in large groups.

Another approach is to use digital signatures. As this is a computationally intensive operation schemes work with fast signature techniques and amortize a signature operation over several packets [10] but this scheme does not tolerate packet loss. BiBa [11] is a fast individual packet authentication signature scheme but re-quires time synchronization between sender and receivers, which limits the authentication rate and also suffers from communication overhead. A Merkle hash tree [12] can be used for authentication and the scheme is tolerant to packet loss but has enormous communication overhead. Erasure codes [13] can also be used for authentication. The scheme performs encoding twice to reduce communication overhead but the scheme fails if a single packet is injected. Graph-based authentication schemes amortize a signature over a hash chain in such a way so as to tolerate packet loss. Hashes can be inserted in strategic locations to make it resistant to a burst loss [14]. In general, graph-based schemes offer probabilistic security guarantee. They do not consider adversarial packet losses caused by attackers. RSA Digital Signature Algorithm can be used for authentication [15]. This scheme is prone to replay attacks and requires use of the RSA signature algorithm which is very costly in terms of processing time.

Each of the schemes for multicast authentication present today suffers from one at least of these drawbacks:

- They are computationally very expensive hence they cannot be used with a wide variety of devices. With the widespread use of PDAs, wireless devices, Internet enabled mobile phones and other low power devices with limited re-sources it becomes infeasible to use computationally intensive techniques for the kinds of applications multicast is targeting such as stock updates.
- They introduce a large overhead communication overhead. With the ever in-creasing use of audio and video streams bandwidth is limited. Wireless net-works also have limited bandwidth. It is unacceptable to clog the network with enormous communication overhead.
- They require time synchronization between the sender and the receivers. With the receivers located at different locations for applications such as online stock quotes, pay-per-view TV, etc., it becomes difficult to maintain time synchronization between the sender and the receivers. Wireless devices are mobile and their distances changes, which changes the network propagation delay frequently. This requires constant resynchronization of the sender and the receivers making it impossible to maintain the service efficiently.
- They are prone to collusion attacks. While senders are few (in most cases it is only a single sender group) and are highly trusted, the receivers cannot be trusted not to form collusions and share keys. Hence it is unreasonable to accept a solution where receivers can spoof one another.

None of these schemes uses the fact that multicast data for commercial purposes will be protected such as pay-per-view TV, etc., so that people without ac-cess cannot see the multicast traffic. This knowledge can be used to add a simple robust multicast packet authentication scheme to any group communication scheme using asymmetric keys.

3. MULTICAST AUTHENTICATION

Multicast authentication is a challenging problem because of the large number of participants involved in the communication and the need to authenticate a large number of packets any of which may be lost. The simplest solution to authentication is if each packet is signed by the sender. The receiver could verify the signature and discard packets whose signatures were not verified. However this solution is unacceptable because of the repeated use by the sender of a computationally ex-pensive sign primitive for each packet and the communication overhead caused by the addition of a signature to each packet. Another solution to authentication is to use hash based message authentication codes (HMACs) as in unicast transmission. This does not work well in a multicast setting if small overhead is required and time synchronization between sender and receivers is difficult to maintain. The use of simple symmetric message authentication codes (MACs) is unacceptable as it would enable any of the receivers to impersonate the sender. Because the stream of multicast packets is implemented using UDP and the loss of packets is accept-able in many applications such as pay-per-view TV, the authentication scheme must tolerate packet loss. Also participants may join at any point in time and they should be able to begin authenticating packets starting from any packet. It is possible to compute signatures in advance and to buffer them for content that is al-ready available, such as applications showing movies over the Internet. However real time multicast applications such as stock and news feeds cannot use signatures that take a long time to compute.

All of the schemes discussed in Section 2 can only perform group authentication and not individual sender authentication. Therefore a sender in a multicast group may be able to masquerade as another sender. However as senders are few in number for large multicast scenarios (in most cases the group is a single sender group) and are trusted, they are not likely to be masquerading as other senders. Receivers are large in number and are not trusted and they may disrupt service by masquerading as a sender. Any multicast authentication scheme must prevent receivers from posing as a legitimate sender. However, it is acceptable to assume that senders will not be posing as one another.

An efficient authentication scheme must
• be able to ensure that the received packets actually originated from a legitimate sender.

- be able to ensure that the received packets were not modified while in transit.
- be able to ensure that packets sent by an adversary are not mistaken as legit-mate packets.
- work with both real time and previously available content.
- be able to ensure that receivers are not capable of posing as senders.
- be able to provide authentication from any packet onwards despite losses in the network.
- reduce the communication overhead by adding a small number of bytes per packet
- not be computationally very expensive

The authentication schemes discussed in Section 2 do not satisfy all of the above mentioned requirements hence there is a need for a multicast authentication scheme.

4. SIM-KM

SIM-KM [6] is an efficient key management scheme to distribute and change keys as required [16] for secure group communication. While we provide a description of SIM-KM to show how asymmetric keys are used for multicast data protection the proposed authentication scheme may be used with any asymmetric multicast data protection scheme to provide multicast group authentication. SIM-KM uses proxy encryptions [16] to split the multicast distribution tree into subgroups when needed. A re-key message combines the subgroups to form a single distribution tree. One node is configured as the Group Manager. It is configured with group and access control information. Other group controllers will join this group manager. Trusted intermediate group controllers may perform proxy transformations. These group controllers are on the data distribution tree with the sender as the root and the receivers as the leaves.

SIM-KM is robust and does not depend on any single controller for its operation. Proxy Functions can convert cipher text for one key into cipher text for an-other without revealing secret decryption keys or clear text messages. This allows a non-trusted third party to convert between cipher texts without access to the clear text message or to the secret component of the old key or new key.

In simple terms, the key generation algorithm generates keys for encrypting the multicast data. The senders encrypt the multicast data using the traffic encryption algorithm and the receivers decrypt the received cipher text using the traffic decryption algorithm. Whenever an intermediary entity wants to change the cipher text (for example, when a membership change occurs in the sub-tree below this intermediate node) it uses the traffic to proxy changing algorithm. The receiver then has to use the proxy decryption algorithm to recover the original clear text. SIM-KM solves the problem of key changing on each membership change by introducing proxy encryptions. However this asymmetric proxy encryption technique differs from other asymmetric key techniques. In other schemes using asymmetric keys the encryption key is freely available and the decryption key is kept a secret so any node can send a secret message to the node with the decryption key. In SIM-KM the encryption key is kept a secret and the decryption key is made avail-able to a selected group of receivers. Fig. 1 illustrates the functioning of SIM-KM.

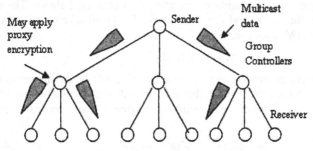

Fig. 1. Functioning of SIM-KM

SIM-KM uses asymmetric proxy functions and keys. The sender has the encryption key, the intermediate nodes have the proxy transformation key and the receivers have the decryption key. El Gamal, RSA or identity based encryption schemes may be used as proxy encryption schemes. It should be noted that SIM-KM does not use the keys as is done in a public key encryption scheme where the encryption key is made freely available to anyone who wants to send data to a particular receiver. In SIM-KM the encryption key is kept a secret and is known only to senders of the multicast data. To ensure that it is not mistaken for a public key encryption scheme we refer to the scheme as an asymmetric scheme. Here we discuss an encryption scheme based on El Gamal encryption. This example is different from [6] because for certain traffic encryption approaches (including

El Gamal) collusion between the intermediate entity and receivers can permit discovery of the encryption key. However, this can be avoided by giving a part of the decryption key to the sender and requiring it to perform a partial decryption before sending the data. This ensures that there is no possibility of deriving the encryption key as shown in the following example:

Let p be a prime, and g be a generator of Z_p = {1, ..., p – 1}. The private key x is an integer between 1 and p – 2. Let y = g^x mod p. The public key for El Gamal encryption is the triplet (p, g, y). To encrypt a plaintext M, a random integer k relatively prime to p – 1 is selected, and the following pair is computed:

$$a \leftarrow g^k \bmod p \qquad (4.1)$$

$$b \leftarrow My^k \bmod p \qquad (4.2)$$

The cipher text C consists of the pair (a, b) computed above. The decryption of the cipher text C = (a, b) in the El Gamal scheme, to retrieve the plain text M is simple:

$$M \leftarrow b/a^x \bmod p \qquad (4.3)$$

In the above expression, the "division" by a^x should be interpreted in the con-text of modular arithmetic, that is, M is multiplied by the inverse of a^x in Z_p. The correctness of the El Gamal encryption scheme is easy to verify. We have

$$b/a^x \bmod p = My^k(a^x)^{-1} \bmod p \qquad (4.4)$$

$$= Mg^{xk}(g^{kx})^{-1} \bmod p \qquad (4.5)$$

$$= M \qquad (4.6)$$

In the Proxy El Gamal encryption scheme the private key is split into x_1 and x_2 such that x = x_1 + x_2. This split can be made when required and there can be a very large number of such possible splits resulting in different values of x_1 and x_2. The sender is given x_1. The sender transforms the data using x_1 after encryption. This is done to ensure that no collusion of intermediate nodes or receivers will succeed in obtaining the decryption key x. Hence there is no possibility of using the decryption key and other information to obtain the encryption key. This ensures that the receivers are unable to impersonate the sender. X_2 is further split into x_3 and x_4 such that x_2 = x_3 + x_4 when a membership change occurs and the decryption key for a part of the multicast data distribution tree has to be changed. The traffic to proxy changing algorithm receives x_3 and the receiver receives x_4. The traffic to proxy changing function and the decryption function are similar to the original decryption function under x_3 and x_4 respectively. The sender performs a partial decryption given by

$$M_1 \leftarrow b/a^{x1} \bmod p \tag{4.7}$$

The traffic to proxy changing function thus performs a partial decryption given by

$$M_2 \leftarrow M_1/a^{x3} \bmod p \tag{4.8}$$

The decryption function performs the decryption by performing

$$M \leftarrow M_2/a^{x4} \bmod p \tag{4.9}$$

The correctness of the Proxy El Gamal encryption function is easy to verify. We have

$$M_2/a^{x4} \bmod p = (M_1/a^{x3} \bmod p)/a^{x4} \bmod p \tag{4.10}$$

$$= (b/a^{x1} \bmod p)/a^{x3+x4} \bmod p \tag{4.11}$$

$$= (b/a^{x1} \bmod p)/a^{x2} \bmod p \tag{4.12}$$

$$= b/(a^{x1+x2)} \bmod p \tag{4.13}$$

$$= b/a^{x} \bmod p \tag{4.14}$$

These proxy encryption schemes have been shown to be as secure as the original schemes [17]. SIM-KM also employs other techniques such as group controllers with varying trust levels and different responsibilities. The scheme also employs dynamic batching techniques to reduce the number of control messages. SIM-KM has been shown to have good performance when compared to other available key management schemes [18].

5. AUTHENTICATION

To provide authentication, a symmetric key is shared among all group members. This symmetric key is a unique shared secret used for authentication. Every time a sender wants to send a message to the group, it adds an index to the packet, a counter "c" and a random number "k". The index is a number assigned by the Group Manager to a particular sender for uniquely identifying it during a multicast session. It then encrypts the packet with the asymmetric encryption key. It then calculates a MAC (Message Authentication Code) on the cipher text using the symmetric key. It then attaches "k" and the MAC to the packet.

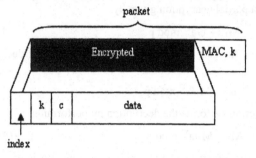

Fig. 2. Packet Structure

The packet structure is shown in fig. 2. The receiver on receiving the packet computes a MAC to ensure that the packet was not modified in transit and was not sent by someone imitating to be the sender. This however does not rule out the possibility of one of the malicious receivers masquerading as a sender. The packet is then decrypted and the value of "k" obtained after decryption is matched with the value of "k" sent in clear text with the packet. As the packet is encrypted by an asymmetric key which is unknown to the receivers there is no possibility that a malicious receiver can create a packet which when decoded produces the same value of "k" without knowing the encryption key. This effectively rules out the possibility of any receiver being able to impersonate a legitimate sender. The index identifies the particular sender providing data source authentication. The receiver stores the last value of the counter received in sequence as c1 and compares it with the value of the counter in the next packet that arrives to prevent a replay attack. The newly arrived packet must fall within the range c1 to c1 + r, where r is the size of the buffer used by the underlying protocol to re-sequence the out of order packets. If the packet already exists in the buffer then the packet is considered a duplicate and is discarded. The symmetric key is generated by the Group Manager and distributed to the group members when they join the multicast group. It may be given along with the decryption key when the members join. The scheme uses a single MAC for message authentication along with a random number, a counter and an index. This reduces the bandwidth overhead considerably and it is not as computationally intensive as digitally signing individual packets. The type of MAC and the size of the symmetric key can be chosen depending upon the context of the application and the sensitivity of the data.

When SIM-KM is used as the key management scheme, the symmetric key is also given to the group controllers. When group controllers perform the data trans-formation they re-compute and replace the existing MAC. The random number "k" is kept as it is. The decryption key is changed by SIM-KM and is communicated to the receivers who need the new key. The symmetric key for authentication remains the same. If another key distribution scheme is being used then there is no need to re-compute and replace the MAC.

6. ATTACKS

This scheme provides message integrity as it allows the receiver to verify that the message is exactly the same as when the sender sent it. Host authentication is also achieved as it allows the sender to be uniquely identified. A number of different attacks [19] are possible against group communications. We describe some of the attacks that are relevant to message authentication and how the proposed scheme would handle these attacks.

6.1 Replay

An adversary may store messages and then send them at a later time. As these packets have been assembled by a legitimate sender, the receivers may be led to believe that they are legitimate packets even though now they are out of sequence. This attack is nullified by having a counter. If packets are replayed then the value of the counter in the packets will be out of the range defined for c and these packets can be discarded.

6.2 Message Modification

An adversary may modify messages that are sent by the sender. The symmetric MAC authentication will fail if the message is modified. As only group members have the symmetric key a non-group member cannot modify the message and attach a MAC that succeeds. A receiver may be able to masquerade as a legitimate sender by modifying the packet and attaching a MAC that succeeds but the random number "k" will not match. There is no way for any adversary or malicious receiver to make a packet with a matching value of "k" as it does not possess the asymmetric encryption key, which is a secret known only to the sender(s).

6.3 Message Insertion

An adversary may insert messages in the stream. There is no way for an adversary to create messages which will be authenticated as legitimate packets. Inserted messages will fail authentication and will be dropped by the receivers.

6.4 Message Deletion

An adversary may delete a message from the stream. Deletion attacks are not ad-dressed by this scheme. It only deals with validation messages that are not deleted. However deleting some messages does not stop the authentication scheme from validating packets that have been delivered successfully.

6.5 Eavesdropping

This paper deals with data source authentication and not with confidentiality but the SIM-KM scheme uses proxy encryptions to secure data. It uses asymmetric keys and only receivers with legitimate decryption keys will be able to decipher the packet.

6.6 Denial of Service

A malicious node can insert packets into the stream to slow down the receiver thus mounting a denial of service attack as the receiver will have to verify the packets. A node that is not part of the multicast session will not be able to make packets with matching MACs and thus will not be able to slow down the receiver as the MAC verification process does not involve decrypting the packet. A malicious receiver can slow down another receiver by inserting packets with matching MACs as it knows the symmetric key but the packet will still be detected as a bogus packet. A malicious sender can send packets to receivers because it possesses the encryption key as well. In this case the denial of service attack cannot be mitigated and the only solution would be to have different encryption keys for different senders. However as discussed in Section 3 senders are trusted entities and are not likely to be disrupting the service themselves. Consider a scenario where multicast is used for conferencing where there are multiple non-trusted senders and authentication is required for such a case then the only solution is to have a separate key pair for each sender. Our scheme would work well is such as case as well. The number of key pairs required will be small as there are few senders.

7. CONCLUSION

In section 2 we have discussed how existing multicast authentication schemes fail to satisfy all the requirements for a multicast authentication scheme. Let us consider a scenario where multicast is used to deliver stock updates to a large number of receivers. Some of these receivers may be PDAs, wireless handsets with limited resource and small bandwidths hence it rules out the possibility of using computationally intensive schemes or schemes with high communication overhead. We compare our scheme with the Multiple MACs scheme, TESLA and Merkle hash schemes. We have not compared schemes that do not tolerate packet loss, are prone to message insertion attacks, etc., because these solutions are not suitable for use in the Internet.

Table 1. Overhead Comparison

Scheme	Overhead per packet	Need Synch.	Comparison
Multiple MACs Scheme	k bits where k depends on the size of the largest malicious receiver coalition	No	Suffers from collusion attack, needs to calculate k MACs before sending out every packet
TESLA	MAC + K_m where K_m is sent once every time period	Yes	Suffers from change in network propagation delay
Merkle Hash Scheme	n*(s + h log n) where n is the number of packets in the data stream, s is the signature size and h is the hash size	No	Suffers from Signature Flooding Attack, Adversarial Packet Loss Attacks, all messages need to be known in advance on sender side
Proposed Scheme	MAC + counter + 2*random number	No	Requires a single MAC computation, does not suffer from known attacks

As seen from table 1 the overhead caused by our proposal is either smaller or comparable when compared to different schemes. It does not suffer from collusion attacks or adversarial packet loss attacks, and does not require any time synchronization. It also does not require multicast data to be known in advance and works well with real time data. Given the basic traffic encryption scheme, this scheme adds only the overhead of a MAC computation. The proposed scheme works better than existing schemes when other scenarios are considered such as Pay-per-view TV, online teaching, news feeds, etc.

8. VALIDATION

We have used PROMELA (PROcess MEta LAnguage) [20] to specify the validation model and then used a tool, SPIN (Simple Promela INtepreter) [21] to validate our model. The model is designed so that it is simple but considers all the at-tacks listed in section 6. The model consists of one sender, one intermediate adversary and a receiver. The sender sends data packets. The intermediate adversary randomly modifies messages, inserts new messages, deletes messages and re-plays messages. Modified messages include messages with wrong MACs, wrong value of "k" in clear text and altered data. Inserted messages include messages that were simply created and added to the data stream as well as messages with correct MACs. Replayed messages are messages that were saved from the data stream and were added to the stream after different time periods. The probability with which the intermediate adversary introduces errors can be controlled. The receiver verifies each packet received to establish if the packet has been sent by the sender or has been inserted/modified/replayed by the adversary.

XSPIN is used to specify the high level model written in PROMELA. As a preliminary check different random simulations were performed with different SPIN options and no errors were found. The verifier was compiled using the exhaustive search option. This option causes a state space search of all possible states and message timings of the modelled processes. Then, the verifier was executed and the output confirmed that our model is free from errors and there are no assertion violations, invalid end states or unreachable states in the design.

We compared the packets modified by the intermediate adversary to those detected by the receiver as packets having errors. In each case it was found that the packets that were randomly inserted, modified or replayed by the adversary were successfully detected by the receiver. The probability of errors introduced by the intermediate adversary was varied from 0 to 100% and it was found that the receiver was able to detect errors independent of the number of messages the adversary modified, inserted, replayed or deleted. The model was found to be free from errors, assertion violations, invalid end states or unreachable states in all cases.

9. CONCLUSIONS

We have presented an efficient robust scheme for multicast group authentication. It can be used with any asymmetric multicast data security protocol for multicast group security (such as SIM-KM) to perform multicast data source authentication. The authentication scheme has no delays, requires no time synchronization, is collusion-resistant, and does not have a large packet overhead. It is simple, works in-dependent of packet losses and is not resource intensive. It is a robust, efficient and scalable solution for multicast data source authentication. The scheme is flexible and does not place any restriction on which asymmetric encryption scheme to use or on the size of the keys and the choice of MACs. The scheme was modelled using PROMELA and validated using SPIN, which showed the scheme is successful in the face of all possible known message authentication attacks.

ACKNOWLEDGEMENTS

Ritesh Mukherjee acknowledges the support of the Natural Sciences and Engineering Research Council (PGS B) scholarship.

J. W. Atwood acknowledges the support of the Natural Sciences and Engineering Research Council of Canada through its Discovery Grants Program and of Concordia University.

REFERENCES

[1] Harney H, Muckenhim C (1997) Group Key Management Protocol (GKMP) Architecture. RFC2094

[2] Harney H, Muckenhim C (1997) Group Key Management Protocol (GKMP) Specification. RFC2093

[3] Ballardie A (1996) Scalable Multicast Key Distribution (SKMD). RFC1949

[4] Mittra S (1997) Iolus: A Framework for Scalable Secure Multicast. In: ACM SIGCOMM '97, pp 277–288

[5] Fiat A, Naor M (1993) Broadcast Encryption. In: CRYPTO '93, Springer-Verlag, pp 480–491

[6] Mukherjee R, Atwood JW (2003) Proxy Encryptions for Secure Multicast Key Management. In: IEEE LCN'03, pp 377–384

[7] Mukherjee R, Atwood JW (2004) SIM-KM: Scalable Infrastructure for Multicast Key Management. In: IEEE LCN'04, pp 335–342

[8] Canetti R, Garay J, Itkis G, Micciancio D, Naor M, Pinkas B (1999) A Taxonomy and some Efficient Constructions. In: IEEE INFOCOM'97, pp 708–716

[9] Perrig A, Tygar JD, Song D, Canetti R (2000) Efficient Authentication and Signing of Multicast Streams over Lossy Channels. In: IEEE Symposium on Security and Privacy, pp 56–73

[10] Gennaro R, Rohatgi P (1997) How to Sign Digital Streams. In: CRYPTO'97, pp 180–197

[11] Perrig A (2001) The BiBa One-Time Signature and Broadcast Authentication Protocol In: 8th ACM Conference on Computer and Communications Security, pp 28–37

[12] Wong CK, Lam SS (1998) Digital Signatures for Flows and Multicasts In: 6th International Conference on Network Protocols, pp 502–513

[13] Pannetrat A, Molva R (2003) Efficient Multicast Packet Authentication. In: 10th Annual Network and Distributed System Security Symposium

[14] Golle P, Modadugu N (2001) Authenticating Streamed Data in the Presence of Random Packet Loss. In: 8th Annual Network and Distributed System Security Symposium (NDSS)

[15] Weis B (2005) The Use of RSA/SHA-1 Signatures within ESP and AH. Internet Draft, Work in Progress, draft-ietf-msec-ipsec-signatures-06.txt

[16] Wallner D, Harder E, Agee R (1997) Key Management for Multicast: Issues and Architecture. RFC2627

[17] Dodis Y, Ivan A (2003) Proxy Encryption Revisited. In: 10th Annual Network and Distributed System Security Symposium

[18] Mukherjee R, Atwood JW (2004) A Comparative Analysis of SIM-KM for Group Key Management. In: CCN 2004, pp 169–174

[19] Rescorla E, Korver B (2003) Guidelines for Writing RFC Text on Security Considerations. RFC3552

[20] Holzmann GJ (1991) Design and Validation of Computer Protocols. Prentice Hall.

[21] Holzmann GJ (1997) The Model Checker SPIN. IEEE Transactions on Software Engineering, 23, 5:279–295

Efficient Loss Recovery Algorithm for Multicast Communications in Active Networks

Marta Barría[1] and Reinaldo Vallejos[2]

[1]Computer Science Department, University of Valparaíso, Chile
marta.barria@uv.cl

[2]Department of Electronics Engineering, Technical University Federico Santa María, Chile
reinaldo@elo.utfsm.cl

Abstract.- A novel highly scalable loss recovery algorithm for Multicast transmissions in active networks that achieves near-optimal implosion and very low latency is proposed. Quasi-minimum implosion is attained by stochastically selecting a sub-set of the loss-affected members as NACK senders. If appropriately tuned, the algorithm selects with high probability only one member as a NACK sender. Near-optimal latency is obtained by minimizing the time taken to select the NACK sender and by retransmitting from the closest possible location. Performance evaluation results show a maximum implosion 4% higher than the optimal value and a low latency.

Index Terms. Multicast Communication, Loss Recovery, Reliability, Active Networks, Multicast Tree.

1 Introduction

Multicast communication offers an efficient way to disseminate information from one or more transmitters to a group of receivers. Reliable Multicast applications require that each destination receive correctly all transmitted packets. Examples of this type of application are software distribution, shared whiteboards, interactive games, network banking and replication of databases [2, 3]. Although there exist lower-layer technologies for providing reliable transmission, the best-effort nature of Internet Protocol hampers error-free packet reception. Reliable multicast requires a scalable recovery of losses. The two main impediments to scale are implosion and recovery latency. Implosion occurs when the loss of a packet trig-

Please use the following format when citing this chapter:

Barría, M. and Vallejos, R., 2007, in IFIP International Federation for Information Processing, Volume 229, Network Control and Engineering for QoS, Security, and Mobility, IV, ed. Gaïti, D., (Boston: Springer), pp. 231–241.

gers simultaneous redundant requests and/or retransmissions from many receivers [3]. The techniques employed to decrease implosion may introduce a long latency recovery. The ideal situation is that the size of the implosion be equal to one and the latency be minimum. For this reason the error recovery mechanisms that have been proposed in specialized literature seek to reduce implosion and latency simultaneously. However, since both objectives are conflictive, algorithms attempt to obtain a compromise between them.

Among the different approaches for loss recovery in Multicast communications, receiver-initiated schemes (receivers detecting a loss send a negative acknowledgement (NACK)) have been shown to perform better than positive acknowledgements (ACK) schemes [11]. One approach to improving reliability is through the use of receiver-initiated protocols with local recovery [1, 3, 4, 8, 9]. A further technique for improving Multicast reliability has emerged from the active networks area [7]. In active networking the routers themselves play an active role by executing application-dependent services on incoming packets. The advantages of using this architecture with reliable multicast protocols are: the cache of data packets allows for local recoveries of loss packets and reduces recovery latency, the global or local suppression of NACKs reduces the NACK implosion problem, and the partial multicast of repair packets to a set of receivers limits both retransmission scope and bandwidth usage. ARM [6], AER[5] and DyRAM [7] are examples of newly proposed reliable multicast protocols that use active networks.

In this article we present a new local recovery algorithm for Multicast communications based on active routers that achieves near-minimum implosion and latency simultaneously.

The rest of this paper is organized as follows: in Section 2 the new error-recovery algorithm is presented; Section 3 contains the performance evaluation of the algorithm; Section 4 provides and discusses numerical examples; and finally, in Section 5 the conclusions are presented.

2 Proposed Algorithm

2.1 Notation

The network is modeled by the graph $G = (V,E)$, where V corresponds to the set of all nodes in the network and E to the set of all its links. The network and the Multicast group are composed of normal routers, active routers and receivers. The routers form the set L, and the hierarchy between them is created using a distribution tree D generated by a Multicast routing protocol [12]. The information is originated in the source, denoted s. The receivers form the set $R = \{r, 1 \le r \le |R|\}$. Hence, all the members of the Multicast group together form the set $M = L \cup R \cup \{s\}$.

2.2 Algorithm

Under normal operation, packets originated at the source are transmitted to all receivers through the distribution tree D. Under error conditions, the proposed algorithm, called Loss Recovery Algorithm for Reliable Multicast (LRARM), is activated. LRARM's operation can be described in the following eight points:

I. If an active router $m \in L$ detects a loss:
    1. It forwards an inhibit message to each of its receivers and its child routers in D;
    2. It executes a Bernoulli random experiment with parameter $p_1(m)$ (to be described below). Upon successful outcome of the random experiment, it sends a NACK up to its parent router in D.
    3. It starts a timer, with timeout $TO(m)$ (described below).
    4. It continues the normal transmission of another received packets.
    5. If $TO(m)$ expires and the requested packet has not been received, m repeats steps 1. through 5. However, the parameter of the Bernoulli experiment now changes to $p_n(m)$ (described below), where n denotes the nth execution of this step (i.e., step 5.) for the unreceived packet.

II. In the case where a receiver $m \in R$ detects a loss, it executes the steps I.1 through I.5 as described above.

III. When an active router receives the inhibit message:
    1. It forwards the message downstream to each of its receivers and its child routers in D.
    2. It refrains from sending a NACK upstream for this packet.

IV. When a receiver receives the inhibit message, it refrains from sending a NACK for this packet.

V. When an active router receives a NACK:
    1. It retransmits the requested packet to its child routers in D.
    2. It eliminates the NACK from the network.

VI. When a receiver receives a NACK, it eliminates the NACK from the network.

VII.   When an active router receives the retransmission of a lost packet:
    1.   If the packet has not been received before, it forwards the packet to its receivers and its child routers;
    2.   Otherwise, it discards the packet.
VIII. When a receiver receives the retransmission of a lost packet that it has received before, that packet is discarded.

Point I is essential for achieving near-minimum implosion by reducing the number of NACK senders (using the inhibit message). The parameter of the Bernoulli distribution is chosen in such a manner that there is a high probability only one potential NACK sender will be selected to transmit the NACK. In addition, low latency is assured by quickly selecting the NACK sender(s) (a process that takes a few microseconds, the time necessary for a CPU to perform the Bernoulli experiment) and by maintaining a copy of transmitted packets in every active router associated with the Multicast group (only those packets with unexpired timeouts are maintained; as timeouts expire without receiving NACKs, the corresponding packets are discarded). Therefore, the closest parent active router to the point of failure is responsible for the retransmission.

2.3 Timeout Values.

Assume that a packet loss has occurred in link $e_{j,k}$ of D. The recovery tree R_k is then defined as the subtree of D, made up of: the first parent active router of k, named $\rho(k)$; the set of active routers of the multicast group that are the first descendents of $\rho(k)$ in D; the receivers of the multicast group, and all the paths that interconnect them. Each recovery tree has its own timeout, calculated upon connection set-up (and when a receiver joins or leaves the group) and known by all its active routers and receivers.

The timeout of R_k, $TO(R_k)$, corresponds to the round trip time between $\rho(k)$ and its farthest member (active router or receiver). Given a leaf $m \in R_k$, $TO(R_k)$ can also be denoted as $TO(m)$.

2.4 Bernoulli Parameter Values.

The value of $p_n(m)$, determined upon connection set-up (and when a receiver joins or leaves the group), is given by:

$$P_n(m) = \begin{cases} \min\left(1; \dfrac{l(m)}{\displaystyle\sum_{\forall m \in R_k} l(m)}\right); \forall m \in R_k; \quad n = 1 \\[20pt] \min\left(1; 2P_{n-1}(m)\right); \forall m \in R_k; \quad n > 1 \end{cases} \tag{2.1}$$

where $l(m)$ is the distance between $\rho(k)$ and member $m \in R_k$. The longer is $l(m)$, the higher is the probability of m being affected by a failure. Hence, because the members affected by a failure are not known in advance, Eq. (2.1) assigns a higher probability of sending a NACK to the leaves (members) of R_k more prone to losses.

3 Performance Evaluation

Implosion is measured as the number of NACKs sent simultaneously per lost packet. Clearly, its optimal value is 1. Latency is defined as the period between packet loss detection and its successful reception at all destinations. If normalized to the timeout, its optimal value is equal to 1.

3.1 Mean Latency

Let $E[L]$ be the latency mean value. Due to the fact that the loss of a packet can occur in any link of distribution tree D, to evaluate $E[L]$, it is conditioned in the link in which the failure occur. Then, the mean latency is given by :

$$E[L] = \sum_{\forall e_{j,k} \in D} E\left[L \mid \text{failure in } e_{j,k}\right] P\left(\text{failure in } e_{j,k} \mid \text{failure}\right) \tag{3.1}$$

If it is assumed that every link has the same probability of being affected by failures, then $P\left(\text{failure in } e_{j,k} \mid \text{failure}\right) = \dfrac{1}{|L_D|}$, where $|L_D|$ is the number of links in the distribution tree D.

If we further assume that NACKs and inhibit messages are not lost, and that $E\left[L\,|\,\text{failure in } e_{j,k}\right]$ is calculated at the iteration at which at least one NACK is sent for the first time and the total probabilities theorem is applied, then:

$$E\left[L\,|\,\text{failure in } e_{j,k}\right]=\left(\sum_{n=1}^{N(A_k)} E\left[L\,|\,e_{j,k},n\right]P\left(n\,|\,e_{j,k}\right)\right) \tag{3.2}$$

where $E\left[L\,|\,n,e_{j,k}\right]$ is the mean value of latency given a failure in link $e_{j,k}$ and at least one NACK sent for the first time in the nth iteration of the algorithm; $P\left(n\,|\,e_{j,k}\right)$ is the probability that at least one NACK is sent for the first time in the nth iteration of the algorithm, given a failure in link $e_{j,k}\in D$; A_k is the set of leaves of R_k affected by the failure; and $N(A_k)$ corresponds to the value of n for which at least one member of A_k sends the NACK with probability equal to 1.

To calculate $N(A_k)$, it is observed that for each leaf $m\in A_k$ there is one iteration of the algorithm in which that leaf sends a NACK with probability equal to 1. Let $N_m(A_k)$, $m\in A_k$ be the iteration in which the leaf $m\in A_k$ reaches, for the first time, the condition $p_{N_m(A_k)}(m)\geq 1$. Eq. (2.1) implies that this condition is equivalent to $2^{N_m(A_k)-1}p_1(m)\geq 1$, which means that $N_m(A_k)\geq 1+\lg_2\left(\dfrac{1}{p_1(m)}\right)$. The smallest integer value that complies with the above inequality is given as $N_m(A_k)=\left\lceil 1+\lg_2\left(\dfrac{1}{p_1(m)}\right)\right\rceil$

Let $N(A_k)$ be the value of n for which at least one of the leaves of the tree A_k reaches the condition $p_{N_m(A_k)}(m)\geq 1$, which implies that $N(A_k)=\min_{m\in A_k} N_m(A_k)$. Then:

$$N(A_k)=\min_{m\in A_k}\left(\left\lceil 1+\lg_2\left(\dfrac{1}{p_1(m)}\right)\right\rceil\right) \tag{3.3}$$

Because failures occur with low probability, and to simplify the analysis without significantly altering the results, it is assumed that the first retransmission of the lost packet is successful. This assumption implies that:

$$E\left[L|n,e_{j,k}\right] = n \cdot TO(R_k) \qquad (3.4)$$

$P(n \mid e_{j,k})$ is given by:

$$P(n \mid e_{j,k}) = \begin{cases} \left(1 - \displaystyle\prod_{\forall m \in A_k} (1 - p_1(m))\right), & n = 1 \\[2em] \left(1 - \displaystyle\prod_{\forall m \in A_k} (1 - p_n(m))\right)\displaystyle\prod_{y=1}^{n-1}\prod_{\forall m \in A_k} (1 - p_y(m)), & n > 1 \end{cases} \qquad (3.5)$$

Using Eqs. (2.1)-(3.5), E[L] can be evaluated as follows:

$$E[L] = \sum_{\forall e_{j,k} \in D} \frac{TO(R_k)}{|L(D)|}\left\{\left(1 - \prod_{\forall m \in A_k}(1-p_1(m))\right) + \sum_{n=2}^{\min\left(l_k,\left(1+\log_2\left(\frac{1}{p_1(m)}\right)\right)\right)} n\left(1 - \prod_{\forall m \in A_k}\left(1-p_1(m)2^{n-1}\right)\right)\prod_{y=1}^{n-1}\prod_{\forall m \in A_k}\left(1-p_1(h)2^{y-1}\right)\right\} \qquad (3.6)$$

3.2 Probability Mass Function of Latency

A more detailed method of characterizing latency consists of evaluating its probability mass function (pmf). Since latency is specific for each recovery tree, the pmf of the latency for a determined recovery tree is evaluated as follows:

Let $p_{T_i}(x)$ be the probability that the latency for the recovery tree T_i is equal to x. In accordance with the results obtained when $E[L]$ was evaluated, we have the following equation:

$$p_{T_i}\left(nTO(T_i)\right) = \begin{cases} \displaystyle\sum_{\forall e_{j,k} \in T_i} \frac{1}{c(T_i)}\left(1 - \prod_{m \in A_k}(1 - p_1(m))\right); & n = 1 \\[2em] \displaystyle\sum_{\forall e_{j,k} \in T_i} \frac{1}{c(T_i)}\left(1 - \prod_{m \in A_k}\left(1 - p_1(m)2^{n-1}\right)\right)\prod_{y=1}^{n-1}\prod_{m \in A_k}\left(1 - p_1(m)2^{y-1}\right); & n > 1 \end{cases} \qquad (3.7)$$

where $c(T_i)$ is the number of links that contain the recovery tree T_i.

3.3 Mean Implosion

Let $E[I]$ be the mean value of implosion, given by:

$$E[I] = \sum_{\forall e_{j,k} \in D} E\left[I \mid \text{failure in } e_{j,k}\right] P\left(\text{failure in } e_{j,k} \mid \text{failure}\right) \tag{3.8}$$

By definition, $E\left[I \mid \text{failure in } e_{j,k}\right]$ is given by :

$$E\left[I \mid \text{failure in } e_{j,k}\right] = \sum_{n=1}^{N(A_k)} \sum_{i=1}^{|A_k|} iP\left(n, i \mid e_{j,k}\right) \tag{3.9}$$

where $P\left(n, i \mid e_{j,k}\right)$ is the probability of sending i NACKs simultaneously in the nth iteration, given a failure in link $e_{j,k}$.-

To evaluate $P\left(n, i \mid e_{j,k}\right)$, let us define $K_{u,l}$ as the set of distinct l tuples that can be formed from $u = |A_k|$ different elements, where l corresponds to the number of leaves of R_k that send a NACK. Let $\vec{k}_{u,l}$ be the uth l-tuple of the set $K_{u,l}$, and m the mth component of $\vec{k}_{u,l}$. The probability $P\left(n, i \mid e_{j,k}\right)$ is given by:

$$P\left(n, i \mid e_{j,k}\right) = \sum_{\forall \vec{k}_{A_k,l} \in K_{A_k,l}} \left(\prod_{\forall m \in \vec{k}_{A_k,l}} p_n(m) \prod_{\forall m \in \vec{k}_{A_k,l}} (1 - p_n(m))\right)^{n-1} \prod_{y=1}^{n-1} \prod_{\forall m \in A_k} (1 - p_y(m)) \tag{3.10}$$

Then, $E[I]$ can be calculated using Eqs. (3.8)-(3.10).

4 Numerical Results

Mean latency and mean implosion were evaluated -using equations from Section 3- for network topologies of 600 nodes randomly generated using the Waxman methodology [12,13] with a 95% confidence level. Multicast groups of different sizes were randomly chosen.

Results for normalized mean latency and mean implosion as a function of the percentage of active Multicast routers in the network are shown in Fig. 1 and Fig. 2, respectively.

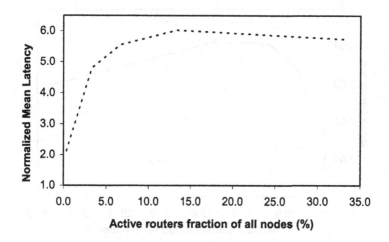

Fig. 1. Normalized mean latency versus the active routers fraction of all nodes

It can be seen that when the percentage of Multicast members in the network is less than 18%, the values for both measures increase to a maximum. However, if this percentage rises (> 18%), the distance between the location of the failure and the nearest router becomes shorter and therefore the latency to recover a lost packet declines.

As regards implosion, we observed that as the number of active routers increases, implosion remains almost unchanged and quite close to the ideal level.

These results clearly reveal the high scalability of LRARM and its ability to simultaneously achieve near-optimal implosion and very low latency.

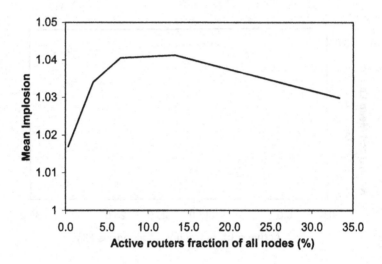

Fig. 2. Mean implosion versus the active routers fraction of all nodes

5 Conclusions

A novel error recovery algorithm for multicast transmissions, LRARM, has been proposed. LRARM simultaneously achieves near-optimal implosion and latency, regardless of Multicast group size. This makes LRARM a highly scalable algorithm with excellent performance.

Acknowledgements

Financial support from Fondecyt Project # 1000055/2000, Chile, DIPUV Project #31/2003, UTFSM Project # 230223 and Fundación Andes is gratefully acknowledged.

References

1. Adamson RB, Bormann C, Handley M, Macker J (2004) NACK-oriented reliable multicast protocol (NORM). Internet Engineering Task Force (IETF) RFC 3940
2. Diot C, DabbousW, Crowcroft J (1997) Multicast communication: a survey of protocols, functions and mechanisms. IEEE JSAC 15:277-290
3. Floyd S, Jacobson V, Liu C, McCanne S, Zhang L (1997) A reliable multicast framework for light-weight sessions and application level framing. IEEE/ACM Transactions on Networking 5:784-803
4. Gemmell J, Montgomery T, Speakman T, Bhaskar N, Crowcroft J (2003) The PGM reliable multicast protocol. IEEE Network 17:16-22.
5. Kasera S, Bhattacharyya S, Keaton M, Kiwior D, Kurose J, Towsley D, Zabele S (2000) Scalable fair reliable multicast using active services. IEEE Network Magazine 14(1): 48-57
6. Lehman L, Garland S and Tennehouse D (1998) Active reliable multicast. In: Proc. of the IEEE Infocom, San Francisco
7. Maimour M and Pham C (2002) DyRAM: a reliable multicast protocol. INRIA Report RR4635.
8. Paul S, Sabnani KK, Lin JC, Bhattacharyya S (1997) Reliable multicast transport protocol (RMTP). IEEE JSAC 15: 407-421
9. Papadopoulos C, Parulkar G, Varghese G (2004) Light-weight multicast services (LMS): a router-assisted scheme for reliable multicast. IEEE/ACM Transactions on Networking 12(3):456-468.
10. Tennehouse DL, Smith JL, Sincoskie WD, Wetherall DJ, Winden GJ (1997) A survey of active network research. IEEE Communications Magazine, pp. 80-86.
11. Towsley D, Kurose J, Pingali S (1997) A comparison of sender-initiated and receiver-initiated reliable multicast protocols. IEEE JSAC 15:398-406
12. Waxman B (1988) Routing of multicast communications. IEEE JSAC 6(9):1617-1622
13. Zegura E, Calvert K, Donahoo M (1997) A quantitative comparison of graph-based models for internet topology. IEEE/ACM Transactions on Networking 5:770-783.

Programmable Network Context Adaptation for Content Delivery Services

Zhaohong Lai[1], Joachim Sokol[2], Klaus-Peter Eckert[3], Alex Galis[1], Richard Lewis[1], Chris Todd[1]

1   University College London, Department of Electronic & Electrical Engineering, Torrington Place, London WC1E 7JE

2   Siemens AG; Corporate Technology, CT IC 2, Otto-Hahn-Ring 6, 81730 München, Germany.

3   FhI FOKUS, Kaiserin-Augusta-Allee 31 D-10589 Berlin, Germany

Abstract. This paper proposes an active/programmable-network-based Service Adaptation Manager (SAM) design to effectively deliver reliable and rich services for multimedia Content Delivery Networks (CDN). It shows that the CDN's service domain comprises two planes: Application Service plane and Network Service plane. The goal of the SAM is to manage the dynamics of the boundaries between these two planes for multimedia CDN (mCDN). The SAM includes three major parts: Service Context Adaptor, Service Adaptation Broker and Network Context Adaptor. A novel algorithm has been proposed to design the Service Context Adaptor. This allows different subsets of service context to be adaptively integrated in order to select the most suitable adaptation modules (such as VPN, QoS or the Optimal Route Service) for the delivered content. The proposed Network Context Adaptor algorithm provides an effective solution for detecting the network topology structure. Also, this paper proposes the design of an adaptive Optimal Route Service for CDNs.

1 Introduction

The advent of content distribution networks (CDN) has significantly improved Internet service performance and has a dramatic impact on the networking industry [3]. However, the traditional vendor-dependent or proprietary CDNs are facing the difficult challenge of supporting new services to customers [1][2] such as personalised services, increased security, flexible pricing etc. The fundamental reason for these difficulties is the strict separation between service layer and other CDN layers. A typical example is that the underlying network layer still only

Please use the following format when citing this chapter:

Lai, Z., Sokol, J., Eckert, K.-P., Galis, A., Lewis, R. and Todd, C., 2007, in IFIP International Federation for Information Processing, Volume 229, Network Control and Engineering for QoS, Security, and Mobility, IV, ed. Gaïti, D., (Boston: Springer), pp. 243–255.

supports single class best-effort service, which cannot satisfy the rich services from the higher layer. As a new generation CDN design, the mCDN project adopts a multi-layer approach as the basis of its architecture, which mainly includes service layer, content distribution layer and network layer. The inter-layer design philosophy provides open interfaces between the different layers. To tackle the boundaries between service layer and network layer, as stated in [4], requires internetworking layers to minimise the gap between the service layer and network layer. This paper proposes an active-network-based Service Adaptation Manager design to effectively deliver reliable and rich services for multimedia CDNs [24] (*multimedia Content Discovery and Delivery Network project*). Firstly, this paper reviews the service deployment problems in traditional network-centric service environments. Then, it analyses the drawbacks of application-centric solutions in service adaptation development. After that, it presents a service-oriented view as the trend for the future service deployment. Based on this, the CDN's service domain is divided into two planes: Application Service plane and Network Service plane. The aim of the Service Adaptation Manager is to provide the required co-ordination between service layer and network layer for mCDN. It includes three major parts: Service Context Adaptor, Service Adaptation Broker and Network Context Adaptor. A novel algorithm is proposed as a key element of the design of the Service Context Adaptor. This allows different subsets of service context to be adaptively integrated in order to select the most suitable adaptation modules (such as VPN, QoS or the Optimal Route Service) for any delivered content. Also, the proposed algorithm for the Network Context Adaptor provides effective means to determine the network topology structure. Finally, how to develop the adaptive Optimal Route Service has been examined.

2. Review in Service Adaptation

2.1 Services adaptation in the traditional network-centric network environment

In traditional network design, services are considered as the one part of the network layer. In [6], *Gbaguidi et al* referred this type of service deployment design as the network-centric based solution. In this framework, services are tied to specific technologies and rely on a dedicated signalling system. For example, the SS7[1] TUP[2]-based switch can only support voice calls while video calls require an ISDN upgrade for every switch. Similarly, only the X.25 or Frame Relay networks support data services. It is clear that, in such an environment, a new service deployment task will be almost entirely implemented within the network and will take years to be completed. Therefore, new service adaptation only can be achieved by relying on the third-party vendors to replace/upgrade modules or install completely new switches.

---

[1] – Signaling System No.7
[2] – Telephone User Part

2.2 Service adaptation in the IP-based network environment

In IP-based network environments, due to the clear separation of service layer and network layers, customers can develop their own services [4]. Typically, web services have been dramatically developed. Fundamentally, IP network is able to support rapidly growing services as IP is an open and connectionless layer 3 protocol. But, as the layer 2-4 protocols are unaware of the service requirements, the existing network treats all packets with the same single 'best effort' class [5]. As a result, this leads to many studies on service adaptation between the service layer and network layer.

In [4], Shenkef et al proposed the application taxonomy as the basis of implementing the service models. The fundamental philosophy of this scheme is that applications are regarded as central to the service structure. Therefore, if one application has been identified, its service type can be recognised and then service adaptation decisions can be made. This work divided network applications into two categories: elastic and real time application. The detailed application taxonomy paradigm is shown in Fig. 1. Based on this application taxonomy, service adaptation can be implemented to some extent. But, there exist obvious drawbacks in this solution such as the narrow service definition. Also, this solution does not fully consider the gap between service layer and network layers.

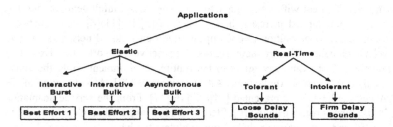

Fig. 1. Application Taxonomy- application classes, associated service offerings.

Compared with [4], *Sun et al* presented a much broader conceptual view on service adaptation in [7]. In their view, the input for adaptation is divided into two types: context-independent and context-dependent. The context-awareness based information is regarded as the implicit input, which leads to the additional elements for service adaptation. Also, a model to construct the adaptive services has been proposed. This model includes three methods: application transparent, application omniscient and application aware methods as shown below:

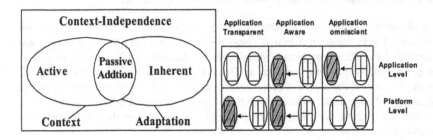

Fig. 2. Context-awareness and Adaptation (Left) and Classification of Adaptation model (Right) [7]

2.3 Service adaptation realisation with active network approach

In [7], based on context-awareness from multiple levels, implicit inputs are taken into account; the adaptation ability is therefore greatly improved. However, the proposed realisation model lacks an analysis of how applications can seamlessly interact with the network layer after they have obtained contextual information from platform level. To deal with issue, the active-network based intelligent solution has been recently popularised in research. As stated in [9][10][11][8], active network provides an innovative solution to open up the traditional closed networks so as to adaptively/intelligently deploy new services. In active network, the Execution Environment (EE) terminology refers to the runtime environment while the active code is called the Active Application (AA) terminology [22]. A wide range of EE and AA designs have been presented [14][15][16][17]. From the service adaptation view, in the Libra project design [10], Steenkiste et al proposed an elegant model to map into EE and AA, which includes two modules: the base service modules and customisation code module. The base service implements shared functionalities, while the customisation code module allows users to "fine tune" the service. Thus, service composition allows the development of new services by combining existing components from the base service module while the service adaptation functionality is implemented by customisation code module. This solution greatly reduces redundancy for deploying new services and effectively improves service adaptation scalability with a lightweight scheme in active network.

3. Service-Oriented View in Content Delivery Network

As discussed above, from the network-centric approach to the existing active network based solution, the service adaptability and scalability has been significantly improved. This evolution reflects the future trend for service adaptation that is moving to the service-oriented architecture design as shown below.

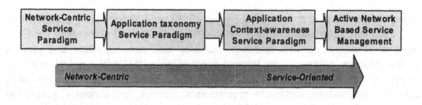

Fig. 3. Service Adaptation Evolution Steps

From the service-oriented point view, Jones defines service as a discreet domain of control that contains a collection of tasks to achieve related goals [24]. Specifically, this domain can be divided into two planes: network service plane (NSP) and application service plane (ASP) as shown in Fig. 4. In the Content Delivery Network context, the Network Service Plane mainly includes the Content Distribution Server (CDS), Metadata Distribution Server(MDS), Edge Servers(EDS) and other ISPs as shown below. The network service provider firstly provides the necessary physical network resource to ASPs like network nodes and its links and bandwidth etc. Secondly, NSPs also offer dedicated and specialised devices for ASPs such as cache machines, leased lines between CDS and EDS etc. The service domain in the application service provider mainly comprises content service provider, end users and other valued-added services etc.

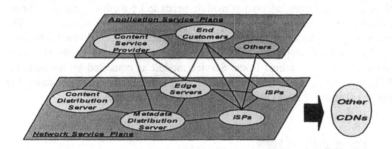

Fig. 4. Two service planes in service-oriented CDN

In such a two-plane service domain, it is apparent if the programmable platform can be deployed between ASPs and NSPs, the goal of CDN's service adaptability, availability and scalability can be effectively achieved. However, the service adaptation tasks will not be able to effectively perform without the support from other service context-awareness components. As discussed in [7], the implicit information derived from context-awareness is the very important data input for service adaptation. In the ASP plane, the scope of the required contextual knowledge comprises user, location, device, content, application and other service context. In mCDN project design, two components[3] have been developed to address these

---

[3] The details of the mCDN project architecture are at [23]

issues: Personalization and Profiling System (PPS) and Internet Media Guide (IMG). The Personalization and Profiling Service PPS is the central component for CDN personalization issues. PPS is capable to deal with personalization and profiles within arbitrary scenarios. An Internet Media Guide (IMG) is a set of metadata describing the features of multimedia content. For example, metadata may consist of the URI, title, airtime, bandwidth requirements, file size, text summary, genre, and access restrictions. PPS and IMG provide the rich context-aware adaptation knowledge for CDN. In line with ASP, the network-aware Service Adaptation Manager is designed in NSP plane as discussed in next section.

4. Service Adaptation Manager Design in CDN

4.1 Service Context Adaptor

The Service Context Adaptor (SCA) is the core part for the Service Adaptation Manager (SAM) design. The SCA aims to effectively and adaptively utilise service context in order to construct service adaptation modules. The service context set is the chain from diverse aspects, which could be either explicit or implicit information from the ASP plane in CDNs. To effectively manage various service context data, the policy for constructing adaptation module needs to be methodically predefined. Based on this policy, the SCA is able to construct different adaptation modules. The example in Fig. 5 shows that the service context space has been divided into three subsets. The service adaptation module is varied according to different subset combinations, e.g. the Optimal Route Service module is consisted by the subset 2 and 3. Some elements are shared by different service adaptation module. For example, the 'Billing' context is part of both VPN and QoS service.

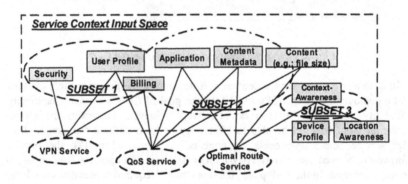

Fig. 5. The flexible Service Context Adaptor

Here, the SCA algorithm is defined as follows. If the service context space is denoted as S, then the new service adaptation module S_m is defined as:

$$(\forall e_1, e_2 ... e_i \in S)(\exists e_1 .. e_n \in S_i)(\exists S_m = S_1 \cup S_5 ... \cup S_i) \quad (1)$$

where S_i is the subset of S and the e_i is element of service context subset. Normally, the S_i is predefined with engineering approach. The condition of triggering a new service adaptation module is that every element's value in S_i needs to reach the predefined threshold. It is difficult to give the exact value for each context element. But, we can define the level value for e_i. Also, the threshold policy set S_p needs to be defined in advance. In this S_p, there are varied policies regarding to different element's value. For example, QoS service can be defined as different classes according to different billing types. When the predefined policy set S_p for S_m is satisfied the following equation, the service adaptation $S_{m.v}$ has real value and then S_m will be triggered by active codes:

$$(\forall e_1, e_2 .. e_i \in S_m)(\exists (r_{e.1} \& r_{e.2} .. \& r_{e.i}) \in S_p) \Rightarrow (S_{m.v} \notin \Phi) \quad (2)$$

here, $r_{e.i}$ is the e_i's rating value and $S_{m.v}$ is the flag for each S_m. There are different rating values for e_i. For example, if there are four bits representing billing's classes, its rating value can range from '0000' to '1111' for total sixteen types. The modular sum of rating value determines the module type of service adaptation. Based on (1), (2) and predefined policies, the Service Context Adaptor therefore can adaptively choose which service adaptation module should be triggered.

4.2 Service Adaptation Broker based on DINA Platform

In the mCDN project, the DINA[4] active platform has been chosen for the adaptation work. A full and detailed review of programmable networks technology is described in [22]. The Service Adaptation Broker has been developed so as to deliver the service adaptation module with the 'on-the-fly' manner for Service Adaptation Manager. As a more advanced variant of ABLE[5], DINA has a modular software architecture that enables deployment, control, and management of active services (sometimes called sessions or active sessions) over networks entities such as routers, WLAN access point, media gateways, and servers that support such services in IP-based networks. Its platform independent interfaces can be used by the active services in order to manage, control, retrieve information or perform other operations in the local node. DINA active platform consists of an Active Engine and a Forwarding Element, namely router, WLAN access point, media gateway, etc. (see Fig.6).

---

[4] http://context.upc.es/principal_licence.htm
[5] http://www.cs.bell-labs.com/who/ABLE/

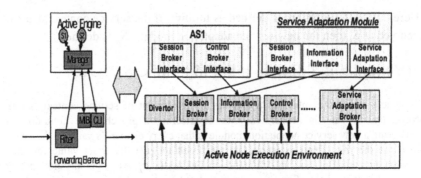

Fig. 6. Active Platform Environment

The modular design of DINA allows the different components to be logically separated. In particular the Active Engine and the Forwarding Element can be either physically separated or co-located at the same machine. This kind of architecture enables DINA to support platforms from different vendors using almost an identical software components implementation. The brokers are modules that give active services the capability to utilize host information and resources and perform operations in the local environment:

1. The Session Broker is the core on the active node. It receives and parses active packets, handles and manages existing services, and it distributes active packets according to requests of the services.
2. The Information Broker Interface provides services to retrieve information such as MIB database of the active host.
3. The Control Broker Interface enables active services to control and configure the active node.

The Service Adaptation Broker is developed as the modular platform that provides open interfaces to specific service adaptation modules such as VPN, QoS and Optimal Route Service modules.

4.3 The objective of Service Adaptation Manager in CDN

Service Adaptation Manager (SAM-Fig.7) is designed to seamlessly manage Service Context Adaptor, Service Adaptation Broker, Information Broker, Network Context Adaptor and Service Adaptation Modules. Its goal is to improve service availability and reliability with an optimal and adaptive approach in the changing CDN environment. Firstly, SAM needs to provide a seamless interface between ASP and NSP service plane as the CDN network layer can be aware of service requirement. Apart from that, as stated in section 4.1, the SCA is the core part of service adaptation decision-making. After referencing to predefined policies, it will select which adaptation module will be triggered and with which level, e.g., QoS service with different levels. Moreover, the network-level context will be taken into account by SAM, which is implemented by the Network Context Adaptor.

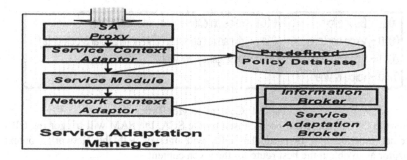

Fig. 7. Service Adaptation Manager

The network-aware service adaptation is a bottom-up solution, taking a passive approach. Typically, when the default network link is congested or broken, the time-sensitive service needs to adapt to this change. Many studies propose network-aware service adaptation [18][19][20][21] based on the application and network transport level, but the limited functionalities can be achieved. Using the built-in functionalities of DINA, the network-level contextual information can be retrieved by SAM, like MIB data from Information Broker. In the next section, it examines how to design the Optimal Route Adaptation Service by SAM.

5. Optimal Route Adaptation Service Module

5.1 The Content Service Context for ORS design

The Optimal Route Adaptation Service (ORS) component design follows a service-oriented approach to allocate network resource for CDN's applications. This is due to the fact that as existing routing protocols like OSPF do not consider service information. As a result, if one unmatched link has been chosen for one multimedia content delivery, content quality and QoS can be expected to severely degrade. The ORS is a typical adaptive service design, which considers service context information from both the ASP plane and NSP plane.

As discussed in 4.1, the type of service module is defined by Service Context Adaptor. The nature of the content is required to define the ORS module. Specifically, the input for Service Context Adaptor needs content metadata information such as content service type, bandwidth requirement and the size of content. One example of content service type is shown in the Table 1. According to this table, ORS will verify the predefined policy database and make different decisions, e.g. the flow reservation required for the '0101' type.

0001 ~ Best effort	0101 ~ mission critical (e.g.; medical video)
0010 ~ voice content	0111 ~ dynamic real-time content (financial stock data)
0011 ~ video content	1000 ~ emergency content
0100 ~ voice & video	

Table 1: Content Service Types

After the ORS module has been chosen by the SCA, the SAM will trigger the ORS internal functionality. In particular, ORS will interact with the Network Context Adaptor as to obtain the best route for the given content.

5.2 The Network Context Adaptor Design for ORS

Network Context Adaptor (NCA) is another key part of the design for Service Adaptation Manager. It is designed to obtain the network-level context-awareness information in dynamically changing network environments. Based on the network-level contextual information, ORS can adaptively choose the optimal route for the given content. The information mainly includes the network topology, the available bandwidth and the link delay contextual information. Of these network metrics, it is vital to obtain the network topology picture so that ORS can know how many links/routes are available for the same application in a given network environment. Most network metrics can be directly obtained from reading the MIB database such as the physical bandwidth, the available bandwidth and the link delay etc. However, it is difficult to obtain and maintain the accurate network topology in a large-scale network, e.g. AS-level [13]. Computation of the complete network topology is a core part for the Network Context Adaptor design. In this paper, we only focus on how to obtain the network topology knowledge in one sub-AS area as ORS and SAM are designed as a distributed system.

- **The algorithm to obtain the Network Topology in ORS**
  In one sub-AS area, the network topology can be deduced by the following (3) and (4) equations. If there are N nodes in one network topology, the total number of possible links φ is given as:

$$\varphi = 2 * C_n^{\,2} \qquad (3)$$

where n is equal to N. The number of possible routes Θ between any two nodes is given as:

$$\Theta = \sum_{r=0}^{n} P_n^{\,r} \qquad (4)$$

where n = N-2. This is can be examined by the following network scenario (Fig.8). In this scenario, one sub-AS area compromises 5 nodes and four stream contents will be delivered from A to A'.

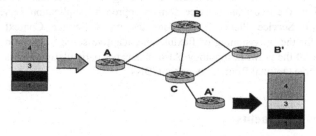

Fig. 8. One five-node's network topology algorithm in ORS

Applying the above equations, from node A to A', theoretically, the number of routes is: $\Theta = \sum_{r=0}^{3} P_3^r = P_3^0 + P_3^1 + P_3^2 + P_3^3 = 16$, as n is equal to 3 (N-2). The total link number is: $\varphi = 2 * C_5^2 = 20$.

Physically, there exist 12 links in this network shown below:

(1) AB, AC, BC, BB', CB', CA', BA,CA,CB,B'B,B'C,A'C;

Then, the total route number from A to A' can be obtained via the following steps:

(2) P_3^0 : AA' = boolean:{0}, as the link AA' can not be found in (1);

(3) P_3^1 : B, B',C = { {AB, BA'}, { AB',B'A'},{AC,CA'}}= boolean:{ {0,0},{0,0}, {1, 1}}={0,0,1}. Thus, only the link ACA' is true.

(4) P_3^2 : BB', BC, B'B, B'C, CB, CB' = boolean:{0,1,0,0,0,0}; → the link ABCA' is true.

(5) P_3^3 : BB'C, BCB', B'BC, B'CB, CBB', CB'B = boolean:{1,0,0,0,0,0}; → the link ABB'C is true;

Therefore, there are 3 links that are available to deliver the content from node A to A' in this scenario. Once ORS has obtained the network topological context information, the SAM will ask the Information Broker to retrieve the minimum available BW for each available link. Finally, ORS can make decisions to optimise content delivery while also maximising network resource utilisation.

6. Conclusion

This paper presents the design of a Service Adaptation Manager (SAM) based on programmable network technology, which provides a service adaptation capability for CDNs. It reviews the main drawbacks of existing solutions for service adaptation and it presents the two-plane service domain approach: Application Service Plane and Network Service Plane. It proposes the novel Service Context Adaptor algorithms for the provisioning of flexible and adaptive service adaptation and the computation of the network topology. Also, this paper particularly addresses how to design adaptive Optimal Route Service for CDNs.

7. Acknowledgements

This paper describes work partially undertaken in the context of the mCDN (FP6-507993) - Information Society Technologies project, which is partially funded by the Commission of the European Union. We thank mCDN consortium for their good co-operation in the project.

8. Reference

1. Hosanagar, K.; et al, Optimal pricing of content delivery network (CDN) services, System Sciences, 2004. Proceedings of the 37th Annual Hawaii International Conference on,5-8 Jan. 2004 Page(s):205 – 214
2. Lazar, I.; Terrill, W., Exploring content delivery networking, IT Professional Volume 3, Issue 4, July-Aug. 2001 Page(s):47 – 49
3. Vakali, A.; Pallis, G., Content delivery networks: status and trends, Internet Computing, IEEE,Volume 7, Issue 6, Nov.-Dec. 2003 Page(s):68 – 74
4. Shenker, S.; Clark, D.D.; Lixia Zhang, Services or infrastructure: why we need a network service model, Community Networking Integrated Multimedia Services to the Home, 1994., Proceedings of the 1st International Workshop on 13-14 July 1994 Page(s):145 – 149
5. Fuin, D.; et al, A novel approach to quality of service in active networks, Local Computer Networks, 2004. 29th Annual IEEE International Conference on,16-18 Nov. 2004 Page(s):760 – 767
6. Gbaguidi, C., et al., A programmable architecture for the provision of hybrid services, Communications Magazine, IEEE,Volume 37, Issue 7, July 1999 Page(s):110 – 116
7. Title 15: Sun, J.-Z.; Sauvola, J., Towards a conceptual model for context-aware adaptive services, PDCAT'2003. Proceedings of the Fourth International Conference on 27-29 Aug. 2003 Page(s):90 – 94

8. Hirschfeld, R.; Kawamura, K., Dynamic service adaptation, Distributed Computing Systems Workshops, Proceedings. 24th International Conference on 2004 Page(s):290 – 297

9. I. W. Marshall, et al, Active Management of multi-service networks, BT Labs, Adastral Park, Martlesham Heath Ipswich IPS 3RE

10. Steenkiste, P., et al, An active networking approach to service customization, DARPA Active NEtworks Conference and Exposition,Proceedings, 29-30 May 2002 Page(s):305 – 318

11. Su Sen, et al, An intelligent network architecture based on active network technology, Communication Technology Proceedings,WCC - ICCT 2000. International Conference on Volume 2, Page(s):1081 - 1086 vol.2

12. Jones, S., Toward an acceptable definition of service [service-oriented architecture], Software, IEEE,Vol22, Issue 3, May-Jun 2005 Page(s):87 – 93.

13. Aho, A.V.; Lee, D.; "Hierarchical networks and the LSA N-squared problem in OSPF routing",GLOBECOM '00. IEEE, 397 - 404 vol.1

14. D. Decasper, Z. Dittia, G. Parulkar, and B. Plattner. Router Plugins: A Software Architecture for Next Generation Routers. In Proceedings of the ACM SIGCOMM '98 conference, pages 229–253

15. D. J. Wetherall et al. ANTS:A toolkit for building and dynamically deploying network protocols. In IEEE OPENARCH '98, April 1998.

16. D. S. Alexander, et al, The SwitchWare active network architecture. IEEE Network, May/June 1998

17. S. Bhattacharjee, et al. An Architecture for Active Networking. In High Performance Networking (HPN'97), NY, April 1997

18. Bolliger, J., et al, 1999, "Bandwidth modelling for network-aware applications",INFOCOM '99. Eighteenth Annual Joint Conference of the IEEE Computer and Communications Societies Proceedings. IEEE, Volume 3, 21-25 March 1999 Page(s):1300 - 1309 vol.3

19. Khan, J.I.; Qiong Gu,2001,"Network aware video transcoding for symbiotic rate adaptation on interactive transport", NCA 2001. IEEE International Symposium on 8-10 Oct. 2001 Page(s):201 – 212

20. Bolliger, J.; Gross, T.R.; 2001, "Bandwidth monitoring for network-aware applications", HPDC 2001. Proceedings. 10th IEEE International Symposium on 7-9 Aug. 2001 Page(s):241 - 251

21. Bolliger, J.; Gross, T.; 1998, "A framework based approach to the development of network aware applications", Software Engineering, IEEE Transactions on Volume 24, Issue 5, May 1998 page(s):376 – 390

22. Galis, A., et al," Programmable Networks for IP Service Deployment" ISBN 1-58053-745-6; pp450, June 2004; Artech House Books

23. mCDN Project public website, http://www.comtec.e-technik.uni-kassel.de/content/projects/mcdn/pub /pages/mCDN_PublicDeliverables.html.

24. Jones, S., Toward an acceptable definition of service [service-oriented architecture], Software,IEEE,Vol.22, Issue 3, May-June 2005,Page(s):87-9

Flow Context Tags: Concepts and Applications

Roel Ocampo[1,2], Alex Galis[2], Hermann De Meer[3], and Chris Todd[2]

[1] Department of Electrical and Electronics Engineering, University of the Philippines, Diliman, Quezon City, 1101 Philippines
[2] Department of Electronic and Electrical Engineering, University College London, Torrington Place, London WC1E 7JE, U.K.
[3] Faculty of Mathematics and Computer Science, University of Passau, 94032 Passau, Germany

Abstract. Context awareness can help build dynamic networks by enabling them to automatically adapt to the user's activities, computational environment, and network conditions. Our approach in building context-aware networks uses flow context: information about the intrinsic and low-level characteristics of flows, as well as the nature of the applications, devices, and the activities, intentions, preferences or identities of the users that produce or consume them. We tag network flows with their associated context, enabling the information to be shared and acted upon within the network and end-devices. We establish the conceptual framework behind this approach and present some application scenarios, particularly in mobility and QoS adaptation.

1 Introduction

Today we find ourselves almost completely blanketed by a plethora of communication networks including those provided by different mobile phone services, privately-owned and public "hotspot" wireless LANs, personal area networks that use Bluetooth, as well as satellite-based mobile communication and Internet services. The diversity of these networks is only rivaled by variety of the features and characteristics of the mobile devices and applications that run on them.

As we shift from one activity to the next, we find it increasingly inconvenient, if not outright difficult, to continuously and consciously adapt to the different devices and connectivity modes appropriate to our activities, as well as to the constant changes in network characteristics and conditions. One way to mitigate this is by designing minimally-distracting [1]

Please use the following format when citing this chapter:

Ocampo, R., Galis, A., De Meer, H. and Todd, C., 2007, in IFIP International Federation for Information Processing, Volume 229, Network Control and Engineering for QoS, Security, and Mobility, IV, ed. Gaïti, D., (Boston: Springer), pp. 257–268.

networks that automatically adapt to changes in conditions as well as users' activities with little or no user intervention, that is, by developing context-aware networks.

In this paper, we discuss the conceptual framework for flow context tagging as an approach in building context-aware networks. We use the term "flow" to refer to distinguishable streams of related datagrams resulting from the activity of a single entity [2], although we adopt a more inclusive, end-to-end view often attributed to sessions. In our approach, flows across the network are tagged with context information, enabling network devices and end-hosts to gain more information about the flow than what would normally be provided by the individual packet headers or obtained only through stateful inspection of the flow at higher layers.

In some of our recent work we mentioned that flow context may be used within the network to trigger adaptation, personalized services, network-wide (rather than flow-directed) management actions, long-term collection of management information and knowledge-based network management. In this paper however we complement those broad usage classes with discussions on possible application areas, with particular focus on mobility and QoS, while outlining future applications in intelligent flow classification and management, overlay routing and content delivery, and in the control of malicious flows.

2 The Context of a Flow

Our use of the term context has its origins from the domain of pervasive and ubiquitous computing. Dey, Salber and Abowd define context as "any information that can be used to characterize the situation of entities ... that are considered relevant to the interaction between a user and an application, including the user and the applications themselves" [3]. In the human-computer interaction (HCI) and ubiquitous computing domains the particular entities of interest are usually the user or the application. For example, context has been defined as the location and identities of nearby people and objects relevant to an application [4]; the elements of the user's environment that a computer may know about [5]; or the state, situation and surroundings of the user and her devices [6]. In our case, however, we are primarily interested in the interaction between users and the network; thus the entity of interest from our point of view is the network flow, as it is the physical (or electronic) embodiment of the user's interaction with the network.

We define the context of a network flow as any information that can be used to characterize its situation, including information pertaining to other entities and circumstances that give rise to or accompany its generation at the source, affect its transmission through the network, and influence its use at its destination. This includes not only the intrinsic, low-level characteristics of a flow, but also the nature of the applications, devices, and the activities, intentions, preferences and identities of the users that produce or consume the flow.

3 Tagging Flows with Context

Recently we outlined the mechanics and architecture of our approach [7,8]. For completeness, we review some of its key elements, which are also illustrated in Fig. 1.

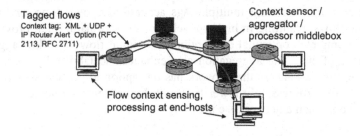

(a) Typical network deployment

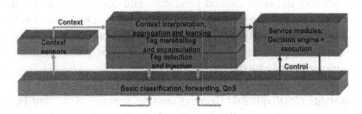

(b) Context tag processing stack

Fig. 1. Functional components of flow context tagging approach

Architecture Context sensing functionality is implemented primarily at end-hosts, where there is rich context information about user and application activity and device capability. Network devices and middleboxes may also perform context sensing either through flow inspection or by processing context information from other sources. Context tags are then assembled and injected along the path of the flow and are intercepted and processed by devices along the flow's path. In some cases the context tags may trigger a control or management action, a service, or an adaptation function within a downstream network device such as a router. End-hosts may also process context tags.

Tag structure Tags are formatted using Extensible Markup Language (XML) and transported within UDP datagrams. XML provides an extensible way to represent context information, and allows the formal specification of languages governing context interpretation. The IP packet header contains the IP Router Alert Option as described in RFC 2113 and RFC 2711.

Tag aggregation Tag processing may also result in the aggregation of information coming from multiple tags accumulated over time, or from multiple flows, resulting in higher-level context information that provides a more complete contextual description of a single flow or a flow aggregate (macroflow). Tag aggregation also enhances scalability by reducing information overload, as the network has the option to process and maintain state for progressively fewer tags with higher-level semantic content as flows approach a network's core.

Ontology An ontology that formally encodes the relationship and properties of the entities within context tags allows the development of a common vocabulary between context producers and consumers within the network and promotes interoperability across domains. Declarative semantics within the ontology facilitate the use of reasoning within the tag aggregation process, and provide a means by which (macro-) flow characteristics and requirements may be derived using inference.

Incremental deployment Context sensing functionality may be added to end-hosts or incrementally on network nodes such as routers, or dedicated boxes may be inserted within the network in order to inspect flows and inject context tags. For nodes that will provide context-triggered services, the service modules and the core router functionalities (classification, forwarding, QoS) do not necessarily have to be closely coupled; the context-related and adaptation functions could reside on a separate device "bolted" onto a conventional router, and SNMP may be used to effect service execution.

4 QoS and Mobility Adaptation

4.1 Mobility adaptation

Context tags may be used as a means by which mobile hosts may announce information on their geographic location or movement to other nodes, or for geographic routing. They may also be used to share other useful information such as device capabilities or battery levels with mobile peers. A flow that indicates a transmitting host with critically low battery levels, for example, may be given priority through the network in order to avoid a costly retransmission.

In this section we describe an application of context tagging to mobility as follows: a mobile node MN (Fig. 2a) requests a multimedia UDP stream from server corresponding node CN. The stream is sent by CN to MN, the latter accessing the network via access point AP_A. MN then moves from the coverage area A of AP_A to coverage area B of AP_B. As it moves, FlowSourceGeographicLocation updates in its context tags allow nodes along the path to directly infer its location and movement.

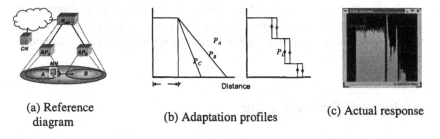

(a) Reference
diagram
      (b) Adaptation profiles   (c) Actual response

Fig. 2. Reference network, adaptation profiles and node response

As MN moves towards coverage area B, router R_{AB} detects through the MN's context tags that it is starting to move within proximity of the coverage area of AP_B. Through a mechanism we call *speculative multicast* the return stream is also sent to AP_B, even while MN has not yet formally handed over to AP_B. Policy settings on the access point AP_B determine whether streams received via speculative multicast are actually sent over the radio interface, or simply cached within the access point. The advantage of having this mechanism is that it offsets the effects of discovery time, or the amount of time before a mobile discovers that it has moved into or out of a new wireless overlay, which often dominates handoff latency [9]. The moment MN joins the new AP it has immediate access to portions of the stream that would otherwise be lost due to handoff latency.

In addition, the type and characteristics of the flow content, e.g. whether its bitrate can be modified either through distillation [10] or by dropping layers [11] are also contained in the context tag. If bitrate modification is possible, an *adaptation profile* (Fig. 2b) specifies the target rate in relation to the probability that it will join a specific access point. We define the *miss penalty* as the number of bits speculatively multicast to an access point that are not actually received by the mobile host because it has not yet joined an access point. A profile P_B with a relatively steep slope reflects a more conservative policy than P_A, as it allows high speculative multicast rates only when a mobile node has a high probability of joining the access point. Consequently it has a lower expected miss penalty. The degenerate case P_C only allows streams to be sent if the AP is actually servicing the MN, which is the behavior seen in many schemes today.

Profile P_D implements a more pragmatic stepwise adaptation, rather than the linear and somewhat idealized profiles shown by P_A and P_B. Figure 2c shows the actual inbound bandwidth on an access point implementing such a profile. The maximum bandwidth received by the access point in this example is when the mobile node is within the coverage area. Even as the mobile node leaves the coverage area, the access point still receives the video stream from the router, although the bandwidth has been reduced by transcoding.

4.2 Implicit QoS signaling

To provide QoS in networks, end-hosts are often expected to either explicitly signal their QoS requirements and undertake resource reservation, or to have sufficient knowledge about the underlying QoS model in order to map application flows to existing QoS classes. However, in [8] we described a scenario that used context tags in implicitly signaling the QoS characteristics and requirements of network flows. We proposed that flow context may be used to: (1) decouple end-hosts and applications from the underlying domain-specific QoS model by providing high-level flow descriptors that can be mapped to a domain's specific QoS mechanisms, (2) provide or expose additional information about the flow to the network in an explicit way to facilitate flow classification for QoS purposes, (3) trigger an appropriate QoS adaptation response on the flow, and (4) identify and label suspicious and malicious flows, or those that are in violation of QoS contracts. This section describes another experiment we conducted to demonstrate some of these aspects.

Simple proof-of-concept We transmitted a video stream with a natural bit rate of approximately 850 kbps, which the network had to reduce to a target 500 kbps based on an adaptation profile similar to those shown in Fig. 2b. A simple (and perhaps default) way for the network to achieve this would be to impose a hard limit on the allowable bit rate of this flow, as shown in Fig. 3, *left*. While this might be acceptable for elastic flows, such context-unaware QoS adaptation might be unsuitable for packet loss- or delay-sensitive traffic such as video, as shown. On the other hand, injecting the appropriate context tags informs downstream adaptors that the flow content may be modified through transcoding. A transcoding adaptor is triggered with an output bitrate parameter setting that corresponds to the 500 kbps target traffic rate. The traffic profile produced by this adaptation and the corresponding video quality are shown in Fig. 3, *center*. The traffic profile shows some "spikes," artifacts of the transcoding scheme used. In order to prevent these, a combination of the bandwidth limiting and transcoding adaptation strategies using adaptor composition results in the traffic profile and video quality shown in Fig. 3, *right*. Occasional and minor degradation of video quality was observed, but the overall quality experienced during the experiment was acceptable.

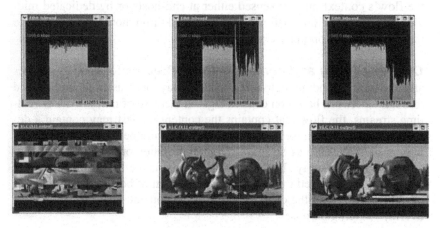

Fig. 3. QoS adaptation strategies. *Left*: Context-unaware. *Center*: Context-aware. *Right*: Context-aware, with adaptor composition

Although not shown here, the function in Fig. 3, right would not be realized properly if band-limiting the flow preceded transcoding its content. This problem may be handled by explicitly stating the interoperability parameters of each adaptor module (or service module as a generalization), specifying the input and output conditions necessary to cascade or compose them [12].

This simple experiment shows how context tags may be used to signal QoS requirements and acceptable QoS adaptation strategies. In this example we have shown implicit signaling, as the sending host had no prior knowledge of the QoS adaptation model existing within the network. In this case it was up to the network to decide which adaptation strategies were appropriate, given the flow's context and the network's QoS goals.

5 Other application areas

Intelligent flow classification and management There are instances where information needed for flow classification such as network addresses or transport-layer port numbers are modified, such as when network- or port address translation (NAT/PAT) are used, or when traffic is tunnelled within well-known protocols such as the Hypertext Transfer Protocol (HTTP) as a stealth technique or as a means to bypass firewalls. As an alternative to each network node performing costly stateful inspection, the flow's context may be sensed either at end-hosts or by dedicated middleboxes, and this information could be shared throughout the flow path so that network may properly classify the flow.

Overlay routing and content delivery Requests for content streams and the corresponding delivered content may be classified and routed through a network based on context tags. In the case of multimedia or real-time streams, the flow that contains the content request may contain a description of QoS, cost, security or reliability requirements that the underlying network may use as basis for a routing decision or to map the flow to an appropriate overlay. In the reverse direction, the flow containing the content to be delivered may contain a description of both the requirements of the requestor and the characteristics of the content, again for routing or overlay mapping purposes.

Mitigating attacks and controlling malicious flows A node equipped with sensors that can detect distributed denial of service (DDoS) attacks or worms propagating through the network may inject a context tag in the reverse path so that upstream nodes may suppress the inbound flows. The tag may contain a description of the malicious flow that upstream nodes may use as a pattern to detect and suppress subsequent attacks, ultimately at or near their sources. This technique may also be explored as a means of controlling spammed email and mitigating its impact on the network. Spam is typically marked, classified or discarded at the receiving end; by the time it has reached its destination, it has already wasted a significant portion of the network's bandwidth. Context tags would enable a network-level response that may also propagate all the way near the source of the spam traffic. This is especially significant in suppressing continuous spam traffic that originates from hijacked hosts on broadband networks.

6 Related Work

Our concept of context-tagged flows seems synonymous with or related to the concepts of "context-aware communications" and "context-sensitive communications." Henricksen et al. use the term context-aware communication to refer to the use of context in communication applications; however, the applications they cited as examples use "communications" in a sense that often pertains to the direct interaction between humans or at the application layer [13]. In addition, the primary consumers of context in these cases were end-applications or even humans, rather than network devices. Context-tagged flows seem to be more related to the general concept of context-sensitive communications (CSCs) in reference to context-triggered, impromptu and possibly short-lived interactions between applications in ubiquitous computing environments [14,15]. CSCs are also defined as a type of communication where channels are established between devices based on some specific contexts, and are used for context dissemination to network entities [16]. Context-tagged flows also share these properties of CSCs and are likewise used for context dissemination to network entities and end-hosts. However, tagged flows provide a very specific approach to the dissemination of context within the network, and present a different persistence model.

Our approach shares some architectural and conceptual similarities with COPS (Checking, Observing and Protecting Services), where middleboxes called iBoxes (Inspection-And-Action Boxes) perform deep packet inspection in order to identify and segregate traffic into good, bad and suspicious classes [17]. Annotation Labels are inserted into packets and used as basis within the network whether a packet is to be forwarded normally, slowed, or dropped. COPS seems to be focused primarily on network protection and QoS, and has a limited notion of context. We believe that our broader view of flow context presents a more general framework and may lead to a wider class of novel and useful applications.

In mobile applications, handoff latency can also be reduced through doublecasting [9], whereby packets within a wireless overlay are simultaneously sent to another base station belonging to another overlay in the network. This however is intended for vertical handoffs between overlays that use different network technologies, as it assumes that the mobile host simultaneously receives on different network interfaces. In multicast-based mobility (M&M) [18] a mobile node is assigned a multicast address and throughout its movement, joins a multicast tree through locations it visits, but only after it has actually moved to the new location. In contrast, in our approach, the inbound stream may actually be sent to the base stations or access points covering the mobile host's next possible locations, even before it has actually moved there.

In the QoS application domain, HQML [19] is an XML-based hierarchical QoS markup language that allows applications to signal QoS characteristics and requirements to end-applications and network elements called QoS proxies. However, it is focused specifically on QoS and on Web applications, and is not designed as a general mechanism for making other types of context information available to network nodes. The Session Description Protocol (SDP) [20] describes multimedia sessions using a short textual description that includes information on media, protocols, codec formats, timing and transport information, while Multipurpose Internet Mail Extensions (MIME) [21] provide high-level type descriptions for different content types such as text, images, video, audio or application-specific data in message streams. Unlike context tags, these schemes deliver flow or session context to end-hosts rather than network nodes, and are limited to very specific application domains. However, the formats and types used in SDP and MIME messages may be reused to describe flows in a high-level way within context tags and our flow context ontology.

7 Conclusion and Future Work

Context awareness can help build minimally-distracting networks by enabling them to automatically adapt to the user's activities, computational environment, and network conditions. Our approach in building context-aware networks considers network flows as entities of interest, and uses context information that encodes the nature, state, requirements and other relevant information that describes these flows. By tagging flows with context, we provide a means by which network devices as well as end-applications can adapt to them, or cause long-term management actions to be performed in an intelligent way.

We have described some application areas where our context-tagging technique may be applied, such as in mobility and moving networks, QoS, intelligent flow classification and management, overlay routing and content delivery, and in the control of malicious flows. We are conducting a more rigorous validation and performance evaluation of our approach in these application areas, and expect to uncover more possible applications in the course of our work.

Acknowledgment. This paper describes work partially undertaken in the context of the E-NEXT - IST FP6-506869 project, which is partially funded by the Commission of the European Union. The views contained herein are those of the authors and do not necessarily represent those of E-NEXT. Roel Ocampo acknowledges support from the Doctoral Fellowship Program of the University of the Philippines.

References

1. M. Satyanarayanan. Pervasive Computing: Vision and Challenges. IEEE Personal Communications, 8(4), August 2001
2. R. Braden, D. Clark, and S. Shenker. Integrated Services Architecture in the Internet: an Overview. Request for Comments 1633, June 1994.
3. A. K. Dey, D. Salber, and G. D. Abowd. A Conceptual Framework and a Toolkit for Supporting the Rapid Prototyping of Context-Aware Applications. Human-Computer Interaction (HCI) Journal, 16 (2-4), 2001
4. B. Schilit and M. Theimer. Disseminating Active Map Information to Mobile Hosts. IEEE Network, 8 (5), September 1994
5. P. Brown, J. Bovey and X. Chen. Context-Aware Applications: From the Laboratory to the Marketplace. IEEE Personal Communications,4 (5), October 1997
6. A. Schmidt, M. Beigl, and H. Gellersen. There is More to Context Than Location. Computers and Graphics Journal, 23 (6), December 1999
7. R. Ocampo, A. Galis and C. Todd. Triggering Network Services Through Context-Tagged Flows. Proceedings of the Second International Workshop on Active and Programmable Grid Architectures and Components (APGAC'05), Atlanta, Georgia, May 2005
8. R. Ocampo, A. Galis, H. De Meer, and C. Todd. Implicit Flow QoS Signaling Using Semantic-Rich Context Tags. Proceedings of the 13th International Workshop on Quality of Service (IWQoS 2005), Passau, Germany, June 2005

9. M. Stemm and R. Katz. Vertical Handoffs in Wireless Overlay Networks. Mobile Networks and Applications. Special Issue: Mobile Networking in the Internet, 3 (4), 1999
10. A. Fox, S. D. Gribble, Y. Chawathe and E. A. Brewer. Adapting to Network and Client Variation Using Active Proxies: Lessons and Perspectives. Proc. 16th Intl. Symposium on Operating Systems Principles (SOSP-16), France, October 1997
11. S. McCanne, V. Jacobsen and M. Vetterli. Receiver-Driven Layered Multicast. Proceedings of the ACM Sigcomm '96 Conference, August 1996
12. M. Yarvis, P. Reiher and G. Popek. Conductor: A Framework for Distributed Adaptation. Proc. 7th Workshop on Hot Topics in Operating Systems, March 1999
13. K. Henricksen, J. Indulska and A. Rakotonirainy. Modeling Context Information in Pervasive Computing Systems. Proceedings of the First International Conference on Pervasive Computing, Zurich, Switzerland, August 2002.
14. S. Yau and F. Karim. An Adaptive Middleware for Context-Sensitive Communication for Real-Time Applications in Ubiquitous Computing Environments. Real-Time Systems, 26 (1), 2004
15. M. Khedr and A. Karmouch. Exploiting Agents and SIP for Smart Context Level Agreements. IEEE Pacific Rim Conference on Communications, Computers and Signal Processing, Canada, August 2003
16. A. Karmouch, A. Galis, R. Giaffreda, T. Kanter, A. Jonsson, A. Karlsson, R. Glitho, M. Smirnov, M. Kleis, C. Reichert, A. Tan, M. Khedr, N. Samaan, H. Laamanen, M. El Barachi and J. Dang. Contextware Research Challenges in Ambient Networks. 1st International Workshop on Mobility Aware Technologies and Applications, October 2004
17. R. Katz, G. Porter, S. Shenker, I. Stoica and M. Tsai. COPS: Quality of Service vs. Any Service at All. Proceedings of the 13th International Workship on Quality of Service (IWQoS 2005), Passau, Germany, June 2005
18. A. Helmy, M. Jaseemuddin and G. Bhaskara. Multicast-based Mobility: A Novel Architecture for Efficient Micro-Mobility. IEEE Journal on Selected Areas in Communications (JSAC), Special Issue on All-IP Wireless Networks, May 2004
19. X. Gu, K. Nahrstedt, W. Yuan, D. Wichadakul, and D. Xu. An XML-Based Quality of Service Enabling Language for the Web. Journal of Visual Language and Computing (JVLC), Special Issue on Multimedia Languages for the Web, February 2002
20. M. Handley, V. Jacobson. SDP: Session Description Protocol. Request for Comments 2327, April 1998
21. N. Freed and N. Borenstein. Multipurpose Internet Mail Extensions Part Two: Media Types. Request for Comments 2046, November 1996

Modelling the Temporal Aspects of Network Configurations

Sylvain Hallé[1], Rudy Deca[1], Omar Cherkaoui[1], Roger Villemaire[1] and Daniel Puche[2]

[1]Université du Québec à Montréal, Montréal, Canada
[2]Cisco Systems Inc., Montréal, Canada

Abstract

One of the main issues with the existing management configuration is the absence of a transactional model, which should allow the network configuration data to retain their integrity and consistence during the configuration process. In this paper, we propose a mathematical framework based on lattice theory allowing the structuring of configuration operations leading to the concept of component and validation checkpoint, and present polynomial-time algorithms for studying these structures. We will illustrate the model by an example of two examples of configuration operations: the deployment of a VLAN service through SNMP and the deployment of a VPN service through the Netconf protocol.

1 Introduction

Among other network management functions, configuration management is still mainly accomplished by proprietary means, be it Command Line Interface (CLI), JunOS or TL1. Recent alternatives like SNMPConf, COPS and Netconf have not yet succeeded in bringing a standard configuration solution. This situation is due to numerous causes: security (SNMPv3), absence of an adequate configuration information model, proprietary equipment instrumentation semantics. Another overlooked factor is the absence of a simple transactional model between agents and manag-

Please use the following format when citing this chapter:

Hallé, S., Deca, R., Cherkaoui, O., Villemaire, R. and Puche, D., 2007, in IFIP International Federation for Information Processing, Volume 229, Network Control and Engineering for QoS, Security, and Mobility, IV, ed. Gaïti, D., (Boston: Springer), pp. 269–282.

ers allowing for the association between management protocol operations (SNMP, COPS and Netconf) and management information.

When configuring a network service that involves multiple equipments, there is an important temporal aspect of complexity of the network service configuration. There are many sequences of configuration commands or operations that must be performed on multiple network elements or equipments, temporal dependencies among these sequences, semantic constraints among their parameters. Moreover, specific groups of commands and parameters belong to the same service or sub-service and must thus be performed together, in an atomic way, even though they affect multiple components or network elements form different network devices. The atomic character of the configuration operations involving a number of parameters is relevant both at device and at network levels.

In this paper, we propose a mathematical framework based on lattice theory allowing the structuring of configuration operations in terms of configuration dependencies. The concepts of component and milestone that we define in terms of paths in the lattice structure help us to simplify the analysis of possible solution paths and provide us with a sound criterion for dividing the deployment of a service into natural macro-steps that serve as validation checkpoints.We will illustrate the model by two examples of configuration operations: the deployment of a VLAN service through SNMP and the deployment of a VPN service through the Netconf protocol, and show preliminary results for validation checkpoints for the latter of these cases.

In section 2, we show by two examples why current management approaches are inedaquate for dealing with the sequential aspect of network configuration. In section 3, the lattice-based mathematical framework for modelling temporal constraints is detailed, and polynomial-time algorithms for studying the resulting structures are presented. Section 4 shows possible applications of this framework and preliminary results obtained for the case of simple Virtual Private Networks, while section 5 concludes and indicates further directions of work.

2 Motivation and Related Work

The deployment of a service over a network basically consists in altering the configuration of one or many equipments to implement the desired functionalities. We can presuppose without loss of generality that all properties of a given configuration are described by attribute-value pairs hierarchically organised in a tree structure [13].

Possible alterations to the configuration typically include deleting or adding new parameters to the configuration of a device, or changing the value of existing parameters. In most cases, the parameters involved in such modifications are both syntactically and semantically interdependent. For instance, the value of some parameter might be required to depend in a precise way on the value of another parameter; the simplest example of such dependency is the fact that an IP address must match the subnet mask that comes with it. More complex dependencies might constrain the existence of a parameter to the existence of another. Recent works have shown how such dependencies can be automatically checked by logical tools on a given configuration snapshot [13].

However, the situation becomes more complex when one wants to actually *deploy* a service from scratch. In addition to constraints on the values of parameters, the dependencies may also impose that the modifications be performed in a specific order. When done in an uncoordinated way, changing, adding or removing components or data that implement network services can bring the network in an inconsistent or undefined state. This fact becomes acutely true in the case where operations must be distributed on multiple network elements, as they cannot be modified all at once. Moreover, while a single inconsistent device can ultimately be restarted when all else fails, there is no such "restart" option when an entire network configuration becomes inconsistent.

However, one of the main issues with the existing management paradigms is the absence of a *transactional model*, which should allow the network configuration data to retain their integrity and consistency during the configuration process.

The network community has proposed different approaches for ensuring the consistency and integrity of the network configuration during the management of network services. The policy-based management using the Ponder language [6] incorporates OCL (Object Constraint Language) [19] to express the dependencies among configuration parameters. Other approaches, based on ontologies [17, 18], use the Protégé Axiom Language and Toolset (PAL) [5] for expressing configuration parameter constraints and queries. Many other constraint languages and tools are also available and can be used to express configuration parameter dependences, such as the Alloy language [16] and the constraint analyser based on it, Alcoa [15]. However, these approaches use constraint languages borrowed from other domains, designed for other purposes. Therefore, they are not adequate to the specifics of network configuration, and they do not tackle the transactional aspect of network configuration.

We will study two examples of configuration management using different paradigms, and stress their weaknesses in this regard. Based on this evidence, we will show what the transactional model can accomplish and what its benefits are in the area of network configuration.

2.1 VLAN Configuration with SNMP

The deployment of a Virtual Local Area Network (VLAN) [3, 11] on a network involves a number of configuration operations falling into four categories:

- specification of the Virtual Trunk Protocol (VTP) domain and operation mode
- VLAN creation
- port allocation
- trunk creation

However, these operations cannot be performed in any order. Some ordering constraints are imposed.

Clearly, the operations belonging to the first group (VTP) are preparation operations on which the operations of the second group (VLAN creation) rely. In the same fashion, the port allocation cannot be done before the VLAN has been created (for the sake of simplicity, we exclude here the case where the port is reserved in advance or dynamically allocated from a pool). This leads to the formulation of a first set of two temporal constraints:

Temporal Constraint 1 All VTP operations must have been done before any VLAN creation parameter is added to the configuration.

Temporal Constraint 2 All VLAN creation parameters must have been added to the configuration before any port allocation or trunk creation parameters are added.

These two constraints entail that the VLAN be created in an *atomic* way: the name, number and other parameters must be specified together and the editing must be done by one manager at a time. If the configuration were to be modified by means of the command line interface, this atomic property would be achieved by having both number and name parameters mandatory within the same command (for example, the Cisco IOS command vlan <number><name>). A similar reasoning can be done for the other modification operations, leading to more temporal constraints.

However, despite these temporal constraints, the SNMP paradigm [2] allows the parameters to be configured independently and has no semantics for the configuration operations. It does not have a transactional model and thus allows inconsistent evolution of the network configuration. The way SNMP ensures atomicity is by providing an editing buffer for VLAN creation (the vtpVlanEditingTable) within the VLAN Management Information Base (MIB) [3]. Only one manager at a time is allowed to own and edit this buffer.

This example illustrates several facts. First, the temporal constraints impose that some of the VLAN parameters be grouped; SNMP does not elegantly enforce this and rather uses an ad-hoc editing buffer mechanism for this purpose.

Second, there are two levels of validation: the first level makes sure that each operation has been correctly made by confirming that the apply buffer operation has succeeded; the second level validates the overall operation and checks whether the VLAN has actually been created.

2.2 Example 2: VPN Configuration with Netconf

In this section we analyse the problems encountered by the Netconf protocol, when dealing with network services that involve multiple equipments and introduce a transactional model that solves these problems.

We illustrate this with an example of an MPLS Virtual Private Network (VPN) service deployment [20]. A VPN is a private network constructed within a public network such as a service provider's network. A customer might have several sites, which are contiguous parts of the network, dispersed throughout the Internet and would like to link them together by a protected communication. The VPN ensures the connectivity and privacy of the customer's communications between sites.

Such a service consists of multiple configuration operations that involve setting the routing tables and the VPN forwarding tables, setting the MPLS, BGP and IGP connectivity on multiple equipments having various roles, such as the customer edge (CE), provider edge (PE) and provider core (PC) routers. In total, a minimum of about 30 parameters must be added or changed in each device involved in the deployment of the VPN. As an example, Figure 1 shows two leaf nodes that must be added, each in its own position, to the configuration tree of a PE router.

Leaf node A is one of the configuration parameters that contributes to the creation of the VPN routing and forwarding tables on the PEs of the service provider. It cannot be added to the configuration of a PE router before the corresponding interface has been configured, which entails, among other things, the addition of leaf node B. Therefore, one can extract a temporal constraint from this relation:

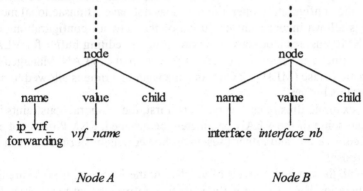

Node A   *Node B*

Fig. 1. Two configuration nodes that must be added for deploying a VPN

Temporal Constraint 3 *The node* `ip_vrf_forwarding` *cannot be added to a configuration tree before node* `interface/number` *has been set.*

Similar dependencies can be extracted for many other pairs of nodes among the 30 parameters involved, based on

- the semantic dependencies among the various components and parameters of the configuration;
- the spatial distribution of the configuration components and parameters;
- the choices of topology and technologies (protocols, device roles and types, vendor software, etc.).

These interdependencies imply a logically simultaneous configuration of the respective parameters on all these equipments. Since these equipments are spatially distributed and configuration operations can only be performed sequentially, this goal can only be achieved by "synchronizing" the configurations on different equipments by carefully setting up *validation points* during the configuration procedure.

The Netconf protocol [12] defines a simple mechanism for network device management. However, its transactional model, which includes a Validation capability, is device-centered, and does not provide a mechanism to ensure the consistency of the configuration that involves correlated configuration steps on multiple devices.

Netconf provides two phases of a successful configuration transaction during a service configuration procedure: preparation and commitment.

During preparation, the configurations are retrieved from the network devices. When all the configurations have been retrieved, the edition starts at service level. The validation at this stage ensures that the network configuration is consistent before the proposed modifications required by the service. To ensure the integrity of the configuration edition, the device configurations are locked, edited and subsequently unlocked. When the service edition has been successfully accomplished, the commitment starts. The validation at this stage ensures that the network configuration remains consistent after the respective modification of the network configurations.

Therefore, taken as is, Netconf does not provide any indication as to where and what to validate.

The previous examples have shown that many configuration operations must be done in a specific sequence, others must be performed together notwithstanding the order and others are mutually exclusive. Therefore, we need a clear temporal representation of the operations to be performed, which will describe all the temporal dependencies, indicate the possible procedural order of operation for various groups of configuration parameters on various devices and indicate the optimal temporal order and distribution of these operations.

3 A Theoretical Model

In this section, we present a theoretical study of the temporal issues described in section 2 by providing a theoretical model of the situation.

3.1 States and Transitions

Let S be a set of "states" representing a unit situation at a given time. In the case of network configuration, states are labelled trees described in section 2.

We call *transition* from a state s_1 to a state s_2 the structural modifications that transform s_1 into s_2. Formally, transitions can be defined as a subset of tuples $T \subseteq S \times S$; there exists a transition from s_1 to s_2 if and only if $(s_1, s_2) \in T$. The tuple (S, T) forms a directed graph G that we call a *transition diagram*.

In the case of the labelled trees we use for modelling device configurations, structural modifications are limited to addition of a labelled node to a leaf, or deletion of a leaf node in the tree. These modifications intuitively refer to addition, deletion or modification of a parameter in the configuration of a device. Therefore, it is possible that no transition exists in either way between two given states: this explains why T is only a subset of all possible pairs of states.

A *path* is a finite sequence of states $<s_1, ..., s_n>$ such that, for any s_i, s_{i+1}, there exists a $t \in T$ such that $t = (s_i, s_{i+1})$. The *distance* between two states, noted $\Delta(s_1, s_2)$ is the length of the shortest directed path linking them.

The configuration problem of the previous section becomes in this system the study of all paths that start from a given configuration, s_s, and end at a target configuration s_t. In addition, one might want to find the shortest of such paths.

However, this system, taken as is, is too general for any practical use. In particular, we must make sure that only solutions that progress towards the target are possible.We hence use path constraints to limit our study to sequences of states that have a meaning and are not degenerate.

A solution is to remove all tuples $(s_1, s_2) \in T$ such that $\Delta(s_1, s_t) < \Delta(s_2, s_t)$.

This condition makes sure that the parameters that are actually added are part of the solution, but not of the start state, and that parameters that are removed are part of the start state, but not part of the solution. Any other modification is out of the way of an acceptable solution. This distance restriction also has for effect of removing any loops in the paths.

3.2 Temporal Constraints

Now that G has been trimmed of any nonsensical states and paths, we can add further restrictions by imposing on the remaining transitions the semantic constraints related to the situation we are trying to model.

For example, in order to respect Temporal Constraint 3 in the case of the VPN deployment exposed in section 2.2, we must remove all transitions that lead to states where node A of Figure 1 is added while node B is not present.

More semantic constraints can be added to further trim the state graph from unwanted states and transitions. The remaining paths satisfy to all defined constraints. Intuitively, these so-called *acceptable* paths can be seen as a semantically desirable candidate solution for transforming the start state into the target final state.

3.3 Structuring Operations

In the minimal VPN example described previously, containing only two provider edge and two customer edge routers, the resulting state graph is composed of over 15,000 states spanning a proportional number of paths. These figures suggest that raw state graphs are far from being meaningful and manageable by hand. However, it is possible to simplify further this graph by studying patterns that can be found in it.

First, we can observe that the remaining graph $G = (S', T')$, induces a partial ordering $\sqsubseteq$ in S' defined in the following way:

$$x \sqsubseteq y \Longleftrightarrow (x, y) \in T$$

The tuple $L = (S, \sqsubseteq)$ forms a bounded lattice [8]; the graph G can also be seen as the Hasse diagram of L. This lattice of possible states and transitions on states can then be studied for interesting properties. It is from these properties that a global procedure describing legal transformations to the configurations will be deduced.

Components

The first step is to recognize the presence of *components*, i.e. of closed groups of interweaved actions. For instance, the parameters that contribute to the creation of the VPN routing and forwarding tables on the PEs of the service provider are bound by constraints 1 and 2. They impose that all VRF actions on a router be done before passing on to another router, and that all VRF configuring must be done before going on to another aspect of the configuration.

Therefore, all actions of VRF configuration on a single router may be done in any order, but must all be done before doing anything else. Such set of n actions thus forms a component and appears as a Boolean n-dimensional cube in the Hasse diagram of the lattice, as shown in Figure 2. The left structure shows a component where three actions, α, β and γ, can be performed in any order, resulting in 6 different paths. The right structure shows a similar Boolean cube for 4 different actions.

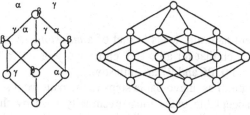

Fig. 2. A closed set of interchangeable operations forms a component

These components act as a "capsule" of operations that must be performed atomically (i.e., that must not be mixed with any other operation).

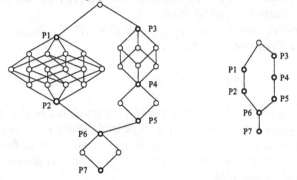

Fig. 3. A complete state graph and its associated reduced state graph

We see that identifying components is an important tool to reduce the
complexity of the state graph. Each component has a unique start and end
point, and can therefore be assimilated to the single edge linking these two
points.

Identification of such components leads to the construction of a reduced
state graph where some edges no longer represent a single transition, but
rather whole sets of transitions (Boolean cubes) that can be performed in
arbitrary order. Figure 3 shows how a reduced state graph can be obtained
from a state graph. One can identify 2, 3 and 4-dimensional Boolean cubes
that are linked together. For example, points P1 and P2 are the endpoints
of a component: all states between P1 and P2 have no contact with any
other state. Since these cubes represent components made of swappable actions, they can be identified as such and be identified with their endpoints
to form a reduced state graph, as shown on the right part of the picture.

Milestones

The notion of component naturally leads to that of a *milestone*. A mile-
stone is an element $x \in S$ such that for all $y \in S$, either $x \sqsubseteq y$ or $y \sqsubseteq x$. For
example, in Figure 3, states P0, P6 and P7 are milestones.

Milestones can be thought of as unavoidable steps in the path from start
to solution, since all acceptable paths must eventually pass by those
points, in the order they appear. Therefore, milestones are good candidates
to divide the modelled process into natural macro-steps of which they are
the boundaries. In the case of Figure 3, two macro-steps can be identified:
the transition from the start state P0 to state P6, and the transition from P6
to P7. The word "natural" is used here, since these milestones emerge from

the set of temporal constraints imposed on the lattice. Different temporal constraints generally lead to different milestones.

The concept of milestone can also be applied to any sublattice of L. In particular, inside each macro-step, there can be local milestones that may be viewed as natural sub-steps. The process can be recursively repeated and yield a natural, hierarchical decomposition of the whole process into nested natural blocks of swappable operations. Hence, states P1-P5 are sub-milestones, or milestones of order 2.

3.4 Computing Components and Milestones

In order to be efficient, the structures defined in the previous section must be able to be found easily and automatically by means of algorithms. In this section, we provide algorithms for finding milestones and for identifying components, and give an overview of their complexity.

Finding Milestones

The first algorithm we present is aimed at finding milestones in a lattice. Its principle is easy: for a state s, we can mark all states reachable from s by a (depth-first or breadth-first) graph traversal starting at s. Similarly, the set of states from which we can reach s can be computed and marked by a traversal of the transpose graph (going "up" instead of "down"). The chosen vertex is a milestone if and only if all vertices of the lattice are marked at the end of the algorithm.

A brief analysis of this algorithm shows that determining whether a given vertex is a milestone takes no more execution steps than the total number n of vertices in the lattice. Therefore, for finding all milestones, it suffices to repeat the algorithm starting at each vertex; the resulting complexity is therefore in $O(n^2)$.

Finding Components

In the same way as the definition of milestones is linked to that of components, the algorithm for finding components relies on the milestone-finding algorithm. We proceed to the same reachability analysis than in the previous section, except that instead of merely marking a vertex as visited, we explicitly state from which original vertex it was reached. At the end of the process, each node has a list of the nodes from which it is reachable, either forwards or backwards. A vertex m is a milestone if all the vertices in L have m in their list.

Then, for each milestone m_1 and its immediate milestone successor m_2, we consider the subgraph of all points between m_1 and m_2. This subgraph is divided into a number of disjoint sublattices $L_1, L_2, \ldots, L_n$. If one of these L_i has no milestone (which can be easily obtained by analysing the lists a second time), then the sublattice $L_i \cup \{m_1, m_2\}$ is a component.

As we can see, the overall complexity of this procedure depends on the maximum level of nesting where milestones can be found. However, a rough worst case can be calculated by supposing there can be no more nesting levels than there are elements in L. At the first step, it takes $O(n^2)$ operations to find the milestones of the first level. It again takes a time proportional to the square of their size to find all sub-milestones found in these sublattices. However, all nested sublattices found after removing the first-order milestones are disjoint. Therefore, the total time needed to find all second order sub-milestones is again in $O(n^2)$, where n is still the total size of L. Since the nesting level of any component is at most n, the total number of steps required is in $O(n^3)$.

4 Applications

The main advantage of the analysis of the lattice that arises from temporal constraints is that it induces a way of synthesising a protocol for the implementation of a service. By placing validation points at milestones, we ensure such checkpoints are optimally placed in semantically sound locations throughout the deployment process. Since these checkpoints reflect the structure imposed by the temporal constraints, they also make optimal points to roll back in case a failure occurs.

We have succeeded in analysing the deployment of a Virtual Private Network for the basic case of four routers and identified six main milestones. This is helpful in practice. For instance, in an existing tool called NetconfMaker [1], the user must manually set validation point in order to obtain a transactional model on top of the Netconf protocol. Due to the large number of possible solution, this is not an easy task. However, by using the approach presented in this paper, it is possible to feed NetconfMaker with scripts enabling it to proceed automatically to the discovery of these validation points.

The granularity of the configuration components and validation operations depends on how tightly the semantic dependences are coupled within the components and the complexity of these components. For instance, in the case of the VPN example, the BGP component can be split into two subcomponents: the first dealing with the creation of the BGP process and the second with the neighbour information configuration. Another component refers to the mutual redistribution of the routing information between the IGP, the static routing used, or the connectivity between PE-CEs and the BGP process. If we take into account the initial underlying sub-services (establishing the connectivity between PE-CEs, between PE-PCs and MLPS), we obtain six components, to which we add the initial constraints, obtained form the customer and the service provider choices.

One aspect of establishing validation points takes into account the hierarchy existing among the configuration transactions. Establishing the network-level validation points ensures the consistency and integrity of the configuration transactions that involve multiple equipments, roles and configuration parameters.

Moreover, the knowledge of milestones and components for a given service allows for the creation of more structured Management Information Bases (MIBs) and Policy Information Bases (PIBs), where the access mechanisms to configuration parameters could be designed according to the temporal dependencies discovered.

5 Conclusion

In this paper, we have shown by examples that configuration parameters in network devices are subject to syntactical and semantic dependencies which, when deploying a network service, may impose that some of the configuration operations be done in a specific order. We also explained how a mathematical framework using lattice theory can model these ordering constraints. The concepts of components and milestones, defined in terms of paths in the lattice structure, help us to simplify the analysis of possible solution paths and provide us with a sound criterion for dividing the deployment of a service into natural macro-steps that serve as validation checkpoints.

In particular, a deeper study of the implementation of an MPLS VPN in a simple case was found to be divided into six ordered main natural components whose internal configuration operations are mutually swappable. These results are in accordance with the intuitive vision of the deployment of this service.

Further work on this concept can lead to a thorough study of the deployment of a number of network services that could allow us to suggest the location of optimal validation points.

References

1. Cherkaoui O, Bétouret F, Deca R (2004) On the Transactional Issues of the Netconf Protocol. Université du Québec à Montréal, unpublished report.
2. Case J, Fedor M, Schoffstall M, Davin J (1990) Simple Network Management Protocol, STD 15. RFC 1157
3. Cisco SNMP Object Navigator. http://tools.cisco.com/Support/SNMP/
4. Clarke EM, Grumberg O, Peled DA (2000) Model Checking. MIT Press, Cambridge
5. Crubézy M (2002) The Protégé Axiom Language and Toolset ("PAL"). Protégé Project, Stanford University http://protege.stanford.edu/
6. Daminaou N, Dulay N, Lupu E, Sloman M (2001) The Ponder policy Specification Language. In Sloman M, Lobo J, Lupu EC. (eds) Policy'2001, Springer, Berlin Heidelberg New York, pp 29–31
7. D'Antonio S, D'Arienzo M, Pescapè A, Ventre G (2004) An Architecture for Automatic Configuration of Integrated Networks. In NOMS 2004
8. Davey BA, Priestley HA (1990) Introduction to Lattices and Order, Cambridge University Press, Cambridge
9. Deca R, Cherkaoui O, Puche D (2004) A Validation Solution for Network Configuration. In CNSR 2004
10. Deca R, Cherkaoui O, Puche D (2004) Configuration Model for Network Management. In Gaiti D, Galmes S, Puigjaner R (eds) NetCon 2004
11. Draft Standard for Virtual Bridge Local Area Networks, IEEE Draft P802.1Q/D1, May 16, 1997
12. Enns R (2004) Netconf Configuration Protocol. Internet draft, June 2004. http://www.ietf.org/internet-drafts/draft-ietf-netconf-prot-03.txt
13. Hallé S, Deca R, Cherkaoui O, Villemaire R (2004) Automated Verification of Service Configuration on Network Devices. In Vicente J, Hutchison D (eds) MMNS 2004, Springer, Berlin Heidelberg New York, LNCS 3271, pp 176-188
14. Hallé S, Deca R, Cherkaoui O, Villemaire R, Puche D (2004) A Formal Validation Model for the Netconf Protocol. In Sahai, A, Wu F (eds) DSOM 2004, Springer, Berlin Heidelberg New York, LNCS 3278, pp 147-158
15. Jackson D, Schechter I, Shlyakhter I (2000) Alcoa: the Alloy Constraint Analyzer, In ICSE 2000
16. Jackson D (2000) Alloy: A Lightweight Object Modelling Notation. Technical Report 797, MIT Laboratory for Computer Science
17. López de Vergara JE, Villagrá VE, Berrocal J (2002) Semantic Management: advantages of using an ontology-based management information meta-model. In HP-OVUA 2002
18. Noy NF (2001) Managing Multiple Ontologies in Protégé-2000. In Fifth International Protégé-2000 Workshop
19. Object Constraint Language (OCL) http://www.omg.org/docs/ptc/03-10-14.pdf
20. Rosen E, Rechter Y (1999) BGP/MPLS VPNs. RFC 2547

Programmable Network Functionality for Improved Qos of Interactive Video Traffic

Brendan McAllister, Alan Marshall and Roger Woods

Institute of Electronics, Communications and Information Technology. (ECIT),
Queens University Belfast,
Queen's Road, Belfast BT3 9DT, UK
b.mcallister, a.marshall, r.woods@ee.qub.ac.uk

Abstract. This paper proposes a novel approach for introducing programmable functions into Internet-type networks. Specifically, the functions are designed to improve the quality of multiple video conferencing sessions when transmitted over DiffServ-enabled IP networks. The scheme operates through the use of the IPv6 hop-by-hop option header. Detailed simulations are presented that show how incorporating the programmable network functionality into the DiffServ routers guarantees the end-to-end delay for basic video playback is reduced by at least 50% with no packet loss.

Keywords: *Video conferencing; Layered MPEG-4; End-to-end delay control*

1 Introduction

The strict end-to-end delay requirements associated with video conferencing, which are in the order of a few milliseconds, make it very difficult to ensure quality playback whenever networks become congested. Providing service quality for these types of interactive applications is very difficult over a network such as the Internet, which has been designed for simplicity. Diffserv [2, 7, 8] goes some way to improve the Quality of Service (QoS) for these applications, however its aggregated approach cannot offer individual guarantees. Work in [3] introduces a scalable approach to streaming media whereby the receiver subscribes to defined levels of video quality depending on it capabilities (available bandwidth). However it

Please use the following format when citing this chapter:

McAllister, B., Marshall, A. and Woods, R., 2007, in IFIP International Federation for Information Processing, Volume 229, Network Control and Engineering for QoS, Security, and Mobility, IV, ed. Gaïti, D., (Boston: Springer), pp. 283–296.

does not look into interactive video conferencing and requires various receiver-driven control protocols.

The proposed work introduces novel programmable network functionality into the current network topology, which operates along with layered video streaming to remark and/or reroute lower priority video traffic. This ensures more video conference sessions can be supported at an increased quality than is currently possible under adverse network conditions. A number of simulations are described which demonstrate this approach.

The paper is organized as follows. Section 2 describes how QoS is currently provided in IP networks and the problems associated with it. The programmable network functionality is introduced in Section 3 while Sections 4 and 5 describe the network simulation environment and present the results obtained using the OPNET Modeller package. Finally Section 6 provides a summary of the results and looks to future work in the area.

2   Video Conferencing over IP

Achieving scalable QoS in the Internet is provided through DiffServ by aggregating flows into a set number of classes. The classification of a packet within a flow is identified by its 'DiffServ code point' (DSCP) value. There are three basic traffic markings, expedited forwarding (EF), assured forwarding (AF) and best effort (BE); EF having the highest and BE having the lowest. Table 1 identifies DiffServ classes and a proposed DSCP marking scheme [4].

Table 1. DSCP application mappings

Service Class	Applications	DSCP Mapping
Telephony	Voice over IP	EF
Interactive Multimedia	Video Conferencing	AF4
Streaming Multimedia	Video on Demand	AF3
Low Latency Traffic	HTTP, Online Shopping	AF2
High Throughput Traffic	SMTP, FTP	AF1
Low Priority Traffic	No BW Guarantees	BE

Fig. 1 shows a typical DiffServ network node configuration. The EF class typically has a low bandwidth requirement but tight delay and loss requirements. These demands are met by ensuring a priority queue (PQ) scheduler within a DiffServ node will always serve the EF queue if a packet is present [5]. The AF and BE queues are serviced with a weighted fair queue (WFQ) scheduler and will be serviced according to the earliest timestamp when no packets are present in the EF queue.

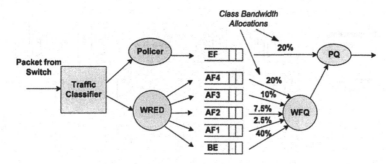

Fig. 1. Typical DiffServ queuing mechanism

Each of the AF classes and BE class are assigned a weight according to the priority and volume of traffic of that class. AF4 being the highest priority traffic with low delay tolerance and BE the lowest priority traffic [6]. Each AF class queue is policed using weighted random early detection (WRED) and each incoming packet is marked with a specific drop precedence indicating the likelihood the packet will be dropped under increasing congestion.

2.1 MPEG-4 Bitstream

For real-time applications such as video broadcast or video-on-demand, the delay tolerance is in the order of seconds and allows for greater compression techniques [9, 10]. This work however primarily deals with real-time video conferencing and so the same level of compression cannot be achieved. The delay tolerance from capture to display for video conferencing is 0.3 seconds [11]. The acceptable network delay is set at 0.2 seconds leaving 0.1 seconds for the encoding and decoding of the video frames. MPEG-4 has the ability to create a layered bitstream of video (Fig. 2), allowing each layer to add to the quality of the decoded video at the receiver. This way, a base video layer of the video stream can be assigned high priority to ensure it receives higher priority than the enhancement layers. The base layer will provide basic quality playback at 10 fps. If decoded along with the spatial enhancement layer, the video would playback at high quality 10 fps. If all three layers are received and decoded in a timely fashion, the destination will receive high quality 30 fps video playback.

  Interactive multimedia traffic is classified into the aggregated flow AF4 and as all the video traffic has low delay requirements, all layers are classified within this class ensuring that they are delivered in the same timely fashion when no congestion is present.

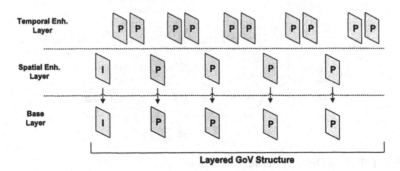

Fig. 2. Video layered bitstream structure

The base layer traffic, being vital to the playback of the video stream, is given the lowest drop precedence value, and the enhancement layers are mapped to high drop precedence values with greater likelihood of being dropped. DiffServ will drop traffic classes using WRED based on their drop precedence values as the queue size within a class increases. This leads to two inherent disadvantages. Firstly, a queue build-up is required before WRED will begin dropping incoming packets with a higher drop precedence, and so a scenario can arise whereby the queue contains a large number of higher drop precedence packets (enhancement layer packets) that create a delay for the incoming low drop precedence packets (base layer packets). The delay incurred by an incoming base layer packet is equivalent to the time it will take for the link to service all backlogged packets in the AF4 class queue. The average delay D, is equal to the size of the queue in packets Q, multiplied by the average packet size P, in bits, divided by the assigned class rate CR, in bits/s assigned to that queue. (Eq. 2.1).

$$(Q * P) / CR = D \qquad (2.1)$$

For example, for a 10Mbps link utilized with 80% background traffic, 2Mbps will be available for incoming video traffic. If the AF4 class is assigned 20% of this bandwidth, then the delay for incoming lower layer packets with an average size of 1000 bytes will exceed the 0.2s delay limit when the queue size increases beyond 20 packets. Delays of this magnitude are unacceptable for interactive applications. The second disadvantage is that enhancement layer packets are being dropped when it may not be necessary, as there may be bandwidth available in an alternative link or class.

3   Programmable Network Functionality

By monitoring the throughput of each link in the DiffServ node, the programmable network functionality can prevent base layer packets being queued, by remarking or rerouting higher layer video traffic whenever the AF4 class throughput is greater than the assigned allocation. In Fig. 3, as the AF4 class approaches the guaranteed throughput assigned to it, the network functionality switches on and performs remarking on the higher layer packets. Consequently they reach the DiffServ output node as AF3/AF2/AF1/BE class traffic. If no spare bandwidth resides in the lower traffic classes the programmable network functionality can mark higher layers packets to be routed over an available alternative route completely away from the congested link leaving the main link free for base layer traffic (Fig. 4).

3.1   Functionality Packet Fields

The concept of individual flow processing by the programmable functionality in the DiffServ aggregated environment may be considered as 'micro-DiffServ' whereby each video flow can request a particular processing treatment. Using the IPv6 hop-by-hop extension header [1], four hop-by-hop option fields are required in the IPv6 header for the network functionality to perform the processing. These fields are 'Split Location' indicating which video layers to remark/reroute, 'Layer ID' indicating which video layer a packet belongs to, 'Original DSCP' records the initial DSCP mapping should it be remarked at some stage and finally a treatment field to indicate the type of processing to perform. The programmable treatments are 'Remark', 'Reroute', 'Remark then Reroute' and 'Reroute then Remark'.

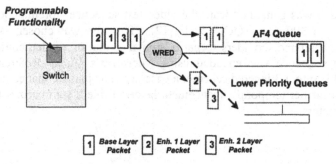

Fig. 3. Remarking higher layer packets

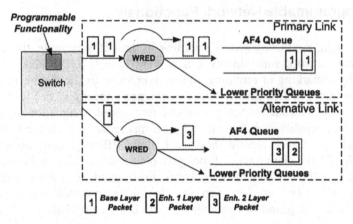

Fig. 4. Rerouting higher layer packets

4   Network Simulation

Fig. 5 outlines the network simulation model used to analyze the ability of the programmable functionality to improve QoS for layered video conferencing under times of congestion.   Each domain contains 4 video source/sinks capable of generating video traffic. The backbone consists of a primary link of 10Mbps along with a smaller alternative (backup) link to allow rerouting within the network. All routers are multi-class DiffServ models to allow remarking.   The network simulator OPNET Modeller was used to develop and simulate the model network.

4.1   Video Source Generation

Layered video was generated from the video test sequence 'foreman.qcif' consisting of a 300 frame QCIF cycle [12].   This clip was chosen as it represents a head and shoulders scenario, similar to that of a video conference.   The sequence was encoded using Microsoft's Visual Reference Software [13] into a 3 layered scheme: a base layer, a spatial enhancement layer, and a further temporal enhancement layer.   Table 2 summarizes the video parameters.

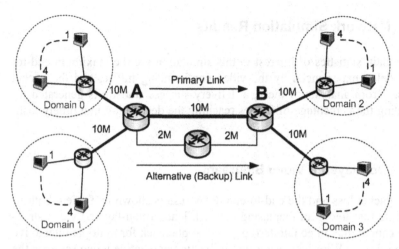

Fig. 5. Network simulation environment

The video traffic profiles in Table 3 were sent over the primary link. To illustrate the ability of the programmable network functionality to support an increased number of video conferences, the results from a non-layered video input (Fig. 6) and a layered video input (Fig. 7) with and without the programmable network functionality were compared.

Table 2. Video traffic generation profile

Source	Destination	Start Time	Stop Time
Domain 0, WKST 0	Domain 2, WKST 0	100	500
Domain 0, WKST 1	Domain 3, WKST 0	200	600
Domain 1, WKST 0	Domain 2, WKST 1	300	700
Domain 1, WKST 1	Domain 3, WKST 1	400	800

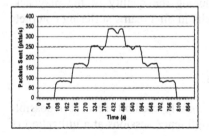

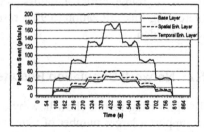

Fig. 6. Non-layered traffic input   **Fig. 7.** Layered traffic input

5   Network Simulation Results

The main statistics of interest in this simulation are the maximum end-to-end delay experienced by the video conferencing traffic, and the packet loss. From analysis of these, a delivery success statistic is generated recording the percentage of frames reaching the destination in a timely fashion.

5.1   Non-layered Video Bitstream

The Packet loss and the end-to-end delay results shown in Table 4 both illustrate that under an increasing network load, a non-layered video structure cannot guarantee uninterrupted video playback for multiple interactive video flows. With increasing link utilization and active video sessions the number of packets dropped increases and the end-to-end delay is sent well above the 0.2s limit.

Table 3. Traffic generation profile

Video Sessions	Packet Loss (pkts/s) Background Link Utilisation (%)			End-to-end Delay (s) Background Link Utilisation (%)		
	70	80	90	70	80	90
1	0	0	0	0.02	0.03	0.18
2	0	0	16	0.03	0.12	0.78
3	0	11	67	0.1	0.38	0.8
4	8	33	120	0.25	0.4	0.83

Fig. 8 shows that as the link utilization increases to 80%, the percentage of frames successfully delivered on time drops below 80% and quickly results in frame errors and loss, reducing the quality of the playback. Increasing link utilization to 90% results in all streams suffering complete loss of video.

5.2   Network Simulation Results

The following results show how by using a layered bitstream it is possible to support a larger number of video conference sessions at a utilization of 80%.

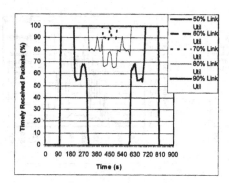

Fig. 8. Timely delivery success ratio

To take full advantage of the properties associated with a layered bitstream transmission, the base layer must be delivered in a timely fashion with no packet loss in the network. Each layered stream has a different DiffServ drop precedence. This is illustrated in Fig. 9 where all layers encounter approximately the same end-to-end delay.

Remarking

By enabling the programmable network functionality within the DiffServ node, it is possible to control the level of higher layer video traffic entering the AF4 queue and so protect the base layer video flow. Setting the packet treatment to 'Remark' the functionality remarks the enhancement layer packets to lower priority aggregated classes when the AF4 class throughput exceeds its class bandwidth allocation. This ensures the end-to-end delay for the base layer traffic is minimized. Fig. 10 shows the result of remarking; from this it may be observed that the delay experienced by base layer packets is much reduced, with a corresponding increase in the delay experienced by the higher layer packets. Though the maximum delay of the enhancement layer packets is greater than 0.2s a significant percentage of the enhancement layer will meet the end-to-end requirements and can be decoded along with the base layer at the receiver. This ensures continuing maximum possible video quality at the destination.

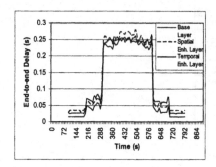

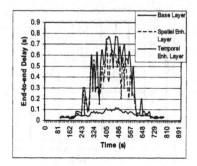

Fig. 9. No treatment: End-to-end delay   **Fig. 10.** Remarking: End-to-end delay

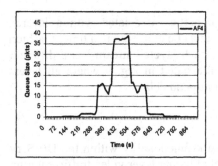

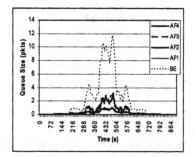

Fig. 11. No treatment:Queue size   **Fig. 12.** Remarking: Queue sizes

Fig. 11 shows the queue sizes generated when no functionality is used and all three layers are queued in the AF4 class. Fig. 12 shows that remarking effectively distributes the higher layers among all the class queues.

Rerouting

Alternatively the packet treatment can be set to 'Rerouting' in which case enhancement layer packets will be rerouted rather than remarked when the class throughput exceeds the allocated bandwidth. The base layer end-to-end delay (Fig. 15) is reduced to less than 0.05s from 0.25s with no treatment and this is mapped to full timely delivery of the base layer bit-stream. Remarking reduced the utilization on the primary link as more enhancement layer traffic is dropped to prevent base layer traffic delay (Fig. 13) whereas rerouting causes the majority of the enhancement layer packets to transverse the alternative link under congestion (Fig. 14).

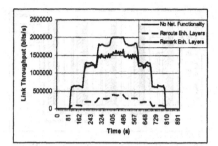

Fig. 13. Primary link throughput

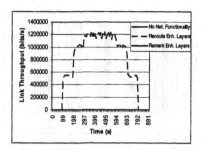

Fig. 14. Alt. link throughput

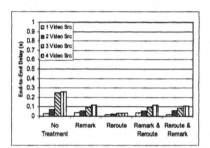

Fig. 15. Base layer delay

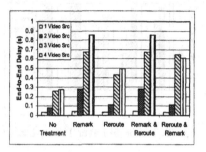

Fig. 16. Spatial layer delay

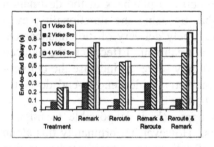

Fig. 17. Temporal layer delay

Programmable Functionality Performance

Fig. 15, 16 and 17 outline the end-to-end delay encountered of each layer for increasing number of interactive video flows. As the results show, the optimizing delivery of the base layer is achieved at the expense of both enhancement layers. However the results also show that in every case the functionality treatments can guarantee base layer video quality playback at the destination.

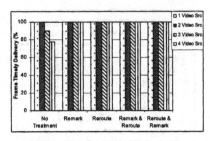

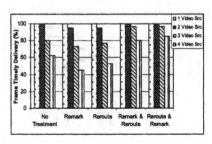

Fig. 18. Base Layer Timely Delivery   **Fig. 19.** Spatial Layer Timely Delivery

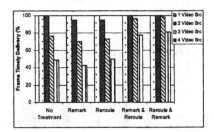

Fig. 20. Temporal Layer Timely Delivery

However, the results also show that in every case the functionality treatments can guarantee base layer video quality playback at the destination (Fig 18). Fig. 19 & 20 illustrate that by using the functionality, even though the packet loss is greater, the timely delivery of the enhancement layers is comparable to that without any treatment. Effectively the reduced packet loss when no treatment is used only serves to increase the delivery of packets which do not meet the interactive video end-to-end delay requirement, sometimes referred to as "badput".

Using a layered video bitstream approach, it is possible to migrate packet loss to the higher video layers. However, unfortunately this alone does not provide a solution capable of delivering uninterrupted error free playback of the basic video elements because of the end-to-end delay suffered by the base layer bitstream. Implementing the programmable network functionality results in a stepped approach to QoS for interactive video. It can guarantee complete timely delivery of all base layer frames for the supported video conference sessions and can offer improved packet loss statistics due to the ability of the network functionalities to direct higher layer traffic to available bandwidth elsewhere on the same link, or onto an alternative link if available.

Table 4. Timely delivery. (90% background traffic utilization)

	Base Layer Frame Timely Delivery (%)		Spatial Layer Frame Timely Delivery (%)		Temporal Layer Frame Timely Delivery (%)	
Functionality	Active Sessions		Active Sessions		Active Sessions	
Treatment	2	4	2	4	2	4
No Treatment	0	0	0	0	0	0
Remark	100	65	45	10	42.5	5
Reroute	100	100	95	55	95	50
Remark then Reroute	100	65	90	62.5	90	56.25
Reroute then Remark	100	85	100	62.5	100	56.25

Additional network simulations for a 10Mbps primary link congested with 90% background traffic have shown that 100% successful timely delivery of the base layer can be achieved when using the reroute treatment as the primary route then only transmits the base layer packets. Furthermore at 90% utilization the network functionality shows significantly increased performance in terms of timely delivery of the enhancement frames (Table 5).

6 Conclusions

The work proposes the introduction of programmable functionality into a DiffServ-enabled IP network in order to improve the network service provided to interactive video conferencing. Using the hop-by-hop option field available in the IPv6 packet when congestion is encountered, the functionality can ensure a stepped reduction in interactive video conferencing quality provided to a layered MPEG-4 bitstream. This prevents the randomized packet losses that can result in a total loss of the video playback. Incorporating the programmable network functionality into the DiffServ router can ensure the timely delivery of the base layer video stream guaranteeing a basic level of video quality under congested conditions. Enhancement layer traffic is directed around the congestion using one of the programmable treatments increasing the level of timely delivered frames and so further increasing the video quality playback at the destination.

Future work will consider a more integrated network environment to simulate multiple points of heavy link utilization over distributed and backbone networks. It is anticipated that once the programmable network functionality has developed to a suitable solution for these practical network environments, a suitable platform for implementation will be investigated.

7 Acknowledgements

The authors acknowledge this work is supported by Xilinx Inc. as part of the PiPPiN project. The authors would like to thank Gordon Brebner and Philip-James Roxby for their guidance and Wilson Chung for his assistance with the technical details of using MPEG-4 for compressed video in interactive applications.

References

[1] W. Stallings, "Data and computer communications", Seventh Edition, Prentice Hall, ISBN 0-13-183311-1.

[2] X. Xiao, L. M. Ni, "Internet QoS: A Big Picture", IEEE Network Magazine, 8-19 March/April 1999 p8-p18.

[3] H. M. Radha et al, "The MPEG-4 Fine-Grained Scalable Video Coding Method for Multimedia Streaming over IP", IEEE Transactions on Multimedia, Vol. 3, No. 1, March 2001, p53-p68.

[4] F. Baker, "draft-baker-diffserv-basic-classes-04" April 2005.

[5] B. Davie et al, "An Expedited Forwarding PHB (Per-Hop Behaviour)", RFC 3246, March 2002.

[6] J. Heinanen et al, "Assured Forwarding PHB Group", RFC 2597, June 1999.

[7] G. Armitage, "Quality of Service in IP Networks: Foundation for a Mulit-Service Internet", Macmillan, ISBN 15-7870189-9, 2000.

[8] S. Blake, D. Black, M. Carlson, E. Davies, Z. Wang, W. Weiss, RFC 2475, "An Architecture for Differentiated Services".

[9] ISO/IEC 14496-2, "Information Technology – Generic coding of audio-visual obects – Part 2: Visual", MPEG-4 Standards, First Edition, December 1999.

[10] I.E.G. Richardson, "H.264 and MPEG-4 Video Compression", Wiley, ISBN 0-470-84837-5, 2003.

[11] S. Mao, S. Lin, S. S. Panwar Y. Wang, "A Multipath Video Streaming Testbed for Ad Hoc Networks", IEEE Vehicular Technology Conference, Orlando, Florida, 2003.

[12] Xiph.org Test Media, http://media.xiph.org/video/derf/, July 06.

[13] S. A. J. Winder, Y. Tung, "ISO/IEC 14496 (MPEG-4) Video Reference Software", Version: Microsoft-FDAM1-2.4-021205.

Characterising Distributed Haptic Virtual Environment Network Traffic Flows

K.M. Yap[1], A Marshall[1], W Yu[1], G Dodds[1], Q Gu[1], Rima T'faily Souayed[2]

[1]Virtual Engineering Centre
Northern Ireland Technology Centre
School of Electrical & Electronic Engineering
Queen's University Belfast
Phone: - +44 28 9097 5588 Fax:- +44 28 9097 4332
Email:- m.yap@qub.ac.uk, A.Marshall@ee.qub.ac.uk,w.yu@qub.ac.uk,
{G.Dodds, Qiang.gu}@ee.qub.ac.uk
[2]Université de Technologies de Troyes,
{Rima.Tfaily,dominique.gaiti}@utt.fr

Abstract: The effective transmission of haptic data in Distributed Haptic Virtual Environment (DHVEs) is a new research area which presents a number of challenges to the underlying network. The transmission of reflected force in these applications has the potential to change the way humans interact with machines and communicate with each other. The future Internet will have to carry multiple DHVE type traffic and it is now established that the best effort service offered by current IP networks is insufficient to meet the needs of these type of applications, which require specific Quality of Service (QoS) from network. The aim of the work presented here is to characterise the traffic generated by multiple DHVE network connections. The approach taken is to develop a simulation model of DHVE traffic based on empirical measurements. Both synchronous and asynchronous real world DHVE traffic is analyzed, quantified and imported into a network simulation. Probability Density Function (PDF) models are subsequently derived for each type of traffic in the DHVE system. The results show the network simulation model compares favourably with the physical network, and can be used to generate a scalable haptic network model where multiple DHVE connections may be examined.

Please use the following format when citing this chapter:

Yap, K.M., Marshall, A., Yu, W., Dodds, G., Gu, Q. and Souayed, R.T., 2007, in IFIP International Federation for Information Processing, Volume 229, Network Control and Engineering for QoS, Security, and Mobility, IV, ed. Gaïti, D., (Boston: Springer), pp. 297–310.

Keywords: haptic, distribution virtual environment, traffic characteristics, tele-operation, network simulation.

1. Introduction

3D virtual environment technologies have been used in numerous research areas. The computer graphics, industry, hazardous industries as well as tele-robotic, education training and interactive advertisement are some areas of application. By definition, a virtual environment (VE) is a space that provides users with the illusion of acting in a real world [12]. However in addition to audio and visual information, the provision of haptic feedback (the sense of touch) can profoundly improve the way we interact with virtual environments. Systems that support interfaces between a haptic device and a virtual environment are called Haptic Virtual Environments (HVEs). HVE uses include military and space exploration; the sense of touch will also enable blind people to interact with each other within a virtual environment. The HVE modalities include graphics (and possibly video), sound and force. Recent research [2] has shown that to have a satisfying experience in interacting with a HVE, the graphics and haptic update rates need to be maintained at around 30Hz and 1 KHz respectively. HVEs can be standalone or distributed. In a standalone HVE, both the haptic virtual environment and the haptic device reside on, or are connected to the same machine. In distributed HVEs (DHVE) otherwise known as tele-haptic systems, the haptic device is separate from the virtual environment and remotely affects and manipulates it. In DHVEs, one or multiple users may interact with the virtual environment, and possibly with other users with haptic devices. Users may take turns in manipulating a virtual object as in Collaborative Environments or may simultaneously modify the same object as in, for example, Cooperative Environments [13]. The DHVE provides the feeling of tele-presence for a single user and the feeling of both tele-presence and co-presence for multiple users.

The effect of network impairments has a direct impact on the sense of human perception during DHVE interactions [1]. Each network impairment affects the sense of force feedback in a particular way. For example, considerable network delay may make the user feels a virtual object either before or after they interact with it on the virtual environment (i.e. it is possible to go through a virtual wall before feeling it). Delay also desynchronizes the different copies of the virtual environment. Packet delay variation (jitter) makes the user feel that the object's mass is variable, and can make the system unstable (e.g. it can produce oscillations on the surfaces of objects). Network QoS performance is generally described using four basic parameters. These are: (i) Throughput: the number of packets that can be transmitted in a fixed amount of time. (ii) Delay: the difference between the time when the packet has been sent and the time when it is received. (iii) Jitter: the statistical variance of delay measured as the average time between two successively received IP packets. (iv) Packet Loss: expressed as a percentage of the number of packets not received, to the number of packets sent. Packet loss can reduce the amount of force felt by the user. A major challenge is therefore to clarify the QoS requirements of collaborative haptic systems such as DHVEs when they are considered for use over the Internet. In particular, the effects of network impairments upon virtual environments need to be quantified. Additionally, an investigation into the suitability of aggregated QoS architectures such as DiffServ [14], in supporting multiple DHVE-type collaborations is required. The work presents in this paper empirically models and characterises DHVE traffic so that scalable haptic QoS architectures may be developed.

2. An Experimental Testbed for Characterising DHVE traffic

In order to examine what multiple DHVE traffic flows look like, it is first necessary to characterise individual DHVE connections. The approach taken here is to set up a test network and run various DHVE applications over it. The collected network traces are then used to generate statistical models of each type of DVHE traffic that can be used in standard network modelling packages such as OPNET [11].

2.1 Haptic Device

The force-feedback haptic device used in the experimental testbed is a PHANToM (Fig.1) which is single point contact haptic device by SenSAble Technologies [4]. The PHANToM's interface main component is a serial feedback arm that ends with a stylus, allowing users to feel interaction forces they would encounter while touching objects. It is capable of 6 degrees of freedom input (measurement) and 3 degrees of freedom output (force feedback). It has three motors, allowing translational force feedback. The force feedback is calculated in proportion to the depth of penetration of the PHANToM cursor into a virtual object. The stylus orientation is passive, so no torque can be applied to the user's hand.

Fig. 1 PHANToM Desktop Devices, Haptic Traffic Generation Devices

The PHANToM can track the position and the orientation of its stylus in an arm workspace of 16cm wide, 13cm high and 13cm deep. The maximum exerted force is 6.4N, while continuous force is 1.7 N. Its maximum stiffness is high (3*103 N/m) to allow realistic simulation of contact with walls and hard objects. The 1000 packets per second sending rate from the PHANToM is greater than that for conventional multimedia applications such as Video, PCM audio or IP telephony, which can range from 30 up to 250 packets per second (depending on the packet frame size used).

2.2 Synchronous and Asynchronous DHVE Test Applications

In order to collect DHVE traffic it is first necessary to run DHVE applications over the test network. To this end, two different DHVE test applications were developed that consider synchronous and asynchronous operation respectively. Both systems work in a client-server arhcitecture. In synchronous operation the local position at the client is only updated upon feedback from the server, while with asynchronous operation the local client updates occur regardless of the feedback data. In synchronous operation, the local client sends local PHANToM position to server and waits to receive the feedback position. In the asynchronous operation, the local client will keep sending new PHANToM position data regardless of the previous position.

2.3 Experiment Configuration

The experimental set-up involves 2 computers that are connected through a gigabit Ethernet fibre optic link running on best effort IP service. Fig.2 shows the configuration of the experimental network.

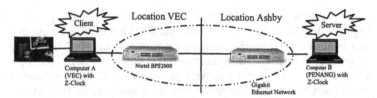

Fig. 2. Experiment Test Bed Setup

In operation, computer A running the client program connects to the PHANToM and generates haptic traffic for computer B which is running the server program. When running, the user holding the PHANToM will experience that he or she is rendering inside a virtual box. The stylus movement is limited by the box's six virtual walls and is unable to go beyond the virtual walls.

2.4 Traffic Collection and Analysis

The network traffic is captured by using a software capturing tool called IP Traffic [3]. The measured network parameters are throughput, packet lost, delay and jitter. The captured traffic is analyzed, imported and customized in simulation software packages called OPNET ACE and Modeler [11]. The captured haptic traffic is converted into tcpdump format before imported into OPNET ACE. Subsequently, OPNET ACE shows the haptic packet format and haptic traffic pattern. OPNET PDF models are customized from captured haptic traffic and implemented in OPNET Modeler simulation network model. The reason for using real-world traffic in the simulator is to gain an accurate baseline haptic model that can be used to generate a better representation of a network's performance when supporting this type of traffic.

3. Experimental Results

3.1 Asynchronous Mode Haptic Traffic Packet and Pattern Distribution

It is important to study what the haptic traffic distribution looks like in order to customize the haptic traffic in the OPNET model. The haptic systems generate 1000 packets/sec and 980 packets/sec in asynchronous and synchronous mode respectively. In asynchronous mode, the data field of a haptic packet is 64 bytes, adding IP, UDP and Ethernet header give a total length of 106 bytes without preamble and CRC header. The length of the data field of a synchronous mode packet haptic packet is 40 because less information is transmitted in this mode (i.e. only the PHANToM's positional data is sent); the total network packet size is 82 bytes without preamble and CRC header. The packet size of the haptic traffic is constant but the inter-packet delay varies. Fig.3 shows the asynchronous mode inter-packet delay from client to server. The synchronous mode results are almost identical to the asynchronous mode and are not shown.

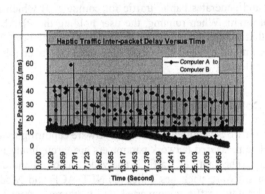

Fig. 3. Asynchronous Mode Haptic Traffic Inter-packet Delay versus time, Client to Server

In Fig.3, it may be observed that most of the inter-packet delays are below 10ms which occur at 1.9ms and 0.1ms with some inter-packet delays experienced at 20ms and 30ms. The maximum inter-packet delay occurs at 59.2ms. There are also a significant number inter-packet delays near zero. These are due to the nature of the steady 1ms time interval of the haptic source application, and after a long inter-packet delay (e.g. 20ms) there are many packets that have been queued waiting to be sent and are then be burst onto the network at rates faster than 1ms. This gives an abrupt movement effect to the user; strategies to optimise the performance of haptic applications over bursty traffic flows are the subject of [1]. The inter-packet delay from Server to Client shows a larger variation than from Client to Server. This is due to the response time of the server computer. The experiment results showed that the server to client inter-packet delay distribution is similar to the client to server packet distribution. The first packet from the server to client occurs 0.7s after the first packet from the client because the server needs time to respond to the haptic traffic from client. The inter-packet delay statistics for both directions are summarised below.

Table 1. Haptic Traffic Inter-packet Delay Summary

	Client to Server (ms)	Server to Client (ms)
Average =	0.999996709	0.998180322
Min. =	<0.01	<0.01
Max. =	59.2	75.3

In the table, the minimum values are less than 0.01ms because of the resolution of the analysis tool at lower time values. The average inter-packet delay is 1ms/packet.

3.2 Haptic Traffic Custom Probability Density Function (PDF)

The next step is to customize the haptic network characteristics in OPNET as there is no generalised distribution that is able to represent haptic traffic distribution. The haptic distribution does not follow a fixed pattern which makes it difficult to generate analytical models of the traffic profile. Therefore, a custom PDF model was developed in order to model this haptic traffic. The inter-packet delay interval is a critical issue which is varying over time. In order to customize the haptic network model, a probability function was created.

Fig.4(a)-4(b) shows the experiment PDF that are created from the asynchronous haptic traffic data. The PDFs of both figures are obtained from over 60000 packet samples. Referring to Fig.5(a), the highest probability is 0.38 at 1.9ms inter-packet time. The second highest probability is at 0.27 at an inter-packet time of less than 0.1ms.

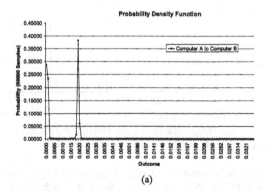

(a)

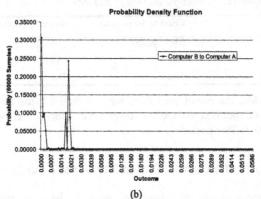

(b)

Fig. 4. Asynchronous Mode Haptic Traffic Inter-packet Time PDF Model, (a) Client to Server (Computer A to B), (b) Server to Client (Computer B to A)

In Fig.4(b), the highest probability is 0.32 at inter-packet time of less than 0.1ms. It is difficult to know the precise inter-packet time at this probability because of the resolution provided by the capturing tools. The second highest probability is 0.24 at 1.9ms. The peak (major) delays occurring in Fig.4 are due to most of the inter-packet delays which are concentrated at 0.1ms and 1.9ms as shown in Fig.3.

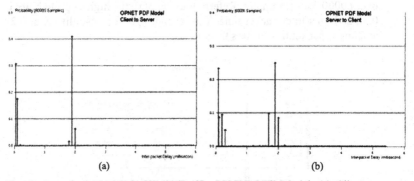

(a)   (b)

Fig. 5. Asynchronous Mode Haptic Traffic OPNET PDF Model, (a) Client to Server (Computer A to B), (b) Server to Client (Compute B to A)

The asynchronous mode probability diagrams in Fig.4 need to be customized into OPNET PDF models as shown in Fig.5; these are created based on the experiment PDF from real world traffic by using OPNET External Model Access (EMA) code method. EMA is an OPNET term that defines the technique for accessing a model external to the OPNET program without using the services provided by the OPNET graphical editors. The synchronous mode PDF models which are not shown here are similar to those in Fig.5 by using the same method discussed here. The probability and inter-packet delay values in Fig.4 are input into an EMA code and consequently compiled to generate OPNET PDF models. The flexibility in customising the PDF model is achieved by changing content of the EMA code. In Fig.5(a), the highest probability is 0.41 at around 1.9ms. In Fig.5(b), the highest probability is 0.25 at 1.9ms and second highest is 0.23 at time of less than 0.0001. The higher probability in Fig.5(a)-5(b) as compare to Fig.4(a)-4(b) is due to normalization of all the probabilities in PDF model. The asynchronous mode PDF model is similar to synchronous mode PDF model but their packet sending rate is different. The asynchronous mode PDF model needs to generate a packet sending rate of 1000 packets/sec but synchronous mode PDF model needs only generates 980packest/sec. The following sections will prove that the custom PDF models for both asynchronous and synchronous mode are able to generate haptic traffic that is closely matched to the experimental haptic traffic.

3.3 OPNET Haptic Traffic Point-to-point Throughput

The asynchronous mode haptic network packet size is 106 bytes without the 12 bytes of Ethernet preamble and the CRC header. Since the haptic packet transmission rate is 1000 packets/sec, thus the throughput will be 848 Kbit/sec. This is closely matched to the simulation throughput of Fig.6.

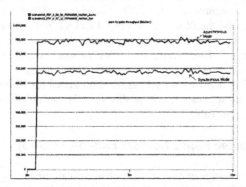

Fig. 6. Asynchronous/Synchronous Mode Custom PDF model Haptic Traffic Point-to-Point Throughput, Client to Server

In synchronous mode, the total network packet size is 82 bytes without preamble and CRC header. Since synchronous model traffic sending rate is 980 packets/sec, the network throughput will be 627 Kbit/sec; closely matched to the simulation throughput result of Fig.6.

3.4 Distributed Haptic Virtual Network Model

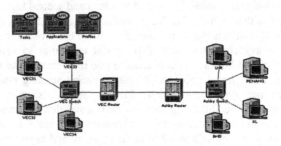

Fig. 7. OPNET Distributed Haptic Virtual Network Model

This section describes the modelling of the two haptic traffic modes in the DHVE network model. Fig.7 shows eight PCs connected peer-to-peer with two switches and routers. The two routers are connected with PPP T3 link while other links are 100Mbps. Four haptic traffic flows are implemented between PCs VEC31-PENANG and PCs VEC32-KL respectively. The PCs VEC31/VEC33 and PENANG/LHR are configured to run a custom application task that simulates an asynchronous mode DHVE application by using the asynchronous mode PDF model created in the previous section. Additionally, the PCs VEC32/VEC34 and KL/BHD are configured to run a synchronous mode custom application by using the synchronous mode PDF model. Effectively, the DHVE network model in Fig.7 is the combination of asynchronous haptic traffic flow and synchronous haptic traffic flow. This network model has been simulated for 10 minutes by using the custom application and profile and the results are presented in Fig.8, Table 2 and Table 3.

3.4.1 Distributed Haptic Network End-to-End Delay

This section investigates the network characteristic under high loading of the distributed haptic network. The simulation results obtained are similar for asynchronous and synchronous modes. It can be observed that background load above 98% results in nearly 10 seconds of end-to-end delay which is totally unacceptable for the asynchronous mode haptic operation.

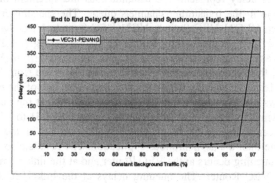

Fig. 8. Distributed Haptic Network Asynchronous/Synchronous Mode End to End Delay VEC31-PENANG(Client-Server), 10%-97% background load.

In Fig.8, the end to end delay drops to 0.02 seconds when the background decreased to 95%-96% but this delay is still unacceptable for haptic applications. The delay drops to 10ms at 94% background loading. From the user perception experiment, a good sense of touch requires a delay of less than 5ms, and this occurs at less than 90% loading. These results are comparable with the results in [2], [10] which describe actual network results.

3.4.2 Distributed Haptic Network Links Queuing Delay

Table 2. Distributed Haptic Network Links Average Queuing Delay (ms)

Background Loading (%)	VEC31-VEC Switch (ms)	VEC32-VEC Switch(ms)	VEC Switch-VEC Router (ms)	VEC Router-Ashby Router (ms)
0	0.029854	0.028118	0.0267862	0.015588
20	0.88529	0.028154	0.0267589	0.054092
50	0.029854	0.099744	0.1004575	0.211428
90	0.220006	0.869559	1.0226898	2.227665
95	2.0812	2.041991	23.976001	3.556528
96	2.908303	2.732627	61.794149	7.137595
97	9.658127	9.030557	214.39641	5.930933
98	1520.362	1539.083	1726.272	6.980548
99	1559.682	1560.1303	1669.125	21.18348

The queuing delay represents the instantaneous measurement of packets' waiting time in the transmitter channels queue. The transmitter channels are between VEC31-VEC Switch, VE31-VEC Switch, VEC Switch-VEC Router and VEC Router-Ashby Router as shown in Fig.7. Referring to Fig.7, the asynchronous mode haptic traffic flows start from VEC31 to PENANG; the synchronous mode haptic traffic flows are from VEC32 to KL. Therefore, the queuing delays on each particular link of the two haptic traffic flows are shown in Table 2. The results show that the queuing delays between VEC32 to VEC switch are lower than VEC31 to VEC switch simply because the synchronous mode application has a lower packet sending rate than the asynchronous application. The results also show that the major queuing occurs at the VEC Router and at the link from the VEC Switch to VEC Router. The queuing delays at the link VEC Router to Ashby Router do not increase significantly compared to the other three links.

3.4.3 Distributed Haptic Network Effective Throughput

Table 3. Distributed Haptic Network Effective Throughput VEC31-PENANG (Client-Server), 60%-99% background load (a) Asynchronous Mode, (b) Synchronous Mode.

Background Loading (%)	Asynchronous Mode (packets/second)	Synchronous Mode (packets/second)
60	981.957045	976.829825
70	991.862847	973.654386
80	999.131579	970.668421
90	987.389474	959.100000
95	793.389474	776.468421
96	509.647368	502.968421
97	77.894737	370.526316
98	37.368421	61.578947
99	60.000000	10.526316

As shown in Table 3, the haptic traffic effective throughput is reduced sharply at 97%-99% background traffic load because of traffic congestion starving the bandwidth available for these flows. The effective throughput is also reduced significantly at 95%-96%. The effective throughput rate is assumed to be normal at up to 90% background traffic load. In summary, the effective throughput from each DHVE machine drops significantly above 90% background load. From the physical experiment, it was observed that at these levels, the user will feel the vibration in the PHAN-ToM and also large abrupt force feedback. At this point the haptic system becomes unstable and the PHANToM is not able to move further.

4. Conclusions and Future Work

This paper has presented a new approach to modelling haptic traffic over IP networks. The aim is to employ conventional network simulation software to simulate large-scale deployment of haptic devices and Distributed Haptic Virtual Environments (DHVEs) over the Internet. The work describes how to successfully generate a customizable haptic traffic PDF model for both synchronous and asynchronous modes of haptic interaction. This is achieved by using empirical traffic profiles obtained from a test network with haptic devices and interactive applications. Results from the simulation model show that the simulation network throughput is closely matched to experimental throughputs of 850Kbit/s and 630Kbit/s in asynchronous and synchronous mode respectively. The simulation results also show that DHVE effective throughput deteriorates sharply above 90% background load. In addition, end-to-end delays of more than 5ms occur at above 90% background loading. Future work will include characterizing the haptic traffic under different QoS IP networks in multi-sensory environments. Differentiated Services will be incorporated into the simulation and experiment networks.

Acknowledgement

This work was supported in full by Industrial Research and Technology Unit Northern Ireland SPUR scheme, research funding of the Virtual Engineering Centre at Queen's University Belfast.

References

[1] Rima Tfaily Souayed, Gaiti, D., Pujolle, G., Wai Yu, Qiang Gu, & Marshall, A. (2003). Haptic virtual environment performance over IP networks: a case study. *Proceedings Seventh IEEE International Symposium on Distributed Simulation and Real-Time Applications, 23-25 Oct. 2003*, 181-9.

[2] Souayed R., Gaiti D. , Yu W., Dodds G., and Marshall A. "Experimental Study of Haptic Interaction in Distributed Virtual Environments", (2004) *Eurohapics 2004*.

[3] ZTI Telecom, http://www.zti-telecom.com/pages/main-ip.htm

[4] SenSAble Technologies. http://www.sensable.com

[5] Kessler, G. D., & Hodges, L. F. (1996). Network communication protocol for distributed virtual environment systems. *Proceedings of the IEEE 1996 virtual reality annual international symposium, mar 30-apr 3 1996*, 214-221.

[6] Kyoung Shin Park, & Kenyon, R. V. (1999). Effects of network characteristics on human performance in a collaborative virtual environment. Proceedings of virtual reality, 13-17 march 1999, 104-11.

[7] Manuel, O., Jesper, M., Joel, J., Anthony, S., & Mel, S. Considerations in the design of virtual environment systems: A case study.

[8] Mejdi, E., Nicolas, D. G., José, R. G., & Dimitrios, M. A scalable network architecture for distributed virtual environments with dynamic QoS over IPv6. *Eighth IEEE international symposium on computers and communications*.

[9] Shirmohammadi, S., & Georganas, N. D. (2000). Collaborating in 3D virtual environments: a synchronous architecture. Proceedings of WET ICE 2000. 9th IEEE international workshops on enabling technologies: infrastructure for collaborative enterprises, 14-16 June 2000, 35-42.

[10] Tom, D., Dan, S., Maxine, B., Dave, P., Josephine, A., & Mike, B. et al. (1999). Technologies for virtual reality/ tele-immersion applications: issues of research in image display and global networking.. *EC/NSF workshop on research frontiers in virtul environments and human-centered computing, chateau de bonas, france*, France.

[11] OPNET 11.0A, Product Documentation, Methodologies and Case Studies, www.opnet.com.

[12] H.G. Hoffman, T. Richard, B. Coda, A. Richards, SR. Sharar, "The Illusion of Presence in Immersive Virtual Reality during an FMRI Brain Scan", *Cyberpsychol Behavior*, vol 6, N°2, pp. 127-31, Apr. 2003.

[13] P. Buttolo, O. Roberto and H. Blake, "Architectures for Shared haptic Virtual Environments", special issue of Computer & Graphics, vol. 21, N°.4, PP. 421-429, July-Aug 1997.

[14] S. Blake, D. Black, M. Carlson, E. Davies, Z. Wang, W. Weiss, RFC 2475, "An Architecture for Differentiated Services".

Security Associations Management (SAM) Model for IP Multimedia System (IMS)

Muhammad Sher, Thomas Magedanz
Technical University Berlin & Fokus Fraunhofer Institute,
Kaiserin-Augusta-Allee 31, D-10589 Berlin, Germany
{sher, magedanz}@fokus.fraunhofer.de
http://www.av.cs.tu-berlin.de/
http://www.fokus.fraunhofer.de/ngni

Abstract. In this paper we propose Security Associations Management (SAM) model which consists of seven security associations & managements based on different technical specifications of Third Generation Partnership Project (3GPP) [1] to develop Secure Service Provisioning Framework (SSPF) [2] for IP Multimedia System (IMS) at IMS Playground within Third Generation beyond (3Gb) Testbed [3] at Fokus, Fraunhofer. The objective of this enhanced security management model is to combine all security associations into single article that deal with the mutual authentication of user and network; to provide security across different interfaces like Ut interface (for HTTP services), Gm interface (air contact) between IMS client and IMS Core, Cx and Dx interfaces (between Home Subscriber Server HSS and IMS core network). It also deals with security when the user is roaming or in home network and security considerations for access networks. The main emphasis of SAM is to propose complete security protection model for IMS network and to the user, therefore only brief description of each security association is provided to understand the architecture and conceptual security model.

Key Words: Security Associations, Security Management, Key Management, Encryption, Network Domain Security, IP Multimedia Systems

1 Introduction

Security and information protection are the focal and central points for all data networks and telecommunication systems but with the emerging of fixed and mobile networks convergence like VoIP, IPv6, WLAN, IP Multimedia System (IMS), Universal Mobile Telecommunication Systems (UMTS) and General Packet Radio System (GPRS) etc., network security becomes critical and important to protect the networks as well as to manage secure communication between users.

Please use the following format when citing this chapter:

Sher, M. and Magedanz, T., 2007, in IFIP International Federation for Information Processing, Volume 229, Network Control and Engineering for QoS, Security, and Mobility, IV, ed. Gaïti, D., (Boston: Springer), pp. 311–325.

As we know that all IP based networks are open and distributed nature of architecture which can enable easy access to services, information, and resources, together with the constant abuse of hackers, curious individuals, fraudsters, and organized crime units. Therefore complex security techniques and mechanisms such as secure data transmission, confidentiality, authentication, data integrity, anti-replay protection and intrusion detection system are the important security consideration features for all IP networks and mobile telecommunication systems.

The proposed security management model is based on different technical specifications of Third Generation Partnership Project (3GPP) [4-7] and consists on seven security associations to provide Secure Service Provisioning Framework (SSPF) [2] for IP Multimedia System (IMS) Playground within 3Gb Testbed at Fokus Fraunhofer [3]. In section 2 we describe briefly IMS technology and Fokus IMS Playground. In Section 3 we present the architecture of proposed security management model along with the security associations and the last section concludes the paper.

2 IMS Technology and IMS Testbed

In the prospect of global trends, the mobile communications world has defined within the evolution of cellular systems an all-IP network vision which integrates cellular networks and the Internet. This is the IP Multimedia System (IMS), namely overlay architecture for the provision of multimedia services, such as VoIP and videoconferencing on top of globally emerging 3G broadband packet networks. The IMS has been standardized by 3GPP [1] and 3GPP2 [8] in the beginning of this decade and is planned for deployment in 3G wireless networks around 2005/2006. Due to the fact that the IMS overlay architecture is widely abstracted from the air interfaces, the IMS can be used for any mobile access network technology as well as for fixed line access technology as currently promoted by ETSI TISPAN within the NGN reference architecture definition [9]. It is important to note, that the IMS defines service provision architecture, and as such can be seen as the next generation service delivery platform framework.

The important entities of IMS are given as:
- P-CSCF (Proxy Call State/Session Control Function):- It behaves like a proxy accepting requests and services.
- I-CSCF (Interrogating Call State Control Function):- It assigns S-CSCF to a user performing SIP registration, charging and resource utilisation.
- S-CSCF (Serving Call State Control Function):- It performs the session control services for the endpoint.
- MRF (Media Resource Function):- It provides media stream processing like media mixing, media announcements, media analysis and media transcoding.
- HSS (Home Subscription Function):- It is the master database of an IMS that stores IMS user profiles.
- AS (Application Server):- It provides service platform in IMS environment.

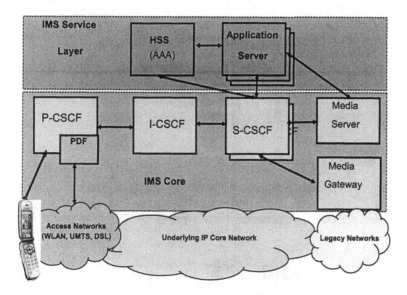

Fig. 1. IMS Architecture

In face of this and knowing the current challenges within the telecommunications market are mainly a consequence of insufficient early access to new enabling technologies by all market players, the Fraunhofer Institute FOKUS, known as a leading research institute in the field of open communication systems, has established with support from the German ministry of Education and Research (BMBF) a 3G beyond Testbed, known as "National Host for 3Gb Applications" [3]. This Testbed provides technologies and related know-how in the field of fixed and wireless next generation network technologies and related service delivery platforms.

As such a Testbed is quite complex by its very nature, FOKUS has coined in addition the notion of technology focused "playgrounds". One of these is the "Open IMS Playground @ FOKUS" [3] where you can find different access technologies, infrastructure components and management tools. FOKUS implemented all core components of the IMS and enriched this base infrastructure with components from commercial vendors. Particularly the field of SDP diversity, promoted within the IMS, is supported by providing different service platforms, such as Open Service Access (OSA) /Parlay, JAIN Service Logic Execution Environments (SLEE), Web Services / Parlay X, SIP Servlets, Call Processing Language (CPL), etc. on top of a multiplicity of access technologies including an exclusive 3G UMTS cell [10].

314   Muhammad Sher, Thomas Magedanz

Open IMS @ FOKUS

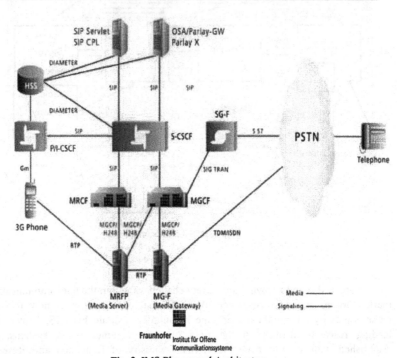

Fig. 2. IMS Playground Architecture

3 IMS Security Management Model

The overall security for IP Multimedia System (IMS) as standardized by 3GPP [1] in its different releases is summarized in diagram 3 and involves following security associations agreements and recommendations:

- Authentication & Key Agreement between IM subscriber and home network
- Security Mechanism Agreement between IM client and visited network
- Integrity Protection and Confidentiality
- Network Domain Security between different Domains
- Existing GPRS/UMTS Access Security

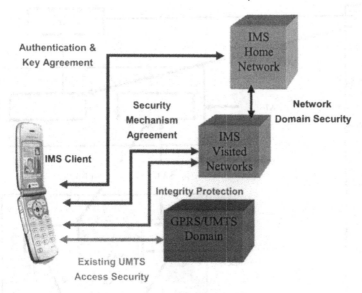

Fig. 3. Overall IMS Security

The architecture of proposed security management model of Secure Service Provisioning Framework (SSPF) for IP Multimedia System (IMS) is provided in figure 4, which presents the following seven security associations (SA1 to SA7) that are mandatory to protect IMS environment for secure and safe communication over wireless and wireline networks in circuit switched (CS) domain as well as packet switched (PS) domain.

- SA1: Authentication and Key Agreement between User and Network

- SA2: Security Management to Protect Gm-interface (Air Interface)

- SA3: Security Management for Cx and Dx interfaces (between IMS core & HSS)

- SA4: Security Management for Roaming Users (visited network)

- SA5: Security Management for Home User (home network)

- SA6: Security Management for HTTP Services (Ut interface)

- SA7: Security Management for Access Networks (GPRS, UMTS, WLAN etc.)

Now we discuss briefly each Security Association and Agreement one by one.

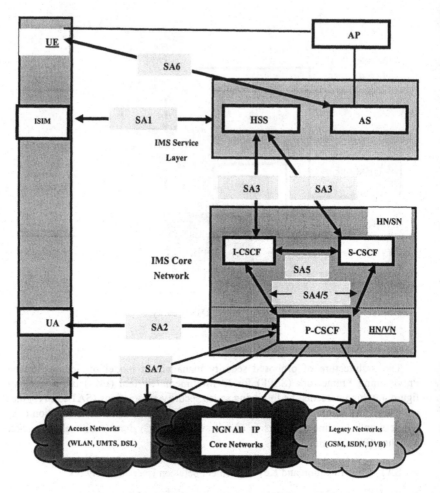

Fig. 4. IMS Security Management Model

3.1 SA1: AKA Management between User and Network

It provides mutual authentication of user and network. The Home Subscriber Server (HSS) is responsible for generating keys and challenges and after that it delegates the performance of subscriber authentication to the Serving-Call State Control Function (S-CSCF). The subscriber will have one user private identity which is called IP Multimedia Private Identity (IMPI) for authentication purpose and one external user public identity which is called IP Multimedia Public Identity (IMPU) which is used for routing purpose.

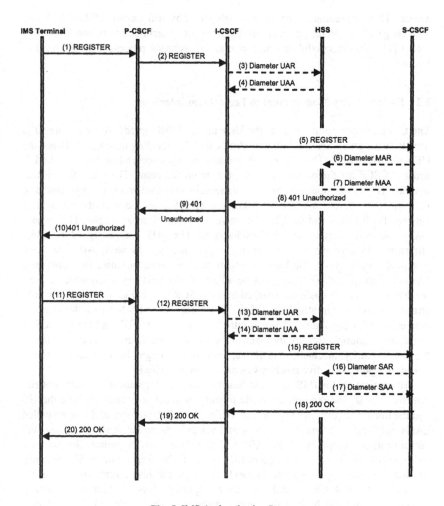

Fig. 5. IMS Authentication Process

The most important module in the IMS security is IP Multimedia Services Identity Module (ISIM), acts as storage for the secret key (K) and Authentication & Key Agreement Algorithm (AKA). The ISIM is normally embedded on the Universal Integrated Circuit Card (UICC) like a smart card based device. The IMS security is based on a long-term secret key (K) shared between the ISIM and the home Network Authentication Centre (AUC), and the AKA performs mutual authentication of ISIM and the AUC and generates Cipher Key (CK) and Integrity Key (IK). By this process the UE and home network have successfully authenticated and establishes a secure communication channel [4]. The device on which the ISIM resides is a temper-resistant and only physical access to it is not sufficient to result in exposing the secret key. It is further protected by the PIN code from unauthorized access. Thus the combination of ownership of physical device USIM/ISIM and knowledge of the secret pin code makes the security architecture of the IMS more robust [11]. The successful authentication and registration process is summarized in figure 5.

3.2   SA2: Security Management to Protect Gm-interface

The Gm reference point connects the User to the IP Multimedia System Core. It is used to transport all Session Initiation Protocol (SIP) signaling messages between the UE and the P-CSCF. This security association manages secure link between the UE and a P-CSCF for the protection of the Gm reference point. The protection of this interface is very essential and therefore its security is considered very important. The IMS in 3GPP Releases 5 and 6 makes use of IPSec as the security mechanism between the P-CSCF and the UE. The Internet Protocol Security (IPSec) [12] is only one of several possible security mechanisms. The IMS was designed to allow alternative security mechanisms over the Gm interface as well. Allowing such openness usually creates backward compatibility problems because, for example, a Release 6-compliant UE would not be able to understand any alternative security mechanism, while it could be attached to a P-CSCF of a higher release that would already support alternatives to IPSec. Therefore, the SIP Security Mechanism Agreement (Sip-Sec-Agree) [13] was introduced to allow the UE and the P-CSCF to negotiate a common security mechanism for use between them. For current releases the only security mechanism is IPSec; however, it might be that some entities already support alternative mechanisms on a proprietary basis.

Authentication for IMS access is based on the AKA protocol but it cannot run directly over IP and requires a vehicle to carry protocol messages between the UE and the home network. SIP [14] acts as vehicle for AKA protocol and it is tunnelled inside SIP and therefore IMS access is obviously to authenticate it. During the authentication of the user, the UE and the IMS also negotiate the security mechanisms for securing subsequent SIP traffic in the Gm interface. SIP Security Mechanism Agreement (Sip-Sec-Agree) [13] is used for this security agreement and the UE and the P-CSCF exchange their respective lists of supported security mechanisms and the highest commonly supported one is selected. The selected security mechanism is used to provide data integrity protection.

Once the security mechanism has been selected and its use started, the previously exchanged list is replayed back to the network in a secure fashion. This helps the network to verify that the security mechanism selection was correct and the security agreement was not tampered with. An example of an attack that would be possible without this feature is bidding-down attack, where an attacker forces peers into selecting a known weak security mechanism [11]. The IPSec ESP (Encapsulated Security Payload) [15] provides both confidentially as well as data integrity and authentication which are mandatory in IP Multimedia System access security. AKA session keys are used as keys for the ESP SAs i.e. IK is used as the authentication key, and CK as the encryption key.

3.3   SA3: Security Management for Cx and Dx interfaces

The Home Subscriber Server (HSS) stores subscriber and service data permanently and this centralized data is utilized by the I-CSCF and the S-CSCF when the user registers or receives sessions through Cx and Dx interfaces. SA3 provides security within the network domain internally for the Cx-interface between HSS & S-CSCF, and for Dx-interface between HSS & I-CSCF and the selected management protocol is Diameter [16] as shown in figure 6. The Diameter messages over the Cx and Dx interfaces make use of Stream Control Transmission Protocol (SCTP) [20] with IPSec for secure communication.

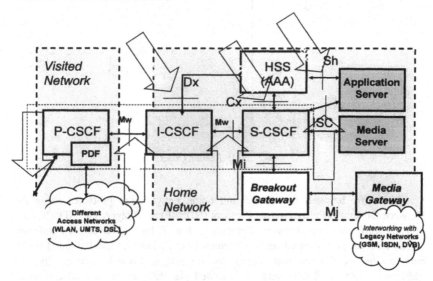

Fig. 6. SIP and Diameter Protocols Bindings

3.4   SA4: Security Management for Roaming Users

It provides security between P-CSCF and S-CSCF & I-CSCF entities which are SIP capable nodes and only applicable when the P-CSCF resides in the visited network i.e. the user is roaming. The IP Multimedia System supports communication between home network and visited network, creating two scenarios weather the IMS terminal is in home network or roaming. In the first scenario the UE's first point of contact to the IMS, called P-CSCF is located in the home network and in the second scenario the P-CSCF is located in the visited network (roaming). The visited network scenario is shown in figure 7. When P-CSCF resides in the visited network than by virtue of the AKA protocol, the shared secret is only accessible in the home network, which means that while authentication needs to take place in the visited network, certain delegation of responsibility needs to be assigned to the P-CSCF, as IPSec SAs exist between the P-CSCF and the UE.

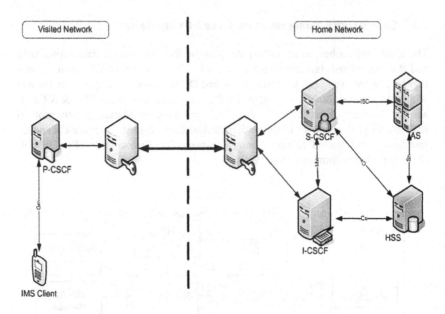

Fig. 7. IMS Roaming User

The traffic between the visited and home network are protected using the Network Domain Security/Internet Protocol (NDS/IP) at IP layer. The NDS/IP only protects traffic between network elements in the IP layer. The security gateway (SEG) enforces policy based security management on inbound and outbound traffic between the security domains like packet filtering or firewall functionality. All traffic within the IMS core network is routed via SEGs when the traffic is inter-domain. For inter-domain IMS traffic protection, NDS/IP is mandatory to achieve confidentially and data integrity.

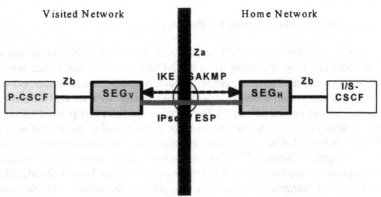

Fig. 8. Inter-Domains Security Gateways

Each SEG is responsible for setting up and maintaining IPSec security associations [12] with its peer SEGs and performs negotiations using Internet Key Exchange (IKE) [17] protocol. Security gateway maintains two SAs per peer connection; one for inbound traffic and other for outbound traffic. The SEG also maintains a single Internet Security Association and Key Management Protocol (ISAKMP) SA [18], for key management and to build up the IPSec SAs between peer hosts as shown in figure 8.

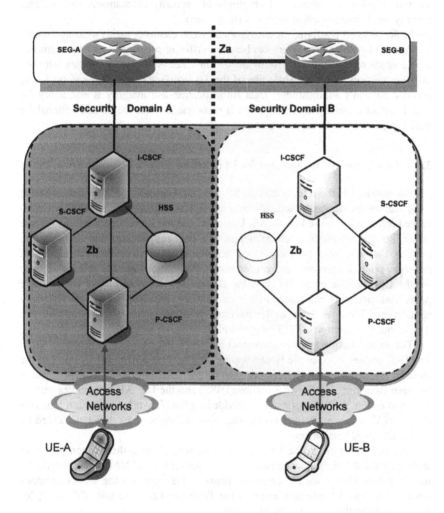

Fig.9. Concepts of Security Domains (Both Users are in their Home Domains)

3.5   SA5: Security Management for Home User

This security association is among P-CSCF, S-CSCF and I-CSCF. It provides security management within the network internally between SIP capable nodes and only applicable when the P-CSCF resides in the home network. The IMS protects all IP traffic in the core network using Network Domain Security/IP (NDS/IP) which provides confidentially, data integrity, authentication and anti-replay protection for the traffic using combination of cryptographic security mechanisms and protocol security mechanisms applied in IP security (IPSec).

In the NDS/IP platform, the interfaces between elements inside security domain are denoted by Zb and the interfaces between different security domains are denoted by Za as shown in figure 9. Use of the Za interface is always mandatory between different security domains while use of the Zb interface is optional and up to the security domain's administrator. Data authentication and integrity is mandatory for both interfaces, while use of encryption is recommended for the Za and optional for the Zb depending upon the nature of data contents.

3.6   SA6: Security Management for Ut interface

The Ut interface is the reference point between the User and the Application Server (AS) that enables users to securely manage and configure their network services-related information hosted on an AS. Users can use the Ut reference point to create public service identities, such as a resource list, and manage the authorization policies that are used by the service. Examples of services that utilize the Ut reference point are presence and conferencing. The AS may need to provide security for the Ut reference point. HTTP is the chosen data protocol for the Ut reference point that performs the functionality to manage data traffic for HTTP based applications. Thus securing the Ut interface means to achieve confidentiality and data integrity protection of HTTP-based traffic.

The authentication and key agreement for the Ut interface is also based on AKA. The IMS defines the Generic Bootstrapping Architecture (GBA) [6] as a part of the Generic Authentication Architecture (GAA) that performs mutual authentication between Bootstrapping Server Functions (BSF) and the UE. AKA generates session keys and enable further applications provided by the Network Application Function (NAF). NAF issues subscriber certificates using an applications protocol secured by the bootstrapped session keys.

The authentication in the Ut interface is performed by authentication proxy. In terms of the GBA the authentication proxy is another type of NAF. Traffic in the Ut interface goes through the authentication proxy and is secured using the bootstrapped session key. The Ut interface employs the Transport Layer Security (TLS) [7] for both confidentiality and integrity protection.

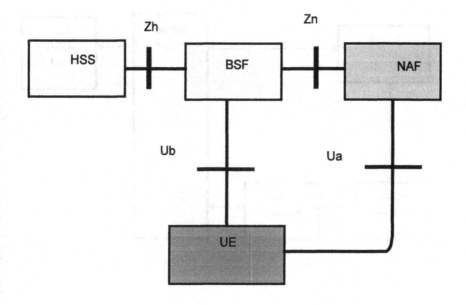

Fig. 10. Generic Bootstrapping Architecture

3.7 SA7: Security Management for Access Networks

This security association manages to protect the user and user's information on the access networks e.g. UMTS, GSM, GPRS, WLAN, DSL and VoIP. The security association takes place independently either in CS service domain or PS service domain. The network access security management architecture consists of User Service Identity Module (USIM), Mobile Equipment (ME), Access Network (AN), Service Network (SN) and Home Environment (HE) [19] as shown in figure 11. The USIM is required for accessing the Packet Switched (PS) domain in General Packet Radio System (GPRS) and identifies the particular subscriber. The USIM contains the security parameters for accessing the PS-domain, International Mobile Subscriber Identity (IMSI), list of allowed access points, MMS-related information.

In serving network, the Serving GPRS Support Node (SGSN) links the Radio Access Network (RAN) to the packet core network in the PS-service domain. It is responsible for performing both control and traffic handling functions for the PS domain. The control parts deal with mobility management and session management. The SGSN also ensures appropriate QoS and generates charging information. In the CS-service domain, the related part is Visitor Location Register (VLR). The authentication and key agreement procedure involves Authentication Centre (AUC) within HE, SGSN or VLR and Mobile Station (MS) networks entities [5].

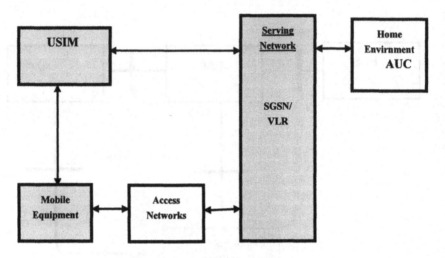

Fig. 11. Access Networks Architecture

4 Conclusions

This paper presents Security Associations Management (SAM) model which consists of seven security associations (AS1 to AS7) which are derived and based on different technical specifications of 3GPP and IETF to provide Secure Service Provisioning Framework (SSPF) for IP Multimedia System. The main focus is that we can be able to understand the complete security management for SIP based application as well as HTTP based services to establish a secure and protected environment based platform for IMS playground within 3Gb (3rd Generation and beyond) Testbed at Fokus, Fraunhofer. The IMS Playground and 3Gb Testbed provide research & development platforms to scientists and engineers in the field of information technology, particularly for Next Generation Mobile Networks.

References

[1]   About 3 Generation Partnership Project at http://www.3gpp.org
[2]   M. Sher, T. Magedanz, "Secure Service Provisioning Framework (SSPF) for IP Multimedia System and Next Generation Mobile Networks" IWWST'05, 3rd International Workshop in Wireless Security Technologies, London, U.K. April 2005, IWWST'05 Proceeding, ISSN 1746-904X, pp. 101-106. *http://www.iwwst.org.uk.*
[3]   IMS   Playground   at   www.fokus.fraunhofer.de/ims   and   3Gb   Testbed   at www.fokus.fraunhofer.de/national_host.
[4]   3GPP, TS 33.203 V6.4.0 (2004-09), 3G Security; "Access Security for IP-based Services (Release 6)".

[5]   3GPP, TS 33.102 V6.2.0 (2004-09), 3G Security; "Security Architecture (Release 6)"
[6]   3GPP, TS 33.220 V6.2.0 (2004-09), "Generic Authentication Architecture (GAA); Generic Bootstrapping Architecture (Release 6)".
[7]   3GPP TS 33.222 V6.1.0 (2004-09), "Access to Network Application Functions using HTTP over TLS (HTTPS)".
[8]   About 3 Generation Partnership Project 2 at http://www.3gpp2.org
[9]   About TISPAN at http://portal.etsi.org/portal_common/home.asp?tbkey1=TISPAN
[10] K. Knüttel, T.Magedanz, D. Witszek: "THE IMS PLAYGROUND @ FOKUS – AN OPEN TESTBED FOR NEXT GENERATION NETWORK MULTIMEDIA SERVICES", 1st Int. IFIP Conference on Testbeds and Research Infrastructures for the DEvelopment of NeTworks and COMmunities (Tridentcom), Trento, Italien, Februar 23 - 25, 2005, Proceedings pp. 2 – 11, IBSN 0-7695-2219-x, IEEE Computer Society Press, Los Alamitos, California.
[11] Poikselkae, M., Mayer, G., Khartabil, H., Niemi, A., "The IMS, IP Multimedia Concepts and Services in the Mobile Domain", John Willey & Sons Ltd, West Sussex, England, 2004.
[12] IETF RFC 2401, "IPSec Security Associations, SAs"
[13] IETF RFC 3329, "Security Mechanism Agreement for the Session Initiation Protocol (SIP)".
[14] IETF RFC 3261, "SIP: Session Initiation Protocol".
[15] IETF RFC 2406, "IPSec Encapsulating Security Payload, ESP".
[16] IETF RFC 3588, "Diameter Protocol".
[17] IETF RFC 2409, "IKE: Internet Key Exchange".
[18] IETF RFC 2408, "ISAKMP: Internet Security Associations and Key Management Protocol".
[19] M. Sher, T. Magedanz: "Network Access Security Management (NASM) Model for Next Generation Mobile Telecommunication Networks", IEEE/IFIP MATA'2005, 2nd International Workshop on Mobility Aware Technologies and Applications - Service Delivery Platforms for Next Generation Networks, Montreal, Canada, October 17-19, 2005, Proceeding Springer-Verlag LNCS 3744-0263, ISSN: 0302-9743, Berlin Heidelberg 2005, pp. 263-272.
[20] IETF RFC 3554, "On the Use of Stream Control Transmission Protocol (SCTP) with IPSec".

A Vision for Reliable Network Services Architecture

Jean Benjamin Belinga   Hanane Oumina   Daniel Ranc

Institut National des Télécommunications
Département Logiciels et Réseaux
9 rue Charles Fourier, 91011 Evry, France
{jean-benjamin.belinga,daniel.ranc}@int-evry.fr
hanane@huawei.com

Abstract. The increasing complexity, heterogeneity and dynamism of networks, systems and services have made our informational infrastructure unmanageable and insecure. The last events in the European telecom operator and IT landscapes showed inherent limits of current network and systems management architectures with respect to availability, resiliency and QoS. This paper presents a new architectural vision, merging well working technologies to tackle the problem complexity of network services management. Particular attention is drawn on the multiple stakeholders environment, where realistically many parties collaborate to fulfill end-to-end service to end users.

1   Introduction

Networks and systems have become so large, complex, and fast, and have assumed so many important tasks that when things go wrong, overburdened IT staffs often can't implement fixes fast enough to avoid mission-critical problems. The complexity of systems and networks keeps growing even beyond human capabilities to handle management tasks for achieving the best benefits from such systems. The last major events, which have occurred in telecommunication world, show an example of some problems the operators face today. These difficulties may become even worse when considering future complex multiple mobile stakeholder environments associating access, content providing, multi-domain transport and metropolitan services to the usual network management context. The aim of this paper is to propose an architecture that attempts to simplify the complexity of this problem area.

2   Problem Definition

Analyzing causes of major network breakdowns in 2004 that have intervened within the telecom operator and IT environment in Europe in term of QoS, availability and denial of service, the first remark to be made is that all impacted systems show some degree of monopolistic architecture either by their centralized structure or by their IT composition.

Please use the following format when citing this chapter:

Belinga, J.-B., Oumina, H. and Ranc, D., 2007, in IFIP International Federation for Information Processing, Volume 229, Network Control and Engineering for QoS, Security, and Mobility, IV, ed. Gaïti, D., (Boston: Springer), pp. 327–337.

The development of IT infrastructures have aggravated network, system and services management complexity due to:

- The emergence of new networking technologies, such as adhoc networking, which are combined with established technologies and that may interface to each other
- The rapidly increasing size of individual networks and the Internet as a whole
- The accelerated development of new technologies, which forces companies to restructure their IT systems more frequently
- The growing pressure on operators of time to market constraints that contradicts a careful and integral validation and testing of systems
- The lack of experience on the multiple stakeholder environment: each operator remains single-oriented; and the fact, that services run under different organizations and administration policies
- The heterogeneity and the independence of resources and components required by these services.

This indicates that IT infrastructures in large companies will grow even more complex in the future. How to adequately administer network services and systems with the inherent complexity, and insure end-to-end services with availability and required quality?

This question calls to a reflexion on the manner of managing the future networks and systems. In this paper, we particularly focus on the multi-operator, multi-stakeholder context: the place where complexity interacts with complexity, with highest constraints on confidentiality and availability.

This research aims at proposing a global architecture to insure the end-to-end service delivery in term of QoS, availability and resiliency; at achieving this aspired solution by building grid-like network with some autonomic features. For this purpose, the research is aimed at merging the following technologies:

- TMF-NGOSS that provides the reference architecture of our system (the eTOM Framework and the Service Framework);
- The features of Grid and Peer-to-Peer systems for achieving interoperability, redundancy and reliability;
- Some primitives of autonomic computing for achieving self-management;

3   Background

3.1   TMF-NGOSS

The TMF-NGOSS (New Generation OSS) [6][7] provides a comprehensive, integrated framework for developing, procuring and deploying operational and business support systems and software. NGOSS principles and tools apply to service providers, software suppliers and system integrators, providing de facto standards for business process mapping and automation.

eTOM. enhanced Telecom Operation Map (eTOM) - is the business view of the NGOSS [5][6]. The particularity of this model is that eTOM considers external actors especially the costumer in the model. It differentiates the long term and the short term business processes in the life cycle of products and services. Two operators communicate with each other in a Customer/Provider way.

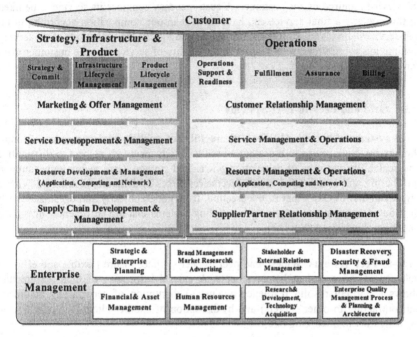

Fig. 1. eTOM Model

3.2   Service architecture

Multi-stakeholder environment. Many emerging real-time and low-jitter oriented services e.g. Video on Demand (VoD) involve a set of distributed stakeholders contributing to the end-to-end service, such as end-user, resource provider, content provider, network operator, information broker, service portal, information carrier. This plurality generates new requirements to the collaborative information exchanges between the telecom stakeholders in order to insure adequate service delivery, to guarantee the contract agreements and also to satisfy the end-user requirements. And what arises from the study of existent monopolistic systems is the lack of experience on the multiple stakeholder environment: each operator remains single-oriented. This "single-minded" point of view is not realistic anymore. Our belief is that in fact many parties are involved in an end-to-end service delivery.

Definition of service. A service is recursively defined as composed of sub-services [8], each sub-service is provided by a single service provider. The key word here is the collaboration of multiple stakeholders to provide a final service to the customer that has the freedom to formulate the properties of its service. In other words, there is no fixed pre-defined portfolio of services offered by the network. But the network has to be able to correlate the sub-services published by the broker to constitute and offer the service required by the customer. A customer may compose its service as he likes. In this context, a final service can have more than one composition according to the sub-services involved to constitute it. A subgoal is to constitute the service, minimizing subservices, with respect to the quality of service that the customer waits for.

3.3   Grid and Peer-to-Peer Systems

Grid systems. Although GRIDs [19] are still not publicly widespread as of today, their architecture seems to represent a promising advance with respect to distribution and scalability in terms of calculation power and storage. Grid technologies support the sharing and coordinated use of diverse resources in dynamic, distributed "virtual organizations" (VOs) – that is, the creation, from geographically and organizationally distributed components, of virtual computing systems that are sufficiently integrated to deliver the desired QoS [17].

Peer-to-Peer systems. Widespread peer to peer services insure flexible and efficient delivery of video and audio documents. A careful inspection of their architecture shows a particular solid resilience against a) disruption of servers (by automatic subcontracting to other servers) and b) disruption of another client (the peer is then exchanged with a working one).

Features of autonomic computing. Autonomic computing is the technology that aims at enabling computing systems to be self-managed with minimal external intervention [15]. IBM defined four main characteristics of autonomic computing systems [16]:

- Self-configuration: With the ability to dynamically configure itself on the fly, a system can adapt immediately with minimal external intervention to the deployment of new components or changes in the IT environment. The system configuration should be done automatically, as well as dynamic adjustments to that configuration to handle changing environments.
- Self-protection: Self-protecting system lets the right people access the right data at the right time and can take appropriate actions automatically to make itself less vulnerable to attacks on its runtime infrastructure and business data. Then system should be capable of detecting and protecting resources from both internal and external attacks, thus maintaining overall system integrity.
- Self-healing: Self-healing systems can detect problematic operations (either proactively through predictions or otherwise) and then initiate corrective action

without disrupting system applications. Then system should be able to recover from faults that might cause some parts of it to malfunction.

- Self-optimization: Self-optimization refers to the ability of the IT environment to efficiently maximize resource allocation and utilization to meet end users' needs with minimal human intervention. Then system should monitor its components and look for ways to optimize its working, like resource allocations, load balancing, and different network traffic optimizations.

3.4   Architectural remarks

From the definition of service, as mentioned earlier, we argue that the deployment issue has to be considered as a critical part of a management framework. This brings two problems for management in multiple stakeholder environment. Firstly, technological differences between domains make it difficult to find a common management mechanism to be used by all operators. Operators utilize different tools and deploy different policies to manage their local networks. Secondly, even if commonly agreed mechanisms and policies exist, the commercial interests (or financial constraints) of operators may prevent their wide deployment.

4   Approach overview

4.1   Computational point of view

The network becomes by itself a true system, and the evolutionary advent of new applications of real time internet gives place to open and dynamic systems based on cooperative distributed networks and other stakeholders like portals, information brokers, content providers... This shift resulted notably in the success of OSS, Business Process based approaches such as the eTOM.

4.2   Framework architecture

Considering the overall network as a federation of multiple collaborating stakeholder networks, each of them insuring a part of end-to-end service, we describe here our vision of the management of such a complex network.

We introduce a new concept based on Grid Computing technology: the Grid Network Management [13][14].

Grid Network Management is a way to simplify the problem of the complexity of the centralized network management and services in a multi-stakeholder environment, while placing a higher notch in architecture, and by applying the principles of virtualization to a system of services and networks management. The objective is to design and to implement an open architecture for the systems and services management in a multiple stakeholder environment, by developing principles generalized for the grids being able to be applied to specific fields. This architecture is directed towards delivering services, and insuring efficient creation of new services within time-to-market constraints.

The architecture reference of our management system is the eTOM architecture. The main idea is to develop a multi-eTOM-based platform making it possible to manage the heterogeneity of network services, to control the problem of interconnection between various stakeholders of the environment, to provide mechanisms making it possible to draw up SLAs and QoS contracts "on-the-fly" ensuring the interconnection between stakeholders and end-to-end service quality management strategy, to design and create functions and applications capable to circumvent various problems resulting from possible flaws in a given stakeholder. In this context, a summarizing term of self-management network may be adequate.

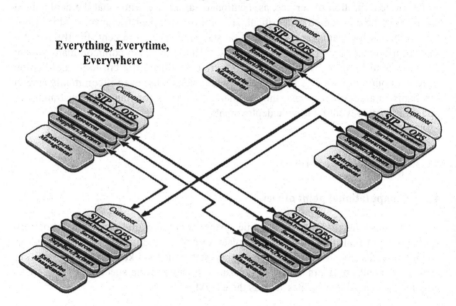

Fig. 2. Partial example of multi-eTOM environment

4.3   Information point of view

At the highest level of the information model is the SLA, which derives information from specifications and cost agreement. It has to be noted that classical SLAs are human-readable but are not powerful enough to provide an end-to-end QoS set-up. There is an emphasis on the SLA concept and its implementation in terms of Service Level Specifications (SLSs), which contain all the technical parameters needed to set-up the corresponding QoS inside a global network like multi-eTOM environment. The proposed approach attempts to cover this emphasis enabling to have instantly provisioned services based on dynamically negotiated SLAs, like in [9][10].

4.4   "Virtualized" service framework

Service management is concerned with end-to-end service delivery quality and management. The focus is on the monitoring and management of SLAs between the customer and internal and external suppliers involved in the service delivery value chain; this make it difficult to adopt an end-to-end strategy for Service Quality Management.We aim to improve the service management by applying the principles of virtualization to a system of services and networks management.

By virtualization [18], we understand the abstraction of our reference architecture – the eTOM framework. It is a set of transformation processes in the virtualization layer during which associations between virtualized entities and "underlying" ones are established and changed.

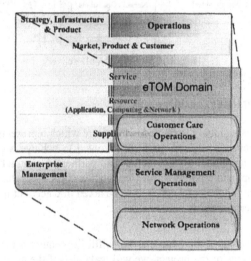

Fig. 3. Virtualization at eTOM layers

The picture above depicts the most noticeable operation layers: Customer Care Operations, Services Operations and Network Operations.

The use of this "virtualized" service framework allows service specification information to be shared between multiple service providers without the need to declare proprietary information. The relevance of a common service framework therefore is fundamental; it not only impacts the practical physical monitoring of performance metrics but also affects the interactions and contractual relationships between all parties involved in the service delivery chain. The following figure considers a scenario of a VoD delivery and illustrates the complexity of multi-party interactions between identified service providers:

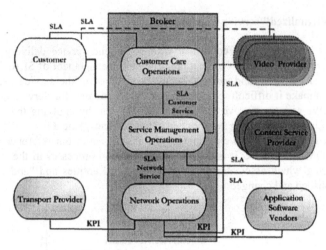

Fig. 4. A scenario of VoD delivery

4.4   Implementations considerations

Our platform is a global distributed architecture which represents a peer-to-peer relationship between two or more partners involved to achieve a common goal. It is characterized by a community that includes all partners, a contract defining the terms of the relationship, and a policy to rule the relationship's lifecycle. As we said above, SLA is one of the fundamental concepts to be taken into account in the architecture in order to offer interoperability.

The agent technology - the Manlets. To fulfill the requirements of SLAs , for the first implementations of the project, we will make use of the agent technology called Manlet (Management Applet), detailed in the project ImaGEnS [11] [12]. Manlets are components of the relevant information that circulates on the (global) network. Manlets feature following main properties:

- Mobility: Manlet is the entity making a Business Process live,
- Polymorphism: their shape, behaviour and properties change according to their location within their lifecycle,
- Autonomy: Manlets follow their path in constant independence,
- Intelligence: Manlets have embedded intelligence that enables adaptative interaction with the environment, lifecycle management, re-routing, re-birth, self-destruction etc.

Manlets all inherit from a generic object implementing all the common and basic features listed above. As shown in the figure above, it can be cloned, can dispatch itself, display itself, can be disposed or can dispose itself, and finally can be archived or archive itself.

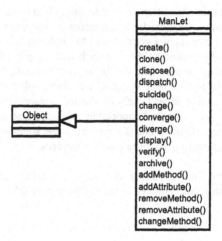

Fig. 5. Manlet generic model - partial UML diagram

Manlets (including all the constraints and requirements of the contract) will index all the partners entering the chain of provisioning the service, and will dynamically carry out the negotiation, the establishment of the contracts with all the requirements of quality of service – thus forming a field of composition of service. It is clear that the dynamicity of ManLet technology makes Service Management very different from traditional Enterprise Management. By the virtualization of domains, the real management in our environment can be formed on a per transaction basis, thus implying dynamics several orders of magnitude larger than found in today's network management systems, whose topology tends to be fairly static. In fact, in our environment the main management resources convert to services, SLAs and QoS requirements across different networking systems. Consequently, the goal of end-to-end management, which has been the target of several management efforts, must become achievable in a multi-eTOM environment.

In our exemple of VoD delivery, we use Manlet as one of the way to chain domains into end-to-end connection. Each SLA interaction in figure 4 depicts a ManLet activity at a particular status of its lifecycle. The chain of all steps and ManLet lifecycle states is to be compared to the notion of TMF Business Process, in the context of multistakeholder environment. It does allow the process to be more efficient in terms of automation, security, availability.

5 Conclusion and related work

The question now is how much various stakeholders can correlate their offers and services to satisfy customer needs and what is the cost of management and optimization of resources in such environment? At last, what is the future of stakeholder's competition and market targets? Can we think on the standardization of service composition that can regulate the offer and the demand of services or are we about to tend to create an on-fly automated on-demand telecom environment?

In this paper, we presented a novel vision to implement a management infrastructure based on a multiple stakeholder approach with availability as a constant focus, and combination of principles with can be applied to network management such as Grid Computer, and peer-to-peer systems. The first implementations using ManLet technology shown in this paper is only one of many ways to chain different eTOM-based domains into an end-to-end connection. We hope that the study present in this paper will lead to excellent results.We presented the arguments for our first implementation – the interaction beetween actors towards a specific agent technology: Manlet.

We are currently implementing the way the actors are connected through Manlet/SLA, and how this is related to the eTOM framework.

References

[1].   Baldonado, M., Chang, C.-C.K., Gravano, L., Paepcke, A.: The Stanford Digital Library Metadata Architecture. Int. J. Digit. Libr. 1 (1997) 108-121

[2].   Bruce, K.B., Cardelli, L., Pierce, B.C.: Comparing Object Encodings. In: Abadi, M., Ito, T. (eds.): Theoretical Aspects of Computer Software. Lecture Notes in Computer Science, Vol. 1281. Springer-Verlag, Berlin Heidelberg New York (1997) 415-438

[3].   Van Leeuwen, J. (ed.): Computer Science Today. Recent Trends and Developments. Lecture Notes in Computer Science, Vol. 1000. Springer-Verlag, Berlin Heidelberg New York (1995)

[4].   Michalewicz, Z.: Genetic Algorithms + Data Structures = Evolution Programs. 3rd edn. Springer-Verlag, Berlin Heidelberg New York (1996)

[5].   enhanced Telecom Operations Map - The Business Process Framework, TeleManagement Forum 2004, GB921 v4.0, March 2004.

[6].   TeleManagement forum www.TMForum.org

[7].   New Generation Operational Support System (NGOSS), NGOSS Release 1.5. TMF GB920. TeleManagement Forum, November 2004.

[8].   Service Model Framework, Release 4.5. TMF GB924. TeleManagement Forum, November 2004.

[9].   SLA Management Handbook, TeleManagement Forum 2004, GB 917-1 v2.0, Member Evaluation version, July 2004.

[10]. Dugeon, O., Diaconescu, A. From SLA to SLS up to QoS Control: the CADENUS Frame-work, WTC'2002

[11]. Ranc, D.,, Vaculova, L., Elmejjad, S., Maknavicius L., Touré F., Daurensan V., Une organisation orienté cycle de vie de l'information pour la gestion des réseaux et services. GRES, Février 2003, Fortaleza-CE-Brésil.

[12]. Ranc D., Vaculova L., Elmejjad S. ImaGEnS: Deliverable v1, v2, v3 An ALCATEL/INT Strategic Collaboration, 2002-2003.

[13]. M. Libicki, Who Runs What in the Global Information Grid: Ways to Share Local and Global Responsibility. RAND Corporation, 2000.

[14]. A. Bodertsky, D. Folk, Knowledge Management for Wireless Grid Operation Centers. 35th Hawaii International Conference on System Sciences. 2002.

[15]. Herrmann, K. , Mhl G. , Geihs K. , Self Management: The Solution to Complexity or Just Another Problem? IEEE Distributed Systems online 1541-4922 2005 Published by the IEEE Computer Society Vol. 6, No. 1; January 2005.

[16]. Kephart,J. O. and Chess,D. M. . The Vision of Autonomic Computing. Computer, January 2003.

[17]. Foster, I., Kesselman, C., and Tuecke, S. The Anatomy of the Grid: Enabling Scalable Virtual Organisations. International Journal of High Performance Computing Applications, 15(3).200-222.2001. www.globus.org/research/papers/anatomy.pdf.

[18]. Graupner S., Knig R., and al.: Impact of Virtualization on Management Systems. HP Laboratories. 33 (2003)

[19]. www.globus.org/

Security Verification of a Virtual Private Network over MPLS

Cédric Llorens1, Ahmed Serhrouchni2
1 Equant, La Défense, France
cedric.llorens@equant.com
2 GET-Télécom Paris, LTCI-UMR 5141 CNRS, Paris, France
ahmed.serhrouchni@equant.com

Abstract. We present in this paper how to assess a VPN (Virtual Private Network) security implemented over the Multi Protocol Label Switching (MPLS) protocol. This assessment is based on the definition of a MPLS/VPN security policy and on a reverse-engineering process performed on the network routers configurations. This paper details the algorithms as well as their asymptotic time complexity required to assess this security policy. Moreover, this paper also suggests an approach to rank a VPN perimeter.

1 Introduction

With the deployment of the Multi Protocol Label Switching (MPLS) protocol used at the network core layer, network operators have developed the Virtual Private Network (VPN) service including Quality Of Service (QOS) and the usage of private IP ranges. A MPLS/VPN security is based on the following security mechanisms; the first one is the network routing mechanism, which isolates the VPNs and guarantees the VPNs integrity within the network; the second is the configuration of the VPNs in the network routers configurations in order to create the VPNs topologies.

To protect a MPLS/VPN, a network security policy must be defined, implemented and checked periodically. The assessment process, required to ensure the application of the security policy, consists of parsing the network routers configurations and verifying the security policy through a reverse-engineering process [1,2]. More precisely, this assessment approach is used to verify the security policy of our MPLS backbone composed of several thousands of routers, representing millions of configuration lines and implementing several thousands of VPNs. It allows to check

Please use the following format when citing this chapter:

Llorens, C. and Serhrouchni, A., 2007, in IFIP International Federation for Information Processing, Volume 229, Network Control and Engineering for QoS, Security, and Mobility, IV, ed. Gaïti, D., (Boston: Springer), pp. 339–353.

at the end the isolation and integrity of the VPNs defined in the routers configurations.

We start by presenting the MPLS and MP-BGP (Multi Protocol Border Gateway Protocol) protocols used to create the Virtual Private Networks. Then, we define a security policy targeting the MPLS/VPN security, its implementation in the network routers configurations (based on a CISCO implementation) and the algorithms (with their time complexity) required to assess this policy. Finally, we conclude by describing how this work will be part of a global "Framework for Network Risk Measurement".

The intended audience covers everyone interested in security assessment and configuration management in the context of network management, including network operators.

2   MPLS and MP-BGP protocols

MPLS is a packet-forwarding technology, which uses labels to make data forwarding decisions. With MPLS, the Layer 3-header analysis is done just once (when the packet enters the MPLS domain). Label inspection drives subsequent packet forwarding. The key idea behind MPLS is the use of a forwarding mechanism based on label swapping that can be combined with a set of different control modules. Each control module is responsible for assigning and distributing a set of labels, as well as for maintaining other relevant control information [3]. A MPLS network is composed of the CE (Customer Edge) devices located in the customer premises and used to interconnect the customer sites to the MPLS network, of the PE (Provider Edge) backbone devices used to implement the value-added services (VPN, QOS, etc.) and to interconnect the customer sites, and of the P (Provider) backbone devices used for switching as shown in figure 1.

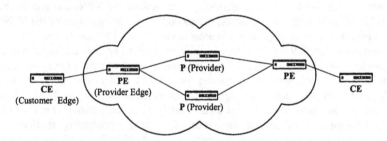

Fig. 1. A MPLS network implementing Virtual Private Networks

A MPLS/VPN is implemented over the MPLS protocol by creating dedicated routing tables per VPN. These routing tables are created thanks to an extension of the Border Gateway Protocol (BGP) protocol named MP-BGP. A VPN or a Virtual Routing and Forwarding instance (VRF) is a dedicated routing table used for connecting a set of sites to a VPN service. The VRFs definitions are defined in the PE routers configurations. Moreover, only the IP prefixes present within the VRF are advertised through the MPLS backbone. So, each MP-BGP advertisement contains for instance a VPNV4 address (including a route distinguisher value (RD) and an ip prefix value) and the Route-target extended community (RT), which will determine into which VRFs the route should be installed.

3   MPLS/VPN security policy

Based on these technical considerations, we present a MPLS/VPN security policy covering the following security sub-areas:
- The MP-BGP routing topology security policy ensures the MPLS/VPNs integrity and availability.
- The MPLS/VPN perimeter security policy ensures the MPLS/VPNs isolation and integrity.

3.1   MP-BGP routing topology security policy

The network routing used both internally and with external partners is critical in an MPLS networking area, and could impact directly the network availability and integrity in case of routing attacks. These attacks are generally based on spoofing, session hijacking, route flapping, route de-aggregation, un-authorized route injection, etc. These attacks are also based on routing architecture design weaknesses, routing bugs, routing attribute, routing cascade failures, etc. [4,5].

The MP-BGP routing topologies could be viewed at 2 levels. The first level considers the Autonomous Systems (AS) and permits to construct a graph of AS connectivity from which, routing loops may be pruned and some policy decisions at the AS level may be enforced. The second level considers the devices within an AS and permits to construct a graph of device connectivity which is generally more flexible, more scalable and provides more efficient ways of controlling the exchange of information.

These two topology levels are critical and must follow defined rules in order to ensure the network availability and integrity. Any violation of these routing configuration rules could generate serious routing instabilities and impacts for the network and its services. In this area, we define the following security rules:

- Security rule: The "MP-BGP AS" graph must be resilient for availability purpose in order to limit the impacts in case of an incident. Moreover, it should be noted that the routing topology generally follows physical/geographic topology mainly due to cost and technical reasons. So, it means that the "MP-BGP AS" graph must be connected and each vertex (AS) is at a minimum 2 edges connected to each of its backbone internal vertex connections. Regarding the other vertex connections, 2 edges connections are required for "partner" MP-BGP links, and 1 edge connection is at minimum required for each of the other links. We will say that the graph is "as-connected".

Moreover, despite all the security features that could be implemented, a model of trust based on common procedures must be defined between the operators in order to avoid any serious impact like the merging of the backbones routing tables.

- Security rule: The "MP-BGP AS router" graphs (one per AS) must be resilient for availability purpose. It means that the graph inside an AS must be complete for a "full meshing" model or biconnected for a "Route Reflector" model. Moreover, the "Route Reflector" model states that any router, which is not a "Route Reflector" client, must be fully meshed with all the similar routers within an AS ("Route Reflector" server). A consequence is that the graph composed of the "Route Reflector" servers must be complete.

Please note that a combination of both designs is obviously possible to avoid a global "full meshing" design, very consuming in terms of router memory and processing, but also to avoid a global "Route Reflector" model design bringing sub-optimal routing issues.

These security rules are checked in the assessment part by computing the routing graphs extracted from the routers configurations.

3.2   MPLS/VPN perimeter security policy

The configuration of a MPLS/VPN in the network routers configurations is also critical for the VPN security, because any configuration errors could impact the VPN integrity and isolation by connecting the VPN to others unwanted VPNs. The mechanism by which, a MPLS/VPN controls the distribution of VPN routing information, is the use of the MP-BGP route-target extended communities. The MP-BGP route-target extended community string follows a predefined format in order to create a VPN by importing or exporting this route-target community. Importing a route-target means that you learn the routes associated to this route-target, exporting a route-target means that you send your routes to this route-target. A VPN is generally configured on several PE routers.

Knowing that any configuration errors could impact a MPLS/VPN integrity and isolation, we define the following minimum set of security rules:

- Security rule: a VPN configuration must be compliant with the service provisioning requirements. For example, a VPN must be only connected to the authorized VPNs. Any error could bring security weaknesses and could impact the integrity and isolation of the VPN.

- Security rule: a VPN configuration must be consistent. Any inconsistency could bring security weaknesses and could impact the integrity and isolation of the VPN. The minimum set of integrity rules are:
  - Any route-target extended community (RT) export statement defined for a VPN must refer (within the MPLS/VPN network) to a minimum of one import statement related to this RT at a PE level (any connection must be bi-directional).
  - Any route-target extended community (RT) import statement defined for a VPN must refer to a minimum of one export statement related to this RT at a PE level (any connection must be bi-directional).

- Unauthorized (in violation with the predefined format) RT import and export statements must not been configured for a VPN.
- Forbidden (used for administration purpose) RT import and export statements must not been configured for a VPN.

These security rules are checked in the assessment part by computing the MPLS/VPN graph extracted from the routers configurations. Effectively, we build from the network routers configurations a MPLS/VPN directed graph where each vertex represent a VPN, and where a directed edge from VPN(a) to VPN(b) is deduced by the MP-BGP route-target extended community import and export statements configured in an asymmetric manner to create a VPN.

In addition to these rules defined for ensuring a VPN isolation and integrity, the VPN perimeter also acts as an important element regarding the VPN security. To provide a first input, we suggest hereafter an approach to rank a VPN perimeter based on the level of potential threats (graph approach, graph and probabilistic approach). This approach is not dependent on the underlying protocol layer (like MPLS BGP, IPSEC, SSL, etc.) used to build the VPN.

3.2.1 Rank a VPN perimeter through a graph and probabilistic approach

It should be noted that this approach only suggests a possible way to rank a VPN perimeter. It does not provide any mathematical proof and accuracy of the measure, but only intends to open potential research areas regarding "network security" measurement.

A Bayesian network is the convergence of the graph and probability theories. In our framework, a VPN graph can be also viewed as Bayesian network under a certain transformation (the graph must be a directed acyclic graph). This approach could permit to quantify the probability that a VPN is penetrated by other VPNs, if we take into account the MPLS graph data and probabilistic distributions. A VPN graph is not by default a directed graph, so if want to compute the perimeter of a VPN_i, then we need to transform the MPLS/VPN graph to a $DAG(VPN_i)$ graph. At this level, the $DAG(VPN_i)$ graph is a tree computed from the node VPN_i and deduced from a spanning tree algorithm for example.

Please note that we voluntary limit our VPN perimeter in this paper to one DAG due to the exponential number of possible DAGs that can be deduced from the initial graph [6]. It should be considered as a major limitation of the current approach and must be generalized in further works.

The main objective consists to define an approach based on the probability to penetrate a VPN in order to rank a VPN perimeter. The basic idea is to sum all the probabilities that could permit to penetrate a VPN. So, more the probability is lower, more the VPN perimeter is better. At last, it will provide an approach to rank a VPN perimeter within different graph topologies

By definition, a Bayesian network is a directed acyclic graph where each node (i.e. a VPN) is a random variable. So, if a Bayesian network is composed of the following random variables $(X_1, X_2 \ldots X_n)$, where X_i is "True" if the VPN_i has been penetrated and "False" otherwise, for $i \in [1..n]$, then the probability value that the VPN_i has been penetrated is [7].

For $i \in [1..n]$ and if k is the number of events for which X_i is in the state "True", then we have:

$$P(X_i = \text{True}) = \sum_{m=1}^{k} P(X_i = \text{True}, X_1(m), X_2(m) \dots X_n(m)) \tag{1}$$

If $(X_i = \text{True}, X_1(1), X_2(1) \dots X_n(1))$, …, $(X_i = \text{True}, X_1(k), X_2(k) \dots X_n(k))$ are mutually exclusive, then we have:

$$P(X_i = \text{True}) = \sum_{m=1}^{k} P(X_i = \text{True} \mid X_1(m), X_2(m) \dots X_n(m)) * P(X_1(m), X_2(m) \dots X_n(m)) \tag{2}$$

If we consider the joint probability distribution (chain rule), where $Pa(X_j)$ represents the parents set of X_j (or causes) in the Bayesian graph, then we have:

$$P(X_i = \text{True}) = \sum_{m=1}^{k} P(X_i = \text{True} \mid X_1(m), X_2(m) \dots X_n(m)) * \prod_{j=1, j \neq i}^{n} P(X_j(m) \mid Pa(X_j(m))) \tag{3}$$

For example, if we consider the following Bayesian graphs (A, B, C) in order to compute the perimeter of the VPN_4 as shown in the figure 2.

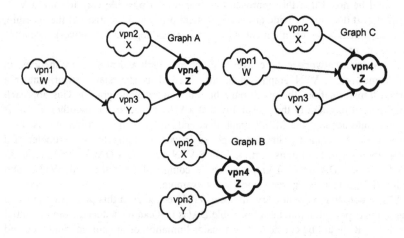

Fig. 2. VPN perimeter : examples of network graph topologies : graph A, graph B, graph C

The graph A shows four VPNs that we can associate to these discrete random variables (W,X,Y,Z). Each random variable has two states, the state "True" means that the VPN has been penetrated and a state "False" otherwise. If we want to rank the VPN_4 perimeter associated to the random variable Z, then we need to fix the following probabilities values:

P(W=True) = 0,5 and P(W=False) = 0,5, P(X=True) = 0,5 and P(X=False) = 0,5, P(Y=True) = 0,5 and P(Y=False) = 0,5, P(Z=True) = 0,5 and P(Z=False) = 0,5

Table 1. Basic VPN penetration probabilities

	W = T	W = F
Y = T	0,8	0,5
Y = F	0,2	0,5

Table 2. Conditional VPN penetration probabilities

	W = T	T	T	T	F	F	F	F
	X = T	F	T	F	F	T	T	F
	Y = T	T	F	F	F	F	T	T
Z= T	0,8	0,8	0,8	0,5	0,5	0,8	0,8	0,8
Z=F	0,2	0,2	0,2	0,5	0,5	0,2	0,2	0,2

So, if we compute the probability that the VPN_2, VPN_3, VPN_4 have been penetrated for the graph B, then we can obtain a VPN perimeter ranking within a network graph topology as described hereafter:

For the VPN_2 (for graph B):
$P(X=T) = 0,5$

For the VPN_3 (for graph B):
$P(Y=T) = 0,5$

For the VPN_4 (for graph B):
$$P(Z=T) = P(Z=T|X=T,Y=T) * P(X=T,Y=T)$$
$$+ \ldots + P(Z=T|X=F,Y=F) * P(X=F,Y=F)$$
$$P(Z=T) = P(Z=T|X=T,Y=T) * P(X=T) * P(Y=T)$$
$$+ P(Z=T|X=F,Y=F) * P(X=F) * P(Y=F)$$
$$+ P(Z=T|X=T,Y=F) * P(X=T) * P(Y=F)$$
$$+ P(Z=T|X=F,Y=T) * P(X=F) * P(Y=T)$$
$$P(Z=T) = 3*0.8*0.5*0.5+0.5*0.5*0.5$$
$$P(Z=T) = 0.725$$

In this example, the VPN_2 and the VPN_3 (0.5) have better VPN perimeter rankings (less exposed to security threats) than the VPN_4 (0.725) in the network graph topology B.

Now, if we compute the probability that the VPN_4 has been penetrated for the graph A, B, C. Then, we can obtain a network graph topology ranking for a dedicated VPN perimeter as described hereafter:

For the graph A (VPN_4):
$$P(Z=T) = P(Z=T|W=T,X=T,Y=T) * P(W=T,X=T,Y=T)$$
$$+ \ldots + P(Z=T|W=F,X=F,Y=F) * P(W=F,X=F,Y=F)$$
$$P(Z=T) = P(Z=T|W=T,X=T,Y=T) * P(Y=T|W=T) * P(X=T) * P(W=T)$$
$$+ P(Z=T|W=T,X=F,Y=T) * P(Y=F|W=T) * P(X=T) * P(W=T)$$
$$+ P(Z=T|W=T,X=T,Y=T) * P(Y=T|W=T) * P(X=T) * P(W=T)$$
$$+ P(Z=T|W=T,X=F,Y=F) * P(Y=F|W=T) * P(X=F) * P(W=T)$$
$$+ P(Z=T|W=F,X=F,Y=F) * P(Y=F|W=F) * P(X=F) * P(W=F)$$
$$+ P(Z=T|W=F,X=T,Y=F) * P(Y=T|W=F) * P(X=F) * P(W=F)$$

$$+ P(Z=T|W=F,X=T,Y=T) * P(Y=T|W=F) * P(X=T) * P(W=F)$$
$$+ P(Z=T|W=F,X=F,Y=T) * P(Y=F|W=F) * P(X=T) * P(W=F)$$

$P(Z=T) = 0.8*0.5*0.8*0.5 + 0.8*0.8*0.5*0.5 + 0.8*0.5*0.2*0.5 +$
$0.5*0.5*0.2*0.5 + 0.5*0.5*0.5*0.5 + 0.8*0.5*0.5*0.5 + 0.8*0.5*0.5*0.5 +$
$0.8*0.5*0.5*0.5$
$P(Z=T) = 0,7475$

For the graph B (VPN$_4$):
$P(Z=T) = P(Z=T|X=T,Y=T) * P(X=T,Y=T)$
  $+ ... + P(Z=T|X=F,Y=F) * P(X=F,Y=F)$
$P(Z=T) = P(Z=T|X=T,Y=T) * P(X=T) * P(Y=T)$
  $+ P(Z=T|X=F,Y=F) * P(X=F) * P(Y=F)$
  $+ P(Z=T|X=T,Y=F) * P(X=T) * P(Y=F)$
  $+ P(Z=T|X=F,Y=T) * P(X=F) * P(Y=T)$
$P(Z=T) = 3*0.8*0.5*0.5+0.5*0.5*0.5$
$P(Z=T) = 0.725$

For the graph C (VPN$_4$):
$P(Z=T) = P(Z=T|W=T,X=T,Y=T) * P(W=T,X=T,Y=T)$
  $+ ... + P(Z=T|W=F,X=F,Y=F) * P(W=F,X=F,Y=F)$
$P(Z=T) = P(Z=T|W=T,X=T,Y=T) * P(X=T) * P(Y=T) * P(W=T)$
  $+ P(Z=T|W=T,X=F,Y=T) * P(X=F) * P(Y=T) * P(W=T)$
  $+ P(Z=T|W=T,X=T,Y=T) * P(X=T) * P(Y=T) * P(W=T)$
  $+ P(Z=T|W=T,X=F,Y=F) * P(X=F) * P(Y=F) * P(W=T)$
  $+ P(Z=T|W=F,X=F,Y=F) * P(X=F) * P(Y=F) * P(W=F)$
  $+ P(Z=T|W=F,X=T,Y=F) * P(X=T) * P(Y=F) * P(W=F)$
  $+ P(Z=T|W=F,X=T,Y=T) * P(X=T) * P(Y=T) * P(W=F)$
  $+ P(Z=T|W=F,X=F,Y=T) * P(X=F) * P(Y=T) * P(W=F)$
$P(Z=T) = 7*0.8*0.5*0.5*0.5+0.5*0.5*0.5*0.5$
$P(Z=T) = 0.7625$

In this example, the graph B (0.725) has a better ranking for the VPN$_4$ perimeter than the graph A (0,7475), and the graph A (0,7475) has a better ranking for the VPN$_4$ perimeter than the graph C (0.7625). The VPN$_4$ is less exposed to threats in graph B.

4   MPLS/VPN security policy assessment

This assessment approach is used to verify the security policy of our MPLS backbone composed of several thousands of routers, representing millions of configuration lines and implementing several thousands of VPNs. It allows to check at the end the isolation and integrity of the VPNs defined in the routers configurations.

4.1   MP-BGP routing topology security policy assessment

The MP-BGP topology information is directly implemented in the router configuration, so we can extract this information by parsing each router configuration belonging to the MPLS/VPN network. For a CISCO MP-BGP implementation, the following statements express it (Each VPN is associated with one or more VPN routing/forwarding instances (VRFs). A VRF defines the VPN membership of a customer site attached to a PE router):

- hostname name : name of the router.
- ip address ip-address [subnet_mask] : define an IP address of a router link. It will be used to find the MP-BGP neighbors.
- router BGP autonomous-system : define the Autonomous System of the BGP (and MP-BGP) process.
  - neighbor ip-address … : define the BGP neighbors if used in the framework of a multi-services backbone (offering Internet and MPLS services for example)
- address-family ipv4 vrf : configure sessions that carry IPv4 prefixes. This is used to establish the VPN routing/forwarding (VRF) table, it refers to the customers BGP sessions where a VRF defines the VPN membership of a customer site attached to a PE router.
  - neighbor ip-address … : define the BGP neighbors
- address-family vpnv4 : configures sessions that carry VPN-IPv4 prefixes, each of which has been made globally unique by adding an 8-byte route distinguisher. This is used to establish the MP-iBGP sessions within the MPLS backbone and the MP-eBGP sessions.
  - neighbor ip-address … : define the MP-eBGP and MP-iBGP neighbors

It should be noted that we will extract all the "ip address" for all the interfaces in order to find the MP-BGP interconnections. This is mainly due to that we have no "configuration" knowledge of the MP-BGP connections such as this router "number 1" is MP-BGP connected with the router "number 2", so we have to deduce it from all the network routers configurations.

The assessment process is composed of the following steps:

1) Extract and validate the MP-BGP information in the network routers configurations (PE and P routers) in order to create the "topology" file with the following format:
   - <router_name> : name : extracted from "hostname name" configuration
   - <BGP_as_id> : autonomous-system : extracted from "router BGP autonomous-system" configuration
   - <BGP_ip_address> : ip-address : extracted from "router BGP autonomous-system" and "neighbor ip-address" configuration
   - <MP-BGP-ipv4> : ip-address : extracted from "address-family ipv4 vrf" and "neighbor ip-address" configuration
   - <MP-BGP-vpnv4> : ip-address : extracted from "address-family vpnv4" and "neighbor ip-address" configuration

- <type_router> : extracted from "hostname" configuration, it states if the router is a P, PE or CE router

and the "repository" file (P, PE and CE routers) with the following format:
- <router_name> : name : extracted from "hostname name" configuration
- <ip_address> : ip-address : extracted from "ip address ip-address [subnet_mask] " configuration
- <type_router> extracted from "hostname" configuration, it states if the router is a P, PE or CE router

This information will be used to build the MP-BGP matrix and to deduce the MP-BGP graphs through a "jointure" operation performed between the "topology" file and "repository" file. The "repository" file is effectively required to determine from all the routers configurations the useful MP-BGP neighbors information. Obviously, it will be applicable for the internal connections knowing that we have the routers configurations. It should be noted that an unsolved "join" line means that the router points to an external connection such as partners. It will also permit to validate any simple inconsistency of the MP-BGP statements (AS definition, Peer-group definition, etc.).

2) Build the undirected graphs:

- Build the "MP-BGP AS" graph: if we consider the topology and repository files as set of data, we can deduce by the following relational algebra query the graph vertices and edges (2 routers are MP-BGP connected if a router MP-BGP neighbor ip address points to a router interface ip address):

    / Determine the MPLS graph vertices */*
    Distinct topology[BGP_as_id]
    / Determine the MPLS/VPN graph edges for each BGP AS areas */*
    For each value in topology[BGP_as_id] do
    / List the BGP AS interconnections equivalent to MP-eBGP sessions */*
    topology[BGP_as_id] as a join repository as b join topology[BGP_as_id] as c
    on
      a[MP-BGP-vpnv4] = b[ip_address]
      and b[router_name] =c[router_name]
    where
      a[BGP_as_id] = value and
      a[BGP_as_id] != c[BGP_as_id];
    Endfor

- Build the "MP-BGP AS router" graphs: if we consider the topology and repository files as set of data, we can deduce by the following relational algebra query the graph vertices and edges (one graph per AS):

    / List the BGP AS areas */*
    For each value in topology[BGP_as_id] do
    / Determine the MPLS graph vertices */*
    Distinct topology[router_name] where BGP_as_id = value

/* Determine the MPLS/VPN graph edges where the routers interconnections are MP-iBGP sessions */
topology[router_name] as a join repository as b join topology[router_name] as c
on
  a[MP-BGP-vpnv4] = b[ip_address] and
  b[router_name] =c[router_name]
where
  a[BGP_as_id] = value and
  a[BGP_as_id] = c[BGP_as_id] and
  a[type_router] != "CE" and
  b[type_router] != "CE"
/* Determine the MPLS/VPN graph edges where the routers interconnections are BGP sessions */
topology[router_name] as a join repository as b join topology[router_name] as c
on
  a[MP-BGP-ipv4] = b[ip_address] and
  b[router_name] =c[router_name]
where
  a[BGP_as_id] = value and
  a[BGP_as_id] = c[BGP_as_id] and
  a[type_router] = "PE" and
  b[type_router] = "CE"
Endfor

As the routing graphs are sparse graphs, we prefer to take an adjacency-list structure in order to have a better time complexity of the various graph operations [9].

3) Check the "MP-BGP AS" graph: we check if the graph is as-connected. If $|V|$ is the number of vertices and $|E|$ is the number of edges in the graph, then the asymptotic time complexity (based on the Depth-First Search algorithm to check connectivity and compute articulation point) is $O(|V|+|E|)$ [8].

4) Check the "MP-BGP AS router" graph: we check if the graph is complete for the MP-iBGP full meshing model and is biconnected for the "Route Reflector" meshing model. Same algorithm and asymptotic time complexity detailed previously.

4.2 MPLS/VPN Perimeter topology security policy assessment

The MPLS/VPN topology information is directly implemented in the router configuration, so we can extract this information by parsing each router configuration belonging to the MPLS/VPN network. For a CISCO MPLS/VPN implementation, the following statements express it:

- ip vrf vrf_name : creates a VRF routing table and a CEF (forwarding) table, both named vrf_name.
- route-target {import | export | both} *route-target-ext-community:* To create a route-target extended community for a VRF.

The assessment process is composed of the following steps.

1) Extract and validate the MPLS/VPN information in the network routers configurations in order to create the "topology" file with the following fields (PE routers):
- <router_name> : name : extracted from the "hostname name" configuration
- <vrf_name> : name : extracted from "ip vrf vrf_name" configuration
- <rt> : *route-target-ext-community* : extracted from "route-target {import | export} *route-target-ext-community*" configuration
- <im_ex> : "export" |"import" : extracted from "route-target {import | export} *route-target-ext-community*" configuration

This information will be used to build the MPLS/VPN graph based on the "topology" file.

2) Build the MPLS/VPN graph:

The first step consists in determining the MPLS/VPN graph vertices. If we consider the topology as a set of data, we can deduce directly the vertices by the field "vrf".

Regarding the MPLS/VPN graph edges, we need to determine the interconnections between the VPNs thanks to the MP-BGP route-target extended community import and export statements.

For consistency and coherency of the network routers configurations, we will use a unique vrf_name within the MPLS/VPN network for a specific VPN.

Due to the asymmetric configuration of the RTs, the "export rule" and "import rule" will determine all the MPLS/VPN graph edges knowing that if a VRF(a) has an export statement with a RT(x) and that the VRF(b) has an import statement with RT(x), then there is a directed edge between VRF(a) and VRF(b). Moreover, it implies that there is also a directed edge between VRF(b) and VRF(a) in order to create a network connection (VRF(b) should have an export statement with RT(x) and VRF(a) should have an import statement with the RT(x)).

So, for each route-target RTx, we must build the lists of the VRFs exporting this RTx and the list of the VRFs importing this RTx as shown in the figure 3.

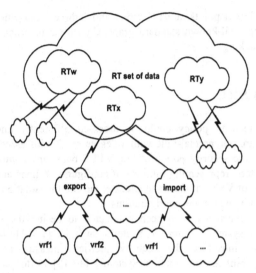

Fig. 3. The RT Trees hierarchy

Now, if we consider the topology as a set of data, we can deduce by the following relational algebra query the graph vertices and edges:

/* Determine the MPLS/VPN graph nodes */
Distinct topology[vrf_name]
/* Determine the MPLS/VPN graph edges */
For each value in topology[rt] do
    /* List the VRF interconnections */
    topology[vrf_name] as a join
    topology[vrf_name] as b
      on a[rt] = b [rt] = value
    where
    /* Directed edges statements */
    a[im_ex] = "export" and b[im_ex] = "import"
    and a[vrf_name]! = b[vrf_name]
Endfor

As the MPLS/VPN graph is a sparse graph by nature, we prefer to take an adjacency-list structure in order to have a better time complexity of the various graph operations [9].

At this level, the VPN security configuration consistency rules are checked during the graph building. The service provisioning rules and the VPNs connections are checked by computing the MPLS/VPN graph connected components. If $|V|$ is the number of vertices and $|E|$ is the number of edges in the graph, then the asymptotic time complexity (based on the Depth-First Search algorithm to check connectivity and compute articulation point) is $O(|V|+|E|)$ [8].

At last, articulation points, a VPN direct and indirect connections, etc. can be deduced by using well-known standard graph algorithms in order to compute the VPN perimeter ranking.

5   CONCLUSION

A MPLS/VPN security policy could be assessed efficiently knowing that the algorithms used are polynomial-time with a degree <= 2. This assessment approach is used to verify the security policy of our MPLS backbone composed of several thousands of routers, representing millions of configuration lines and implementing several thousands of VPNs. It allows to check at the end the isolation and integrity of the VPNs defined in the routers configurations.

Considerable researches have been conducted to define the security metrics (measures) for a system (Computer System) such as [10,11]. Moreover, other publications also introduce the security metrics (measures) to assess risk management capabilities (Information Systems) [12,13] or to provide a general framework for security measurement and assessment, however a global definition of the security metrics (measures) for a network is missing.

Thanks to the experience gained during the development of the router configuration validation tool [1,2], we will engage our efforts to define a detailed framework for security measurement of a network and its services. It will include the definition of the network security attributes, the definition of the security metrics (measures) and the definition of a global "Framework for Network Risk Measurement".

REFERENCES

1. D. Valois, C. Llorens, Network Device Configuration Validation, Proceedings of 14th annual FIRST conference, Hawaii, 2002.

2. C. Llorens, D. Valois, Y. Le Teigner, A. Gibouin, Computational complexity of the network routing logical security, Proceedings of the IEEE international Information Assurance Workshop, Darmstadt, Germany, pp. 37-49, 2003.

3. E. Rosen, A. Viswanathan, R. Callon, Multiprotocol Label Switching Architecture, Internet Engineering Task Force, www.ietf.org, Proposed standard, 2001.

4. N. Feamster, Practical verification techniques for wide-area routing, ACM SIGCOMM Computer Communication Review, Volume 34, Issue 1, pp. 87-92, 2004.

5. N. Feamster, H. Balakrishnan, Towards a logic for wide-area Internet routing, Proceedings of the ACM SIGCOMM workshop on Future directions in network architecture, pp. 289-300, 2003.

6. R. Robinson, Counting unlabeled acyclic digraphs, in C.Little editor, Combinatorial Mathematics V, volume 622 of Lecture Notes in Mathematics, Springer, pp. 28-43, 1977.

7. Finn V.Jensen, Bayesian Networks and Decision Graphs, Springer, ISBN 0-387-95259-4, pp. 1-30, 2001.

8. R.E. Tarjan, Depth First Search and Linear Graph Algorithms, conference record of Twelfth Annual IEEE symposium on Switching and Automata theory, New York, pp. 114-121, 1971.

9. G. Brassard, P. Bratley, Fundamentals Of algorithmics, Prentice-Hall, ISBN 0-13-335068-1, pp. 219-258, 1996.

10. Common Criteria, the common criteria represents the outcome of a series of efforts to develop criteria for evaluation of IT security that are broadly useful within the international community, for more information see: http://www.commoncriteria.org

11. R. ORTALO, Évaluation quantitative de la sécurité des systèmes d'information, Thèse de Doctorat de l'Institut National Polytechnique de Toulouse, Rapport LAAS 98164, 19 mai 1998.

12. J.R. Williams, G.F. Jelen, A framework for reasoning about assurance, Project report supported by National Securiy Agency, contract number MDA904-97-C-0223, 1998.

13. W.A. Wulf, D.M. Kienzle, A practical approach to security assessment, MOAT project report supported by DARPA, contract number N66001-96-C-8527, 1996.